Craig Schuftan was born in Sydney in 1974. He spent the nineties hoping that the breakthrough of alternative rock might lead to a more widespread social revolution in attitudes and ideas, while at the same time working to prevent this from happening by eagerly consuming every Gen-X-marketed fad under the sun. Since then, he has worked as a producer and presenter at Australia's national youth broadcaster, triple j, and written two books on music and popular culture, *The Culture Club* (2007) and *Hey! Nietzsche! Leave Them Kids Alone!* (2009).

Craig Schuftan

ENTERTAIN US!

ABC
Books

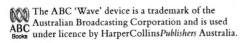 The ABC 'Wave' device is a trademark of the
Australian Broadcasting Corporation and is used
under licence by HarperCollins*Publishers* Australia.

First published in Australia in 2012
by HarperCollins*Publishers* Australia Pty Limited
ABN 36 009 913 517
harpercollins.com.au

HarperCollins*Publishers*
Level 13, 201 Elizabeth Street, Sydney NSW 2000, Australia
Unit D1, 63 Apollo Drive, Rosedale, Auckland 0632, New Zealand
A 53, Sector 57, Noida, UP, India
1 London Bridge Street, London, SE1 9GF, United Kingdom
2 Bloor Street East, 20th floor, Toronto, Ontario M4W 1A8, Canada
195 Broadway, New York, NY 10007, USA

National Library of Australia Cataloguing-in-Publication entry:

Schuftan, Craig.
  Entertain us: the rise and fall of alternative rock in the nineties
  978 0 7333 2884 8 (pbk.)
  Australian Broadcasting Corporation.
  Popular culture—History—20th century.
  Music—Social aspects—History—20th century.
  Social movements—History—20th century.
  Art and society—History.
306

Cover design by Brad Cook and Matt Stanton
Cover illustrations by Brad Cook
Background cover image by shutterstock.com

For Ben and Jess, and whatever happens next

Introduction

Musicians often tell us that they write songs because they don't hear anything they like on the radio, because the sound they most want to hear simply doesn't exist in the world. In the same way, I wrote this book because I wanted to read it, or something like it. I'd read a lot of interesting books on grunge and alternative rock in America, a great history of Britpop, and plenty of articles and essays on Madchester, neo-punk, nu-metal, riot grrrl, Radiohead and Rage Against the Machine. But what I wanted was a book that could tie all these stories together, to tell the tale of alternative music on both sides of the Atlantic from 1990 to 2000, from Sonic Youth's major label debut, through the rise and fall of Grunge and Britpop, right up to Radiohead's *Kid A*. As I set about writing it, I realised there was no way of describing these albums and the people who made them without also describing the world they lived in — no Jesus Jones's 'Right Here Right Now' without the fall of the Berlin Wall and the end of communism in Europe, no *Nevermind* without the Gulf War. I found that Urge Overkill's 'Girl, You'll Be a Woman Soon' was inexplicable without some understanding of America's economic decline in the 1970s, grunge and riot grrrl alike had as much to do with talk shows and therapy culture as they did with punk rock, and Britpop made far more sense as a means of coping with globalisation than it did as a riposte to Nirvana. So I'm pleased to say that the book you now hold in your hands is both the one I wanted to read and something a little bit more.

Entertain Us! is a tale of two cities, a book about rock music, culture and society in England and America. For the most part, I wrote about alternative bands from other parts of the world only when they made

1

some significant impact in the UK or US charts, which means that, with the sole exception of Silverchair, there are no Australian bands mentioned. Nevertheless, it is a very Australian book, written at one remove from both England and America, from a peculiarly if not uniquely Australian point of view. The book's slightly idiosyncratic playlist — where Stone Temple Pilots, Happy Mondays, Denis Leary, the Smashing Pumpkins, Suede, the Breeders, Blur and Body Count mingle freely — might seem odd to an American reader, but will be instantly recognisable to anyone who spent the nineties listening to Australia's national youth broadcaster, triple j. I'm grateful to the station for providing me with such an eclectic musical education, since I believe it allowed me to see, even at the time, that *Nevermind* and *Modern Life is Rubbish* had more in common than the flag-waving rhetoric of the period had us believe.

From the start, I imagined this book would have a large cast of characters, and cover a broad spectrum of musical styles. But considerations of time and space meant that I had to set some limits. I decided to write about rock, as opposed to pop, dance or hip-hop, because it seems to me that in the nineties, this particular way of making music became a focus for arguments about art, entertainment and ideals in a way that other genres did not. As the decade went on, rock itself broke up into many different subgenres, and absorbed ideas and influences from other forms of music — hip-hop in particular — and I've tried to explain how and why this happened. But I've limited my definition, for simplicity's sake if nothing else, to artists who had been seen with a guitar in their hand or in their band at some point during the nineties. So Ice-T and Beck made the cut, whereas Björk — whose music had become almost completely electronic by 1991 — did not.

I've chosen to focus on alternative rock as opposed to other varieties, though I realise this is a confusing term. These days, 'alternative' signifies a particular kind of guitar noise that might include Nirvana and Beck, but probably not Pavement — who are now considered 'indie'. But I've chosen to revive the term's original definition, as it might have been understood in 1990 — as music fostered by or in some way informed by the post-punk underground scene of the mid to late eighties, or music that continued in that vein after alternative music broke through to the mainstream in 1991. So my definition includes the Stone Roses, Faith No More, PJ Harvey, Nirvana, Pavement and No Doubt. What it doesn't include is groups like R.E.M., U2, Metallica or the Cure. All these artists did important work in the nineties, but because they were already signed to major labels and had some degree of commercial success in the eighties, I've only written about them briefly, if at all. Within the world of alternative rock itself, I've given far more space to bands that had hits and commercial success than I have to those who didn't because what interests me in this period is the point where underground ideals met the mass media. I've written about the late-nineties indie scene — the underground diaspora that grew up in the shadow of grunge and Britpop's mainstream success, fostered by labels such as Matador, Drag City and Chemikal Underground— only briefly.

There are, of course, plenty of other bands that meet all my criteria that don't appear in this book, or are only mentioned in passing, including some of my personal favourites. I decided that the best way to write a coherent and exciting story at a manageable length was to leave out the stories of a few artists whose music — while interesting in itself— made a little less of an impact on the wider world in the period I was writing about (the Dandy Warhols and Supergrass, for instance), or whose conceptual world was simply so elegantly self-contained that it could be removed without harming the rest of the book — as was the case with Tool and Ween.

Historians, as E.H. Carr once pointed out, usually have a bee in their bonnet of some kind, and I can't deny that this is true of me. This book is not a polemic, but it does have a point. In *Entertain Us!* I hope, to some extent, to dispel the hazy cloud of classical gas that is already starting to gather around the nineties, particularly the early part of the decade. The period between the release of 'Smells Like Teen Spirit' and the death of Kurt Cobain less than three years later is, we're now being told, a golden age of rock, the likes of which we may never see again. This suits those who profit from the back catalogues of dead or ageing rock stars, but is far less interesting or useful to those of us who hope to preserve or revive their ideals.

'When youth culture becomes monopolised by big business, what are the youth to do?' asked Sonic Youth's Thurston Moore in 1991. The singer went on, answering his own question. 'I think that we should destroy the bogus capitalistic process that is destroying youth culture: mass marketing and commercial, uh… paranoia behaviour control. And the first step to do is to destroy the record companies.' Moore, like his friend Kurt Cobain, was a new kind of rock star, with ideals and ethics forged in the crucible of punk, making his way through the world of corporate entertainment. Over the next ten years, Moore's underground peers would find themselves similarly thrust into the maw of a billion-dollar music industry, the supposedly airtight network of mergers, megastores and MTV, whose foundations had been laid in the eighties by the success of pop stars like Michael Jackson and Madonna. Once there, these idealistic types had to reconcile their principles with the new demands being made on them as entertainers.

Most found this impossible. Because they saw their art as a means of expressing their dissatisfaction with the state of the world, and held a belief that music could play a role in improving it, they realised early on that their job was not to entertain but to complain, and to keep on complaining, even when people insisted there was nothing to complain about. Looking back on the decade now, and at all that's happened since, I believe they were right to do so. Nothing seems more premature, or more disingenuous than those voices in this book that urge their peers and their fans to take it easy, to chill out, to stop worrying so much about everything, to take music and politics less seriously, to do the tour, play the hits and take the money. Nothing is more frightening than the moment, late in 1993, when Kurt Cobain declares that he is tired of complaining, that he wants to lead a normal life, to watch TV and shop and celebrate Christmas like everybody else. Nothing, save perhaps its transatlantic equivalent, the easy-listening nightmare depicted in Blur's 'The Universal', wherein Damon Albarn resolves to stop making trouble and follow the path of least resistance. 'If the days just seem to fall through you,' he advises, 'just let them go.'

Albarn and Cobain were justified in believing that there was something abnormal about the artist's incessant need to make trouble — complaining wasn't always the artist's lot. In my last book, *Hey!*

Nietzsche! Leave Them Kids Alone!, I tried to show that artists were, to some extent, forced into this role by necessity roughly two hundred years ago. Faced with a world that was becoming less fair and less free, they sought to preserve what they saw as authentically human values, and rejected those of the new industrial society. As a result, they became outsiders, consigned to the margins of modern life. Two centuries later, in 1990, they were still there. The commercial breakthrough of grunge in 1991, and the subsequent arrival of Britpop in 1994, seemed to promise an end to this state of affairs. Both offered a hopeful vision of radical art reconciled with popular culture, the outsiders finally let back in. Both were touted as youth revolts, the disenfranchised kids of the eighties taking control of the media and making their voice heard. Both made the mistake of assuming that the basic problem of the artist's alienation could be fixed by music, that once the wider world accepted and embraced alternative rock and its unlikely stars, the rest would take care of itself. Subsequent events showed that this was by no means the case. Alternative rock was accommodated on the media spectacle's terms; its complaint was tolerated on the understanding that its radical message would go largely unheard.

The repackaging of alt rock as nostalgia represents the final phase of this process, the revolution safely locked away behind glass, and I can't pretend that this book won't benefit from it. But it's my sincere wish that the story I've told here should do more to undermine the canonisation of nineties music than to help the process along. I've tried, as much as possible, to take the masterpieces out of their frames, to kick our heroes out of the hall of fame and dump them on the street, to put the music and the people who made it back into the world they hoped to change. If the result reads sometimes like a litany of failure, a succession of stories about artists who find — for one reason or another — that they are unable to live up to their ideals, it's because I want very much to refute the view of rock history promoted by anniversary specials and box sets, which assures us that we can accept Classic Hits in lieu of the realisation of their authors' best hopes for the world.

'Music means time,' said Jeff Buckley in 1994. As the singer sat in a radio studio and picked out five pieces of music that turned his world upside down, Buckley told triple j's Richard Kingsmill that for him, songs are 'the things that keep time in your life.' The music industry knows this, of course. It makes a great deal of money from nostalgia — whether it be the nostalgia of thirty-something music fans who bought Pearl Jam and Pulp records in their teens and twenties, or the nostalgia of those born after 1991, who wish that they had been old enough to participate in the music wars they grew up hearing so much about. But just because our wish to return to the past can be exploited for profit doesn't make the impulse itself a bad one. Nostalgia, as Buckley suggested, invites us to reflect on our lives and all that's changed in the world and ourselves over their course. As such, it can become a force for cultural and social change. When a stray object, sensation or song unexpectedly takes us back to an earlier time, we're confronted with the often staggering discrepancy between the promises of our past and the reality of our present. We're reminded, essentially, that things could be other than they are, that everything has changed, and could change again.

The past, and what we do with it, is a recurring theme in this book. It's full of stories about musicians rediscovering and coming to grips with music's history — Kurt Cobain and Richey Edwards poring over the legacy of punk, Kim Deal re-imagining Led Zeppelin, Liz Phair picking up *Exile on Main St* by the scruff of the neck and giving it a good talking-to, Damon Albarn digging through Justine Frischmann's second-hand vinyl LPs, Beck snapping up second-rate sixties folk albums in the thrift store, Gomez and Mercury Rev rediscovering what cultural critic Greil Marcus called the 'old weird America'. Because they drew so much from music's past, many of these artists were accused, at one time or another, of wanting for real inspiration, just as musicians who draw on the sounds and styles of the nineties today will be. The argument is as misleading and counterproductive now as it was twenty years ago. New bands inevitably take their influences from the past. ('Of course we do,' said a friend of mine. 'We can't be influenced by the future.') And this shouldn't be a problem, since the past, as their older siblings and parents constantly remind them, was a golden age. But when new music sounds too much like old music, older listeners accuse their heirs of betraying their legacy. What made music great in the seventies/eighties/nineties, they say, is that it was original — so you must be original too. This double standard, ironically, encourages exactly the kind of shallow dabbling that further convinces older music fans that we are now adrift in a postmodern wasteland of reference and pastiche, where nothing is happening because history is over.

This, of course, is no more true in 2012 than it was in 1992. History, despite what we might like to think, goes on. We make it every day, by living our lives, listening to music, involving ourselves in social life and politics, but also in the way we construct and reconstruct our idea of the past. In their different ways, all the artists whose lives and careers I've documented here were involved in this ongoing process, as they sought to make good on what Walter Benjamin called 'the promises of the past'. When they looked back at history, they saw not a hall of fame, but a shambles; not a litany of heroes, but a long list of unfinished business. This is exactly how the story of music in the nineties strikes me today, and this is the restless spirit in which I hope this book will be received.

1990

Trust the Kids

'I don't know what it is, but they're probably the best band in the world right now'.[1] The year was 1989, and Paul, seventeen years old, was talking about the Stone Roses, a four-piece rock group from Manchester whose debut album had already turned the UK's independent music scene on its head. Their single 'Fools Gold' had recently landed in the UK Top Ten, and many critics and music fans would have agreed with Paul that they were indeed the best band in the world. It certainly came as no surprise to the group themselves. 'We feel we're the only British group worth exporting since the Sex Pistols,' John Squire told *Rolling Stone*.[2] And according to the band's singer, Ian Brown, it had always been thus. 'We always knew we were special,' he told *Melody Maker*'s John Wilde.[3]

Unlike most of his colleagues in the UK music press, Wilde remained unmoved by the excitement surrounding the band. 'Five years from now,' he wrote, 'the Stone Roses will be seen to be of no significance whatsoever.' Roses hype, Wilde insisted, was mostly wishful thinking, 'an excuse to rave up the dying months of an uneventful decade in music'. He asked the band's fans to explain themselves. What's so great about the Stone Roses? 'It's the attitude,' they replied.[4] This answer failed to convince Wilde, but it revealed a lot about the band's appeal. The Stone Roses had an attitude that went beyond the usual rebellious rock and roll stance. Theirs was an attitude to the future — that it should be embraced — and an attitude to the past — that it should be destroyed. 'Has anyone ever said anything to you that really hurt?' asked a TV interviewer. Brown furrowed his brow and stared down at his enormous flared jeans. 'That we're influenced by the sixties,' he replied.[5] This kind of talk made the Roses instantly heroic to an audience too young for punk and sick to death of baby boomer reruns. An American journalist once gave the band what he thought was a compliment by comparing them to the Rolling Stones. 'Rolling who?' Brown shot back. 'It's 1990, innit?'[6] And this wasn't bluff either — the Stones had already asked the Roses to support them on their Steel Wheels tour. But the Best Band in the World had no interest in supporting the Former Best Band in the World. The Stones' offer was, they said, 'a joke, a fuckin' bore'.[7]

Critics of the band were quick to point out that the Roses had risen to a position from which they could afford to look down on the Rolling Stones by playing loose, funky, psychedelic and vaguely menacing rock that owed a substantial debt to Jagger and Richards. But while their attitude was a little ungrateful, it wasn't necessarily hypocritical. Brown, as *Q* magazine noted in its profile on the band, was of a generation that had learned to distinguish heroes from recordings, and to treasure the latter over the former.

Heroes let you down, but records last forever. Brown asked Wilde to 'name me one band that's lasted', and he couldn't, of course.[8] Rock and roll had been around for almost forty years, and no-one had managed to get to the end of rock's obstacle course without selling out, losing their edge or kicking the bucket. Mick Jagger in 1990 was an embarrassing old man in a designer suit, putting on a pantomime of rebellion in order to fuel a global money-making machine. 'So insincere,' said Brown, 'it's just patronising.' But the records Jagger made in the sixties said, and continued to say, that you could change your world; that you could rip it up and start again. To the Stone Roses, it seemed as though the legacy of the Rolling Stones was best served by destroying the Rolling Stones as soon as possible. 'We're against hypocrisy, lies, bigotry, show business, insincerity, phonies and fakes,' they declared.[9]

This policy extended to their press as well. Often, they declined to do interviews altogether, opting instead to have 'a bit of a chat' with the music press. 'Artificial situation, innit?' said Brown of the standard Q&A format.[10] 'You've got to try to get through these conventions,' he insisted. 'It's not easy.' John Wilde would have agreed that this was the case. Having sat with the band for an hour and tried in vain to get them to say something interesting for *Melody Maker* about their music, Wilde asked them straight up why it was that the Best Band in the World had nothing to say. 'We could've come along with prepared statements and snappy quotes,' Brown explained. 'That would be false though, and that's what we don't want to be. It's important to be sincere. Everything you do should come from your heart.'[11]

The Stone Roses would attempt to do away with these two most repetitive and artificial institutions of the entertainment industry — the interview and the tour — with their masterstroke of 1990 — Spike Island. 'You'll never see us do a full-scale tour,' Brown explained. 'You can't give it your best, can you? Four days in and you'll be like that [slumps forward], like a cabbage, going through the motions.'[12] The idea was that, instead of traipsing across the country doing a nightly facsimile of inspiration, the Stone Roses would play one inspired concert, and the nation would come to them. And rather than doing the usual endless round of interviews and appearances, the band would invite the world's media to sit at their feet for a single pre-gig press conference. 'What are your ambitions?' asked one journalist who'd made the pilgrimage. 'Change the world,' said Brown, 'end poverty, make everybody 'appy. I'll do me best, know what I mean?'[13]

The Stone Roses, sadly, did not make everybody happy at Spike Island. The *NME*'s reporter concluded that, 'the last ten minutes aside, the Stone Roses didn't blow anybody's minds'.[14] A twenty-one-year-old fan named Noel Gallagher was less diplomatic. 'It was a shit gig,' he later recalled. But he also claimed that it was there, at Spike Island, that the inspiration for his own world-beating indie rock band was born — and this, as the *NME*'s Roger Morton noted, was perhaps more the point. 'The foreign journalists who came to see the new rock gods in person probably went away feeling conned. But they were looking for the wrong thing in the wrong place.' The Stone Roses could be stadium gods if they chose, said Morton, 'but that would be selling their souls to sixties showbiz devils, and the band have their own participatory nineties groove to follow. A more approachable, danceable, communal groove.'[15]

Factory Records boss Tony Wilson had noticed the first signs of this 'Spike Island spirit' in May 1988. These were the glory days of acid house, the merger of American electronic dance music and ecstasy that had transformed both club culture and indie rock in the UK in the last moments of the 1980s. 'What have we here,' said Wilson to himself as he looked into the eyes of the dancers at Factory's Ibiza-themed 'Hot' night. A new spirit, which was also an old spirit — a bit 1968, a bit 1976: 'A bit like being part of the French Revolution, I gather, from what people said who were at the French Revolution.'[16] Noting that the crowd was applauding the DJ rather than the singer — 'the medium, not the message' — Wilson concluded that a new egalitarian ideal was at large: no more rock gods, no more heroes, a poetry made by all, everybody is a star. For Ian Brown, whose musical ideal was formed as much by nights like 'Hot' as by the Jesus and Mary Chain, this was the point of Spike Island. 'I'm not performing,' he said. 'I'm just participating.' This was why he preferred the chat to the interview, the outdoor riot to the concert tour, the perfect disaster to the well-executed show. 'I'm somehow always getting people to participate rather than spectate … I'm not interested in being spectated, I'm interested in the group being a catalyst to spark things.'[17]

By the end of 1990, it was possible to point to a number of significant 'things' that the Stone Roses had made possible. The shape of UK music had changed dramatically. Two years previously, the BBC's Radio 1 and *Top of the Pops* had been the private playground of eighties MOR megastars such as Phil Collins, or soap actors with record contracts such as Kylie Minogue and Jason Donovan. Now — thanks to the Roses' example — the nation's charts and playlists were being invaded by scruffy, mouthy bands with loud guitars and dirty minds. The Happy Mondays, Inspiral Carpets, the Soup Dragons, Primal Scream, and The Farm all had records in the Top 40 and songs on the radio, and everybody agreed this was a very good thing. '1990 is proving to be the year the eighties forgot,' wrote *NME*'s Simon Williams, 'the resurgence of the underdogs wherein the pop pups chomp savagely back.'[18] Such was the mood of optimism that even a baggy-by-numbers racket like Blur could be considered future hit-makers. 'Randall, or whatever his name is, has definite star potential,' wrote *Melody Maker*. The old guard seemed finally to be making room for the new, and the future of music looked as though it was in good hands. 'It's gonna be really nice,' said Mark Gardener from Ride, 'when you can put the radio on in the daytime, and maybe every other record is good, whereas for ages it's been a load of shit.'[19]

The Sundays were another of Britain's great white hopes for 1990, and the band happily admitted to having benefited from the Stone Roses' pioneering excursion into the national chart. But the Sundays were very different to the Roses — their debut album, *Reading Writing and Arithmetic*, contained no dance beats or wah-wah licks, and their interviews were entirely free of the Madchester bands' cocky bluster. 'I don't think we'd take it upon ourselves to be hopes for the nineties,' said guitarist David Gavurin. In the early eighties, Gavurin reminded the *NME*'s reporter, there was a lot of talk about a new spirit in music, and a lot of excitement over post-punk bands like U2 and Simple Minds 'storming' the pop charts. What good had it done? 'It's not quite as simple as thinking about what's alternative now getting into the mainstream. You've got to hope that it's going to lead to something in the future.'[20]

But what might that 'something' be? Ian Brown had undoubtedly had his tongue not too far from his cheek when he said that he planned to change the world and make everybody happy. But in May 1990 this kind of talk did not seem nearly as ridiculous as it might have twelve months earlier. Emboldened by recent events — the fall of the Berlin Wall, the first free elections in East Germany and Romania — music journalists made hopeful parallels between pop and politics, the likes of which had not been heard since 1968. At the Spike Island press conference, *Spin* asked the Roses if they thought that 'the radical change in British music and the revolutions in Eastern Europe could have been linked with the end of an old decade, people seeing the oncoming nineties as a chance to create cultural and social change?' 'That could have something to do with it,' said guitarist John Squire. 'Human beings have realised they can make things change.'[21] 'I don't see it being naïve or hippy-ish that people will come together,' Brown insisted in early 1990. 'I believe they will because they have to.'[22]

New Sounds for a New World

'We put MTV into East Berlin,' said Viacom's Sumner Redstone in January 1990, 'and six months later the wall came down.'[1] To consolidate this victory, and leave viewers in no doubt that revolutions in pop were inextricably linked to — if not solely responsible for — changes in global politics, MTV began broadcasting a new station promo later that year. The viewer was shown brief highlights from the network's playlist — Snap!'s 'The Power', Deee-Lite's 'Groove is in the Heart', Aztec Camera's 'The Crying Scene', Iggy Pop's duet with Kate Pierson, 'Candy', and a new song by Faith No More, 'Falling To Pieces'. Faith No More's livewire singer Mike Patton leered into the camera, as the voice-over guy drove home the message. 'New sounds,' he said, in a voice usually reserved for Bruce Willis movies, 'for a new world.'[2]

Implying that the end of an oppressive socialist regime was in any way connected with the launch of a new video by Snap! might seem glib. But the image of a great barrier collapsing, of a divided country — and a divided world — being reunited, was inspiring and contagious in 1989. 'When the old geo-political maps were ripped to pieces,' wrote Dick Hebdige, 'the reversibility of binary terms like "left" and "right" were suddenly made public.'[3] This new way of looking at the world spiked the usual draft of optimism that goes down at the start of a new decade with something stronger, a desire to rejoin and reconnect, to make whole what had been divided by doing away with outmoded distinctions. In their own way, MTV's priorities for 1990 — which included a techno hit from Frankfurt, a romantic duet featuring a punk icon and a new wave chanteuse, and Deee-Lite's five-way collaboration between a Russian DJ, a Japanese producer, a funk legend, an afrocentric rapper and a New York performance artist — reflected this new mood.

In October, The Cult's Ian Astbury staged a two-day festival in California called A Gathering of the Tribes. The bill, featuring Soundgarden, Ice-T, the Indigo Girls and the Charlatans, suggested a new world in which eighties subcultures like post-hardcore, rap, folk and psychedelic indie rock could finally meet as equals. But these inter-genre handshakes were already taking place within music itself. The Stone Roses had made guitar music that ravers could dance to, and the Happy Mondays' shambolic punk-funk was being remixed for clubs by house music DJs like Paul Oakenfold and Andy Weatherall. Candy Flip and the Soup Dragons had covered the Beatles and the Stones respectively, but had done it over sampled hip-hop breaks and Jamaican dub effects. And Jesus Jones had fused guitar noise with techno on their album *Liquidizer*, whose cover image of a pop-art blender gave notice of singer Mike Edwards's vision: in the nineties, we would use technology to mix music together. 'It's very easy to make guitar music, and it's very easy to make dance music,' he said in 1990. 'The difficulty is in trying to combine the two.'[4] For the members of EMF, however, there was nothing difficult about it. The band had begun in 1989, when the six original members decided 'to have a laugh', as keyboardist Derry Brownson later said, by putting on a rave in the forest. When Ian Dench joined the group later that year, he suggested they start recording songs, and asked singer James Atkin what they should sound like. 'Dance stuff with guitars,' Atkin replied. 'And that,' Dench told *Q* magazine, 'is the only time we've ever talked about how EMF was going to sound.'[5] They signed with EMI after their fourth gig, and the label's head of A&R proudly described them as 'the best band EMI have signed since the Pet Shop Boys and before that the Sex Pistols'.[6] 'Unbelievable' was released as a single in the UK in August 1990, and had become an anthem by the end of the year

In England, dance-rock bridged a gap between the rave and the gig. 'Amazingly,' wrote *i-D* magazine's Mike Noon, 'it is no longer an unfashionable thing for an indie music fan to be seen dancing to

Soul II Soul.'[7] In America fusion meant bringing black music closer to white, which, in 1989, meant finding a way to mix hip-hop with metal. In 1987, Rick Rubin had brokered the first major summit between the two forms with Run-D.M.C. and Aerosmith's 'Walk This Way'. But while the wall that separated black pop from white rock had been symbolically ripped apart in that song's video, in real life, it remained intact. Red Hot Chili Peppers' singer Anthony Kiedis felt that music in the late eighties was still heavily segregated, with bands always having to be placed 'in some rigid category, like black radio, white radio, CHR radio, AOR radio'.[8] Now, new albums by the Chili Peppers, Fishbone, Primus and Living Colour suggested that this musical apartheid might soon be overturned by a coffee-coloured funk-metal for the nineties.

Faith No More's January 1990 single 'Epic' was one of the new music's first real success stories, a proper fusion of hip-hop and hard rock which seemed to combine all the best elements of both genres, and more besides. Patton spat out his verses in the blustery style of Run-D.M.C. as the band hammered out bass-heavy beats. Then, as the song lurched into its chorus, he instantly shifted gears, wailing and snarling like Johnny Rotten after singing lessons. Guitarist Jim Martin let fly with joyous seventies-style hard rock licks that gave way, after a while, to a strange, melancholy solo that sounded like it owed more to Schubert than Sabbath. And as the song came to an end, and the rest of the band faded to silence, a lone piano played a stately blues. 'It's a musical hybrid,' exclaimed CNN's *Showbiz Today*, 'that combines heavy metal and rap with African drum rhythms, classical piano and jazz.'[9]

No-one, in 1990, had ever heard anything quite like it, and the band were quizzed endlessly about their genre-busting sound — how did they come up with it? 'Everybody in the band is very different from one another,' explained Martin. 'We all have different musical tastes and styles.'[10] Martin was an unreconstructed rock animal with a taste for the bizarre, while bassist Billy Gould had roots in metal and a keen interest in hip-hop. Keyboardist Roddy Bottum was classically trained, and well-versed in jazz and cabaret, while drummer Mike 'Puffy' Bordin wore his hair in dreadlocks and listened to Metallica. Patton's tastes, meanwhile, ranged all over the musical map, from the industrial clang of Einstürzende Neubauten to the soothing strings of Mantovani.

Bordin, Bottum, Martin and Gould had been playing together in San Francisco since the mid eighties. They started out in a style Gould later described as 'psychedelic, but still with a groove', and began looking for a singer who could 'scream and yell and basically just provoke people'.[11] An eighteen-year-old zine writer and sometime radio announcer named Courtney Love joined the band for a spell in 1982, but left soon after. They hired Chuck Mosley in 1983, but after dragging the non-singer 'kicking and screaming' through four years of recording and touring, the band parted ways with him following the release of 1987's *Introduce Yourself*, and embarked on what Martin later described as a 'scary' period, writing music for a band without a singer, or any clear direction for the future. But Martin's penchant for weirdness eventually led him to an avant-rock group called Mr Bungle, and its singer, Mike Patton. The twenty-year-old Patton was handed a tape of the band's new music, and over the next month composed lyrics for it. By the end of January 1989 the songs were recorded, and six months later *The Real Thing* was released.

Describing the effect Patton's singing had on Faith No More's music, Billy Gould offered that 'his voice kind of elevates it'.[12] This was understating the case by a long shot — Patton instantly made himself essential to the band. While most elements of the group's musical approach were in place by the time *Introduce Yourself* was recorded, Mosley's undistinguished bark had tended to flatten out what they were trying to achieve. Patton's melodies picked out the pop hooks that Bottum's parts hinted at, and his powerful voice blew them up to stadium proportions. His high, clear tone cut right through the band's dense blocks of noise, and when they quieted down, he could croon in your ear like Sinatra. 'Ugh, get the old singer back,' complained Jim Bob of Carter the Unstoppable Sex Machine after hearing *The Real Thing*. 'This bloke's voice is really horrible, isn't it?'[13] But Jim Bob was in a minority. When *Rolling Stone* asked the band what the main difference between Faith No More Mark 1 and Mark 2 was, Patton hit the nail on the head when he replied, 'I can sing.'[14]

MTV began playing the video for 'Epic' in January, and not long after, *The Real Thing* reached number 11 in the Billboard Top 20. Faith No More's shows rapidly filled up with much younger fans than they'd had in the late eighties, kids who might have been listening to MC Hammer or Mötley Crüe last week, but had caught 'Epic' on MTV and wanted to see what Faith No More was all about. This new popular audience came at the expense of their old one, many of whom felt that Faith No More had sold out. But the band had already decided they could do without these people. 'San Francisco,' Bottum observed, 'is full of these assholes who say "you shouldn't eat at McDonald's, it's politically uncool". And then you ask them why *and they don't fuckin' know!*'[15] Bottum and Gould had cable installed in their share-house so they could watch MTV, partly because they liked MTV, but mostly because they knew it would annoy the kind of San Fran hipsters who believed anything popular had to be bad, the very same people who were now turning their backs on Faith No More. 'I don't see the point of limiting accessibility out of stubbornness,' said Gould. 'There's always been this misconception that "commercial" equals "stupid". Just because something is accepted by a lot of people, doesn't mean there isn't some interesting thought behind it, you know?'[16]

In November 1989, Billy Gould and Roddy Bottum made a promotional appearance on *Billboard Top 20*, a televised rundown of the national chart. 'And now, here to count them down, a funk-rock band with a new album,' said host Bella Shaw, as the camera cut to Gould and Bottum, wearing the kind of smirks on their faces that suggested they knew they were somewhere they should not be.[17] As they read out the list, it became clear why — underground rock bands did not appear in the Billboard Top 20 in 1989. They stayed where they belonged — underground, and left the business of pop to pop stars. Johnny Gill, Glenn Medeiros, Mariah Carey, New Kids on the Block and Michael Bolton, who was 'Back in the charts again with "When I'm Back on My Feet Again",' as Bottum, reading carefully from his autocue, informed the nation. Having wrapped up the countdown, Bottum and Gould recited, in cheesy unison, 'We're Faith No More, and we'll see *you* on the chart!'[18] This last was scripted, like everything else, but unmistakably aimed at those 'assholes' in San Francisco — who of course wouldn't see it, being too busy watching PBS or listening to Primus.

Onstage, Patton began incorporating bits of the Billboard Top 20 into the band's set. Stick-in-the-muds who'd paid their money to hear

'We Care A Lot' — from the band's pre-pop days — were rewarded with a medley version where Patton would throw in whole verses from the New Kids on the Block's 'Right Stuff', or Madonna's 'Vogue'. He sang the Nestlé commercial straight, and responded to the crowd's requests for Sabbath's 'War Pigs' with a note-perfect version of Van Halen's 'Jump' or the Commodores' smooth-as-silk seventies hit, 'Easy'. Patton was having fun — getting off on the goofy thrill of singing pop songs just as he had on *The Real Thing*, which is, if nothing else, a great pop album. But he was also provoking the audience, making people mad — including Jim Martin, who made no secret of his distaste for such material. Onstage, he would pointedly light up a cigarette and stand to the side while Patton and the rest of the band jammed on the Top 20.

By the time Faith No More had found its way onto MTV, the group's former lead singer, Courtney Love, had gone through some ups and downs. Having parted ways with the band, she'd started a short-lived group with her friends Jennifer Finch and Kat Bjelland, appeared as a 'punk rock extra' on an episode of *Quincy*, and spent three years working as a stripper at LA clubs such as the Seventh Veil and the Star Strip. 'But then I had to quit,' she later explained, 'because they kept playing songs by Faith No More. There's nothing worse than having to dance topless to your old band.'[19] Love spent some time in self-imposed exile in Alaska before moving back to LA to start 'a band that everybody would hate' called Hole. On the way, she decided to stop in Seattle, Washington, home to a thriving scene of long-haired post-punk bands like Mother Love Bone, Soundgarden, the Screaming Trees and Mudhoney. As she rode the Greyhound bus into town, Love's head was filled with daydreams about Mudhoney's Mark Arm and Kurt Cobain, the lead singer of Nirvana. But Love was no groupie. 'When I get my band together,' she thought to herself, 'you are gonna open for me.'[20]

We Wanna be Free

'People were literally saying to each other: "Have you heard? The Scream have rocked out." It was like something dirty had happened.'[1] Publicist Jeff Barratt recalled the release of Primal Scream's second album in 1989 as the moment the indie music scene turned its back on the band. They'd fallen a long way in a relatively short space of time. In 1986, Primal Scream had been hailed as heroes — that year's 'Velocity Girl' was so influential that it had created a genre in its own right, a wave of bands that played chiming melodic rock on twelve-string guitars, mouthing vaguely psychedelic lyrics from beneath bowl-shaped haircuts. But this was a development Primal Scream's singer Bobby Gillespie almost immediately tried to distance himself from. For Gillespie, music was about 'melody, sex and violence', and the fey, jangle-pop groups that sprang up in the wake of 'Velocity Girl' seemed to him to be deficient in the first category and totally lacking in the other two.[2] Primal Scream ran a mile from the twelve-string aesthetic on its second album — the band members grew their hair long, donned leather jackets and embraced balls-to-the-wall biker rock. If this move had been intended to alienate them from the indie crowd, it worked. But having escaped from indie's small-minded ghetto, Primal Scream appeared to have nowhere else to go. They wanted to start a riot — or at least make people dance, but their new direction was so far from the UK's idea of dance music at the end of the eighties as to be laughable.

Toward the end of 1990, Primal Scream's label boss Alan McGee put the band on a six-month tour to try to drum up some much-needed excitement over the album. But this only made matters worse — playing unfashionable music for tiny audiences and an indifferent music press began to wear the band out, and Gillespie considered calling time on Primal Scream. In any case, he saw little point seeing through the rest of the tour. The band cancelled their remaining European dates and flew home from Barcelona in March 1990 — to a pleasant surprise, as it turned out. In the band's absence, a new Primal Scream single had been prepared for release, and Creation Records had received roughly 7500 advance orders for it. The company's publicist Laurence Verfaillie — who had been dreading the prospect of touting a new Primal Scream record to a rock press that had all but written the band off — suddenly found she had the easiest job in the world. 'It was incredible,' she said. 'I was phoning the likes of *Blitz* and *The Face* to ask if they'd got the record, and hearing the track playing in the background. It was overwhelming.'[3]

The record in question was 'Loaded', a remix of the song 'I'm Losing More Than I'll Ever Have' by Andrew Weatherall. The DJ had grafted the band's country-rock ballad onto a drum loop from a tune by Edie Brickell and the New Bohemians, and rebuilt the song from the floor up — beginning with the bass, gradually adding slide guitar, horns, backing vocals, Andrew Innes's wild wah-wah solo and the barest flicker of Gillespie's voice. The result was somewhere between Coldcut's 'Paid in Full' remix and the Rolling Stones' 'You Can't Always Get What You Want' — a cutting-edge dance record that somehow sounded like you'd been hearing it your whole life. Well before its official release in March, 'Loaded' had become an end-of-the-night anthem at raves and clubs across London and beyond.

'Loaded' reversed Primal Scream's fortunes in an instant — the band Creation couldn't give away six months earlier were now music press darlings. Everybody wanted to talk to Bobby Gillespie, and he was more than happy to oblige, since he had a few things to get off his chest. 'It's 1990 but sometimes you wouldn't know it,' he told Jack Barron. 'What really fucks me off is that we're into a new era in music and bigots on both sides of the rock-dance fence are still too dumb to realise what's going on. It's like, the Wonder Stuff have a song called "Who Wants to be the Disco King?" I think that is fucking disgusting, deeply offensive. They might as well have just called it "Who Wants to be a Nigger?" since the song implies that white rock is intelligent and has something to say and black dance or disco music is banal and only for idiots to dance to.'[4] Gillespie had come to realise that the weekly music papers, with their separate indie and dance charts, were perpetuating this kind of musical bigotry. 'It shouldn't be like that,' he insisted. 'It's all just music really.'[5]

Primal Scream's follow-up to 'Loaded', 'Come Together' sampled Jesse Jackson on stage at Wattstax in 1972. 'Today on this program you will hear gospel and rhythm and blues and jazz,' he said. 'All those are just labels: we know that music is music.'[6] A soulful choir sang 'come together as one', heralding the arrival of music's new borderless world. Meanwhile, Terry Farley's mix on the other side of the single preserved Gillespie's original vocal, 'I'm free, you're free'. The record's euphoric sound and optimistic lyrics suggested the arrival of a new hippy movement for the nineties, as did the simultaneous release of records like the Stone Roses' 'One Love' and the Soup Dragons' 'I'm Free'. There were other signs too, of a return to the spirit of '69 — the Roses had already invited the comparison by staging events like the rave at Alexandra Palace in north London, and the one-band Woodstock at Spike Island. The year's most fashionable men's haircut was a kind of grown-out mop top directly descended from the one worn by The Byrds' Roger McGuinn in 1967; album covers and videos by the Happy Mondays, Deee-Lite, De La Soul and Soho sprouted flowers and paisley spirals; the style magazine *i-D* emblazoned its covers with slogans like 'Positivity', 'Fresh' and 'Feel Free', and the July 1990 issue of *The Face* announced 'The 3rd Summer of Love' next to a photograph of a sixteen-year-old model from south London named Kate Moss wearing a feather headdress.

But 1990 wasn't all about peace and love. 'We're not into wearing fucking daisies in our hair and shouting "karma fucking peace man". Fuck that,' said Wilbur, a baggy-trousered Manchester teen interviewed by Mike Noon. 'We like the violence'.[7] Many writers noted the aggressive edge to the new psychedelia — the accusative 'you' in the lyrics, the stony-faced stares under the bowl cuts. The Stone Roses' debut had a lot more hate songs than love songs on it; music writer Peter Kane claimed that the band dispensed with bells and beads in favour of 'a rather harsher, streetsussed code for urban survival'.[8]

Soho's 'Hippy Chick' had flowers in its video, but also sampled a shotgun in its chorus. And Bobby Gillespie described Primal Scream's psychedelic odyssey, 'Higher than the Sun' — released in September — as a 'Street Fighting Man' for the oncoming decade. Rave culture and indie rock in the UK had prescribed peace and love as an antidote to Thatcher's conservatism. But by the summer of 1990, her police force's continued attempts to thwart this new youth culture by shutting down raves and parties had forced those who supported it to adopt a more radical, confrontational stance. Speaking to *Rolling Stone*, Factory Records' Tony Wilson rejected the idea that the scene was 'non-political'. 'Nothing has been as political as this,' he said, 'where the police are trying to close you down and the British government is going berserk over your parties.'[9] To dance in the streets in 1990 was to pick a fight in the streets, and this — according to Andy Weatherall — was the real subject of 'Loaded'. If it was a peace and love anthem, it was one that recognised that you might have to fight for peace and learn to hate those opposed to love. It was, he said, a record to play at your warehouse party as the police kick down the door.[10] The fuzz would be met with a canned rebuke in the form of the spoken-word sample that opens the song: We wanna be free, to … to do what we wanna do! And we wanna get loaded, and we wanna have a good time! And that's what we're gonna do.[11]

We're the Load of Crap

The movie dialogue heard at the start of Primal Scream's 'Loaded' had also been sampled two years earlier in another song — 'In 'n' Out of Grace', by the Seattle-based four-piece Mudhoney. Peter Fonda's freedom rap wasn't the only thing the two groups had in common. Like Primal Scream, Mudhoney had spent the late eighties mining a vein of loose, loud psychedelic garage rock at odds with both mainstream pop and the underground scene from which they'd emerged. Bobby Gillespie and Mudhoney singer Mark Arm were both devotees of Roky Erickson's 13th Floor Elevators, and had in common a taste for biker chic and sixties exploitation films (Mudhoney's name was taken from a movie by one of the kings of the genre, Russ Meyer). The members of Mudhoney and Primal Scream also shared a considerable appetite for drugs — especially speed and ecstasy — which played a decisive role in the history of both groups. It was ecstasy that drew Gillespie to rave culture and gave Innes the idea of collaborating with Weatherall; while Mudhoney might never have existed if drummer Dan Peters hadn't been high as a kite when Arm and guitarist Steve Turner asked him to join the band.[1]

But if the band shared many of the Scream's influences, they seemed — as of 1989 — to have done a more convincing job of synthesising these into something of their own. Seattle's relative isolation from both the US indie network and the LA-centric rock mainstream allowed its music scene to develop in highly idiosyncratic ways. The city's bands were fired by punk, but had, by the late eighties, begun to grow their hair long and play rambling acid-fried guitar solos in defiance of indie orthodoxy. They rocked out in a semi-ironic fashion that let the audience know that they knew it was stupid, but they did it so well that nobody particularly cared how seriously they took it. They bought old sixties and seventies effects units because they were cheap and no-one else wanted them, and flaunted their bad-taste qualities while making no secret of their very sincere enjoyment of the sounds they produced. Two of these outmoded devices combined to give Mudhoney the title of their 1988 EP, *Superfuzz Bigmuff*. The record came wrapped in a sleeve featuring hand-drawn comix-style lettering and a black-and-white photo of the band in full flight — sweat, bead necklaces, dinged-up guitars and hair everywhere. It looked, in 1988, like a thing from another world — or another time.

In 1989, Mudhoney's record company, Sub Pop, flew a British journalist named Everett True to Seattle at great expense so that he could cover the scene. True returned like a colonial explorer, with tales of a strange, wild beast roaming America's northwest — the bastard offspring of hardcore and Creedence Clearwater Revival, raised on a diet of beer and ecstasy, driven half crazy by post-industrial boredom and long, cold nights. 'Raging primal grunginess,' wrote True, in his profile on Mudhoney. 'Ultimate gnarly gristly gory grossly grainy, grimy garage group.'[2] In the midst of the UK's highly politicised and fashion-conscious music scene, at a time when polite jangle-rock and third-rate Velvet Underground copyists seemed to define the limits of what bands could achieve, news of a genuine rock freakout in the forest caused no small amount of excitement.

After 'Loaded' Primal Scream's Bobby Gillespie was fired with enthusiasm for even more bold genre collisions, as the band began working on an album that would fuse psychedelic rock with dub, hip-hop, free jazz and post-rave chillout soundtracks. But hearing one of the early results of this experiment — a cover of Roky Erickson's 'Slip Inside This House', Mark Arm declared that Primal Scream had 'butchered it' by removing the guitar riff.[3] The comment was telling — while Gillespie was attempting to make a record that sounded like the Rolling Stones, The KLF, Jane's Addiction, Sun Ra, Lee 'Scratch' Perry and Sly Stone all at the same time, Mudhoney seemed to be writing the same song over and over again. The band's aesthetic, which had seemed so promising only two years earlier, now appeared worryingly limited, and Mudhoney's highly anticipated debut album, released in 1989, sounded like a group stuck in a rut — playing the same kind of noise as they had on their earlier EPs, but without the sense of urgency or conviction. The UK press lost interest, London's love affair with Seattle appeared to be on the rocks, and Mark Arm was on the defensive. 'Fuck you!' he told the *NME*. 'We used to do E years before you guys over here did.'[4]

In a sense, Mudhoney had simply become victims of the UK music scene's notoriously fast news cycle. A geographically small country served by three competing weekly papers created a constant demand for next big things — and an alarming tendency to lose interest in them if they failed to come up with any new tricks within three months of being discovered. American musicians had grown used to watching this carnival ride with a kind of bemused disbelief. Unless, of course, they were taken for a spin themselves. 'We'd say, "It's all hype, what a load of crap,"' as Mark Arm recalled, 'and then the next thing you know, *we're* the load of crap.'[5]

But there were other, more specific reasons why Mudhoney's star fell so dramatically after 1989. When the band talked in interviews about the qualities they admired in music, they used words like 'sick', 'poorly played' and 'messed up'.[6] Mark Arm's lyrics were mostly confined to themes of disease, failure and degradation. He wrote — by his own admission — only two kinds of songs, songs about dogs and songs about sickness. The band's taste in retro moved in a similar direction. To Mudhoney, the sixties was fun because it was cheap, and a good joke. The seventies was even better because it was bloated and in poor taste. They loved the cornball kick of old fuzz pedals and old biker movies, and happily admitted to stealing riffs from their favourite garage-rock tunes. But unlike the British positivists, Mudhoney had no vision of tomorrow — they weren't using all this stuff to invent the future, just playing with it because there was nothing else to do. 'I think you're kind of fooling yourself as a rock band if you think you're doing anything really original,' said Arm.[7] Hearing Peter Fonda talk of freedom and partying on 'Loaded' was quite a different proposition to hearing the same speech in the midst of a Mudhoney EP — where the first spoke of possibilities, the second made an ironic joke of their disappearance.

In the midst of British music's prevailing 'positivity' vibe, Mudhoney's lack of ambition and obsession with failure seemed perverse. 'We don't have time for negative thinking,' said the Stone Roses in 1990.[8] But in the American underground, there seemed to be all the time in the world — negativity was encouraged, and failure became popular. In Seattle, Mudhoney played a festival with Tad and Nirvana called Lame Fest, while their record label did a brisk trade in T-shirts with the single word 'LOSER' emblazoned across the front in bold type. 'The loser,' explained Tad's Kurt Danielson, 'is the existential hero of the nineties.'[9] Dinosaur Jr's J Mascis had declared that it was his ambition 'not to have ambition',[10] and Mascis's friends in Sonic Youth had paid tribute to the guitarist's legendary apathy in their song 'Teenage Riot'. 'It'd take a teenage riot to get me out of bed right now,' sang Thurston Moore.[11] In Chapel Hill, North Carolina, indie band Superchunk had a hit with a song called 'Slack Motherfucker', in which singer Mac McCaughan confirmed Mark Arm's suspicion that rock history had come to an end. 'Everything's bought,' he yelped, 'and everything's used.'[12]

Meanwhile, in Austin, Texas, director Richard Linklater staged the first screening of his film *Slacker*, which included a scene where a young musician hands out flyers for his band's gig. 'We've changed our name,' he says. 'We're the Ultimate Losers now.'[13] This was a wise decision — in the American underground, the rhetoric of UK indie had been completely reversed. No US band, at the dawn of the nineties, would describe themselves — as the Stone Roses had — as 'the best band in the world'. In fact, any notion of success had to begin with the realisation that you were the worst.

Male, White,
Corporate Oppression

'How many times have people asked you if you've sold out in the past few months?' asked MTV's Dave Kendall. 'You're the first,' deadpanned Thurston Moore.[1] In June 1990, after ten years as an underground attraction, Sonic Youth had released its major label debut, and in the four weeks since, Moore had already become used to dodging this question — as well as awkward attempts to ask it without asking it, like Kendall's. It was difficult to answer — not because the band had anything to hide or defend — but because the concepts behind the question itself were so poorly understood. 'We've been on an independent label for ten years,' Moore explained. 'When we first started, we had nowhere else to go. The idea of being on a major label was so far-fetched ... the only alternative was to put out records yourself, which is what we did.'[2] Moore went on to describe how bands like Minor Threat and Black Flag, having no hope of interesting record companies in what they did, created their own labels — SST and Dischord — for distributing their music and touring America, and how those labels and others like them went on to support the careers of many more bands, including Hüsker Dü, Dinosaur Jr and Mudhoney. All of this would have been news to the majority of Kendall's viewers. For most of the eighties, the world of MTV and the world of SST were so sharply divided that the idea of crossing over wouldn't have crossed most indie musicians' minds.

But by 1990, the gap was closing. 'There's been a lot of progress made since then,' said Hüsker Dü's Bob Mould of the mid eighties.[3] In an interview with triple j, Mould said he felt that the idea that 'noise and melody and thoughtful lyrics can coexist' had become much more widely accepted. Underground music was becoming more popular and as a result the ad-hoc 'network of people whose floors you could sleep on' (as Mould described it) was growing to resemble something closer to a music industry.[4] By the end of the eighties, the difference between being signed to an indie or a major was becoming academic. 'It's just as much big business as the major labels,' said Sonic Youth drummer Steve Shelley to Dave Kendall.[5] But if the indie scene was turning into big business, it had already become clear by 1989 that it wasn't always good business. Tired of losing friends and being ripped off, the members of Sonic Youth decided, toward the end of that year, that if they were going to be signed to a record label it might as well be one that knew how to make money and pay its artists. The band cast a sideways glance at corporate America, and this time, found their gaze returned. David Geffen's DGC Records was interested and, after some counselling from Mould on how to negotiate a deal that gave them creative control over the direction of their music and the presentation of the band, Sonic Youth signed a contract with the label early in 1990.

DGC kept its word and left Sonic Youth alone in the studio, and the band turned in a record that was every bit as ferocious, wilful, noisy and arty as its last two. Even when *Goo* flirted with pop, it sounded like the band members were doing it because they wanted to, rather than because they had been told they had to write a hit. But while the music itself remained free of corporate meddling, the album's cover was almost a different matter. Sonic Youth had chosen an image by the underground artist Raymond Pettibon, based on a paparazzi photo from the trial of Myra Hindley, one of the perpetrators of the United Kingdom's infamous Moors murders in the sixties. Pettibon rendered the image in his usual low-rent comic-book style, and added a caption: 'I stole my sister's boyfriend, it was all whirlwind, heat, and flash. Within a week, we killed my parents and hit the road.' Geffen executives had a fit over the picture. 'This is going to be difficult for us to sell in some chains because of the world "killed",' they protested. 'Can't you change it?' Here, Mould's advice proved invaluable — the band stuck to its guns, and insisted that it could not. 'It's not just decoration,' explained Kim Gordon, 'it's important to us.'[6] '*Goo* needed an image of a strong, dangerous woman on its cover, because it was, as Moore explained, 'a very pro-women, and pro-men who are pro-women, record' — the album gave notice of a coming war between the forces of male, white, corporate oppression and those who hoped to liberate the planet from their control.[7]

Since the late eighties, Gordon had been dreaming of a revolutionary alliance between hip-hop and punk rock — two camps with a grudge against The Man teaming up to bring him down once and for all. After all, if the forces of oppression were male, white and corporate, it stood to reason that the liberating army would be female, black and indie. A summit between the queen of noise and the crown prince of hip-hop was subsequently brokered by *Spin* magazine, and Kim Gordon and rapper LL Cool J sat down to talk in September 1989. But despite (or perhaps because of) Gordon's high expectations, the encounter was disappointing. She talked about artists causing trouble and subverting mainstream culture; he said he just wanted to help people have a good time. 'Music is fun,' he insisted, 'that's why I don't get too political.'[8] She tried to talk about Iggy Pop; he said he liked Bon Jovi. 'She realised here was someone she was totally attracted to as an entertainer,' Moore said later, 'but their cultures were so divided.'[9]

On *Goo*'s first single, 'Kool Thing', Gordon called the rapper to account. After two minutes of thrilling noise-pop, the band broke down into a vamp, with Moore's guitar steaming in the background like a kettle about to boil. 'Hey, Kool Thing,' said Gordon, 'I just wanna know, what are you gonna do for me? I mean, are you gonna liberate us girls from male, white, corporate oppression?'[10] There was no answer from Kool Thing. Instead, the voice of a real black pop radical — Public Enemy's Chuck D — appeared alongside Gordon's, talking about 'fear of a female planet'. The phrase — a twist on the name of Public Enemy's 1990 album, *Fear of a Black Planet* — suggested that Gordon's dream of a sixties-style alliance between young militant rappers and feminist art-terrorists might not be so far-fetched after all. Gordon and director Tamra Davis, dreamed up a video for the song that alternated shots of Chuck D and the band with footage of Kim wearing a beret and carrying a machine gun. According to Moore, these images would give visual form to one of the album's central ideas, that 'women are the true anarchists of our society'.[11] 'For a woman,' Gordon told the *NME*, 'there was something very appealing about wanting to be an anarchist or a terrorist. I think it's very appealing myself. A woman fully clothed with a gun in her hand is probably the most sexy image you can ever see.'[12] Much to Geffen's relief, the band eventually decided against this particular version of the video. But the story shows why Pettibon's cover art was so important to the band. The image of a punk rock girl with a gun and a motive was, for Kim Gordon, a symbolic refusal of corporate control.

The Non-service Industries

Late in 1989, Joey Santiago, Kim Deal, David Lovering and Black Francis of the Pixies were rehearsing songs for a new album at Cherokee Studios, when Los Angeles was hit by a medium-sized earthquake. As the walls began to shake, they dropped their instruments and ran for the exits. 'We got outside in the car park,' said Deal, 'where there were all these guys from heavy metal bands scared shitless.'[1]

The sight of these supposed tough guys shaking in their snakeskin boots simply confirmed something Francis had suspected for years — that LA rock's badass image was nothing more than a pose. 'Rock and roll,' he told *Melody Maker* in 1990, 'has become an artificial experience. It's got nothing to do with rebellion. Rock music is just part of mass culture now. It's all acceptable. Nothing is extreme, dangerous or subversive.' Looking around at the stuff in the charts, Francis saw nothing but fake hard rock — nothing on MTV, he said, 'is gonna frighten my mother'.[2]

LA metal bands dressed like they were the end of civilisation, but their music was pure pop — fun for all the family. The Pixies were the literal reverse of this — they looked like they were dressed by their mothers, and sounded like the apocalypse. In 1989, Black Francis had worn plaid shirts tucked into jeans and talked cheerfully about how he just wanted to make 'cool rock tunes'.[3] Then *Doolittle* came out, and it sounded like the last days — songs about dead monkeys, alien girlfriends, a great flood and a serial killer on a surfboard; avalanches of noise and screaming interspersed with moments of unsettling quiet and ghostly harmonies. 'The Pixies,' wrote Simon Reynolds in a 1989 *Melody Maker* feature, 'are what's left when all the obstacles and absences that once prompted rock and roll into being have faded away or been catered for, and all that remains is the urge to holler, shriek and whoop it up for the arbitrary, unnegotiable hell of it.'[4] This was pretty close to the mark, but at Cherokee later that year, the band began working on a song that sounded more like Reynolds' description of their music than anything they'd done before — one minute and fifty-two seconds of thunderous garage punk and incomprehensible screaming. The tune's title, 'Rock Music', suggested this was the last the band had to say on the subject, and maybe all there ever was to say.

Underground rock, it could be argued, had already reached this point years earlier with bands like the Jesus Lizard, Butthole Surfers and Big Black (whose singer Steve Albini produced the Pixies' *Surfer Rosa*). But while there could be no doubt that Big Black's *Songs About Fucking* would frighten your mother, your mother never listened to college radio or read *Subterranean Pop*, so she would never hear Big Black. Your mother did, however, listen to the American Top 40 and read *People* magazine and, by 1990, the Pixies had made appearances in both. Here — in the world of Milli Vanilli, Michael Bolton and Paula Abdul — terror, despair and madness seemed like genuinely new ideas.

That their music was considered remarkable at all was, Francis believed, a sad indictment on rock and roll. In the midst of a growing furore over the introduction of 'Parental Advisory' stickers — applied to albums like Jane's Addiction's *Ritual de lo Habitual* to warn parents of their unsavoury content — Francis suggested that good rock and roll probably *should* come with a warning sticker, and Deal agreed with him. 'Rock and roll should be nasty, dirty, horrible, disgusting,' she insisted. 'Rock and roll should be like pornography. I'm all for it.'[5] Here, the Pixies believed they had history on their side. You didn't have to go to some punk-rock hellhole and watch Gibby Haynes from Butthole Surfers murder a sex doll while screaming into a megaphone to get a load of existential horror. 'Go to the museum and look at paintings,' Francis said. 'All that kind of thing is a complete staple for the non-service industries.'[6]

Francis's neat phrase could have served as a description of any major art movement since the industrial revolution, but he most likely had Surrealism in mind. As a college student, Francis was profoundly influenced by the Surrealists — his transformation from Charles Kittridge Thompson, former Teenager of the Year, into Black Francis, full-time debaser, had as much to do with Luis Buñuel as it did with Hüsker Dü. Francis instinctively grasped the connection between Dada poet Hugo Ball's 'bosso fataka oo oo' and garage rock's 'ding a ding a dang a long ling long', and set about bringing the two closer together — a feat which made the Pixies sound, as the *NME* put it, 'like the world's best-read garage band'.[7] In 1989, Francis told triple j's Tim Ritchie that he wrote songs the way André Breton used to watch movies — randomly — and set Dali and Buñuel's *Un Chien Andalou* to music in 'Debaser'.[8] Like Breton, he calmly accepted murder and mayhem as the necessary obverse of civilisation — 'I've got nothing against crime and murder particularly,' he told *Melody Maker* in 1990, 'but maybe it's just not for me'[9] — and wrote songs about serial killers the way Surrealists like Man Ray used to talk about Jack the Ripper — with admiration, and a touch of envy.

That Francis and the Pixies should do all this while wearing plaid shirts, short haircuts and cheerful smiles (as Deal always did onstage), was not so contradictory as it might first seem. Francis was a big fan of the films of David Lynch, 'where you get totally sucked into the lives of these ultra-normal people and then you suddenly realise something's not quite right'.[10] Lynch's TV series, *Twin Peaks* — which went to air around the time *Bossanova* was being recorded — was set in a picture-perfect American north-west logging town that, on closer inspection, turned out to be teeming with horrors: drugs, madness, ritualistic killings, messages from outer space, and terrifying hallucinations. The plot revolved around the death of a homecoming queen who turned out to be 'filled with secrets'. Everything was normal, but nothing was what it seemed to be. The same could be said of the Pixies' *Bossanova*, an album of teen-dream pop tunes, whose lyrics were steeped in UFO paranoia — from the conspiracy tale of 'The Happening' to the space romance 'Velouria'. Listening to late-night talkback radio shows in LA, Francis had discovered a rich seam of alternative information lying just below the surface of the normal world, 'all these people phoning in with these tabloid UFO stories', he recalled. 'Mary from Burbank talking about the aliens that killed her husband.' As an employee of the non-service industry, Francis felt it was his job to give form to these undercurrents whether the world was ready to see them or not.[11]

The only problem with having a job in the non-service industry was that it wasn't really an industry at all. To make money, you had to move into another industry, the entertainment industry, and the Pixies had already taken several steps in this direction, signing with a major label in America, and making videos for MTV. They were immediately accused of selling out, but Francis had no time for such stuff. 'You gotta get paid,' he said. 'You gotta get paid so you can buy stuff.'[12] As Kim Deal pointed out, rock music was almost by nature sold out. People playing acoustic guitars for friends in their living room could be pure art, but 'the minute anybody signs a record contract,' she said, 'they sell out'.[13] And yet Deal could already see that working with Warner/Elektra in the US was leading the band into territory she wasn't quite comfortable with, as its A&R teams set about grooming the band for stardom. 'Boy,' she said in a college radio interview, 'do they have some dumb ideas.'[14] Francis, on the other hand, appeared to be enjoying his new role as an indie pop star. 'I used to hate it when people chanted along with the songs,' he told the *NME* in October, 'but now I take it as an indication that people like us.'[15] His willingness to face the monstrosities in his subconscious had prepared him for the fact that one of these was a desire for attention, his determination to say what was on his mind gave him no reason to hide the fact from anyone. In late 1990, Francis's portrait had appeared on the cover of a Dutch magazine under a quote from the interview inside, where he proclaimed: 'I am the Pixies.'[16]

The music business was changing the Pixies, but the Pixies were also changing the music business. Even LA was changing. In 1989, an eighteen-year-old guitar player named Rivers Cuomo moved to the industry capitol from his home in Connecticut, certain that his ability to shred like Steve Vai and Yngwie Malmsteen would soon make him a metal superstar. But after spending a year working at Tower Records on Sunset Boulevard, he learned that nobody in LA cared much for axe heroes anymore. 'They played music in there eight hours a day, through my whole shift,' he explained. 'And they weren't playing Yngwie, they were playing Sonic Youth and the Pixies.'[17] Cuomo hated the stuff at first, but eventually came around to its peculiar charms, and found that his own musical approach was changing as a result of his non-stop exposure to noisy college rock. He stopped practising solos, and started trying to write cool rock tunes. By the end of 1990, he had cut off his hair.

Double Seriousness

In March 1990, Primal Scream's 'Loaded' had demanded freedom. Three months later, the Soup Dragons announced that it had been accomplished, with a cover of the little-known Rolling Stones song 'I'm Free'. Over a lazy hip-hop shuffle, singer Sean Dickson spat out Jagger and Richards' lyrics in a stoned-sexy drawl: 'I said I'm free to do what I want, any old time.'[1] Reggae singer Junior Reid popped up in the middle eight like a ragamuffin Rousseau, to remind the listener that freedom is natural ('free like a butterfly free like a bee'), nothing to be scared of ('don't be afraid to feel freedom!') and for everyone — indie-rock guys and dreadlocked toasters alike. 'I just wanted to make the perfect record for this period of time, in this year, on this planet,' said Dickson in an interview with the *NME*.[2] He had certainly come close. Rave culture and ecstasy made a mockery of class divisions as surely as the new indie-dance fusion had trashed the wall that separated black dance music from white guitar pop. 'I'm Free' was suffused with this new, egalitarian spirit — a giant, all-encompassing, end-of-the-night dance-floor hug, which promised an end to Thatcherite self-interest and indie miserabalism alike.

But it was Manchester's Happy Mondays — whose single 'Step On' had reached number five in the national chart in April — who truly epitomised this new borderless youth culture. The band's 1988 album *Bummed* had combined elements of funk, disco, post-punk, classic rock and sixties pop in a slightly shambolic and utterly unique form of danceable guitar rock. By 1990, their collaboration with DJ Paul Oakenfold had allowed their scruffy funk to reach the ears of London's most fashionable club-goers. But the band remained honest-to-goodness working class: a half-dozen uncouth youths from the outer suburbs of Manchester, who'd decided to start a band because — as lead singer Shaun Ryder realised all at once while watching David Essex in *Stardust* on TV one night in 1980 — it beats working.[3]

In April 1990, *Q* magazine's Chris Heath followed a whole troupe of Mondays devotees to a show in Paris. 'They're just normal youths,' insisted one. 'They dress the same as us.' 'No,' another pointed out, 'we dress like them.'[4] It hardly mattered who had started it. The point was that the Happy Mondays were real, and their fans loved them for it. 'There's been nothing like the Mondays since the Sex Pistols,' said another fan. 'They're not manufactured ... they don't give a toss.'[5] Jack Barron, reviewing the Mondays' new album *Pills 'n' Thrills and Bellyaches*, agreed that the band's lack of pretension and artifice set them apart. The Mondays, he wrote, had 'the bullshit detector buzz of oiks on the street'. Barron praised the single 'Kinky Afro' for its 'matter-of-fact waywardness welded to a blunt honesty'.[6] *Vox*'s reviewer confirmed that the Happy Mondays were the real deal. 'This is what they honestly are,' wrote Betty Page, 'what you hear is no contrivance.'[7]

By the time *Pills 'n' Thrills and Bellyaches* was released, the Happy Mondays had reached number five in the UK charts for the second time with 'Kinky Afro', and were earning enough money from their hits to make all their Armani dreams come true. But Ryder saw no problem with the band becoming rich and famous, as long as they kept it real — and so far that had been the easiest thing in the world to do. 'We'd go down to London to meet journalists and we'd only be ourselves,' he explained, 'we wouldn't even think of ourselves as a band.'[8] Nor did he believe that his fans would begrudge him his newfound fame, or the opportunities it afforded him to get out of it and have a good time. 'They should cherish the success,' he insisted. It wouldn't improve the fans' situations, but they would understand it as symbolic. 'I'm sorry for the people who are still stuck in the shit,' he said, 'but I can hardly take the whole of fucking working-class Salford with me, can I?'[9]

He couldn't, but by April 1990 some of those still stuck in the shit were already beginning to wish the Mondays had stayed there. Because they identified so closely with the group, the fans felt they ought to have a say when it did something they didn't like, and many were uncomfortable with the sight of the Happy Mondays playing 'Step On' on *Top of the Pops*. 'It's our band,' said one of the Paris contingent, 'we don't want 'em in the charts.'[10] The fans' frustration was understandable — they had, up until recently, been the proud owners of an authentic youth culture, a dynamic regional scene built on a real relationship between themselves and the band they'd chosen to represent them. Now that relationship was being stretched too far over too great a mass of people, and the scene was disappearing as a result. But when *Q*'s Chris Heath relayed the fans' complaints to Ryder after the Paris concert, the singer was furious. 'That's really nice of them, isn't it?' he snapped. 'They've never had a real life have they, them idiots? They live in some sort of fuckin' dream world.' In the real world, Ryder insisted, you have to seize opportunities.[11] 'This is real for us,' he said later. 'It's our only way out.'[12]

By this point, it had become clear that the Mondays, like many of the artists who supposedly embodied the new egalitarian spirit, were themselves products of Thatcher's regime, and that their ideals were shaped more by her politics than by those of the old indie left. While they objected in principle to her government's conservatism, and resented her police for shutting down their parties, when they sang or spoke of freedom, they tended to do so in Thatcher's terms — the freedom to earn and spend, or the freedom to seize opportunities and make something of yourself. 'Positive thinking, that's all we've ever believed in,' Ian Brown told Nick Kent at the end of 1989, 'you've got to make things happen for you.'[13]

'Do what you're doing,' sang Shaun Ryder on 'Loose Fit', 'say what you're saying, go where you're going, think what you're thinking sounds good to me.'[14] The song's lyrics seemed to draw parallels between the baggy clothing styles then in fashion, and the coming end to a decade of uptight conservatism. 'Won't be no skintights in my wardrobe today / fold them all up and put them all away.'[15] But Ryder was no pop socialist. Six months earlier, the singer had rehearsed the idea for 'Loose Fit' in an interview with *Melody Maker*. In this first draft, he'd given a clearer definition of freedom, Ryder style. 'I just wanna be able to go where I want, do what I want, spend what I want and how I want. Even if I'd been born with loads of money, I'd still be into racing cars, abseiling, taking humungous lots of drugs and knocking about with John Paul Getty III. Just having a good time, like now.'[16] To Nick Kent he'd been even more frank. 'We all wanna make a fookin' pile,' he said. 'But at the same time I think we've got, like, principles.'[17]

Whatever these were, they had nothing to do with maintaining an island of resistance to the corporate world. Ryder dismissed the whole notion of selling out as a 'trendy, studenty hippy idea' left over from the oppositional eighties — the world of Billy Bragg, Paul Weller, Red Wedge and Alternative Comedy. 'Fuck,' he said, 'I thought we were past all that.'[18] The fans who'd turned on the band because they'd started making money reminded him of the crusty hippies and students smashing up Trafalgar Square in the Poll Tax Riots on the evening news a few weeks earlier. 'It's like, over in England, when someone gets a nice car, and some bastards smash it up because they haven't got one,' he said later. 'Shitpots. It's just daft.'[19] Backstage at the Paris show, with the fans' betrayal still fresh in his mind, Ryder dismissed the record company reps that reminded him he still had some interviews to do for French TV. 'Can't you see?' he said. 'I'm in a double-serious mood here.'[20]

On 28 November 1990, Margaret Thatcher resigned as Prime Minister of the United Kingdom. 'Now,' said Billy Bragg, in an interview with the *NME*, 'if we, the generation that have had our political ideas moulded by Thatcher, can be bothered, we could start to dismantle the legacy of selfishness and greed with which she has divided the country.'[21] But the early signs were not good. The Inspiral Carpets' Clint Boon, asked to share his feelings on Thatcher's resignation in the same article, said, 'We couldn't give a fuck'.[22]

Freedom isn't Free

'Once we get out of the eighties,' said Dennis Hopper in the 1990 film *Flashback*, 'the nineties are gonna make the sixties look like the fifties.'[1] Jesus Jones's Mike Edwards had no more doubt that this was true than he did that he was a better guitarist than Eric Clapton. 'There's nothing he could do that I couldn't,' he told the *NME*. 'He's crap, really boring. I'm a loads better player.'[2] Hell-bent on inventing the future, Edwards had little time for rock's past. One month earlier, he'd shoved George Harrison in the back at a skate contest, and said he'd gladly do it again. 'There's nothing I could say to those people,' he insisted, besides, 'why haven't you made any decent music in the last twenty years, you wanker?'[3] Modernists, as Peter Conrad observed, have always enjoyed pretending to be vandals, and Edwards was modern to the core. 'The past has never received so little respect,' wrote Simon Williams in his *Spin* profile on Jesus Jones, 'the future has never felt so close.'[4]

Jesus Jones marked the end of history with a single, released in September 1990. 'Right here, right now,' sang Edwards, 'there is no other place I wanna be.'[5] The song had begun to form in Edwards's mind after the fall of the Berlin Wall at the end of 1989, and continued to develop during the extraordinary events that followed, as communism collapsed all over Eastern Europe. In January 1990, Edwards saw these events at close range as Jesus Jones travelled with two other bands — Crazyhead and Skin Games — to play a concert in post-revolutionary Romania. The country was a mess, but the people's optimism was infectious. For the visiting bands — whose members belonged to a generation that had grown used to the idea that revolution was something you'd only ever get to see in reruns — it was almost too good to be believed. 'You can't escape the clichés,' said Crazyhead's singer, Porkbeast, 'this whole thing is about peace, love and freedom. Fuck it, go for it!'[6] The three bands played at a sports arena in Timisoara, and the *NME*'s reporter described Mike Edwards taking the stage and introducing 'a song he wrote for the Romanian people'.[7] 'I saw the decade in when it seemed the world changed in the blink of an eye,' he sang. 'Bob Dylan didn't have this to sing about, you know it feels good to be alive.'[8]

Certainly there were real grounds for this kind of optimism. The people of Eastern Europe could look forward to a life without communism. They were at last free to determine their own political future, and to express themselves without restraint. Meanwhile, the end of the Cold War also promised a brighter future for the West. Economists and political commentators on both sides of the Atlantic saw a great opportunity for renewal on the horizon, as money that had been tied up in ever-escalating defence spending during the eighties could be re-routed to repair some of the damage Reagan's and Thatcher's economic policies had done to their respective countries. 'Even the cautious editorialists of the *New York Times* agree that the military budget could be cut in half with ease,' wrote RL Borsage.[9]

US President George Bush agreed that the post-Cold War world offered new opportunities. 'We're beginning a new era,' he announced on 8 August 1990. 'This new era could be full of promise, an age of freedom, a time of peace for all peoples.' But Bush went on to sound a darker note, warning that even as communism was collapsing, there were new forces at work, forces that could undo the hard-won peace the world was now enjoying. 'If history teaches us anything,' he reminded his audience, 'it is that we must resist aggression, or it will destroy our freedoms.'[10] Bush was referring to the invasion of Kuwait — a small Arab nation few Americans had heard of in 1990 — by the Iraqi leader Saddam Hussein several days earlier, and the purpose of his address was to announce that the US would be sending military forces to the Gulf to protect neighbouring Saudi Arabia from the threat posed by Iraq. Operation Desert Shield, Bush said, would show Hussein that America and the world would not tolerate aggression, and quickly 'stabilise the turbulent Middle East'.[11]

The Gulf crisis instantly put a stop to any talk of Post-Cold war defence budget cuts, as the Pentagon, as Borsage put it, began 'mobilising against the threat of peace'.[12] Soon, US forces were massing in the Gulf, and the president's earlier talk of a purely 'defensive' mission had modulated into a declaration of war. Shortly after Bush addressed the nation, *Rolling Stone*'s Michael Azerrad stood side of stage at the UK's Reading Festival, and watched the Pixies play a song with only one lyric line — 'it is time for stormy weather'[13] — repeated over and over again. 'Hearing it played during the Persian Gulf crisis is eerie,' wrote Azerrad. 'Hearing it played to 50,000 kids with no future is downright chilling.'[14] The crowd might be in face paint and love beads, but the Third Summer of Love, Azerrad felt, was fading fast.

It was the Gulf War, and not the imminent demise of Margaret Thatcher, that Shaun Ryder had in mind when he wrote 'Loose Fit'. 'Gonna buy an air force base, gonna wipe out your race, get stoned in a different place.'[15] The lyrics came to Ryder as he and the Mondays' dancer/percussionist Bez sat on a couch in an LA recording studio and watched the war play out on TV — images of smart bombs and Scud missiles cut up with flashy news graphics and commercial breaks. The war, as many observers noted, seemed made for TV, 'a deft mix of *Star Wars* technological precision and *Top Gun* guts and glory', as technology writer Jon Katz put it.[16] To Danny Schechter, an investigative filmmaker, it seemed as though Bush's generals had planned their offensive with one eye on the TV ratings. 'The first bombs fell at 6.40pm, Eastern time,' he wrote, 'just in time to juice up the national news with live footage.'[17]

The viewing audience quickly became hooked. Sonic Youth was supporting Neil Young on an American tour, and found that the war had already become very popular — Young's fans waved 'Fuck Iraq' banners as Sonic Youth played Sabbath's 'War Pigs'. Every night, after the show, the band members sat in their hotel rooms and watched the war on TV, 'like a hot new mini-series', as Thurston Moore put it.[18] Ride, My Bloody Valentine and Nirvana were all making albums at the time, and they all had the TV on constantly — every coffee break, every second of downtime was filled with images of multicoloured military fireworks over the desert. The Gulf War, in fact, was so successful as a piece of entertainment that it was hard to believe it was really happening. It had all the thrills of a Hollywood action movie, but seemed, in the end, to be no more important. 'Go where you're goin', Kill who you're killin',' thought Shaun Ryder, as the news logo faded into a commercial, 'sounds good to me.'[19]

It was appropriate that the Happy Mondays' freedom ode should have been inspired by the war, since the war — as Bush never wasted an opportunity to remind people — was about freedom. Americans and people of other Western nations cherished a way of life in which they were allowed to do what they wanted, go where they wanted, and buy what they wanted. But these freedoms had to be protected. Military recruitment ads were appearing on American television, showing montage scenes of wholesome-looking recruits fighting it out in the desert. A song played on the soundtrack, in which a soldier sang longingly of his hometown from his bunker in the Saudi Desert. 'My hometown is not like this,' he wailed, 'but that's all right with me. See I'm out here for my hometown, 'cause freedom isn't free.'[20] The man was a professional singer, not a real soldier. But the real soldiers, according to *Spin* magazine, were also singing. A DJ for armed forces radio in Riyadh, Saudi Arabia, told the magazine's reporter that he was getting a lot of requests for Pat Benatar's 'Hit Me With Your Best Shot', N.W.A's 'Fuck Tha Police' and Guns N' Roses' 'Knockin' on Heaven's Door'.[21] But the real hit of the war, the song taken up as an anthem by American bomber pilots as they homed in on their targets, was a song about being in the right place at the right time, about the dawning of a new era full of possibilities. 'Right here right now, there is no other place I'd rather be.'[22]

1991

A Popular Consensus

EMF's 'Unbelievable' was released in the US in June 1991, and reached number one on the Billboard charts two months later. The band were raved over by Axl Rose, and taken on tour as support by Jane's Addiction and the Red Hot Chili Peppers. Everywhere they were mobbed by fans who had seen them on MTV. The *NME*'s David Quantick met some at an LA show, and asked them what all the fuss was about. 'They're cute, if you think about it,' replied one girl, 'and you can dance to it!' 'I like their hair!' said another. 'And I like Extreme's hair!' 'It's good dance music!' the first girl added. 'It's new, it's like Jesus Jones and they're all from London!'[1] The band, meanwhile, had embarked on what *Q* later described as 'a lifestyle of monumental hedonism — drugs, girls, drugs and girls, girls on drugs'.[2]

All in all, EMF was doing well — far better, certainly, than most British bands did in the States in the early nineties. But they weren't happy. 'Their most abiding anxiety,' said *Q*'s Matt Snow in September 1991, 'is credibility.'[3] Songwriter Ian Dench worried that EMF might soon be nothing more than a line in a Billboard Annual, another band of cute guys with nice hair who had a hit and disappeared forever. 'I hope we're not just another pop band,' he told *Spin*.[4] Dench liked pop, and insisted that it was important for music to be accessible. But what worried him about EMF being labelled a pop group were the 'associations' that went with it — that they were a manufactured band, that they couldn't really play, that they were popular simply because they were cute and had good hair.

This, in 1991, was a real cause for concern. Two years earlier, a group named Milli Vanilli released a fresh-sounding pop-soul album called *Girl You Know It's True*. Catchy tunes like 'Blame It on the Rain', 'Baby Don't Forget My Number' and 'Girl I'm Gonna Miss You' made the record a hit, and in February 1990 singers Rob Pilatus and Fab Morvan appeared at the Grammys to accept their award for best new artist. Ten months later, they gave it back, after it was publicly revealed that neither Rob nor Fab had sung a single note on *Girl You Know It's True*, or at the many concerts and TV performances they'd given throughout the year. The defrauding of millions of unsuspecting listeners with false music became one of the year's biggest news stories. In the future, warned CBS's news presenter, 'you might have to think twice about what you think you're hearing'.[5] As a result, English groups like EMF, who relied heavily on sequencers and samples in their live performances, found themselves skating on very thin ice in America. Critics noted that when the band smashed up their gear at the end of their set, the sound coming out of the speakers remained curiously unaffected.

The Milli Vanilli saga seemed to prove what many American rock fans and critics had long suspected — that the pop industry was guilty of deceiving and manipulating its audience. The music was shaped in the studio using computers and other gadgets to make it sound more radio friendly, concerts were over-rehearsed, pre-fab affairs where the group's sound was augmented and in some cases replaced by programmed synths and backing tapes, and the public was being fooled into buying this stuff instead of real music by real bands. 'All the kids will eat it up,' observed Kurt Cobain in his journal, 'if it's packaged properly.'[6] That this might be a problem was seen by rock artists and the critics who supported them as virtually self-evident — real music was better than artificial stuff for the same reason that fresh fruit was better than Coke. The Red Hot Chili Peppers offered their 1990 album *Mother's Milk* as a healthy option in a music market otherwise full of artificial junk. 'Basically, it's fucking good for you,' explained the group's bass player Michael 'Flea' Balzary. 'Music is a direct expression from the heart, or it should be.' Flea singled out synth-pop duo the Pet Shop Boys as 'indicative of what's happening in the pop music industry' — studio-bound boffins doing 'pop bullshit for the sake of money'.[7]

Rock musicians like Flea had long distinguished guitar music as the antithesis of pop bullshit. But in the 1980s, rock itself seemed to have submitted to this process to a frightening degree. 'Rock and roll has become an artificial experience,' complained the Pixies' Black Francis. In 1988, Billy Corgan met D'Arcy Wretzky at a concert by the Dan Reed Network. 'You can tell this band was put together by a record company,' said Corgan, as they stood outside after the show. The songwriter knew he was watching a choreographed performance by a fake rock band when he saw the way the singer moved onstage. 'Real people in bands don't jump around like that,' he insisted.[8] Critics felt that this kind of market-researched rock was one of the most unwelcome developments of the last ten years. In the eighties, wrote *Rolling Stone*'s Anthony De Curtis, rock and roll became 'terminally safe', joining a rock band 'about as rebellious as taking a business degree — and if you got lucky, more lucrative'.[9] In the eighties, argued Legs McNeil in the *NME*, 'instead of Sex, Drugs and Rock and Roll, we ended up with fear and addiction and corporate sponsorship of rock and roll'.[10] As the decade came to an end, critics like McNeil and De Curtis saw an opportunity to clean house; to call time on an era of pre-fab rock, and hasten the return of real music.

In the early nineties, rock musicians and critics took great pains to let the audience know there was a difference. Joe Carducci's influential book, *Rock and the Pop Narcotic*, published in 1990, argued for a precise re-definition of rock as the real-time interaction of bass, drums and guitar, as opposed to its opposite — pop — which relies heavily on technology and is created according to a formula. The following year, Thurston Moore explained the meaning of a Sonic Youth poster for Dave Markey's camera in *The Year That Punk Broke*. The poster featured a Raymond Pettibon drawing of a girl performing onstage. 'This picture represents the fact that it's a live gig, see? This is the singer singing *live*,' he said. 'It's not a clone. It's not a fake. This shit's fuckin' live, man!'[11]

But if rock could be redefined as real rock, there was also the possibility that pop might be redefined as real pop — genuinely popular music as opposed to the stuff that is, as Nirvana's Krist Novoselic put it, 'rammed down people's throats'. For many, the problem with pop in 1990 was not so much that it was popular, but that its popularity was manufactured, that people only consumed it because they'd been brainwashed into doing so, or because the music industry made sure that they would never know any better. The idea that mass culture is a form of manipulation had been a staple of cultural criticism in America since the post-war period, when refugee intellectuals from Nazi Germany began to see disturbing parallels between advertising in America and the propaganda used by fascist leaders in Europe. Capitalism, according to German sociologists Theodor Adorno and Max Horkheimer, destroyed consumers' critical self-awareness, and left them vulnerable to exploitation. This pessimistic view had to be rethought in the 1960s after the advent of rock and roll, which seemed to have pulled off the neat trick of *using* mass culture to *critique* mass culture. But by the early nineties, after ten years of sensationalised politics and blockbuster albums, many had returned to Adorno's unsparing critique, or something like it.[12] 'Audiences do, in fact, interpret messages variously,' wrote media critic Herbert Schiller in 1989's *Culture, Inc.*, 'but when they are confronted with a message incessantly repeated in all cultural conduits issuing from the commanders of the social order, their capacities are overwhelmed.'[13]

Singer-songwriter Sinéad O'Connor had no doubt that this was the case in 1990. Seeing the music industry up close had given her a sense of just how much hype and manipulation was involved in 'breaking' an artist. Radio stations and record companies collaborated to manufacture hits and keep everything else off the air. 'That's not an honest representation of what people like,' she complained. 'How can it be?'[14] O'Connor believed that the chart success of her own minimally produced and emotionally raw music constituted proof that what people wanted and what the pop industry was giving them were two quite different things. 'People don't want to hear what's on the radio,' she said, 'people are screaming out for something more.'[15]

In July 1991, music writer Gina Arnold saw this 'screaming out' for herself at Lollapalooza, as she watched 9,000 people cheering the Butthole Surfers and shouting along with the chorus of 'Cop Killer' by Body Count. The next day, she drove from San Diego to Los Angeles to interview Nirvana. She listened to a pre-release copy of the band's new album on the car stereo, and as the chorus of 'On a Plain' roared out of the speakers, she thought to herself that 'if the world were a better sort of place, it'd be a hit single'.[16] Arnold saw nothing wrong with artists having hits and playing for huge audiences as long as they deserved them. She believed it was possible to create genuinely popular rock music outside of corporate manipulation, that pop music could become, as Sinéad O'Connor had suggested, a genuine expression of what people like.

It was this vision of pop as a democratic rather than a commercial process that guided independent bands and labels in America through the eighties, a vision fostered by DIY heroes like Ian MacKaye of Fugazi, Beat Happening's Calvin Johnson, and fanzine writer and label boss Bruce Pavitt. What excited Pavitt about the indie scene in Seattle was not its obscurity, but its popularity — a popularity that was created by genuine local enthusiasm, and not, as Pavitt later put it, by 'this industry that's manufacturing bands'.[17] The name Pavitt gave to his record label expressed this idea perfectly — Sub Pop. You have been deceived by MTV, it seemed to say. Hidden below the surface of what you are told to buy, is something people actually like.

The mainstream success of Soundgarden showed that Pavitt's instincts had been correct — a band whose music most industry heads would have regarded as commercial suicide only two years earlier now had an album in the charts and a hit on MTV. The members of Soundgarden — singer Chris Cornell, guitarist Kim Thayil, drummer Matt Cameron and bass player Ben Shepherd — were all veterans of the Seattle indie scene, and Thayil had in fact played a key role in its formation. It was he who had introduced Bruce Pavitt to his future Sub Pop business partner, Jonathan Poneman, with the idea that the two might start a label to release Soundgarden's debut single, 1987's 'Hunted Down'. Since then, however, the band had made a jump from the alternate universe to the real one, having signed to A&M records in 1989. Their major label debut, *Louder than Love*, had brushed the Billboard Top 100 in 1990, and the band had toured with Guns N' Roses.

If any of Soundgarden's peers or fans had worried, upon learning this, that the band would soon be spending ten thousand dollars a night on strippers and drugs, or that Cornell might soon be seen putting his foot up on the foldback amp and pointing at the crowd, they needn't have. Like Mudhoney, Soundgarden was a band composed of smart guys; smart enough to steer well clear of mainstream metal's 'paaarty and fantasy crap', as Thayil put it, smart enough to know that rock itself was slightly stupid.[18] Their biggest hit to date was a song called 'Big Dumb Sex', a venomous put-down of LA's metal monsters, written by musicians who — like their indie peers — treasured a vision of music as a communal experience, in which the rock singer is, in the end, not so different to the fans. The highlight of a Soundgarden show was not, as in mainstream metal, the elevation of the singer on a cherry picker over the audience, but the singer's descent into the crowd. This 'cool little bonding thing', as Kurt Cobain called it, was the ultimate expression of indie rock's musical democracy.[19] Music writer Grant Alden watched Soundgarden play at the Bumbershoot music and arts festival in Seattle. 'Chris Cornell finished the night in the mosh pit,' he later recalled, 'and it felt like we had all finally won.'[20]

Soundgarden's breakthrough suggested that the world might be about to become, as Gina Arnold had hoped, a better sort of place — a place where real bands with great songs filled stadiums, topped the charts, and got played on the radio. There would still be rock stars in this new world, but they'd be better ones, rock stars who knew about punk and had some awareness of feminism. The promise of alternative music, it seemed, was about to be realised. By 1990, alternative rock had been alternative for so long that people seemed to have forgotten what it meant — it had become shorthand for a style of music, when in fact, it had always been more like a party in opposition. Now, in 1991, alternative bands had finally got the majority of the vote, and were about to take power.

But this argument assumed that alternative music would survive its trip to the top of the charts with its message and its ideology intact — and there were already signs that this might not be the case. 'I don't think the mechanisms that exist in the mass media are sensitive enough to what we want to do,' explained Fugazi's Guy Picciotto, 'that's why we don't sign to a major.'[21] Picciotto and his bandmate Ian Mackaye insisted that the alternative revolution could not take place at the expense of the bands' independence. As far as Fugazi was concerned, there could be no collaboration with the commercial media. Calvin

Johnson too, felt that the world-wide network of labels, bands and fans that had been established over the past decade ought to remain — as it had always been — fiercely and proudly outside of corporate control. 'As the corporate ogre expands its creeping influence on the minds of industrialized youth,' he wrote, 'the time has come for the international rockers of the world to convene in celebration of our glorious independence.'[22] Johnson's call-to-arms was printed on the flyer for 1991's International Pop Underground Convention, a gathering of the world's indie tribes held over a week at the Capital Theatre in Olympia, Washington, featuring bands, film nights and stalls. Fugazi, the Nation of Ulysses, Mecca Normal and L7 all played at the festival, and many more bands and musicians came along to enjoy themselves, including Soundgarden.

Had the band not read Johnson's warning printed on the flyer, 'no lackeys to the corporate ogre allowed'?[23] To the festival's hardcore indie ideologues, Soundgarden must have seemed like opportunists — a great underground rock band who had sold out their fans and the community that supported them so as to make more money and become more famous. But to Soundgarden's Matt Cameron, such people seemed less like idealists and more like snobs — cultural elitists trying to preserve a make-believe revolution while a real one was taking place right under their noses. Wandering around the IPU convention, the drummer spotted a pile of T-shirts with the legend 'Kill Rock Stars' printed on the front. Cameron asked if he could buy one. 'No, man,' said the guy with the stall, 'you're a rock star.' Cameron walked away. 'What a close-minded idiot,' he thought to himself.[24]

Last Chance

In June 1990, as Geffen's executives tried — and failed — to have *Goo*'s cover art toned down, a similar crisis was unfolding at Warner Bros. This time the issue was sex, rather than violence. The LA-based rock band Jane's Addiction had just delivered its second album, *Ritual de lo Habitual*, along with a cover designed by the group's singer, Perry Farrell. It was a photo of a wall-sized assemblage, in which three papier-mâché figures — one man and two women — lay naked on a mattress, surrounded by religious paraphernalia, with golden halos burning behind their heads. Nine out of ten of Warner's distributors refused to carry the album in its then current form, and the label told the band it would need a more 'family friendly' version to sell in the chain stores.[1] Jane's Addiction had already been through this two years earlier with its previous record, *Nothing's Shocking*, the cover for which had been rejected on exactly the same grounds — that its depiction of female nudity would not play well in the heartland. Farrell had always had a feeling that he was slightly out of step with the world. 'I don't feel part of everything,' he told *Melody Maker* in 1989. 'I feel like I'm speaking a foreign language.'[2] Born Peretz Bernstein, his stage name was a pun on the word 'peripheral'. Now, once again, he found himself on the outside, forced to assert his belief in nature, art and beauty in a world that saw only what was profitable as worthwhile. 'A woman is the most attractive creature nature has to offer a man,' he wrote. 'Why then is it such a shame to see her unclothed? I feel more shame as a man watching a Quik Mart being built.'[3]

Many of the songs on *Ritual de lo Habitual* argued for a clearing of the moral slate, wiping away the Judaeo-Christian idea of sin and

55

punishment along with the non-values of capitalism. 'Been Caught Stealing' was a proud tale of shoplifting, in which Farrell broke into joyous Cab Calloway scat-singing over a monster Sly Stone groove. Stealing, he insisted, is only wrong if you respect the notion of private property; since Farrell respected nothing but beauty and art, he could walk out of the Quik Mart with whatever he liked, whenever he liked. 'Hey alright,' he sang, 'if I get by, it's mine.'[4] 'Stop' was an affirmation inspired by surfing, in which the force of the ocean stood opposed to the world of manufacture and mass media, 'that smokestack and that goddamn radio!'[5] 'Three Days' was an arty epic inspired — like the album's cover — by Farrell's tryst with his girlfriend Casey Niccoli and a woman named Xiola Blue. And 'Ain't No Right' was virtually the band's manifesto, a setting-to-music of William Burroughs's famous maxim, 'Nothing is true, everything is permitted'. 'Ain't no wrong,' sang Farrell in his helium whine, 'ain't no wrong and there ain't no right. There's only pleasure and pain.'[6]

Farrell's insistence on pleasure and contempt for Christian morals sometimes gave the impression that he was a Satanist, while his fondness for red and his passing resemblance to the ruler of the underworld added to the effect. 'Do I look like the devil?' he asked MTV's Kurt Loder. 'A little, huh?'[7] But his philosophy was not so much satanic-by-default as Christian-in-reverse. He believed that what Christians called sin was divine, and that hell was reserved for those who denied pleasure to themselves and others. 'I think they all should die,' he replied, when asked what he thought of Walmart's corporate censors. 'They should go to hell, and then see what fuckin' life is really like. People just don't leave you alone — if they're not trying to take your money, they're trying to take your fun.'[8] The replacement of youth culture's holy trinity by their opposites — fear, addiction and corporate control — was, in Farrell's view, the result of a deliberate attempt by certain interested parties to deny people their fun, and then make it look as though fun itself was a problem.

In 1991, social critic and feminist Camille Paglia scoffed at the idea of a 'conspiracy of white, male heterosex, greedy capitalists using the media as a tool to keep the people down and twist their thinking'. This, Paglia claimed, was nothing more than leftist paranoia. 'The media is very commercial,' she insisted, 'it's driven by what people want.'[9] But if Paglia was correct, then the songs Americans wanted to hear more than any others in the first half of 1991 were the songs most played on US radio: Paula Abdul's 'Rush Rush', Mariah Carey's 'Someday', and Bryan Adams's 'Everything I Do'. For some, this was a horror too great to contemplate. Perry Farrell, for one, had little doubt that there was male, white, corporate oppression at work. 'Alternative bands, it's almost like they're taboo-ed off of rock stations,' he told Kurt Loder. 'I've been in this business for ten years,' he went on, 'I just get the feeling that … something's real fishy about it. These bands, to me, in every respect they broke ground. But you know, maybe someone else got the billboard, or the publisher of some piece-of-shit magazine just shmeared their face all over it.' Loder asked Farrell if anything could be done about it. 'Oh,' he replied with a smile, 'I'm doin' somethin'.'[10] What Farrell was doing was putting together a travelling rock and roll festival, with a line up of what he considered cutting-edge bands from music's past, present and future. Lollapalooza would feature performances by Living Colour, Fishbone, Rollins Band, Nine Inch Nails, Siouxsie and the Banshees, and the rapper Ice-T, with his new hardcore group, Body Count. There would be good food, circus acts and art installations, and the night would end with a farewell performance from his own band, Jane's Addiction. 'I mean come on,' he told Jim Greer, 'it's the summertime, why wouldn't you go?'[11]

By offering a day of real fun, Farrell hoped to expose, once and for all, the fake fun offered by the mainstream media. Janet Jackson's 'Love Will Never Do (Without You)' had been a huge hit in 1991, and plenty of people would be going to her shows over the summer. But when they went, what would they get? A dozen or more songs, an encore, a few fireworks. 'It's like she's giving you a salad,' Farrell explained in a TV interview, 'but all she's giving you is lettuce. I'm giving you the lettuce, the cabbage, the …' Farrell trailed off, momentarily unable to think of any other vegetables.[12] But his point was made — Jackson had only pop R&B to offer, Lollapalooza had industrial-strength dance music, funk-rock fusion bands, one honest-to-goodness hardcore hero, a high priestess of goth and the Butthole Surfers — who virtually constituted a circus on their own. For the same price, Lollapalooza would give you ten times as much flavour.

But Lollapalooza wasn't just about giving people more bands for their buck. Farrell was suspicious of ordinary rock shows for the same reason he was suspicious of ordinary rock stars. It was all a bit too much like a political rally or a school hall, with the leader up the front and everyone standing obediently in place. Lollapalooza was modelled on British music festivals like Reading, where people could walk around, talk, and interact. They might wander out of the Nine Inch Nails show and into a Greenpeace booth, go looking for a taco and end up learning about smart drugs. As they roamed about the festival, ideas and cultures would mingle and interact. 'I want to see what happens with a major exchange of information,' Farrell explained. 'I don't like the idea of the world being controlled by the news media. We need to exchange ideas somewhere else, another forum. The cafés aren't being used anymore, so let's try a festival.'[13] Farrell's hope was that Lollapalooza would act as a catalyst for ten years' worth of alternative music and culture, and that the combustion of all these ideas in the highly charged atmosphere of a rock festival might lead to real change in the world. On the last night of the tour, Farrell stood on the stage and laid it on the line. 'This is it, homeboys,' he said, at the end of Jane's Addiction's set. 'Youth revolution! Last chance, let's get on with it.'[14]

One year earlier, Allan Moyle's film *Pump Up the Volume* had been released in cinemas. The movie starred Christian Slater as a nervous geek with a secret life as a pirate radio DJ called Hard Harry, whose show becomes a cult hit with high school kids. He plays all the music they never play on the radio — Ice-T, the Pixies, Concrete Blonde, Primal Scream, Soundgarden and Henry Rollins. And he says all the things no-one ever says — how much it sucks being a teenager, how selfish parents are, how fucked up it is to be living at the end of history in a world you can't afford. Harry quickly becomes a hero to his audience, and when he is pursued and harassed by the FCC for broadcasting illegally, the show itself becomes a cause for his disenfranchised listeners to rally around. The film ends with a showdown, where Harry's fans face off against the police and the school principal. They're ready to fight, until Harry talks them down and gives himself up — but not without a final message for his people. 'It's time,' he says. 'It begins with us. Not with politicians, or the experts or the teachers, but with us.'[15] Harry is led away in handcuffs, and the kids resolve to do what they can to change their world.

If Farrell was hoping for a showdown of this kind between the kids and the powers-that-be at Lollapalooza, he didn't get it. Not that the festival hadn't been a success — if nothing else, it proved that what Billboard called 'popular music' was not the only thing that was popular in 1991. 'The fact that none of us gets played on the radio, to be able to pack arenas and all, it shows people want to hear this.' But his call to arms on the final night was met with baffled looks, and more than a little embarrassment on his behalf. 'When I said it, I really shrank,' he told *Rolling Stone* critic David Fricke the next day. 'Because I felt like, right, these guys could give a shit. This isn't gonna happen: they are just too happy with life.'[16]

Spending Our Children's Inheritance

Early in 1991, in a shed behind a suburban house in Tacoma, Washington, Nirvana began jamming on a new song brought to the group by singer Kurt Cobain. The band — Cobain, bassist Krist Novoselic and drummer Dave Grohl — had been writing material for its second album since April the previous year, and already had some promising new tunes — but this did not look like it was going to be one of them. Like their friends in Mudhoney, the members of Nirvana had a keen sense of irony — they knew rock and roll was clichéd and stupid, but had decided to keep doing it anyway. And yet this new offering, Novoselic felt, was a little bit too stupid. The song was basically 'Louie Louie' — the old bar-band staple — played fast and loud. As such, it also bore a strong resemblance to Boston's FM rock radio classic 'More Than a Feeling', which was also derived from 'Louie Louie'. Cobain was happy with both of these associations, but Novoselic told him he thought the song was a joke, which only seemed to make the singer more determined to make something of it. The new tune might have been a joke, but he had a feeling it was, at the very least, a good one.

Cobain's new song reflected the singer's eclectic musical taste — it had the crooked pop sensibility of R.E.M., the heavier-than-hell intensity of post-hardcore bands like the Jesus Lizard, and the unashamed rock power of an Aerosmith tune from the seventies — long hair and fists in the air. But it was the influence of the Pixies that would turn the piece around and convince Novoselic it was worth keeping. Cobain had, by his own admission, spent the last two years trying to rip off the Boston quartet's earth-shaking attack. The good news was, as Black Francis himself explained in 1989, it wasn't all that hard to do. 'We use basic dynamics,' he told triple j's Tim Ritchie, 'play loud, play quiet, play loud, scream: anything to get attention.'[1] As Nirvana slowed Cobain's new song down and took it apart, it began to show real promise. The gloriously stupid 'rocking out' chorus was balanced by a quiet, melancholy mood in the verses, the basic banality of the riff now seemed to have something interesting to say about rock's basic banality.

Any further doubts Nirvana had about the worth of the new song were swept away by a home-town gig at the OK Hotel in April 1991. The crowd went nuts from the moment they heard it — the entire room seemed to heave in time to Grohl's almost funky drum part, the audience screamed along with the chorus despite the fact that neither they — nor the band themselves — had the slightest idea what Cobain was hollering about. Suitably encouraged, Nirvana recorded the song in May with producer Butch Vig. Cobain — as usual — finalised the lyrics minutes before the tape rolled. Knowing Cobain didn't like to sing a lot, Vig kept the first take, which seemed the freshest, and recorded a few vocal overdubs.[2]

The song, now called 'Smells Like Teen Spirit', was the first successful stab at recording tracks for the new album that was also to be Nirvana's major label debut. Geffen had signed the band at the end of 1990 after repeated recommendations from Sonic Youth's Kim Gordon, but the label did not, as of July 1991, seem to have particularly high hopes for the Seattle trio. Nirvana was a college-rock phenomenon, and Geffen execs expected its album to do no better than Sonic Youth's *Goo*. The label's promotional muscle had been thrown behind other, more lucrative prospects — the simultaneous release of Guns N' Roses two *Use Your Illusion* albums, and the debut by a group called the Nymphs. Geffen shipped only 45,000 copies of Nirvana's *Nevermind* in the week of its release. 'Smells Like Teen Spirit' was released as a single to college radio, and a promotional video was made — although the label's head of promotion did not believe for a moment that MTV would play it.[3]

The band set out on a European tour in support of the album, and received a warm welcome in England — where the *NME*'s Steve

Lamacq had given *Nevermind* a 9/10, and predicted it would be 'the big American alternative album of the autumn'.[4] Nirvana, to some extent, revived the UK music press's hopes of finding rock's noble savage in the forests of the American northwest. 'What else are you gonna do,' said Cobain, by way of explaining his choice of career, 'work in a gas station and pay off a car?'[5] Cobain's trailer-park origins combined with the band's unashamedly heavy sound seemed to offer all the low-rent thrills Mudhoney had promised in 1989, but without the older band's cynicism. 'Nirvana,' wrote the *NME*'s Keith Cameron in September, 'have an unsettling intensity that's far removed from the Mud boys' tongue-in-cheek rifling of the history books. Nirvana's music shudders with frustration, born out of small-town ennui and disgust at the reactionary nature of mainstream American culture.'[6]

Here, Cameron, like many listeners, picked up on what Novoselic elsewhere described as the 'us versus them'[7] feeling the band had shared while recording the album. Novoselic was appalled at Bush's decision to take the country to war. 'I was so angry that it was so wrong,' he told Cameron. 'It was such a fuckin' lie.'[8] Cobain, meanwhile, was also angry about the war. but even more incredulous at a teenage nation that would seemingly rather listen to Paula Abdul or Guns N' Roses than do anything about it. Where were the protest songs? Where were the riots? Why, the singer wondered, was his generation so apathetic? 'Most people would just as soon forget or say "never mind" than to take a can of spray paint, or start up a band,' he told Cameron. 'People just don't do things anymore.' This, according to Cobain, was the meaning of the album's title.[9]

If all of this suggested the singer had hopes of a youth uprising in the coming decade, his next answer confirmed that this was true. Cameron asked for an explanation of 'Smells Like Teen Spirit' Cobain gave him a manifesto. 'No longer is it taboo for the tattooed to take their generational solidarity and shove it up the ass of the Byrds-and-Herman's-Hermits-loving disgraces we call parents,' he said. The singer spoke of a new movement 'posing as the enemy to infiltrate the mechanics of the empire and slowly start its rot from the inside. It's an inside job — it starts with the custodians and the cheerleaders.'[10] Here,

Cobain was riffing on a page from his diary, in which he had been plotting a teenage revolt for some time.

Like most young people born after 1967, Cobain had been told all his life that there was a rock revolution, and that he had missed it. The twenty-somethings of the nineties were left with the feeling that any future youth revolt would have to take place in the shadow of the old one, and would most likely come up short in the comparison. As Nirvana toured Europe with Sonic Youth in August 1991, Thurston Moore quizzed the bands' fans about 'the state of young rock and roll'. 'Well I think it's a real problem,' offered a fan, 'y'know for me the sixties are the only real rock and roll, and you can only try to copy it.'[11] *Details* magazine's Julian Dibbell interviewed kids in the Michigan area a few months earlier, and found most were nostalgic for a time they never knew. 'You see those TV specials,' said one, 'they just amaze me, just what people thought, how they felt, their philosophies. You don't really see that as much today.'[12]

But the TV specials' endless reiteration of the achievements of 1968 also begged questions. If that revolution had been a success, then the world ought to have improved since the sixties, and this was clearly not the case. If there had been a great revolt in the name of love, peace and social justice, why was America, in 1991, divided by hate, fighting a war, and killing black kids on the streets? The gleeful mangling of the Youngbloods' sixties hit 'Get Together' that later appeared on *Nevermind* in which Novoselic sings the words 'everybodyloveyoursisterandyourbrother' in a strangulated whine, said all there was to say about Nirvana's view of the Age of Aquarius.[13]

For Cobain, the image of the sixties — endlessly rescreened in the orgy of nostalgia that accompanied the twentieth anniversary of Woodstock in 1989 — jarred badly with the reality of the eighties. He began to harbour a sense of deep resentment toward an older generation that, it seemed, had brought him up on dreams of freedom, fun and revolution, and then dumped him in a world where the idea of being able to buy your own house was little more than a joke. 'The 1980s kids felt cheated,' wrote sociologist Donna Gaines in 1990. 'They felt that our parents loved us more, that schools were better, that life was easier.' In her book *Teenage Wasteland*, Gaines described how the affluent economy of the sixties gave way to the economic hardships of the seventies, and how this drastically changed climate pushed the divorce rate up and 'eroded the patriarchal structure of the American family'.[14] A 1970 study showed that two-thirds of parents felt that they 'should be free to live their own lives even if it meant spending less time with their children' and more than half agreed that they had a right to live well and spend what they earned 'even if it means leaving less to the children'.[15] Thus the great libertarian experiment of the sixties appeared to have soured into the selfish ethos of the 'me decade'. These, in turn, became the heaven and hell of the children born in the meantime, including Kurt Cobain who, in a 1989 band bio, listed 'divorces' along with 'the Beatles' among Nirvana's influences.[16]

The harsh economic climate of 1990 was, Cobain believed, to a large extent the result of Reaganomics gone awry. 'The Reagan years have definitely set us back to where the average teenager feels sort of lost,' he told a radio interviewer in 1991. 'There isn't much hope.'[17] But who had voted for Reagan? Films like *Flashback* or the TV show *Family Ties* encouraged the idea that the baby boomers had mellowed into easygoing liberals, or were still out there trying to start the revolution, while their children — having rebelled against them — became greedy materialists. But this wasn't exactly true. In the year before Reagan became president, *Esquire*'s Sara Davidson noted that 'people who in the flowering of the sixties gave their children names like Blackberry and Veda-Rama have changed them to Suzy and John. The parents are, as they say, "getting their money trip together". The successful ones are buying homes, Calvin Klein suits, and Porsches.'[18] Kurt Cobain had no doubt about it. In a list of his favourite things compiled in late 1990, just below 'I like to have sex with people', the singer wrote, 'I like to blame my parents' generation for coming so close to social change and then giving up: the baby boomers became the ultimate yuppie hypocrites.'[19]

Cobain began to sense that any future upheaval would have to be inter-generational — the spirit of the original revolt could only be revived by destroying and replacing those who had carried it out — since they had proved unworthy of its high ideals. For this to happen, teenage America would need to be shaken out of its apathy and isolation. Late in 1990, Cobain added a further item to his list of favourite things. 'I like to dream,' he wrote, 'that someday we will have a sense of generational solidarity amongst the youth of the world.' Everybody was going to have to get it together. It might sound like a cliché, but Cobain felt it was the truth. 'Revolution,' he told his diary, 'is no longer an embarrassment.'[20]

During his visits to Olympia, Cobain had met and begun dating zine writer and musician Tobi Vail, who — along with her friend Kathleen Hanna — was already plotting a riot of her own. The three talked a lot about punk rock and teenage revolt in 1991, and the thrust of their discussions could be judged from Cobain's diary entries from the time, in which his earlier feelings of ennui and distant longing for generational solidarity had been replaced by manifestos and to-do lists. 'I am in absolute and total support of: homosexuality, drug use, creativity through music and art, journalism, love, friendship, family, and full-scale, violently organised terrorist-fuelled revolution,' he wrote. The singer warned ageing eighties yuppies of 'the uprising of your children, the armed and de-programmed crusade, littering the floors of Wall Street with revolutionary debris'.[21]

Cobain's revolt in the name of love and creativity would end with an assault on the stronghold of male, white, corporate oppression. But it would begin — as Hard Harry had promised in *Pump Up the Volume* — in the high schools of suburban America. It would begin where the forty-somethings least expected it to — at youth clubs and pep rallies. Its literature would fly out of the school photocopier right under the librarian's nose, its instigators would know one another by secret handshakes and sign their manifestos in blood behind the bike sheds. Before you know it, Cobain warned, 'your children have taken over'.[22] One night, as Cobain, Vail and Hanna hatched their plans, Hanna declared, 'Kurt smells like teen spirit!' and spray-painted this slogan on the wall of his apartment.[23] The gesture made a huge impression on Cobain. He later spoke of how proud he was to think that Vail and Hanna thought of him as 'someone who could inspire' — although whether they thought this or not, it was not quite what they meant.[24]

In any case, it was a perfect name for a song — especially for a song that made kids scream and jump up and down, a song that sounded a bit like 'Louie Louie', 'More Than a Feeling', and a hundred other songs that had made kids jump up and down over the past thirty years. The band kept playing it as they toured Europe and the UK, and the response got better and better. The shows were getting bigger too — the gigs in October had crowds double the size of the ones they'd played in September. 'We'd get to the gig,' Grohl later recalled, 'and it was fucking chaos.'[25] The sudden swell in numbers could be explained using just three letters — MTV. That month, the network had started playing the 'Smells Like Teen Spirit' video in its 'Buzz Bin' category. MTV got so many requests for the clip that it was moved into daily rotation. By November, the unthinkable had happened — Nirvana had a hit. 'Smells Like Teen Spirit' climbed steadily up the Billboard chart over the rest of the year, and showed no signs of slowing down.

Sales of the album grew in proportion. In the last week of December, Michael Jackson's *Dangerous* dropped down to fifth position, and was replaced at number one by *Nevermind*. The upset, according to *Rolling Stone*'s Kim Neeley, was not quite as dramatic as it seemed, since Jackson's album sold only 50,000 fewer copies than Nirvana's. But as Soundscan's Mike Shallet pointed out, the number one spot had a symbolic meaning for the public that facts and figures couldn't budge. 'That's the way Americans think,' he reminded Neeley. 'The [New York] Giants won the Superbowl — but does anyone remember who they beat?'[26] The symbolism in this case was particularly hard to resist, since this wasn't the usual clash of the chart titans, in which Madonna beats Michael, only to be trounced by The Boss or Bon Jovi. A record by a band no-one had ever heard of, which had hardly been promoted at all, had knocked Michael Jackson off the top of the chart. A revolt from below had taken place, and pop's reigning monarch had been deposed by a band of grunge punks from Seattle.

By the end of the year, Nirvana was so famous, and 'Smells Like Teen Spirit' had caused such a sensation, that journalists really were starting to get the impression that Kurt Cobain somehow embodied and spoke for his generation — a generation no-one had really expected would speak at all until the song came blasting out of the radio. And it was only after all this happened that Cobain found out what Hanna had really meant when she'd said he smelled like teen spirit. Early in 1991 the cosmetics company Mennen had launched a new range of deodorant sprays for girls called Teen Spirit, and it was a whiff of this — and not the zeitgeist — that Hanna had caught that fateful afternoon.

Nirvana's anthem for a generation had been accidentally named after a product that exploited teen culture for profit — this made for a good joke, but it also drew attention to an idea already at work within 'Smells Like Teen Spirit' — the flipside to the song's righteous rage and idealism. Cobain's lyric invited the listener to 'load up on guns and bring your friends', but immediately followed this call to arms with the line 'it's fun to lose and to pretend' — his invitation to join in the revolution came with the proviso that it might only be make-believe, and would probably fail in any case. The whole song maintained this curious game of is-it-real-or-isn't-it: did the singer actually believe in the youth revolt he was singing about? Or was he singing about the impossibility of its ever coming to pass? Cobain had told Keith Cameron that the song was about generational solidarity. But the song's lyrics painted quite a different picture — of a teenage nation that would rather drink and go to rock shows than kill their parents and hit the road. His revolutionary army, once assembled, wanted nothing more than to be distracted: 'here we are now, entertain us'.[27]

Cobain's ability to switch at lightning speed from hopefulness to cynicism was one of the quirks of his artistic personality. 'My lyrics are a big pile of contradictions,' he admitted. 'They're split down the middle between very sincere opinions and feelings that I have and sarcastic and hopefully humorous rebuttals towards cliché bohemian ideals that have been exhausted for years.'[28] Here, Cobain described the basic thrust of 'Smells Like Teen Spirit' two years before the fact. The song's demand for freedom by any means necessary was utterly sincere. The singer's conviction that the whole idea was corny and a waste of time was equally heartfelt. Even as he called on the kids to march on Wall Street, the singer knew all too well that youth culture, from the Beatles to punk, had as much to do with shopping as it did with social change, and that teen spirit had always smelled like money.

There was no reason to think that the youth revolt of 1991 would, like the revolt of 1968, be resolved in a protracted shopping spree. The kids, as Perry Farrell observed, were just a bit too happy with life to want to change their world in any significant way. 'People are so spoiled,' said Krist Novoselic in November 1991. 'They have VCRs, cheap gasoline and forty channels and they're not going to rock the boat.'[29] You could rant and scream about how the world was going to hell all you wanted, and the response from teenage America would always be the same — oh well, whatever, never mind. It was appropriate that 'Smells Like Teen Spirit' should sound like 'Louie Louie', because Cobain knew, at some fundamental level, that for all his revolutionary plots and high ideals, the song was most likely destined to be nothing more than that — a song for kids to drink and dance to. 'Stupid and contagious. Here we are now, entertain us.'[30]

And yet there were encouraging signs on the horizon. Or rather, there were signs of imminent disaster that, if your hope was to stir your audience out of its apathetic stupor, could be taken as encouraging. 'Personally,' Novoselic told the *NME*, 'I'm looking forward to total economic collapse. They're putting so many band-aids on the economy right now, Bush is pumping money into the banks, but it won't be long before they go down.'[31] Novoselic predicted a new depression on the way, which would make the thirties look like the fifties. What would happen to teen spirit without the affluence that fuelled it? What kind of culture would be created by kids who no longer had the option of spending their way out of alienation? Cobain saw a brief window opening up — a gap between expectation and reality in which real change might occur.

But the gap was closing fast. As 'Smells Like Teen Spirit' continued its climb up the national chart, Mennen cosmetics launched a new campaign to capitalise on their brand's unexpected injection of indie-rock cred. 'Deodorant made for your generation,' read the ads. By 1992, the brand held a quarter of the market share for teenage girls in America. That a song which raged bitterly at the exploitation of teen culture for profit should turn out, after the fact, to have been named after a deodorant that exploited teen culture for profit was already bizarre. That the song's success should then in turn be successfully exploited by the deodorant's manufacturer in order to increase its profits was merely the first in a long series of crazy-making ironies that Nirvana would be confronted with over the coming year.

Asked, in a BBC interview, if he'd heard any good music since he'd been in the UK, Nirvana's Kurt Cobain sang a catchy refrain he'd heard on the radio: 'There's no other way, there's no other way.'[32] This was the chorus and title of the second single by London-based four-piece Blur. Careful finessing by the band's record company had ensured that the band's sound was very much of the moment. Label manager Andy Ross was very keen on the dance-fusion sound of the Happy Mondays, and encouraged Blur to incorporate breakbeats and samples into their music. Ross's tireless promotion of 'the indie-dance crossover' eventually earned him the nickname 'the Andy-dance Rossover' from guitarist Graham Coxon, but his instincts proved correct.[33] 'There's No Other Way' was, as the band later admitted, a dud until Ross talked them into grafting a drum loop from a Run-D.M.C. record onto it. Released in April 1991, 'There's No Other Way' went to number 8 on the UK chart, and the music press became interested. 'Blur,' wrote music journalist Simon Williams, 'are going to be massive.'[34]

To the *NME*'s Danny Kelly, Blur seemed to have something sorely lacking in most other post-Madchester bands — teen appeal. 'I see this girl every morning at my local station,' wrote Danny Kelly in the *NME*. 'Fourteen, fifteen, she scrawls the names of the latest girlie-pop heroes on the side of her holdall.' As 'There's No Other Way' climbed up the chart, Kelly saw a new name appear on the girl's bag. 'To the legends KYLIE, JASON, CHESNEY was added the word BLUR.'[35] That his music should appeal to American indie rockers as much as it did to South London teenagers would hardly have come as a surprise to singer Damon Albarn, who saw no limits to the group's crossover potential. 'We're romantic enough to believe that we can have our cake and eat it,' he told Kelly, 'that we can appeal to everyone.'[36]

Dealing with Things

In Penelope Spheeris's comedy *Wayne's World*, a TV executive tries to convince one of his sponsors that rising public access stars Wayne and Garth are worth investing in. 'Kids can relate to this show,' he says. 'These guys aren't phonies. Kids can spot phonies — they're very smart.' The sponsor — who owns a chain of amusement parlours downtown — is unconvinced. 'Kids know dick,' he grunts. 'I watch 'em in my arcades. They stand there like laboratory rats hittin' the feeder bar to get a food pellet. But as long as they keep pumpin' in the quarters, who gives a shit, right?'[1] The TV execs, in their polo necks and boxy late-eighties suits, laugh indulgently at the old man. They represent — in the film's terms — the greed, ambition and exploitation of the decade just gone. Wayne and Garth, with their flannel shirts, abiding love of rock, and commitment to not selling out, embody the ideals of the nineties, where artifice has been replaced by authenticity.

Kurt Cobain was no phoney — but he wasn't so sure the kids could spot one. 'I do feel a duty to warn the kids of false music that's claiming to be underground or alternative,' he told Michael Azerrad.[2] Cobain wasn't speaking in the abstract here — he had one band in particular in mind — Pearl Jam, the Seattle-based five-piece whose debut album, *Ten*, had been released just one month before *Nevermind*. Krist Novoselic agreed. 'Those guys are not an alternative band! They're a hard rock band.'[3] The bass player insisted that Pearl Jam was a classic example of the depths the music industry would sink to as it strove to exploit the new teen angst for profit. 'Record companies are such schemers,' he said.

Pearl Jam's singer, Eddie Vedder, was very upset by this snub from Nirvana, whose music he admired. He was also confused by it, and with some justification. Pearl Jam was not, after all, Milli Vanilli. Pearl Jam was a real band made of real people who played their own instruments, wrote their own songs, and had come together in order to play music. If the new authenticity was about the sincere expression of personal feelings, the removal of hype and artifice, and drums, bass and guitar, then Pearl Jam passed on all three counts. Vedder had loathed the scheming and schmoozing of the music industry from the moment he laid eyes on it. He walked out of the launch party for *Ten* — where he'd gritted his teeth and shaken the hands of the record company people for only as long as he could stand — in a furious huff. 'That was unlike anything I've ever experienced in my life,' he said afterward, 'and I never want to experience it again.'[4] The band eschewed the excesses of a rock and roll lifestyle — asked in New York whether he'd indulged in any hotel room-trashing while on tour, Vedder replied, 'I think I left the towels kind of messy.'[5] Even social chitchat was too much like pretence for Pearl Jam. 'They despise small talk,' observed *Rolling Stone*'s Kim Neeley, 'cutting right to the existential chase.' The band met Neeley on the observation deck of Seattle's space needle, where Vedder got right down to the meaning of it all. 'Life is, like, so much to live, and we don't know how long we're gonna be here,' said the singer, as he leaned over the deck into the night. 'All I really believe in is this fucking moment, like right now.'[6]

Twelve months earlier, there had been no such thing as Pearl Jam, and Vedder was just another aspiring singer-songwriter — living in southern California, surfing and working the night shift at a gas station to pay the rent and support his music habit. One day, his friend Jack Irons, who at the time played drums for the Red Hot Chili Peppers, gave Vedder a cassette tape with some demos on it by a Seattle trio — Stone Gossard, Mike McCready and Jeff Ament — who were looking for a singer. Vedder listened to the tape on headphones at work, and then went surfing the next morning, with the band's churning seventies-style rock still ringing in his ears. He hadn't slept for days — he'd been working all night, writing songs all day, and surfing in whatever spare time he had left. As he surfed, song lyrics came to mind — the content of which surprised him. Vedder would later tell interviewers that he wrote the songs while surfing, although he joked once or twice that he had written them while sleeping. 'I woke up,' he said, 'and there they were.' Both stories, in a sense, were true. 'The sleep deprivation came into play,' he later recalled. 'You get so sensitive it feels like every nerve is exposed. I started dealing with things I hadn't dealt with.'[7]

What Vedder hadn't dealt with was his childhood. The singer's biography had many parallels to Kurt Cobain's — the familiar litany of divorce, re-marriage and abandonment played out to a soundtrack of FM radio hits, so common to their generation. But Vedder's tale had a few extra twists — his parents had separated shortly after he was born, and he grew up believing that his mother's second husband was his biological father. Vedder was eighteen when he finally learned the truth, by which point his father was dead.

Vedder turned all this over in his mind as he surfed and sang to himself. By the afternoon he'd composed three songs with interlocking themes, which together formed a mini-rock opera about a child from a broken home who grows up to become a serial killer, and is later sentenced to death. 'Alive' told of the young man's attempts to deal with the death of his father, and of an incestuous relationship with his mother that followed. In 'Once', the son is driven mad by the rage and resentment he feels toward his parents. 'I got a bomb in my temple that is gonna explode,' he sings.[8] The bomb goes off, and carnage ensues. 'Footsteps' is the last act of the tragedy, in which the young man, facing execution, confronts his parents and lays the blame for his wasted life squarely at their feet. 'Did what I had to do,' he sings. 'If there was a reason, it was you.'[9] Vedder recorded the three songs over the demos he'd been given, copied them onto a cassette (whose label read 'The Best of the 70s and 80s'), sent them back to the band in Seattle, and waited.

The rock opera was as unfashionable a concept in 1990 as it had been at any time since 1976. But Vedder had an abiding love for *Tommy* — The Who's classic song cycle of 1969 — which had sustained him through his teenage years. *Tommy* gave the singer a taste for epic drama, big choruses and rock-as-storytelling. But it also forged an important link in his imagination between the tension and release of rock music, and the idea of healing psychic trauma by confronting and 'letting go' of past experiences. In *Tommy*, the deaf, dumb and blind kid eventually discovers that his disabilities are psychosomatic — the result of his repressed unhappy childhood. In a dramatic moment of revelation, Tommy confronts his past, and finds he can speak again. Confrontation leads to understanding, understanding leads to redemption. These were the terms in which Vedder saw the songs he'd written. He'd locked away the hurt and resentment he'd been feeling toward his family, and had been driven half crazy as a result. But by expressing these feelings through music, he'd been healed, and had attained a state of psychic equilibrium.

The subject matter of the songs showed that he was all too aware of what might have occurred if he hadn't — a scenario described by author Douglas Coupland in 1991 as an 'emotional ketchup burst'.[10] In Vedder's universe, music was a safe means of expressing desires which society could not tolerate — the desire to kill, or the desire to sleep with one's mother. The reputation of Sigmund Freud, in 1991, was at one of its lowest ebbs — but Vedder still held a basically Freudian view of culture and society. Freud believed that human nature is essentially destructive and evil. We must repress our natural impulses in order to get along with others, but in doing so, we become neurotic. In therapy, we identify these hidden desires in ourselves and speak their names aloud — thereby robbing them of their power. When we make art, we represent them in code. Vedder's idea of what rock music was for, in 1990, was somewhere between these two. Like all Amercians born in the sixties, the singer grew up in a media environment saturated with Freudian concepts, ('repressed', 'ego', 'subconscious') and came of age in the shadow of a social revolution underwritten by a grossly simplified version of Freud's philosophy — in a nutshell, 'better out than in'.

It was his ability to deal with past trauma, as much as his affecting baritone that told Ament, Gossard and McCready that Vedder was the right man for the job. 'Eddie's whole trip seemed to relate to us in a good way,'[11] Gossard later recalled. Gossard and Ament had both been members of a group called Mother Love Bone, whose trip had come to an untimely end in July 1990 when singer Andrew Wood died of a heroin overdose. The songs Vedder had written suited the musicians' sombre mood and the 'period of turmoil and reflection' they had undergone since Wood's death, while also hinting at the possibility of redemption in the future.[12] The singer was flown to Seattle for an audition, and was subsequently invited to join the band. They played their first show as a five piece (with drummer Dave Krusen) in October, were signed to Epic Records by the end of the year, and had finished their debut album three months later. The record, Gossard later explained, was 'a quick and spontaneous kind of thing', recorded in two weeks with many songs written in the studio.[13]

The apparent speed and ease with which the group had achieved all this had a lot to do with the subsequent sniping about Pearl Jam not being a 'real' band, and even the musicians themselves felt, as Gossard later put it, 'a little undeserving' of their success.[14] Critics were suspicious of the apparently thrown-together nature of the group, which raised the old spectre of the 'manufactured' band, whose membership had been assembled, Monkees style, by a scheming record company. While this was untrue, the band members' guilty conscience regarding their fairly short history together was betrayed by the image they chose for the cover of *Ten*. Jeff Ament's design — which showed the band members clasping hands in a circle — was meant, he said, to give the impression of 'being really together as a group and entering into the world of music as a true band'.[15]

Pearl Jam's relatively recent arrival on the scene also suggested that they might be bandwagon-jumpers. Nirvana had been around since 1987, Soundgarden since 1986. Both were now signed to major labels, but the fact that they had spent the majority of the late eighties driving their own vans, booking their own gigs and sleeping on people's floors gave them a right to call themselves 'alternative'. The members of Pearl Jam, on the other hand, had played only a handful of shows together before they were signed.

But the amount of time Pearl Jam had spent together before their breakthrough meant very little, if anything at all, to the thousands who saw the band play live in the months following the release of *Ten* in August 1991. Likewise, the arguments Cobain and Novoselic had been using to explain why Pearl Jam's music was fake (for example, that *Ten* contained too much lead guitar playing) seemed academic at best, pedantic at worst in the face of the overwhelming physical force Pearl Jam now generated at its shows, and Vedder's extraordinary rapport with the crowd. In a TV interview in New York, Vedder quipped that he had given up surfing for music, but Gossard was quick to correct him. 'You still surf, every night in the crowd. He kinda does this "crowd surfing" routine,' Gossard added, for the interviewer's benefit. 'It's pretty cool.'[16] Vedder's surfing — which on some nights took him all the way from the stage to the mixing desk and back — was heavily symbolic for Pearl Jam's audience. It implied a bond of trust between the singer and the fans, a bond they had sensed while hearing the band's records, and found confirmed at its concerts.

Toward the end of 1991, for a variety of reasons — not the least of which was the surprise success of 'Smells Like Teen Spirit' — the power to determine whose band was real and whose band was phoney passed from the hands of critics, ideologues and musicians into those of a growing popular audience. The kids decided Pearl Jam was a real band for reasons that had nothing to do with the group's underground credentials — or lack thereof. Pearl Jam was real because audiences believed in Eddie Vedder. And they believed in him because he was honest — more so, some felt, than Kurt Cobain. Vedder gave voice to many of the same feelings and experiences Cobain did — he sang about being a child of divorced parents, about growing up as a lonely outsider and feeling alienated from modern life. But unlike Cobain, Vedder never hid behind irony or sarcasm. Nothing summed up the difference between Nirvana and Pearl Jam quite so eloquently as the covers of the albums the two bands released in 1991. *Nevermind*'s bitterly ironic photo of a baby swimming toward a dollar bill on a fishhook could not have been more different from the redemptive image of brotherhood featured on the cover of *Ten*. If Nirvana's music was, as 'Smells Like Teen Spirit' had it, 'a denial', Pearl Jam's was an affirmation. And where Cobain confused his audience with surreal word games and non sequiturs, Vedder — as music critic Simon Reynolds noted — told stories.[17] Not happy stories by any means, Vedder's muse was as dark as Cobain's. But he usually gave his listeners a moment of deliverance at the end, even if the deliverance came through tragedy, as in 'Jeremy'. Best of all, he offered up these tales in a warm, comforting singing voice that evoked distant memories of seventies FM radio hits, while constructing an image of the singer in the listener's mind as someone honest, human and real. 'Pearl Jam's Eddie Vedder sings with the emotion most singers lack in today's rock business,' wrote one fan. 'Unlike a certain so-called "Seattle" band, he does a lot more than scream. Jealous, Kurt?'[18]

Learning and Hugging

'Sorry,' said a slightly embarrassed Stone Gossard, having just made an off-colour joke in a 1991 TV interview, 'I've been on a bus for a month with nine guys.'[1] Pearl Jam had been touring with the Red Hot Chili Peppers throughout autumn, and the shows had been — according to Eddie Vedder — 'amazing'.[2] The Chili Peppers new single 'Give It Away' had been given a huge boost by high rotation on LA's influential KROQ and, as other stations across the country followed suit, the shows began to sell out. The Chili Peppers lapped up the attention, playing white-hot funk while — more often than not — wearing nothing more between them than four well-placed socks.

In October Anthony Kiedis and Flea were interviewed by music TV presenter Erica Ehm, and were asked — not for the first time — 'What is it with you guys and your penises?' For Kiedis, such questions said more about a society that felt the need to ask them than he could ever say in a song. 'The existence of sexual energy is such a natural part of life,' he explained to Ehm. 'When you feel comfortable with a particular aspect of life and sex and you sing about it ... then you're normal in my opinion.' What was really crazy, the singer insisted, was the 'right-wing Judaeo-Christian' attitude that tries to ignore and suppress sexual urges, until they become 'something sick and terrible'.[3] Like Vedder, the Chili Peppers' singer believed that society's problems had to do with repression, and his belief that what is secret should be uncovered applied to feelings as much as it did to penises. Music, he said, 'is an exorcism of emotions. Artists build up so much inside of themselves based on their lives that without the ability to express that in some form of art ... well, personally, I would go crazy.'[4]

In *Rolling Stone*'s annual 'Hot' issue for 1991, comedian Jerry Seinfeld had identified the 'Hot Attitude' for the coming year as 'earnest'. 'Everyone's tired of bullshitters,' he said. 'It's like we're tired of the package — show us what's inside.'[5] Never less than earnest, and frequently unpackaged, the Red Hot Chili Peppers embodied this red-hot mood better than any other band by the end of 1991. 'Is there such a thing as indecent exposure?' asked a radio interviewer, shortly before the tour with Pearl Jam got underway. 'I'm sure there is,' replied Flea, 'but I don't think we could ever be accused of it.' For the Chili Peppers, the sharing of body parts and personal feelings — on stage and off — was the decent thing to do. But 'every time an ugly, greedy person shows their face,' Flea added, 'that's indecent exposure.'[6] Sex was cool, feelings were cool. Money, the band insisted, was not — although money accompanied by feelings was acceptable. In 1990 the band signed to Epic for $5.7 million. When Warner Bros' Mo Ostin learned he'd been out-bargained, he called Kiedis, Flea, drummer Chad Smith and guitarist John Frusciante individually to congratulate them and wish them good luck. Kiedis was 'so touched by his human-ness' that he called a last-minute pow-wow, after which the Chili Peppers decided to go with Warners instead — for 10 million.[7]

'Give It Away' was an anthem for the new era of renunciation and sharing, inspired by an episode from Kiedis's past. In the early eighties, Kiedis had briefly dated the new wave singer Nina Hagen. One day, while rummaging through her wardrobe, he'd come across a jacket he liked — Hagen told him to keep it, insisting that she'd rather make him happy by giving it away than own a closet full of clothes she'd probably never get around to wearing. 'It's important to give things away,' she said, 'it creates good energy.'[8] For Kiedis — who had grown up in LA during the transition from the 'me' decade to the Reagan era, and had been told all his life that he had to take what he could get and keep it — this was an extraordinary thing to do, and the phrase 'give it away' had stuck in his mind ever since. The finished song was a high-powered rap in favour of the renunciation of property, in which Kiedis observed 'greedy little people in a sea of distress' and declared himself 'unimpressed by material excess'.[9] New producer Rick Rubin suited the music to the mood — banishing from the studio any piece of equipment designed after 1975, and recording the song like the eighties never happened. Having shrugged off the layers of digital sheen that had obscured their funk on earlier releases, the Chili Peppers stood as defiantly naked on record as they did on stage.

Rubin was also instrumental in helping Kiedis to share his feelings, something he and the band had resolved to do after the disappointingly flat *Mother's Milk*. 'We still want to explode in your face,' Flea explained. 'But we have other emotions we want to express.'[10] Kiedis and Flea had been devastated by the death of the Chili Peppers' original guitarist Hillel Slovak from a heroin overdose in 1988. 'A completely unexpected bummer,' said Kiedis, 'that will probably make us sad 'til the day we die.'[11] Slovak's death had also given the singer a considerable scare — he had gone into rehab for his own drug addiction and was, by the time the band came to record with Rubin, completely clean. But this created problems of its own. Flipping through the singer's notebooks one day, Rubin came across some lines Kiedis had written about his days as a drug addict and the distance his new-found sobriety had put between himself and his friends. 'What's this?' asked Rubin. 'Oh,' said Kiedis, embarrassed, 'that's just a poem.'[12] Kiedis hadn't even thought about sharing it with the band, but the producer talked him into it. The result was an affecting ballad called 'Under the Bridge' — a real breakthrough for the Chili Peppers, which proved they could emote as well as explode.

According to Kiedis, Slovak's death and his own subsequent battle with addiction made the Red Hot Chili Peppers stronger, and gave them a new sense of purpose. 'By losing Hillel,' Kiedis said, 'I gained a greater respect for my own life and also for the relationships and love I share with my friends.'[13] On the 1991 tour, the band practised a backstage ritual before every show that symbolised the new bond the group had forged. Kiedis, Flea, Frusciante and Smith would stand in a ring, hold hands, slap each other and hug it out, in what Kiedis called a 'soul circle'.[14]

Tragedy brought the group closer together, but it also gave them a story. In the eighties, the Red Hot Chili Peppers had been stuck in a perennially goofy LA party pose. By the dawn of the nineties, they had turned this partying into part of a narrative, in which they were seen to have partied too hard, pushed things too far, descended into hell, clawed their way out of it, and come out stronger. In this way, the group embodied Seinfeld's zeitgeist better than the comedian did himself. Seinfeld had declared that earnest was hot but he diluted the candour of his eponymous TV show with generous quantities of irony, and instituted a firm 'no learning, no hugging' rule for himself and co-writer Larry David.[15] But learning and hugging would prove to be important features of the cultural life of the nineties — and essential pursuits for any LA party band hoping to make the transition from the old decade to the new.

In October, Mötley Crüe declared the 'Decade of Decadence' over with a hits compilation that marked its beginning in 1981 — the year Reagan was inaugurated — and its end in 1991 — the year *Nevermind* and *Ten* were released.[16] Already, the archetypal Sunset Strip party band had moved into a slightly changed mode of presentation — they were now survivors, rather than purveyors of good times. The confessional mood of the day demanded that the excesses of the eighties be presented as a mistake, for which you had suffered, and were now 'dealing with'. *Spin* magazine's Bob Mack met Anthony Kiedis at a party at the singer's Hollywood home in August, and saw a very different scene to the one that the phrase 'party at rock star's home in LA' would have conjured three years earlier. No drink, no drugs, no strippers — just diet soda, 'natural tobacco' cigarettes, and a handful of B-list celebrities — a few actresses, one Beastie Boy, and one rehab doctor to the stars, warmly embracing each other as Kiedis manned the barbecue. It was, Mack concluded, 'very LA, very nineties'.[17]

Later, Kiedis told the reporter about how he had written the song 'My Lovely Man'. 'I was in my room, missing Hillel, and I just started crying,' said the singer. 'I couldn't stop, so I wrote that song.'[18] Five years earlier, a confession of this kind from the singer of an LA funk-rock band would have seemed as absurd as a Hollywood party without coke and bikini models. But it was no longer enough to simply stick out your chest, turn up the guitar, whip out your cock and fight like a brave. 'To be strong may only conceal a rickety scaffolding of denial,' said Robert Hughes in a lecture on 'The Culture of Complaint' delivered earlier that year in New York. 'To be weak is to be invincible.'[19]

1992

Platform Double Suede

By way of showing their gratitude to Kim Gordon for recommending them to Geffen, Krist Novoselic, Dave Grohl and Kurt Cobain decided to pay the favour forward. 'Since our record has done so well,' said Novoselic in a 1992 radio interview, 'we can open up the door for other bands from where we come from.' The bass player talked excitedly in interviews about Mudhoney, the Melvins, Dinosaur Jr, Hole and the Jesus Lizard. He also took care to mention Gordon's own band, Sonic Youth, whose Geffen debut had sold barely a tenth of what *Nevermind* had. 'People ask me why they haven't sold 500,000 records,' said Novoselic, 'and my only answer is that people are fucking stupid.' Nirvana saw its role within the mainstream as educational. 'If we are important, it's to bring a lot of underground bands to the surface,' Novoselic insisted, 'so that some kid from the mainstream will understand there's more to life than just Poison or Mötley Crüe.'[1]

Cobain had already used his newfound clout to help one of his favourite underground bands, Urge Overkill, by inviting the group to support Nirvana on its American tour. The Chicago trio — Eddie 'King' Roesser, Nash Kato and Blackie Onassis — had, by 1992, finessed their music from a post-hardcore racket into a sound closer to that of classic rock acts like Cheap Trick and Aerosmith, mixed with a generous shot of lounge-lizard cool. But the members of Urge were not content with simply sounding like they'd recorded their music in the past. They wanted to live there, full time. 'This is our lifestyle,' declared Blackie Onassis in 1990. 'We are here to resurrect the era of the swinger.'[2] The band outfitted themselves in crushed velvet suits, patent-leather shoes and gold medallions so as to firmly locate themselves in what they believed was the peak period of American culture — 1967 to 1971. Back then — in the era of moonlight dancing, Vegas and *Playboy* magazine — America, they insisted, was a fun place: 'We'd like to bring that back,' said Onassis. Over the next couple of years, the band's aesthetic seemed to shift forward in time slightly, as they embraced Kool and the Gang, Cheap Trick and white flared pants. In 1992 they came closer than they ever had to their ideal when they recorded a version of Neil Diamond's 'Girl, You'll Be a Woman Soon' — not so much a cover of the song as a mystical communion with one of the band's all-time heroes. 'Who are we,' asked Blackie, 'to speak of a deity such as Neil?' The band then went on to speak about him for at least four more paragraphs in a rapturous tribute to the man who minted their peculiar aesthetic.[3]

By 1991, the so-called 'decade that taste forgot' had begun to acquire a certain hip cachet among indie scenesters. The IPU convention had included in its program a *Planet of the Apes* movie marathon and a disco-dancing contest, and Sonic Youth's patronage was already turning the Carpenters into a hipster phenomenon. In July 1991, the *NME*'s Stuart Maconie visited the members of a group called Jellyfish in their San Francisco share house, and found them living in a miniature seventies pop museum — the walls plastered with Kiss and Farrah Fawcett posters, the band members sleeping under *Dukes of Hazzard* doona covers and passing their spare time with an *H. R. Pufnstuf* jigsaw puzzle.[4] Six months later, in Minneapolis, John Wozniak of the group Zog Bogbean began working on a song about his girlfriend called 'Sex and Candy'. Even though the lyrics described events that took place in the eighties, Wozniak started throwing in 'all these weird disco-era references that I was making up, you know, "platform double suede".'[5] These words already had some pop culture currency — platform shoes had made a comeback thanks to videos by Deee-Lite and Kylie Minogue, and, in London, critics were beginning to take notice of a band called Suede with a penchant for seventies glam.

In 1988, the *Washington Post*'s Jefferson Morley had wondered why there were no movies set in the seventies. 'Why is it,' he asked, 'that there's never been a seventies revival?'[6] By the end of 1991, *Spin*'s Celia Farber felt confident that it was underway. 'Get your bell-bottoms out,' she wrote, 'this is going to be fun.'[7] Farber wrote excitedly about John Travolta's dancing and the unparalleled delights of seventies junk food, and interviewed the founders of The 70s Preservation Society — two former yuppies who had dropped out of the present into the past and decided to stay there. 'We had all this eighties angst,' said the society's co-president Cliff Chenfield, 'and we just decided we couldn't do it any longer. Out of this angst came a revelation that what we really loved were the days of our youth, the great 1970s.'[8] In Tim Burton's *Beetlejuice*, Michael Keaton punished a yuppie interior decorator by zapping him out of his eighties power suit and into seventies leisure-wear. Chenfield had done the same to himself, as a form of regression therapy. In the seventies, Chenfield insisted, 'people were a lot happier and a lot funner than they are today. It was a silly, fun time.'[9]

The idea that the seventies were a fun decade didn't really hold up to serious scrutiny — in fact, most commentators agreed that the end of the sixties marked the beginning of a period of steady economic and social decline. In a 1991 article for *Rolling Stone*, Walter Russell Mead described how, in the 1950s, the miracle of the post-war economic boom had fostered the idea that life would get better with each passing decade. Americans, it had been said, would eventually be so well-off that the five-day working week might soon become a thing of the past. 'The affluent society had arrived,' he wrote, 'the leisure society would be next.'[10] But by 1970, this future was already disappearing from view — the escalating cost of the war in Vietnam led to an inflation panic, and wages began to fall. Here, Mead confirmed what Urge Overkill's pop-culture radar had earlier led them to believe. '1972 was the peak,' Mead insisted, 'since then, the decline has been relentless.'[11]

This slow-motion collapse created the world that twenty-somethings like Kurt Cobain, Eddie Vedder and Blackie Onassis grew up in, and subsequently took for granted. 'For us,' wrote Jefferson Morley, 'everything seemed normal. I remember wondering why people were surprised that prices were going up — I thought that's what prices did.'[12] As the cost of living rose, wages fell, businesses closed, and employees were laid off. Families moved with alarming frequency from town to town in search of work, and when the pressure became too much, they separated. The landscape of cities like Detroit and Chicago changed dramatically as the factories that had supported them closed, and the social and racial divides that had lain beneath the surface of these once-thriving economies were aggravated by desperation and ennui. By the mid seventies, the leisure suit had become fashionable, but the leisure society it had been designed for was nowhere to be seen. And while an argument could be made that the non-appearance of utopia was silly, few would have agreed that it was fun.

The generation born at the end of the sixties had fond memories of the seventies — as most people do of their formative years. Seventies nostalgia, like all nostalgia, reflected a basic preference for childhood over the complexities of adolescence and adult life; the repeated insistence that the seventies were a more innocent time simply indicated that the speaker was innocent in the seventies. But even this rose-tinted view could be unexpectedly tainted by the harsh economic and social pressures of the period. *The Real Live Brady Bunch* theatre show, which debuted in 1990, tapped an almost universal fondness for the syndicated seventies TV hit among Gen X audiences. But the show's appeal to seventies kids was based to a large extent on its premise — two single-parent families coming together, making whole what had been broken. And the show's success was based not on its original evening time-slot, but on the later reruns, broadcast in the afternoon. The result was guaranteed to resonate with what Steven Daly and Nathaniel Wice, the authors of 1995's *Alt. Culture*, later described as 'a latchkey generation experiencing a 50 per cent divorce rate'.[13] In 1991, Elizabeth Moran penned an open letter to Robert Reed, the actor who played Mike Brady. 'Bob,' she wrote, 'you'll be our dad forever.'[14]

Although the 1970s failed, in every significant way, to live up to the promises of the sixties, this only seemed to make them more appealing to seventies revivalists in the nineties. The seventies, Celia Farber insisted, were actually 'much cooler than the sixties, because the sixties tried so hard to be meaningful, and radical. If I see one more balding intellectual on TV saying, "You see, we thought we could change the world", I will drop dead from boredom.'[15] Faith Soloway, co-creator of the *Real Live Brady Bunch*, agreed. 'Ex-hippies look at Jefferson Airplane records and pine,' she explained. 'Twenty-somethings watch seventies reruns and giggle.'[16] Farber and Soloway acknowledged that seventies culture was decadent, and had been produced by a society in decline. But they maintained that it was preferable to that of the sixties *because* it was bad.

This reversal of values was born of necessity. Baby boomers seemed to have got all the good culture — along with the good neighbourhoods and the good jobs — before anyone else did. By the time their children grew up, there was nothing left for them except the things no-one else wanted, the forgotten detritus of the decade that taste forgot — crushed velvet suits, Neil Diamond records, Farrah Fawcett posters and Fluevogs. 'Those of us who never got to protest,' said Soloway, 'are left with *The Brady Bunch* and *Saturday Night Fever.*' The decade that produced these things wasn't classic or cool or significant, but it didn't need to be. 'It's ours,' Soloway explained.[17] For a generation that felt as though it had inherited nothing much, this was of no small importance.

Bad culture has one distinct advantage over good culture — it's cheaper. This quirk of America's cultural economy worked for Urge Overkill on two levels. The low critical standing of seventies music and fashion in the eighties made it very cheap, and thus easily available to struggling young musicians living in one of post-industrial America's more blighted cities. 'We've been touted as these fashion horses, but we're just blessed that we live in Chicago,' said Kato. 'We invented a million-dollar look on a shoestring.'[18] New records and clothes were expensive, but Cheap Trick albums and white flared pants could be bought at thrift stores for next to nothing. But this principle applied to ideas and moods in the same way that it did to objects. The period itself was considered a failure, which meant that, like the Wicker Park neighbourhood of Chicago where the band members lived, it had been abandoned. And just as the city's vacated neighbourhood had provided a space for its artists and musicians to create their own community, so the vacant spaces of seventies music and fashion offered vast tracts of cultural real estate for those artists to colonise.

With 1992's 'Girl, You'll Be a Woman Soon', Urge Overkill moved into this abandoned space and made itself at home, padding its way into a sunken living room with a cocktail, and sinking its toes into the shagpile carpet. Being able to appreciate all this stuff required imagination, certainly, 'the perspective and the goofy genius' as the *NME*'s Stuart Bailie put it, to turn seventies junk into art.[19] The fetish for the sixties in the eighties worked on a very simple level — the sixties were classic and original, their leftovers desirable for that reason. Enjoying the seventies required a leap of the imagination — it was, more than anything, a creative act. But this was a task Urge Overkill approached with relish — as did many other groups who were exploring the decade at the time, including Soundgarden, Spin Doctors and Jellyfish. As Nash Kato gleefully indulged himself in the hitherto taboo mannerisms of a seventies soft-rock entertainer, one could feel the thrill of a group that had believed it was living in a used-up world discovering an abandoned city right on its doorstep. 'That's the thing,' wrote Pere Ubu's David Thomas in 1993. 'It's that American thing. Get all you can before it's too late. No, it's too late now. But you can still catch up to the echoes.'[20]

Useless Generation

In March 1992, UK retailer Our Price Music ran a series of ads on the back of England's weekly music papers for a new in-store promotion. 'Sounds of the 70s' promised '50 classic albums at fab and groovy prices'. The discounted selection included titles by The Doors, Led Zeppelin, Wings, the Sex Pistols, The Clash, T-Rex, Carol King, The Sweet and Madness. 'So never mind the bollocks,' urged the copy, 'get down to your local Our Price Music now!'[1]

For those who were old enough to have participated in the music wars of 1976–1978, the idea of The Clash being lumped in with Carol King — not to mention the sight of the phrase 'never mind the bollocks' spelled out in a pink lava-lamp font — may well have provoked some involuntary puking. But English music writers had been noting, of late, the emergence of a new generation of musicians and fans for whom the ideological divide between Led Zep and the Pistols meant nothing much at all. The four members of Lush — Miki Berenyi, Emma Anderson, Steve Rippon and Chris Acland — were all around ten or eleven years old when the Sex Pistols played the 100 Club. Rippon spent that weekend in a holiday caravan in Bognor with his parents. Anderson recalled sitting in the back seat of her mum's car in the summer of 1977, having a competition with her friend to see how many punks they could spot on the King's Road. 'There's one! I've seen three now. How many have you seen?'[2] Being too young to have got caught up in the movement's politics, Lush saw no contradiction in pledging their allegiance to punk and ABBA — both, to them, were sounds of the seventies, and could be appreciated as such.

Many music writers found this refreshing. By the nineties punk had — to a slightly lesser extent — become to England's indie scene what Woodstock rock was to America's: 'old people's youth music', as music critic Simon Frith called it.[3] To those born in the late sixties, punk, more often than not, meant the self-righteous older brother or cousin who told you that you couldn't listen to *Are You Experienced?* because it was for hippies, or the bore at the pub who lectured you about how bands now just aren't as good as they were in the seventies. You should have been there, they'd say. On 13 October 1990, music writer Simon Dudfield went to the London Falcon to see a new group called the Manic Street Preachers — four skinny kids from south Wales, their hair spiked up with liquid soap, playing would-be punk anthems for a sceptical crowd. 'So you like 'em then?' an older punter asked Dudfield. The man laughed when Dudfield told him he did. 'I'll play you some proper punk records some time.'[4]

Like Dudfield, the Manics — Nicky Wire, Sean Moore, James Dean Bradfield and Richey Edwards — were at infants school in 1976, so they missed punk. But they saw the reruns. Bradfield told music journalist Steven Wells how, at the age of seventeen, he'd turned on the TV one night and caught Tony Wilson hosting a tenth anniversary punk special, with clips of The Clash playing live and the Sex Pistols saying 'fuck' on Bill Grundy's *Today* show. Then he changed the channel and saw the striking Welsh miners being 'kicked to crap by police and starved back to work by the Tories'.[5] Something clicked, as Bradfield began to realise that punk was not ancient history, but an abandoned work in progress. The band formed later that year, released a single called 'Suicide Alley' in 1989, and an EP, *New Art Riot*, in 1990. Their trebly buzz-saw guitar sound and wordy, political lyrics showed the influence of the first two Clash records. But the band happily mixed pure punk with Public Enemy, Guns N' Roses, the Rolling Stones, Bacharach and David, and whatever else they felt they could use. 'Everybody lives out what's gone on in the past,' said Richey Edwards. 'We're all about second-hand ideas. What else can we do?'[6] As Edwards spoke, Wire sat beside him on the hotel bed, making collages with a Sex Pistols calendar, an Irish pop magazine, and a glue-stick.

By this point, the Manic Street Preachers — with their sloganeering lyrics and spray-painted T-shirts — could not have been more out of step with the mood of British youth culture if they'd been a mariachi band. 'A speed band in an E generation,' wrote the *NME*'s Steven Wells in 1991, 'slogan-vomiting missionaries for violence in the garden of good vibes.'[7] The Manics were spiky where Madchester was baggy, uptight in a loose-fit scene. In the midst of the Third Summer of Love they seemed like the worst kind of party poopers, using an outdated language (punk) to complain about a non-existent problem (capitalism). 'The E generation still faces the long suicide of work every Monday morning,' Edwards claimed. 'Music is useless if it keeps on promoting hedonism in a war zone.'[8]

But if the Manic Street Preachers appeared, at first, to have arrived fifteen years too late, by 1992 it seemed more likely that they had arrived just one year too early. In January 1991, Bradfield had said that he found it 'offensive' that pictures of the Inspiral Carpets were on teenagers' bedroom walls.[9] By the end of the year they had most likely been taken down. Madchester's optimistic bubble had been burst — after the war, hedonism no longer seemed appropriate. It had been replaced by the art-for-art's sake retreat of shoegaze — which the Manics hated even more.

Described by one observer as 'a small coterie of like-minded musicians who shared a suffocating admiration for My Bloody Valentine's *Isn't Anything*, shoegaze bands played dreamy pop songs with half-whispered vocals, wreathed in layers of noise. The name was originally a put-down — a reference to such groups' tendency to ignore the audience in favour of their much-loved guitar pedals. By the end of 1991, the scene had produced a handful of inspired records, including strong singles and EPs by Chapterhouse and Slowdive, and at least two truly great albums — My Bloody Valentine's *Loveless* and Ride's *Nowhere*. But while shoegaze music could be thrilling, the bands themselves were not. They looked ordinary, did nothing interesting on stage, and had nothing much to say on the subject of politics, society or the state of the world. For those who believed that rock and roll had anything to do with glamour, danger, sex or subversion, this was disappointing to say the least. The *NME*'s Danny Kelly wrote shoegaze off as a 'pleasurably engulfing but dangerously bland and determinedly apolitical sound'. A Manic Street Preachers fan, busily putting up posters for the band's February show at Leicester University, was far less diplomatic. 'Slowdive and Chapterhouse are all fucking shitty bands that don't mean anything. They just look at their feet and go on about fuck all!'

The Manic Street Preachers' essential difference from their contemporaries had won them a devoted school of fans, for whom the band provided everything indie rock was missing in 1992. The girl told music journalist David Quantick that the Manic Street Preachers spoke to her in a way that no other band did. They were the only group, in 1992, that could tell her why life was empty and society was shit. 'If they didn't exist,' she said, 'I'd kill myself.'[10] This, according to Richey Edwards, was one of the reasons he started the band. 'When I was a teenager,' he told Steve Lamacq in May 1991, 'I never had a band who said anything about my life. That's why we're doing this.'[11]

But the Manic Street Preachers weren't just about giving kids a little bit of hope. Edwards saw youth culture in general, and rock and roll in particular, as a means, rather than an end. The quotes they slipped into interviews and the slogans painted on their shirts betrayed the debt the group owed to Guy Debord and the Situationist International, the revolutionary avant-garde movement whose texts and slogans had played an instrumental role in the student uprising of Paris 1968. Following the twentieth anniversary of this event in 1988, the Situationists' activities and legacy had undergone a reappraisal. Debord's *The Society of the Spectacle* had been reprinted, new books by cultural critic Greil Marcus and music journalist Jon Savage demonstrated the debt that punk owed to Debord's theories, and an exhibition of the Situationists' publications and posters had toured Britain. Debord had been a poet leading an art movement, but gave up poetry and kicked all the artists out of the movement once he realised that the fetishisation of art was preventing the improvement of real life. As long as you're writing about it, painting it and selling it, he believed, your refusal to participate in the Society of the Spectacle would simply add to the spectacle. In an article published in *Esquire*, Greil Marcus argued that this was precisely the reason why rock and roll was dead in 1992. 'Rock and roll,' he wrote, 'no longer seems to say anything at all that is not instantly translated into the dominant discourse of the day.'[12] From Debord and Marcus, the Manic Street Preachers learned that their band could only be the method, the goal had to be the transformation of everyday life. When the goal had been achieved, there would be no need for the band anymore. 'Personally,' said Edwards, 'I just want to make rock and roll redundant.'[13]

But this was easier said than done. The Manic's record company, for instance, had an obvious interest in keeping their revolt symbolic, rather than actual. The group had been signed by Columbia Records' Tim Bowden in 1991. He did it, he said, 'because they were the most exciting thing I'd seen since The Clash in 1976, which I also signed'.[14] At the Leicester University gig in February 1992, Bowden, wearing a suit and shaking hands with industry folk, told the *NME* that the band was brilliant, but harmless. 'They're no more anarchistic than anyone their age,' he explained. 'They're pissed off about where they live, they're pissed off about unemployment; but they're not so pissed off that they can't enjoy themselves and express themselves. And that's what young people are meant to do.'[15]

Bowden was right, of course. Enjoy themselves, express themselves — that's what young people are meant to do. What they're not meant to do is take up arms and destroy capitalism. And as long as they're being entertained by rock bands that can act out their appetite for destruction in a safe, symbolic form, there's no chance of this happening. This, the Manic Street Preachers knew, was how rock and roll worked and, as of 1992, it didn't seem like their band was going to be any exception. Already they could feel their provocations turning into shtick, their riots and smash-ups becoming ritualised. Nicky Wire told music journo David Quantick that the show in Leicester was 'like looking into an abyss'. Wire had thought for a moment about trying to start a fight, tearing the place up, doing something — but had thought better of it. 'Nothing would have changed,' he said.[16] The band could feel reality and representation drifting apart — somehow the gap between art and life would have to be closed.

In May 1991, the Manic Street Preachers played a show at the Norwich Arts Centre, and were interviewed after the gig by Steve

Lamacq for a feature in the *NME*. Lamacq had made no secret of his reservations regarding the band; he was convinced by neither their music nor their rhetoric, and had accused them of having a 'manufactured' image, like that of notorious early-nineties punk-posers Birdland. Lamacq described the interview backstage in Norwich as 'thirty minutes of friendly enough discussion and vitriol'. The session ended with a last word from Edwards. 'The thing is,' he told Lamacq, 'for us, it's really hard to convince you that we are for real.'[17]

Edwards would give it one more shot before Lamacq went home. 'I know you don't like us,' he said, as he and Lamacq walked off alone together, 'but we are for real.' Lamacq watched, frozen, as Edwards took a razor blade out of his pocket and started cutting the words '4 REAL' into his arm. 'We're not the next Birdland,' he said, his voice trembling as blood poured down his arm. 'We do mean what we do.'[18] Nicky Wire later described the event to *Q* magazine as a triumph. 'It proved we were real,' he said. But Edwards himself seemed less convinced. Two weeks after the interview with Lamacq, music writer James Brown asked the guitarist whether he felt foolish about what he'd done. 'No,' said Edwards. 'I feel just like the rest of this country — banging my head against the fucking wall.'[19]

Mass Rioting in America

In March 1992, the LA-based hardcore group Body Count released its self-titled first album, which the band's frontman Ice-T described as 'a rock album with a rap mentality'.[1] While he'd made his career as a rapper, Ice had always been a big fan of hardcore and metal — he cited Ministry, Cannibal Corpse and Slayer as favourites at the time — and had relished the opportunity to show this other side of his musical personality on stage and in the studio. Early signs suggested he'd made the transition with relative ease. Body Count's set was one of the highlights of Lollapalooza, and the album was getting good reviews. *Village Voice* gave it an A–, *Rolling Stone* praised its metal chops and 'sonic intensity'.[2]

But while *Entertainment Weekly*'s reviewer had her tongue firmly in her cheek when she called Body Count 'moronic, sexist, profane, gratuitously violent and morally reprehensible', President George Bush, when he described the band as 'sick', most definitely did not. And yet this thumbs-down from the White House pleased Body Count's frontman more than all the other reviews put together. How does it feel to be dissed by the president, asked Allan Light. 'It makes me feel good,' said Ice, 'like I haven't been just standing on a street corner yelling with nobody listening all this time.'[3]

Body Count had come to Bush's attention thanks to a song called 'Cop Killer', a first-person revenge fantasy inspired by a lifetime of harassment by Los Angeles' finest. 'It's a shot at the cops who are basically out of control,' Ice explained to MTV.[4] He made it clear that he didn't hate cops as a rule — at Body Count shows Ice would often preface the song by reminding people, 'Yo, there's some good cops out there'. He was also at pains to point out that the song was written from the point of view of a character, and no more confirmed that he was in favour of killing police officers than 'Space Oddity' proved David Bowie had been to the moon. 'We ain't never shot a cop,' he reminded Kurt Loder. 'Yet.'[5] But he'd certainly thought about it. 'I have many days of my life that I just wanted to go out there and kill the fucking pigs,' he told music journalist Alan Light.[6]

LA Hardcore had a long history of anti-cop songs, going back to the days when LA police chief Daryl Gates's force was doing its darnedest to drive Black Flag out of Hermosa Beach. The band retaliated with a single called 'Police Story', which had a Pettibon-designed sleeve showing a police officer with a gun in his mouth and the legend 'make me come, faggot'. Ronald Reagan paid no attention to this — or anything else hardcore bands might have to say about life in America in the eighties — because hardcore was underground. But now the taboo on the tattooed had been lifted. Body Count's record came out on Warner Bros, which had recently merged with Time to form one of America's largest and most powerful corporations. And being a public company, Time Warner was answerable to its shareholders, one of whom was Charlton Heston.

The veteran Hollywood actor was appalled that the company saw fit to release 'Cop Killer', and at the next stockholder's meeting, he took the floor to register his disapproval. 'To a hushed room of a thousand average American shareholders,' he later recalled, 'I simply read the full lyrics of "Cop Killer" aloud.' 'I got my 12-gauge sawed-off / I got my headlights turned off / I'm 'bout to bust some shots off / I'm 'bout to dust some cops off.' As Heston read these words in his commanding baritone, he looked out at the room and saw 'a sea of shocked, frozen, blanched faces'.[7] At another meeting later in the year, Heston led dozens of LA police officers in a protest, and called for Warner to withdraw the album. 'The right to free speech,' he insisted, 'has its limits.'[8] A growing chorus of public figures and politicians stepped up to denounce the song — including New York's Governor Mario Cuomo, who described 'Cop Killer' as 'ugly, destructive and disgusting', and Oliver North, who called for Time Warner to be brought up on charges of sedition. Meanwhile, three major national chain stores refused to carry the Body Count album, and Time Warner — who had defended the song from the beginning — began to receive bomb and death threats in the mail. The company was eventually forced to rerelease the record without 'Cop Killer'.

For Ice-T, the hypocrisy of all this was obvious. 'They're like, "Well, I'm down with freedom of speech, but he shouldn't have said that." That's bullshit.'[9] But the rapper also insisted that, in the increasingly hysterical debate over 'Cop Killer', too much was being made of the first amendment. This wasn't about constitutional rights, he told a college newspaper, it was about human rights. 'We have to turn it around and say "we don't need the constitution".'[10] Ice-T — like many American artists — reserved the right to imagine, and if necessary realise, a completely new America if the current version wasn't up to scratch. Far from being treasonous, this was, he argued, very American. 'This country was founded on the things I talk about,' he reminded *Rolling Stone*. 'We had a revolution or we would be under the Queen. We just celebrated July 4th, which is really just national Fuck the Police Day.' If it happened once, it could happen again, he insisted. 'People want America to be fair.'[11]

By the time Ice said this, Los Angeles had already had a Fuck the Police Day of its own — a whole week of them, in fact. On 29 April, a jury had acquitted four white LAPD officers charged with the brutal beating of a black man named Rodney King early in 1991. Crowds of protesters gathered in front of the Los Angeles County courthouse and on street corners nearby, and by the evening, these demonstrations had become riots, which soon engulfed the city. By the following Monday, fifty-three people were dead and hundreds of cars, homes and businesses had been destroyed over six days of burning and looting. Ice-T, who had been talking for years about the trouble brewing in the city, declared that he was 'fucking Nostradamus. I predicted this shit'. But he and many others in the hip-hop community were also quick to point out that it didn't take a genius to have seen it coming: twenty years of poverty and police harassment had made LA highly combustible. The King verdict might have been the spark, but as Public Enemy's Chuck D pointed out, 'We gotta be smarter than that.'[12]

In the weeks and months following the riots, there was a great deal of public speculation as to their underlying cause. Vice President Dan Quayle blamed the more general decline of traditional family values in America; White House press secretary Marlin Fitzwater agreed, and traced the disappearance of these core values to the liberal ideals and social policies of Lyndon Johnson's Great Society. 'Many of the root problems that have resulted in inner city difficulties were started in the sixties and seventies,' he said. 'They have failed; now we are paying the price.'[13] Both Fitzwater and Quayle echoed the claims of an influential conservative thinker named Charles Murray, who had been arguing for five years that the social programs instituted in the sixties had done more harm than good, and that black Americans would have been better off if the conservative policies of the fifties had been allowed to run their course. The events in LA following the Rodney King verdict seemed to many to have proved conservatives like Murray correct. Race riots, they concluded, were — like AIDS — a punishment for earlier indulgences.[14]

But not everyone endorsed this view. In his 1992 book, *The Culture of Contentment*, the economist JK Galbraith took Murray to task for trying, as he put it, 'to get the poor off the consciences of the comfortable'.[15] Murray's argument, Galbraith said, served the interests of a powerful new class that had emerged in the early seventies. This new class, according to Galbraith, had spent the past two decades promoting laissez-faire capitalism as the answer to all of society's ills, insisting that social problems could be more effectively dealt with by giving tax breaks to corporations than by spending money on welfare. But this, Galbraith argued, had been done in bad faith. The real goal had been to ensure the continuation of business as usual. In an editorial published in 1992, *Billboard* magazine's Timothy White argued that the end result of all this had been nothing less than the creation of a new underclass, whose problems could always be blamed on a decline in 'values' and treated with calls for law and order, more police, harsher penalties. 'The Reagan and Bush administrations have effectively reversed nearly forty years of gains in civil rights while fostering racial demagoguery that destroys the powerless by pitting them against one another, cunningly implanting fear and hatred in a society — and then stepping in to "rescue" the populace with the sort of massive, heinous repression that can take a century to undo.'[16]

For many musicians — whose basic sympathy for the downtrodden was here mingled with a metal-head's appetite for chaos and destruction — the sight of LA in flames was curiously hopeful. Kids who were too happy with life would do nothing. But kids with no jobs, no health care and no other outlet would, it seemed, rise up and take what was theirs. Having watched the burning and looting on a hotel TV in Milan, Faith No More's Mike Bordin said, 'It's almost good to see, in a way, because you see that maybe through something like that, something could change.'[17] Meanwhile, at the level of national politics, others saw fresh opportunities in the wake of the riots. The question of what caused LA to go up — the erosion of family values or the decline of social services — would be a key point of debate in the 1992 presidential election. And it was in this context that Body Count's 'Cop Killer' became a political football. 'That's some shit,' said Ice-T in August. 'Maybe we should be running for office. I'm not even in the race, and they're tripping off what I say.'[18]

Mega Distribution

Kurt Cobain believed that Geffen's corporate clout could help bring punk to the people. 'That's pretty much my excuse for not feeling guilty about why I'm on a major label,' he told the *NME*.[1] Jennifer Finch, of the LA-based punk group L7, agreed. The band had recently moved from Sub Pop to Slash, an indie shopfront owned by a Polygram subsidiary. 'We wanted mega distribution,' Finch explained in a 1992 TV interview, 'so everybody in really small towns could get our record as well as in big cities.'[2] For Finch, as for many in America's indie underground, there was no contradiction in being a punk band on a major label. Indie had never really been anti-consumerist, but had rather promoted what Simon Frith refers to as a 'people's version of consumerism', founded on the idea that record buyers had a right to real choice outside of market manipulation.[3] 'People are tired of listening to the stuff they usually have to listen to on the radio,' Finch told triple j's Michael Tunn. 'They wanna hear new, different stuff — a variety, as it were.'[4] If music by great bands was now widely available in stores and on the radio, this could only be good news for artists and consumers alike. 'It's great,' said Finch. 'It's about time we can walk into a 7–11 and hear something cool.'[5]

But the transition from the underground to the surface still had to be made with care. However pure L7's intentions might have been, the band knew how it looked, so they made sure that their audience knew that they knew this too. Like Nirvana, the members of L7 became masters of the delicate art of ironically pretending to sell out in order to defuse the accusation that they might have sold out. They played the New Music Seminar — a series of music industry showcases that were held in New

York each year — but reserved the right to call it names afterwards on MTV's *Headbanger's Ball*: 'New Music Slime-inar!' 'New Music Semen-hour!' 'New Music Schmoozin' 'er!' Jennifer Finch and Suzi Gardner gleefully riffed on the corporate rock showcase's handle while host Riki Rachtman tried to get the interview back on topic. 'What was that like?' he asked. ''Cause you guys started in the "underground scene", so ...' 'Yes,' Finch interrupted, all too aware of what was coming next. 'We manipulated the underground scene and took everything we could for what it was worth, and moved on.'[6]

This was a joke, but also true in a sense. L7 had abandoned the underground in order to sell more records — not to make more money, but to spread the message those records contained. Meeting the band in March 1992, Steven Wells found a group with 'a good deal more political integrity than one might initially expect', with a set of beliefs formed during the conservative Reagan years, and given an extra kick by the fuss made over 'family values' in the wake of the LA riots.[7] The band made no secret of these beliefs. 'Get George Bush out of office,' said lead singer Donita Sparks in another MTV interview, 'and more bush in office!'[8] In the back-to-the-fifties doctrines espoused by Bush and Quayle, L7 heard a declaration of war on those who didn't fit the republican vision of family — in particular single mothers. They also felt that such rhetoric would only encourage the actions of extreme right-wing groups such as pro-lifers Operation Rescue: 'Human rights violators,' according to Sparks, 'who block off clinics so women can't get in to have abortions.'[9] The band had, in late 1991, organised and played at the first Rock for Choice benefit. Their new album, *Bricks are Heavy*, contained a number of odes to those the band felt were fucking up the world, including 'Wargasm', a furious swipe at Bush's bread-and-circuses politics, and 'Shitlist'. 'When I get mad and I get pissed,' warned Sparks, 'I grab a pen and I write a list / of all the people who won't be missed / you've made my shit-list!'[10]

The album was preceded by a single, 'Pretend We're Dead', a rock anthem pulled off with all the cool-as-shit insouciance of Joan Jett, who the band loved. The song, Sparks explained, was about 'people not caring, not paying attention to what's going on, politically, socially'.[11] It railed against middle-class conformity and the politics of average America ('they're neither moral nor majority'), but saved its real fury for a teenage nation that would rather say 'never mind' than get involved. The song insisted that it was possible for the band and its fans to 'turn the tables with our unity', but warned that nothing would happen if they maintained their stance of sullen detachment. 'They can't hear a word we've said,' sang Sparks, 'when we pretend that we're dead.'[12] The song's central image of a zombie-fied nation revived an old horror movie cliché to give shape to a real fear — that a generation that couldn't learn to think or act for itself might already be dead. L7's anthem insisted that to unthinkingly accept the messages of politicians and the media they abuse was to 'say "no" to individuality'.[13]

'Think for yourself,' was, as music journalist Michael Azerrad has argued, a central tenet of punk philosophy in the eighties, and perhaps the only slogan that bands as diverse as Black Flag, Minor Threat, Fugazi, Sonic Youth and Big Black might all comfortably rally around.[14] The exciting thing about 1992 was the way that this message seemed to be spreading: the idea that the popular music of the nineties might be using mass-media channels to encourage free thought rather than to suppress it. The new bands were attracting bigger and bigger audiences. But their suspicious attitude toward authority figures — rock stars and politicians alike — compelled them to encourage these audiences to determine their own thoughts. 'To just go out and follow someone in some stupid band thinking he's the spokesperson for a generation,' said Krist Novoselic, 'hey, you should try harder man.'[15] 'My politics are: be yourself,' said Sindi Valsamis of the Lunachiks in 1991, 'and hope everybody else wakes the fuck up.'[16] Talking to Riki Rachtman on *Headbanger's Ball*, Jennifer Finch seemed confident that conformity was on its way out in the nineties. 'Do you think there's bands that are gonna try to copy L7?' asked the TV host. 'No,' replied Finch, 'because I think the trend right now is to be unique and individual.'[17]

Those in the media who were being paid to spot trends had already been following this one for some months. Mega distribution had made alternative music mega popular, and the individual, non-conforming fashion of its non-rock stars was becoming fashionable — the cut-off fatigue shorts and flannel shirt that Eddie Vedder had been escorted out of Harrods for wearing in 1991 were already on department store mannequins by the summer of 1992. 'Out of the mosh pit, onto the catwalk,' wrote the UK style magazine *i-D*, 'designers in New York have gone grunge crazy.' The story went on to describe how the fashion capital's designers had 'bowed to the US's fastest-growing subculture and embraced the buzzsaw guitars of Sonic Youth, Unsane, Helmet and the Lunachicks'.[18] Diesel's campaign slogan for the new season was 'The Alternative Energy', and Henry Rollins appeared in a series of ads for Gap clothing, which, the copy insisted, was 'for individuals'.[19]

It was now popular, it seemed, to be different. But the contradiction inherent in this was immediately apparent, and Rachtman, in his interview with L7, spotted the problem right away. Finch had claimed that it was fashionable to be an individual. 'But if everyone's trying to be unique and individual …' said Rachtman. 'Well,' Finch interrupted, 'then they're copying that trend!' Here, the interviewer and his guest pulled back slightly, as if from an abyss. The problem was an impossible one — how could youth reject middle-class conformity without the rejection itself becoming a kind of conformism? How could the constituents of the alternative nation turn the tables with their unity without saying no to their individuality? 'Aaaaah,' said Rachtman with a smile, aware that things had become too serious, 'I don't wanna analyse this stuff!'[20]

A Small Victory

As the studio audience quieted down, comedian Roseanne Arnold — hosting *Saturday Night Live* in February 1992 — threw to the band: 'It's the Red Hot Chili Peppers!' A cheer went up, but as soon as the group appeared on screen, it was clear that something was wrong. Anthony Kiedis, Flea and Chad Smith were shirtless and in shorts, Kiedis's muscular arms adorned with silver bands. Rock stars for the nineties — they looked tough but humble, sexy without being glamorous. John Frusciante, however, wore an unfashionable cardigan over layers of dirt-coloured clothes and hung his stubbly head low. The guitarist looked like he was in a completely different band and, as the Chili Peppers' performance of 'Under the Bridge' got underway, he played like it too. Frusciante wrong-footed Kiedis from the start, throwing tricky rhythmic shifts and complex chords into the song's intro. The band tried gamely to get things back on track, Smith grinning hopefully from behind his drum kit. But Frusciante's playing became more and more obtuse by the second. He drowned the chorus in an ocean of noise, and sabotaged the tune's emotional pay-off — the falsetto cry of 'under the bridge', which he normally sang — by howling incomprehensibly into the microphone. Kiedis felt as though he'd been stabbed in the back.[1]

It was around this time, just before the Red Hot Chili Peppers' 1992 world tour got underway, that John Frusciante came to a realisation that would change his life. 'If I was going to follow the path I wanted to follow,' he later explained, 'I couldn't do the things that were being demanded of me as a Red Hot Chili Pepper.'[2] His path had been mapped out for him by the complex guitar improvisations of Frank

Zappa — whose music he'd studied at length — and by the bizarre non-career moves of the French conceptual artist Marcel Duchamp — whose work he'd been devouring on the tour bus. Frusciante had learned from his heroes that great artists must reinvent their art from moment to moment. What was being expected of him on *Saturday Night Live* was the exact opposite of this. The massive success of *Blood Sugar Sex Magik* had turned the Red Hot Chili Peppers into entertainers, which now made his job to reproduce note-perfect versions of the things he'd played on the record, and to do this every night in every city of the world for the next three months for huge audiences who had paid good money to hear him do so. For Frusciante, being an artist meant being able to do whatever you liked. Being a rock star, it seemed, meant doing as you were told. The guitarist quit the band just moments before a concert in Japan in May 1992. He secluded himself in his house in LA's Hollywood Hills, with 'no obligation to do anything for anybody', and spent his time recording avant-garde music on a four-track tape recorder, and taking heroin.[3]

For alternative rock bands entering the mainstream in the early nineties, mega distribution had one very unfortunate side effect: mega repetition. The new music was being played on the radio and being sold in shopping malls across the world. This gave alternative bands many more places to play, and allowed them to play much bigger venues. But the vast majority of the people who came to these shows were interested in songs, rather than bands. They'd heard the group's hit on the radio, or seen the video on MTV, and when they went to the concert, they wanted to hear that song again, just the way they were used to hearing it. Record companies, tour promoters and TV show producers — mindful of this, and not wanting to cause confusion or alienate their audiences — also expected the group to play the single it was promoting, and to do it faithfully. For many of the musicians involved, this was a considerable shock. This wasn't the non-service industry anymore. It wasn't even the-we'll-serve-you-when-we-feel-like-it industry of indie rock. This was the actual service industry, where markets had to be serviced, the goods delivered exactly as advertised. 'I was expressing myself spontaneously' was no more acceptable as an excuse from a musician who had turned in a non-standard performance than it would be from a Starbucks barista who had alarmed a customer with a too-hot latte.

But the industry's need for standardisation worked on a number of levels — not just from one performance to another, but also from album to album. Roddy Bottum, Billy Gould, Mike Bordin, Jim Martin and Mike Patton learned this the hard way in 1992. Faith No More had toured America and Europe relentlessly through 1991. As the tour wound up and the band went into the studio, the label looked forward to consolidating this new market with a strong follow-up from the kings of the rap-rock genre. 'I think they were expecting a lot of repetition on this record,' explained Patton in 1992. 'I think they would have been really happy if we'd just made the same record again.'[4] But this was in no sense what the label got. By the time Bordin, Gould, Bottum, Patton and Martin started preparing their new album, they had played the songs from *The Real Thing* almost every night for over a year, and the experience had changed them profoundly. 'It made us not want to be a funk-metal band,' explained Billy Gould.[5]

The band's third album was eclectic to the point of being schizophrenic, veering wildly from death metal to smooth-as-silk soul, from country and western to pop R&B. In fact, the only thing Faith No More didn't do on *Angel Dust* was the one thing its record company was counting on — the winning combination of rap rhymes and guitar heroics that had made 'Epic' a million-seller. 'You seem to have left the funk-metal thing behind,' remarked MTV's Vanessa Warwick, after hearing the new material. 'Well, we all hate it,' replied Patton.[6] It was fair to say that Faith No More's paymasters felt the same way about the band's new direction as the band did about its old one. The label was not at all happy with *Angel Dust*, and furious with the group for sabotaging its own success.

Faith No More understood that the manufacture of scenes, genres and trends was an essential part of the selling of rock music. 'It's an industry,' said Gould, some years later, 'they sell millions of records, they've gotta have some form of standardisation to move big units, they have to be able to categorise and box things.'[7] But the band had no interest in helping this process along, because its members were — as

Bordin put it — 'too fucked-up and individualistic' to work to formulas.[8] 'We're talking about music and we're talking about individuals, and talking about doing something interesting too,' Gould explained. 'And that's where the conflict is.'[9] *Angel Dust* argued for human values over industrial ones — its unrepeatable, unpredictable music was designed to resist any form of categorisation. And its message was directed as much at the group's rapidly growing audience as it was at the business.

Record companies liked to say they were giving the people what they wanted, and used this pseudo-democratic logic to justify every kind of banality. But Gould, having seen a lot of the people over the previous twelve months, was not so sure they knew what they wanted anymore. 'I think the public have been trained to accept what the industry gives them,' he told triple j's Richard Kingsmill. 'They've been rewarded for doing that.'[10] Push the feeder bar, get a pellet — the audiences Faith No More met on tour in 1991 seemed to have no more discernment than lab rats. 'The kind of crowd we draw is … I don't know if gullible is the word,' said Patton, 'but … easy. It's so simple.'[11] The singer's attitude to this audience might have been contemptuous, but it wasn't condescending. Most bands that played stadiums were well aware of how brutally simple the psychology involved was, but proceeded with the operation anyway, in the belief that the audience simply didn't know any better, and never would. Patton's view gave the crowd some credit — he was determined to shake them out of their stupor and thereby give them back their dignity — as well as his own.

The experiments the band had begun in 1990 — where the kids yelled out for Sabbath and got the Commodores — were taken to fresh heights of absurdity on the 1991 tour as Faith No More set out to violate its audience's expectations in every way — they played elevator music for metal-heads and deathcore for pop fans; one night Patton would be drinking his own piss out of a shoe, the next he'd be operating a coffee percolator on stage, making fresh cups for the entire front row while the band played a fifteen-minute vamp. When the audience booed him, Patton gave them flowers; when they cheered, he told them to shut up. When the kids pushed the feeder bar at a Faith No More show, they were given a shoe full of piss or a cup of coffee or a gorilla mask — anything but the thing they were hoping to get.[12]

Faith No More would not give the crowd what it wanted at the show for the same reason the band wouldn't give its record label what it wanted in the studio. The band had been told they had to make another funk-metal album because that's what the audience wanted to hear. But the audience only wanted this because it had been trained, over a lifetime, to expect rock bands to repeat themselves on cue. The notion that the band was serving the needs of its fans by sticking to the formula, playing hits and signing autographs was a myth, designed to conceal the fact that both band and fans were in fact serving the industry. Since the real result of this, from Faith No More's point of view, was boredom for the band and alienation for the audience, the group set out to sabotage the process at the point where it was most volatile and most vulnerable — in the moment when the fans meet the band.

'We love you, you're so awesome!' a fan exclaimed, rushing up to Patton after a concert. 'Don't say that,' begged Patton.[13] This scene was, of course, straight out of *Wayne's World* — a reprise of the moment when Wayne and Garth, having attempted to keep their cool in the presence of Alice Cooper for barely a minute, prostrate themselves on the floor and chant, in unison, 'We're not worthy!' But while this might have been funny in a movie it was, for Faith No More, deeply disturbing in real life. The cold stares they gave their gushy fans came from a real concern for their humanity — they refused to treat the kids like lab rats, or to allow them to behave as such. Only in this way could the band keep making art in a situation where it was expected to make money, only in this way could the relationship between Faith No More and its fans be dragged out of *Wayne's World* and into the real one. 'I sometimes find myself being so absolutely stupid to these people,' said Bottum, 'just to get the point across that I am nothing — you are everything.'[14]

Be True to Yourself

The first Lollapalooza tour in 1991 had played to audiences of around 15,000 people. But that was before Nirvana. By the time Lollapalooza 2 hit the road in July 1992, *Nevermind* had sold over four million copies, and the public's interest in alternative music had grown considerably as a result. 'This year,' wrote *Rolling Stone*'s Jon Katz, 'everyone wants to be alternative.' Attendance for Perry Farrell's travelling circus almost tripled, with over 40,000 people turning out to see Soundgarden, Ministry, Pearl Jam and the Red Hot Chili Peppers at San Francisco's Shoreline Amphitheatre. For Farrell, the meaning of this was clear. 'What Lollapalooza 2 has proved,' he said, 'is that there is a serious market for a youth counterculture. That's the bad news.'[1]

Some of the acts featured in the line up felt the same way. 'This whole thing is entertainment for the leisure class,' said Kim Thayil of Soundgarden. 'I'm tired of the lie that alternative music somehow offers something that's anti-corporate.' For Thayil, the irony of seeing 40,000 kids 'affirming their alternativeness' by wearing virtually indistinguishable variants on his own band's jeans-and-flannel style merely confirmed that 'alternative' itself was an exhausted concept.[2] Earlier in the year, as the band toured with Guns N' Roses, Thayil had hoped that Soundgarden's new fans would see them as 'an alternative to what people would like them to listen to'.[3] But now that MTV and commercial radio were learning 'the new science' as Henry Rollins called it, Soundgarden was exactly what the industry wanted the fans to listen to.[4] Alternative rock, Thayil insisted, was now simply rock.

This would have been a problem if alternative music had nothing to offer beyond its alternative-ness. But the new rock was markedly different from the old model, and — in many ways — much improved. For one thing, it was dirtier. 'These guys are studio computer geeks,' concluded *Spin*'s review of Def Leppard's *Adrenalize*. 'There's no recklessness, no danger, no dirt. It's so clean, so homogenised.'[5] The new music, by contrast, was all about dirt. There were no keyboards or layered vocal harmonies — the guitars were distorted, the playing was loose. The bands didn't dress up in shiny pants and tease out their hair; they dressed down in old jeans and dirty boots and left their hair lank and unwashed. Band names gave notice of the new aesthetic — Soundgarden, Skin Yard, Screaming Trees, Pearl Jam, Mudhoney, Blood Circus, Treepeople — the references to nature and the human body signalled a decisive turn away from artifice and showbiz. But the name given to the musical movement as a whole — grunge — said it best of all. The new rock exposed all that the old rock had tried to scrub away or sweep under the carpet. 'Grunge,' wrote music journalist Grant Adler, 'has risen from the shores of a stagnating culture like some great, unkempt beast.'[6]

Grunge wasn't a new style; it was an absence of style. 'There's no glamour in Nirvana,' noted Keith Cameron in the *NME* in 1991, 'no glamour at all, in fact.'[7] Cobain's look was arrived at by default, by not choosing a look — he simply wore the clothes he wore to keep warm in Seattle, and left his hair the way it looked when he woke up in the morning. Layne Staley of Alice in Chains — whose album *Dirt* epitomised the new non-aesthetic — told *Q* magazine's Mark Cooper that his band was 'trying to take a long hard look in the mirror instead of putting on make-up and lights and candy-filling things up'.[8] Staley's assertion demonstrated the way in which grunge's aesthetic revolution implied a moral one — no make-up was better than make-up for the same reason that the truth was better than a lie — the same reason why Anthony Kiedis liked Sinéad O'Connor from the moment he laid eyes on her. 'I knew,' he later wrote, 'that someone who would shave her head was tough and real and couldn't give a fuck.'[9] Jerry Seinfeld had been right — in 1992 everyone was tired of bullshitters, and the title of Nirvana's second single from *Nevermind* summed up the new mood precisely — come as you are.

Without all the make-up and digital sheen, it was now possible to see that rock stars were, in the end, not so different from their fans. This, it was felt, was also a great improvement, as was the fact that the new non-rock stars seemed to accept, and even embrace it. 'Why go through all the traumas and tribulations to be in a band and be successful if success just means you're separated from your audience?' asked Billy Corgan, lead singer with the Smashing Pumpkins. 'It should be the other way around.'[10] Asked what he was looking forward to about Lollapalooza 1992, Eddie Vedder said, 'Just hanging out and talking to the crowd.'[11] The singer took a Polaroid camera with him into the mosh, and took pictures of his heroes: the fans, who warmly embraced him as one of their own. This was the good news about Lollapalooza. The crowd might have been there to affirm their alternativeness, but that affirmation stood for something important — the long hair and flannel shirts spoke of music's new consumer democracy, where the fans looked the same as the bands because — in every important sense — they were. 'Who were the stars of Lollapalooza '92?' asked photographer Maxwell Hudson in *Spin*. 'Ministry? Pearl Jam? Fact is, the answer is you.' Hudson praised 'the sense of community, the sense of belonging, the knowledge that you matter, your heroes on stage fully aware that your voice — and wallet — speak volumes.'[12] The rock star had been killed, and no-one in rock's new republic would miss him.

Even some of those who'd been superseded by the revolution had to admit it was probably for the best. 'God bless it, it was due,' said Jon Bon Jovi. The quintessential late-eighties rock star could see that the new music was, in many important ways, more honest than the old. But where some of his contemporaries were busy trying to learn the new science — washing the stuff out of their hair, buying flannel shirts and moving to Seattle — Bon Jovi accepted that he could only honour the new reality principle by resisting the temptation to emulate it. 'Be true to yourself,' he told himself. 'Do not grow a goatee.'[13]

1993

A White Man's Mentality

On stage in Orlando, early in 1993, Stone Temple Pilots launched into a performance of a song called 'Sex Type Thing'. As the tune's signature riff rang out into the Florida night, music writer Jonathan Gold observed a primitive grunge ritual taking place on the edge of the mosh pit. 'Two sweaty jock dudes,' he wrote, 'lunge at each other again and again, high fives extended, bellowing like male mooses in rut.'[1] These guys — and others like them — had made 'Sex Type Thing' a huge hit at the end of 1992. It was dark and heavy and serious, like much of the new music, but it was also a great hard rock song about wanting to get with a chick real bad — a 'Whole Lotta Love' for the nineties. As singer Scott Weiland barked, 'I know you want what's on my mind / I know you like what's on my mind / I know it eats you up inside / here I come', the jock dudes — in their low-slung jeans and goatee beards — closed their eyes, pumped their fists, and thought about getting laid.[2]

Sadly though, these guys were missing the point. If they'd seen Dave Mustaine from Megadeth talking about 'Sex Type Thing' on MTV's *Headbanger's Ball*, they would have learned that this was a song about the objectification of women by the music industry and the world at large. Weiland, talking to *Spin*'s Katherine Turman a few months later, confirmed this. 'I don't think of myself as a political writer,' he sighed. 'But there are some things that are important — everyone's individual rights are as important as everyone else's.' 'Sex Type Thing', Weiland explained, was about the way rock's male-dominated culture conspired to deny women these rights. 'The white man's mentality,' he said, 'that women are just objects of sex, not respected as individuals.'[3]

That male hard-rock singers should feel the need to speak about a woman's point of view at all in 1992 was mostly due to the influence of Kurt Cobain — whose sympathy for women was as boundless as his contempt for sexists and misogynists. By mixing a feminist sensibility with heavy, Zeppelin-esque rock — a type of music that had been largely untouched by such stuff up to this point — Cobain became the first major male, white rock singer to offer a serious critique of his own maleness and whiteness. The shock of this alone had turned heavy music on its head, and made party-metal bands look instantly out of date and out of touch. In 1993, Thurston Moore met Gene Simmons of Kiss backstage at the Santa Monica Civic Center. According to Moore's tour diary, 'Gene kept wanting to know where all the groupies were, and how he could have been standing there for twenty minutes and not gotten laid yet. I tried to tell him about the nineties, but I don't think he grasped the concept.'[4] The new humility had brought with it a new sensitivity, and it was no longer possible, in 1993, to play power chords without understanding and criticising the power relations they served to perpetuate. Scott Weiland — by his own admission — was no 'poster boy for the feminist movement'.[5] But as an alternative rock singer in the early nineties, he felt compelled, at the very least, to acknowledge its existence — even if his audience did not.

'You're all white, all good looking, and it looks like you've got lots of money,' Weiland told the audience at a show in Orange County, California. A huge affirmative cheer went up from the guys in the crowd. 'No, no,' the singer protested, 'I'm not sure that's a good thing.'[6] For most of the previous two centuries, being a rich white man had been a very good thing — at least if you were rich, white and a man. But by 1992, it seemed, the jig was up. 'Now everyone is sick of white men,' wrote *Rolling Stone*'s Jon Katz in August of that year, 'the white men who practised slavery and fought to preserve it, the white men who beat up gays and raided their bars, the white men with briefcases who launch and carry out every war, the white men on campus who cling to self-serving curricula, the white men in corporations who ravage the environment.'[7] Katz failed to mention the white police officers who beat Rodney King, or the white jurors who acquitted them — but his point was made. The white man's legacy was disgraceful. A badge handed out to visitors at an exhibition of emerging artists held in New York read, 'I can't ever imagine wanting to be white', and many white men already preferred to imagine they were not.[8] Cobain confessed to his diary that he felt guilty about being a 'white middle-class male' and deferred instead to 'the superiority of women and the negro'.[9] Had the singer attended Lollapalooza '92, he could have assuaged his guilt — if not actually changed his sex and skin colour — by buying a T-shirt from the Refuse and Resist booth bearing the slogan: 'I used to be a white American, but I gave it up in the interest of humanity.'[10]

It was time to call this pale beast — ravaging the planet, objectifying women, waging war and oppressing minorities — by his real name. 'Asshole,' said Denis Leary, in a stand-up routine that became a hit single early in 1993. Leary painted an unforgiving picture of the 'average white suburbanite slob', reading 'porno and books about war', driving his gas-guzzling car, 'sucking down quarter-pounder cheeseburgers in the old-fashioned non-biodegradable styrofoam containers'. 'And,' he reminded the rest of the world, 'there ain't a goddamn thing anyone can do about it. You know why? Because we got the bomb.'[11]

But the asshole in the song, and assholes like him, had made a lot of enemies. If all the enemies banded together there might yet be an end to the rule of white men — and this was Jon Katz's hope in 1992. 'Almost every other sexual and racial group,' he declared, 'is fighting them with every means at hand.'[12] These means included the very same ones that the white man had used as tools of oppression for so long. Words like 'nigger', 'dyke' and 'queer' were reclaimed by those they had been used against, as was the word 'slut', which Kathleen Hanna, singer with the band Bikini Kill, painted on her stomach with lipstick. Hanna, too, was certain that the long reign of white men must soon come to an end, for the good of the planet. 'We're Bikini Kill,' she'd announced on the band's first EP, 'and we want revolution, girl style, now!'[13] But rock and roll being a teenage sport, her war was one of girls against boys rather than women versus men. 'White boy,' she sang in 1993, 'don't laugh, don't cry, just die!'[14] Hanna's defiant yelp leapt out from behind a powerful, primitive racket that made most boy-punk bands of the early nineties sound about as punk as Toto. Men said Bikini Kill couldn't play, of course. But the band's music wasn't made to please male critics or musicians — it was meant to terrify them. Bikini Kill was the sound of white boy rock and roll being killed in its sleep with the weapon it had used to oppress music's minorities for almost three decades; rock's equivalent to the business suit or the nuclear bomb — the electric guitar.

Your Whole Fucking Culture

'One of the bitterest disappointments of my life has been the failure of women to contribute anything interesting to rock and roll,' said feminist and social critic Camille Paglia in September 1991. 'In the past twenty years, nothing is stopping a woman from picking up a guitar.'[1] Songwriter Juliana Hatfield wondered whether the problem wasn't genetic, and suggested that girls might simply lack the chromosome that produces great lead guitar playing.[2] But Kathleen Hanna was convinced that the non-appearance of the female Jimi Hendrix had nothing to do with biology or laziness, and everything to do with male power. The singer started attending punk shows when she was in high school in Portland, Oregon, and learned quickly that a woman's place at such events was not on the stage with a guitar, or even in the mosh, but slightly to the side, holding her boyfriend's jacket. Hanna's college education had taught her to look for power relations in everyday events, and in the world of indie rock she found plenty — an interlocking system of behavioural codes and bogus common sense that conspired to keep girls off the stage. Contrary to Paglia's assertion, Hanna realised that just about everything was stopping women from picking up guitars, a realisation which made her even more determined to do so. Hanna formed Bikini Kill with Tobi Vail and Kathi Wilcox in October 1990, and the band played its first show with Bratmobile — another all-girl punk band — on Valentine's Day 1991.

Within the world of punk, Hanna saw male power being perpetuated in three ways. First was the old 'Yoko Ono' argument

— that women were a danger to men's art and therefore shouldn't get involved in bands.[3] Second was the macho culture of the pit — where the aggressive behaviour of muscular, shirtless 'Rollins Boys' made dancing dangerous for girls, and the widely practised (but never discussed) habit of groping in the mosh made it downright scary. Third was the fuss made over guitar technique, which guys in bands used in order to shut down girls' attempts to rock before they'd even started playing, a practice Hanna viewed as not only unfair, but profoundly un-punk. Hanna saw punk as democratic and anti-elitist. The important thing was the idea that anyone could play — if the rules said you couldn't, the rules would have to go. 'You don't make all the rules!' sang Hanna in 'This is Not a Test', 'I know what I'm gonna fuckin' do, me and my girlfriends gonna push on through!'[4]

With Bikini Kill, Hanna, Vail and Wilcox did away with the pillars of punk's sexist hegemony in three swift strokes. They formed a band with no men in it, so that no man would have to worry about one of the girls 'breaking up the band'. They instituted new rules for dancing, which said that only girls were allowed up the front. And they trashed the elitist dogma of technique by playing badly. 'The fact that we weren't taking guitar lessons and getting really good before we let anybody see us was really perceived as the hugest "fuck you",' said Hanna.[5] 'Men,' said Vail, 'could barely deal with it.'[6] Girls, on the other hand, loved it. By the middle of 1991, Bikini Kill was getting mail from fans all over the country, praising the band for making the scene safe and fun for girls, and for inspiring them to pick up guitars and make a noise of their own. By August, there were more bands springing up. The IPU convention in Washington DC opened with Girl Night, featuring performances from Mecca Normal, the Spinanes, Bratmobile, 7 Year Bitch and the members of Bikini Kill. Vail would later describe the night as 'a punk rock dream come true'.[7] For Tracy Sawyer of Heavens to Betsy — which played one of its very first shows at Girl Night — it was 'the most incredible thing in the world'.[8]

Over the next twelve months, the thing got more and more incredible. By December 1991, it was a movement, with a name — riot grrrl — and a manifesto, published in Hanna and Vail's Bikini Kill zine. Here, riot grrrl declared the rules of rock and roll null and void as far as women were concerned: 'We don't wanna conform to your [boy] standards of what is and what isn't.' The document called on riot grrrls to 'create revolution in our own lives every single day by envisioning and creating alternatives to the bullshit Christian capitalist way of doing things', and to 'take over the means of production in order to create our own moanings'.[9] Riot grrrl had, by the summer of 1992, built an underground media empire out of paper and cassette tape — a cross-country network linked by hundreds of self-published zines, homemade recordings, and girls with guitars and typewriters. Chapters in Washington, Portland, Seattle, Austin and a dozen other cities held weekly meetings in kitchens, bedrooms, diners and apartment-house laundries.

Riot grrrl bands and zinesters had, by this point, done a far better job of realising Kurt Cobain's teenage revolution than Cobain had himself. Cobain had dreamed of fighting male, white, corporate oppression with a revolutionary teen army, communicating by way of Xeroxed flyers and bonded by secret handshakes. But Nirvana, in 1992, was not a revolt; it was a multi-platinum rock band. Emily White of the *Chicago Reader* had dinner with Hanna, Vail and Fugazi's Ian MacKaye in April, and watched Hanna almost choke on her vegetable mash when she saw Cobain's face under the *Rolling Stone* logo. 'Can you believe this?' asked MacKaye, leafing through the magazine. 'This is just so weird.'[10] Hanna had perhaps already seen the phrase she'd given her friend — 'Smells Like Teen Spirit' — splashed across the front of the magazine in February, alongside a photo of the stars of *Beverly Hills 90210*. Even though Cobain had initially refused to speak to the magazine after this, he had, by March, relented, and Nirvana appeared as the lead story in *Rolling Stone* the following month. The cover — which showed Cobain wearing a blank expression and a hand-made T-shirt that read 'CORPORATE MAGAZINES STILL SUCK' — was funny. But it was funny in an ironic way, and irony — as MacKaye pointed out in a new Fugazi song — 'is the refuge of the educated'.[11] The selling of Nirvana only confirmed Hanna's belief that mass media could not be trusted to deliver riot grrrl's message intact. Controlling the means of production allowed you to make your own moanings — handing them over to Geffen, MTV and *Rolling Stone* allowed corporate America to take your moanings and make whatever it wanted with them — usually money.

Conversations like the one taking place over the dinner table at MacKaye's house that evening had taken on a new sense of urgency by the end of 1992. Many musicians and label owners in America's indie underground had become aware that Seattle was running out of bands, and that A&R reps were already looking for fresh scenes elsewhere in the country. In Chapel Hill, Chicago, Austin, Portland and Boston, a new thought began to form: 'We're next' — a thought that could inspire anything from dread to elation depending on one's politics. Already the media were becoming interested in riot grrrl, which, from a magazine editor's point of view, had it all — a regional setting, disaffected youth, generational angst and a dash of sex appeal. Stories of varying degrees of quality and accuracy appeared in the *New York Times*, *Newsweek* and the *Washington Post*. But by the time *USA Today* got in touch in September, Hanna had called on riot grrrls to hold a 'press block'. Desperate journalists and editors had to cobble together stories based on second-hand reports, spiced up with accounts of 'the way in which various scenesters hung up on them'.[12]

This last description came from *Spin*, which also found itself on the wrong end of the press block having already run a story on Bikini Kill that made Hanna 'feel exploited'.[13] Riot grrrl had decided from the beginning that it would make its own news, and nothing in its members' recent experiences had given them any reason to change their minds. *Spin* could offer the usual platitudes about 'getting your message to a wider audience'. But the message was getting out in any case. Ada Calhoun, seventeen at the time, was working as an intern at the magazine in 1993, and found a pile of comics and zines under the sink in the apartment she was staying in. 'The one that instantly changed my life,' she later recalled 'was Bikini Kill Fanzine #2. I went straight to the copy store and made copies for me and all my friends. We studied it like it was a textbook. I sent a fan letter to the address on the back. I started doing my own zines.' *Spin*'s article would do nothing more than turn riot grrrl into a lifestyle accessory, actions like Calhoun's had already turned it into a way of life. 'I carried the BK zine around with me in my backpack like it was an amulet that would protect me from the indignities of high school,' she said, 'which in a very real way it did.'[14]

Stories like this showed why riot grrrls needed no encouragement from Hanna or Vail to maintain the movement's blackout in the winter of 1992. Media outlets assumed that riot grrrls would talk to them, since they — like the Seattle bands — would appreciate the 'exposure'. But exposure was the one thing they didn't want — many riot grrrls described the experience of seeing stories about the movement in the media as being akin to having someone sneak into your room and read your diary. Riot grrrl was that increasingly rare thing in the early nineties — a real youth culture — a 'girl culture', as the manifesto insisted, built on stories, songs, art and shared ideals. It existed in defiance of corporate control, and not as its research and development division, and this alone was reason enough to protect it. 'It's just something that's really important to me,' one riot grrrl told the *New York Times* shortly before hanging up the phone, 'and I'm afraid of it being exploited.'[15]

Dirty

'This is a dirty country,' announced Kim Gordon in July 1992. 'It's full of music and pornography.'[1] Sonic Youth had just released its second album for Geffen, *Dirty*, in which America's filth was exposed for all to see. The band had no doubt as to who was to blame for the mess. 'I've been around the world a million times, and all you men are slime,' sang Thurston Moore on the single '100%'.[2] In 'The Swimsuit Issue', Kim Gordon took the role of an office worker whose life was being made miserable by her sleazy boss. 'Don't touch my breast,' she snarled, 'I'm just workin' at a desk.'[3] Gordon's character could have been based on any one of the 9920 women who filed workplace harassment complaints in the United States in 1992 — a statistic that had doubled since the previous year — most likely as a result of the media coverage of Anita Hill's complaint against Supreme Court Justice Clarence Thomas in October 1991. Sonic Youth made its position on the matter clear in 'Youth Against Fascism'. 'I believe Anita Hill,' sang Moore in a punkish sneer, going on to describe protesting kids 'Bangin' pots and pans / We're gonna bury you man!' — an account of a real event later in the year, when riot grrrls marched on Washington in a show of support for Hill, making an unholy racket with thrift-store percussion and a capella punk rock.[4]

Dirty's sleeve art was designed by the visual artist Mike Kelley — an appropriate choice considering that Kelley's work was seen as definitive of a new messy aesthetic (sometimes referred to as 'clusterfuck') that had revolutionised the art scene in much the same way that grunge had changed the face of youth culture. The album cover showed a close-up photo of a hand-made children's doll — one of hundreds Kelley had been collecting over the last few years. The toys had already appeared often in Kelley's art, sometimes stitched together into giant mutant animals, at other times exhibited with photographs of human genitals pinned to their stomachs. 'I became very interested in toys as sculpture,' Kelley later recalled. 'But it's almost impossible to present them that way, because everybody experiences them symbolically.' Kelley quickly discovered the truth of Marcel Duchamp's old maxim — that 'it is the viewers who make the painting' — as visitors to his exhibitions began telling him what the toy sculptures were about. 'People went on about how the work was about child abuse. What was my problem? Why was I playing with these toys? Had I been abused? Was I a paedophile?' Confused by this at first, Kelley soon came to realise that his work had unintentionally hit a nerve, just below the skin of America. 'I did a bit of research,' he said, 'and I discovered how culturally omnipresent the infatuation with child abuse was.'[5] By 1993, even the most casual observer of America's media-scape would most likely have agreed with Kelley's conclusion. This, after all, was the year when the daydreams of the eighties morphed into the nightmares of the nineties, after a man named Evan Chandler accused Michael Jackson of sexually abusing his thirteen-year-old son while the latter stayed with Jackson at his Neverland ranch.

In October 1991, Roseanne Arnold stood before an audience of over a thousand people in Denver, Colorado. 'My name is Roseanne,' she said, 'and I am an incest survivor.' Arnold went on to describe the ordeal she had been subjected to as a child, and the recent resolution she had made to conquer her fears, confront her parents, and move on with her life. As she spoke, she was — according to *People* magazine — 'interrupted more than twenty times by applause'. Arnold later told the magazine that she had been inspired to speak up about her experience by the story of former Miss America Marilyn Van Derbur Atler, who had revealed her own history of abuse in *People* some months earlier. Before that, Arnold said, 'I was still in a huge place of denial.'[6] Arnold's turn of phrase was a relatively new one. Constructions like 'in a hurting place' and 'in a healing place' had entered the lexicon via the wave of confessional TV talk shows that had sprung up in the late eighties, in particular Oprah Winfrey's, which pioneered what *Time* magazine's

Richard Zoglin described in 1989 as 'the talk show as group therapy session'.[7] Winfrey, in a landmark episode of her show that aired in 1986, had told her audience how she herself had been raped at the age of nine by an older cousin, and the spectacle of guests confronting their parents over the abuse they had suffered as children soon became a common sight on *Oprah* and similar programs like *Ricki Lake* and *Donahue*. By 1992, on any given day of the week, one could turn on the TV and see ordinary Americans stand in front of a studio audience with a microphone and share painful memories from their early years. As they spoke, members of the crowd would whoop and cheer and, emboldened by the guest's confession, slowly come forward with their own stories.

Meanwhile, in the makeshift meeting places of the punk underground, similar scenes were taking place. The sight of riot grrrls sharing tales of childhood abuse at meetings or onstage at shows was a common one, and the movement's literature teemed with stories of harassment, rape and incest. 'At its concerts, Bikini Kill urges audience members to show how they have been sexually exploited,' wrote one observer, 'hundreds of riot grrrls have thus brought a historically shameful secret — incest — out of the closet.'[8] Kathleen Hanna spoke about her own abuse as a child and sang about it in the Bikini Kill song 'Suck My Left One', a revenge fantasy in which a victim of incest turns the tables on her father. The singer led by example with her frank confessionals, enshrining at the movement's heart the idea that speaking about trauma would rob it of its power, and allow grrrls to move from a place of denial to a place of strength.

In her piece on riot grrrl for the *Chicago Reader*, Emily White noted that all of this was 'very much of our time. Incest in particular has become a national obsession, our highest-rated horror the gothic violation of the inner child.'[9] The notion of an ideal girl-state that is shattered on contact with the world of men was, according to White, key to riot grrrl culture; the importance the movement's writers and theoreticians placed on the word 'girl' indicated to her that 'their utopia lies in the past'. Riot grrrl style, with its thrift-store baby-doll dresses and kiddie accessories, served as a form of symbolic resistance — reviving the 'wild, unafraid girl' who disappeared on contact with patriarchal society, and enlisting her in the fight against oppression.

Zine writer Carla Costa told author Kaya Oakes about walking into a record shop with a friend in 1993, and having the shop assistant greet them by saying 'Hey, riot grrrls'. They looked the part, with their bleached blonde hair, barrettes and thrift-store dresses, but Costa didn't really know what a riot grrrl was — she'd acquired her style from two other bands: Oregon trio Babes in Toyland and LA-based punk quartet Hole.[10] While neither of these groups was officially connected with the movement, they had enough in common with riot grrrl bands for fans of one to be able to embrace the other. But this lead to a certain amount of confusion in the media as to who was a riot grrrl and who was not, and the fact that these two bands had arrived at a similar dress code to riot grrrl by a different route only added to the confusion. Hole singer Courtney Love adopted what the *Washington Post* described as 'a kind of kindergarten-whore approach in her dress' — baby-doll dresses worn with barrettes, ripped stockings and smeared lipstick. Both Love and Babes in Toyland's Kat Bjelland claimed to have invented the look, both were correct — the 'kinderwhore' style evolved out of a mixture of punk provocation and thrift-store chic adopted by Babes in Toyland at a time when Love actually played in the line-up in the late eighties. '3–4 baby barrettes, Great Lash mascara,' wrote Love in a kinderwhore shopping list. 'Xtra vintage white slip, Bobbi Brown taupe eyeshadow.'[11] The look spoke of damaged innocence and difficult childhoods — a major preoccupation of both groups. 'She screams sweet hell in her old white nightie,' sang Bjelland, 'with rips and tears she's too aware.'[12] In an interview with *Melody Maker*'s Everett True, Bjelland shared a frightening story about the time she found a scratch on her mother's Kenny Rogers album, and received a beating for a crime she didn't commit. After hearing this, and Babes in Toyland's debut album late in 1990, True concluded that 'only a complete dork could mistake their music for anything but the sound of a fucked-up childhood'.[13]

Likewise, only an insensitive dork would criticise their lack of technique. 'Kat pretty much doesn't bother singing,' noted True, 'preferring to scream out her anguish instead.'[14] For Bjelland, 'good' vocal technique, as defined by male rock critics, did not allow for the full expression of female rage. The idea that women should sing beautifully was, like the expectation that they should apply make-up with care — a form of oppression, the notorious 'male gaze' translated into musical terms. The word 'singing' itself was, Bjelland felt, inadequate to describe what she did, and carried with it unwanted expectations of good female behaviour, which was why she preferred the term 'spirit yelling' — a phrase that suggested that Babes in Toyland saw its music as closer to primal scream therapy than rock and roll. This was not too far from the truth. As with riot grrrl, Babes in Toyland sought forms of expression that were specifically female, which meant harking back to the last time that girls were girls — the pre-teen, prelapsarian world of childhood. Babes guitarist Lori Barbero explained that the group's name was meant to suggest 'three retarded musicians beating hell out of their instruments, treating them like little toys'.[15]

The title of Hole's debut album, *Pretty on the Inside*, spoke volumes about how rock's new authenticity applied to women. The look of grunge marked an important shift in rock style away from the aspirational looks of the eighties to a new unplugged, unpackaged realism. So too, for women, the goal now was to reveal rather than to construct; if images of Madonna, Grace Jones and Cyndi Lauper had told girls that they could be whatever they liked, the sight of Courtney Love with her make-up half wiped off and her dress torn to shreds offered a new possibility — that girls could finally be themselves.

This was a long way from the vision of girlhood promoted by the Republican Party and the Christian Coalition at the time — a fact Love acknowledged by painting the words 'Family Values' on her stomach in a *Vanity Fair* photo shoot. But it was inevitable that male, white, corporate oppression should be terrified by the sight of the women whose innocence it had stolen fifteen years earlier finally wiping off their lipstick, ripping up their party-dresses and screaming their hearts out. In her 1990 book, *The Beauty Myth*, Naomi Wolf argued that the standards of beauty set by *Vogue*, *Cosmopolitan*, *Playboy* and MTV had nothing to do, in the end, with female beauty, and everything to do with male fear. 'The beauty myth,' she wrote, 'is summoned out of political fear on the part of male-dominated institutions threatened by women's freedom.'[16] Kurt Cobain, who married Courtney Love in February 1992, and appeared with her in the *Vanity Fair* photos holding the couple's newborn baby, Frances Bean Cobain, appeared to be paraphrasing Wolf, as he praised his wife for 'choos[ing] not to function the way the white corporate man insists. His rules for women involve her being submissive, quiet, and non-challenging. When she doesn't follow his rules, the threatened man … gets scared.'[17] Love, for her part, had no desire to join a moral majority that — as L7 had already pointed out — in reality was neither. 'I prefer being part of a minority,' she told *Newsweek*. 'It makes me feel special.'[18]

None of Our Business

By 1992, many alternative rock bands had attracted the 'wider audience' their adherents had always insisted they deserved. But by the following year, most of these bands were hoping this new audience would go away. The problem was one of definition. Alternative rock had, for almost a decade, defined itself by its oppositional stance toward mainstream values. 'I'm different, I'm special, nobody likes me,' as Kim Thayil put it. 'That worked for us for years.'[1] It had still worked as late as 1990, when Jane's Addiction's freaky rock circus hit the American South — the outright hostility the band provoked from redneck rock fans was, as bassist Eric Avery concluded, a good thing. If they weren't alienating sexists, racists and macho tough guys, they probably weren't doing their job.[2] Alternative music reversed the values of the mainstream. Since it was music for freaks and outcasts, you could be sure that as long as you were making yourself unpopular with popular people, you were doing well.

But the success of Nirvana had upset this system. Dave Grohl noticed new faces at the band's gigs from almost the moment 'Smells Like Teen Spirit' went into MTV rotation: 'That guy looks like a jock,' the drummer thought to himself. 'What's he doing here? Hmmm, maybe this video thing is attracting some ... riff raff!'[3] By 1992, Nirvana shows were full of what Cobain described as 'racists and homophobes',[4] and it was no more possible to tell these guys that 'In Bloom' was a critique of their mentality than it was for Scott Weiland to tell the dudes in Florida that 'Sex Type Thing' was a feminist anthem. Alt rock's educational value appeared to have been overrated — instead of Nirvana making football jocks smarter, football jocks were making Nirvana look stupid. Cobain was determined to get rid of them. In the liner notes to *Incesticide* — a beat-the-bootleggers compilation of early Nirvana material released in December 1992 — the singer told his less enlightened fans, in no uncertain terms, to get lost. 'If any of you in any way hate homosexuals, people of different color, or women, please do this one favor for us — leave us the fuck alone! Don't come to our shows and don't buy our records.'[5]

If it was MTV that had attracted these boobs to the band in the first place, then Nirvana would have to find a way to get itself off MTV. Early in 1992 Cobain had wished out loud that Nirvana had put a clause in its contract to limit the number of times its songs were played on TV and radio, but since this was impossible, he simply resolved that the band's next album would be one that TV and radio would not want to play. Nirvana began planning its follow up to *Nevermind* in late 1992, and Cobain told journalists that it would be 'raw, abrasive and eight-track'. He wanted to 'really test [MTV viewers], shove something totally aggro in their face and see if they could handle it'.[6]

Since Nirvana's new goal was to alienate rather than to appeal, Butch Vig's radio-friendly rock production could be of no further use to the band. Cobain considered working with Jack Endino — who'd recorded Nirvana's debut, *Bleach* — but eventually settled on Steve Albini, the former frontman of post-hardcore pioneers Big Black, whose production credits included two of Cobain's favourite records — the Pixies' *Surfer Rosa*, and the Breeders' *Pod*. The producer had no real love for Nirvana's music, but he did have a certain amount of sympathy for their position; the idea of America's biggest rock band setting out to sabotage, rather than to expand the market for its music appealed to Albini, who had made a career out of alienating audiences. To give Nirvana an idea of the kind of sound they could create together, Albini sent Cobain a tape of a record he'd just made with a British group called PJ Harvey whose singer, Polly Jean Harvey, was the embodiment of Albini's musical ideal in 1993. Harvey's tastes were extreme, her music was totally unique, and she refused to pander to her audience for any reason. She was, Albini believed, 'a genius'.[7]

If Nirvana wanted to frighten people with its new album, it could do a lot worse than to follow the lead of PJ Harvey, whose music was inspired as much by horror movies as it was by the blues. The group had formed early in 1991, and had spent the rest of the year writing songs and playing gigs. But while trying to translate the excitement of their live show onto tape, Polly Harvey, drummer Rob Ellis and bassist Steve Vaughn had found their attempts frustrated by a common enemy — the home stereo volume-knob. 'With a record,' explained Ellis, 'you don't have the final say over the volume at which the music is played. People can turn it down.' The band's solution was to arrange its songs as a filmmaker would direct a murder scene — lulling listeners into a false sense of security, only to make them jump out of their seats when they least expected it. PJ Harvey incorporated long, unsettling, too-quiet passages into its songs where, as Harvey put it, 'you want people to think: "There's something not quite right about this — what is it?"' That way, Ellis explained, the band could 'con people into thinking, "Oh this is a bit quiet, I'll turn this up", and then maybe they'll get a shock when the loud bit comes in'.[8] This approach was a neat fit for Harvey's songwriting, which also dealt in shocks. 'Extremes, to me are really important,' she said, 'either really happy or really sad. Extremes of loud and quiet are good too.'[9] PJ Harvey combined both on its single, 'Sheela-na-gig', where Harvey cut together ancient words from druidic fertility myths with lines from the musical *South Pacific* while her band slid with sickening ease from a tense, muted strum to a full-throttle roar.

But 'Sheela Na-Gig's violation of expectation was still not quite violent enough, according to Ellis. 'You want to be able to go from a whisper to a scream, like that,' he said, snapping his fingers. Albini, who virtually invented quiet/loud/quiet with *Surfer Rosa*, was enlisted for the second album, and helped the band refine its attack. The result was *Rid of Me* and its title track was the ultimate rock horror show. Harvey's desolate moan drew the listener in, Albini's perverse mix kept her voice a little too far away for comfort. To the lover who thought he'd washed his hands of her, Harvey offered a quiet but assured threat: 'No, you're not rid of me.'[10] And sure enough, just like a monster in a movie, Harvey — who had seemed safely contained behind bars in the verses — suddenly leaped into the front of the song's frame in the chorus, which Albini recorded at roughly three times the volume level of the rest of the song.

In June 1993, Albini set out on a tour with his own band, Shellac. In Australia, the producer talked excitedly about the improvised sections he and the group were building into the songs. 'We're really enjoying it,' he said in an interview with triple j. 'Well, you might be enjoying it,' responded Richard Kingsmill, 'but what's it doing for the audience?' Albini, in his precise, measured way, replied without hesitation. 'Really that's not of interest to us,' he said. 'That's none of our business. There's a point doing it in front of other people because you want them to see what you're doing,' he went on, 'but it is almost an entirely selfish concern.'[11]

Albini talked at length in the interview about other artists he admired — the Jesus Lizard, the Jon Spencer Blues Explosion, Slint and PJ Harvey. 'Bands that have produced something I've never heard before,' he said, 'that made me rethink my notion of what music is about.' He played Suicide's 'Frankie Teardrop', and told Kingsmill the story of the band's disastrous support tour with The Cars in 1979. As he related the tale of the New York duo being bottled off the stage every night by an audience that had paid to hear snappy new wave pop, it became clear that this story was, for Albini, a kind of moral fable, in which Suicide represented his rock and roll ideal — the unique, unclassifiable, self-determining artist doggedly refusing to cater to the demands of a mass audience, reserving the right to scare the pants off a crowd who wanted only to be entertained.

Albini's contempt for Nirvana's *Nevermind* came from its failure, in his eyes, to live up to any of these principles. Butch Vig's radio-friendly mix had levelled off the band's noisy peaks, his use of double-tracking had smoothed Cobain's unusual voice into a standard rock croon, and the whole album had been made with an eye on the market, with the aim of getting Nirvana on the radio. Now they wanted off it — and this suited Albini perfectly. Work on the new Nirvana album began in February 1993, at Pachyderm Studios in rural Minnesota, where *Rid of Me* had been recorded six months earlier. Albini suggested to Cobain that he pay for the recording with his own money, and instituted a strict lockdown on the sessions. No one besides the producer, the band and one engineer would be allowed near Pachyderm. News of all this sent Geffen into a panic — and with some justification. The new Nirvana album was most certainly being made with the wider audience in mind, but not in the way the band's record company was hoping.

Fragments

In Douglas Coupland's *Generation X*, the narrator, Andy, introduces the reader to his friends by explaining where they're from — and then wonders why he bothered. 'Dag is from Toronto, Canada, Claire is from Los Angeles, California ... but where you're from feels sort of irrelevant these days ("since everyone has the same stores in their mini-malls," according to my younger brother).'[1] The spectacular success of what economist Theodore Levitt described in 1983 as the 'swaggering global corporation' had ensured this.[2] Over the past ten years, super-brands like McDonald's, Coke and Marlboro — freed from earlier restrictions on global trade by the laissez-faire policies of Ronald Reagan — had spread their products, stores and logos over half the world. After the fall of communism in Europe, they quickly covered the other half. In May 1990, cultural theorist Dick Hebdige opened the business section of a newspaper and saw an advertisement for investment opportunities in the former Eastern Bloc in the form of a map, 'which looked like one of Hitler's wish-fulfilment scenarios drawn up on his last day in the bunker'. The map showed Central and Eastern Europe 'caught in a pincer movement' by branded arrows, as swaggering global corporations homed in on new markets.[3]

In 1984 philosopher Jean-François Lyotard had described a world where 'one listens to reggae, watches a western, eats McDonald's for lunch and local cuisine for dinner, wears Paris perfume in Tokyo'.[4] Ten years later, all of this could be done as easily in Moscow. McDonald's 1990 TV ads, which showed furry-hatted Russians tucking hungrily into Big Macs, celebrated the opening of the chain's first store in the former Soviet capital as a great victory, symbolic of a new borderless world. But the ad's theme song — 'sweet dreams are comin' true / and there's no difference between me and you' — hinted at a more sinister side of globalisation.[5] 'This isn't entertainment, it's a front for global domination,' wrote Hugh Gallagher in 1992, as he sat alone in a hotel room watching MTV for seven days straight.[6] Gallagher's sleep-deprived brain was plagued with visions of dystopia, a world remade in MTV's image. 'Ancient customs are abandoned, religions fall to pieces.' But to Suede's Matt Osman, it seemed as though this had already come to pass. 'I went to Vienna,' he told *Select* magazine, 'and I could have been anywhere.'[7] As the reach of the global brands expanded, thousand-year-old cultures were being replaced by American dreams. 'That's something I don't really care for,' said US comedian Bill Hicks in London in November 1992. 'The Americanisation of the world.'[8]

As Hicks spoke, the members of Blur were in a studio not far away, putting the finishing touches on an album whose central theme was the Americanisation of Britain. 'Sunday, Sunday here again a walk in the park,' sang Damon Albarn. 'You meet an old soldier and you talk of the past / He fought for us in two world wars / The England he knew is no more.'[9] 'I do feel our culture is under siege,' the singer explained. 'We should be proud of being British.'[10] Albarn had known for some time that he was living in a cultural colony of the United States, but his sense of national pride had been stirred by more recent events.

In May 1992, Blur had set out on a lengthy American tour. The band's timing could not have been worse — this was the precise moment when any lingering admiration American critics might have had for the 'Brit-Pack' sound of the previous year had been swept away by the arrival of grunge. Blur's early hits now sounded dated, and its more recent material was, from an American point of view, even less appealing. The pace of rock radio in 1992 had been set by the stately plod of groups like Alice in Chains and Soundgarden and, in this context, the caffeinated pogo of Blur's new single 'Popscene' was even more out of place than the band's old crossover shuffle. 'It sounds dope at this speed,' said the Beastie Boys' Mike D, as he played 'Popscene' at 33rpm on the *NME*'s turntable. 'The beat was too nervous,' explained Ad-Rock. 'You had to slow it down.'[11] But the biggest problem of all for Blur in America was the simple fact that it was a pop group in a market obsessed with rock. Albarn tried — as indie rockers had done since indie rock began — to tell himself that he was losing because he was special. 'Maybe one of our weaknesses is that we're too clever,' he mused. 'Fundamental, hormone-titillating rock fills halls. But it takes a fuck of a lot more intelligence to be a pop group.'[12] But being in a clever pop group was cold comfort in a season when pop was less popular than it had ever been.

So America rejected Blur, and Blur dealt with this by drinking. 'And drinking,' as Graham Coxon later recalled. 'And drinking, and drinking.'[13] The more they drank, the worse they played, and the worse they played, the more they drank. Gigs deteriorated into punch-ups, and were cut short or cancelled. As the band's reputation began to precede it, the turnout at shows — not great to start with — dwindled to almost nothing. But the tour dragged on regardless, and the longer it went on, the more homesick Damon Albarn became. As he lay one night in a generic hotel room somewhere in Nowheresville USA, he realised that he missed Britain, and that he missed it because he was British.

Albarn had already begun to figure this out early in 1992, as he sat on the floor at his girlfriend Justine Frischmann's house and listened to her records — the Specials, Madness, XTC, The Jam, The Fall. 'Fuck,' he thought to himself, 'we are something. We are part of a heritage of British bands.'[14] For a group undergoing a perpetual identity crisis, whose biggest hits to date had described nothing more than the feeling that there wasn't really much to say, this was no small realisation. In Japan, Albarn hoisted a small Union Jack aloft for the *NME*'s photographer.[15] On tour, Blur began writing new songs with lyrics that told stories of English life. The post-shoegaze abstractions that had plagued Albarn's lyrics in 1991 — 'I can't feel / 'cause I'm numb' — were replaced by real-life details — he wrote about buying blue jeans on Portobello Road, a family sitting down to a Sunday night dinner, washing a shirt collar with new soap. The band swapped lazy funk and shoegaze drone for Beatles-esque pop and music-hall waltzes. Even their wardrobe was given an overhaul — Albarn's loose-fit T-shirts and trainers disappeared, the band's new photos showed them wearing Mod jackets, Fred Perry shirts and Doc Martens boots.

When he heard Blur's new music, and saw its new image, Dave Balfe, Blur's label boss at Food Records, was certain that Albarn, Coxon, Alex James and Dave Rowntree had lost their minds. The US tour had been a disaster, but it should at least — Balfe felt — have taught the band that the new sound for 1993 would be American, not British. Balfe, as an avid reader of the music press, had seen this coming for some time. The self-flagellating mood of early 1992, when UK critics had collectively thrown their hands in the air and declared baggy dead and shoegaze over, had been further encouraged by the rude health of American rock. Chris Global, writing in the *NME*, complained of the 'cancer of say-nothing niceness' in British music, and declared that 'the only cure is grunge'.[16] The revolutionary rhetoric continued in a piece by Keith Cameron published the following month. 'Lollapalooza was the spark, Nirvana fanned the flames, and by the end of 1991 a regular forest fire was out of control, putting paid to any dead wood,' wrote Cameron. 'This is the sight, sound and smell of rock and roll, if not being reborn, then at least recovering its soul and its sense of humanity.'[17] Here, as with the initial breakthrough of Mudhoney in the late eighties, a fortuitous meeting of Sub Pop's 'trailer trash' marketing pitch and the UK music press's class-based fantasies had worked in grunge's favour. The *NME* praised the Screaming Trees as backwoods savants, 'banging their hairy heads, they almost don't realise exactly what it is they're doing',[18] and quoted the Lemonheads' Evan Dando saying, 'I won't have anything to do with the lavish treatment record companies lay on. I'd rather take the bus and sleep on the floor' — despite the fact that Dando had said no such thing.[19] But the facts would only get in the way of a good story, and the story — The Return of Real Rock — was too good to resist. When Blur returned home from the States in July 1992, the UK music press was full of American guitar bands: Pearl Jam, Alice in Chains and the Red Hot Chili Peppers. For Blur, at this particular moment in time, to suddenly rediscover Madness seemed to Balfe to be merely perverse. When he heard the album in December 1992, he strongly recommended to the band that they scrap Stephen Street's bright, poppy production and hand the master tapes over to Butch Vig for a remix.

But for Blur, a Seattle makeover was out of the question, and when the album was released in May 1993, it soon became clear why. According to the band, *Modern Life is Rubbish* was not only pro-British and anti-American in a general cultural sense, it was specifically pro-British pop and anti-American rock. 'Our last album killed baggy,' Albarn told *Melody Maker*. 'This one will kill grunge.'[20] As the interview went on, Blur's singer began to say things that very few people, in the heady atmosphere of 1992, had been prepared to say — that the authenticity of the new guitar rock might be overrated, for example, or that its rebellious stance might be nothing more than a pose. Chris Global had argued in the *NME* that grunge was preferable to shoegaze because it 'at least challenges things'; Cameron had cheered Nirvana on for leading a rock revolution in the name of humanity.[21] But Albarn wasn't buying any of it. 'Don't tell me Nirvana have changed the face of American rock,' he scoffed. 'No-one should kid themselves that anything happens in America unless the establishment thinks there's a buck in it for them.'[22] Music writers entertained and encouraged the romantic notion that grunge represented a youth revolt against corporate control when in fact, Albarn insisted, grunge was simply the new, slightly hairier face of Coca-colonisation.

Albarn's labelmate, Jesus Jones's Mike Edwards, believed that grunge had more to do with nostalgia for the seventies than revolution in the nineties. This was bound to be a sore point with Edwards, whose song 'Right Here Right Now' had been taken up as a campaign anthem by presidential candidate Bill Clinton, only to be ditched in favour of Fleetwood Mac's 'Don't Stop'. 'Rock music in the past reflected the society we lived in,' he told music writer Jonathan Bernstein. 'It's stopped doing that now, it's stopped being representative.'[23] Bernstein — noting that Edwards was on the defensive, having to 'consolidate his position in an America now enamoured of dirty, stubbled rock realism' — pointed out that grunge was nothing if not representative of its audience. Edwards declared that this, if it was true, was 'immensely sad — that this sort of apathetic miserabalism is all that we can expect from this new generation'.[24] Albarn was similarly disgusted by the angst and apathy of grunge singers. His feeling about the state of the world in 1993 was perhaps not so different from that of Kurt

Cobain and Eddie Vedder. But Albarn believed that the songwriter's task was to describe and critique this state of affairs; his models for musical excellence at the time were the detached, third-person style of the Kinks circa 'Dedicated Follower of Fashion' and the kitchen-sink realism of the Specials' Terry Hall. Therefore, he saw grunge's self-absorption as cowardly and unproductive. 'What have they got to say for themselves?' he asked, '"I'm fucked up" — fantastic.'[25]

But unlike Edwards, Albarn did not accuse grunge bands of peddling nostalgia, probably because he knew he couldn't afford to. The idea for Blur's new direction had come to him, after all, from a feeling of homesickness — his vision of the future was based on a memory of the past. Blur insisted on British nostalgia over the imported American variety, but there was no question of whether or not to look back. What else could one do in 1993? Alex James and Graham Coxon had known since they were at art school in the late eighties that there was nothing new under the sun. Their fellow student, Damien Hirst, later recalled that this was perhaps the single most important thing that he'd learned there. 'Before I went to Goldsmiths,' he told *Interview* magazine, 'I sort of tried to be original. But there's just so much in the world, and so much of it is derivative. At Goldsmiths we were kind of freed — you don't have to worry about that!' Hirst pointed out that art had, to some extent, always been about copying: 'Everybody has always ripped everybody off since the beginning. But what I think is different about our generation is that we never felt the need to be original.'[26]

This generational trait had proved very useful to Blur as it made its way through the future-obsessed UK music scene in the early nineties. They may have copped their haircuts from the Stone Roses, their guitar sound from My Bloody Valentine, and their beats from Run-D.M.C., but they saw no reason to feel guilty about it. 'I don't claim that we are stunningly original,' Albarn told the *NME*'s Simon Williams in 1991.[27] The members of Blur had grown up in a media-saturated world — by the time they started the band, they had heard and seen everything, and had long since given up on the idea of doing anything for the first time. 'That's what modern life is about,' said Albarn, 'people learning about love from television.'[28] Twelve months later, on the side of a building near Marble Arch tube station, the singer spied a piece of graffiti that, to him, said everything there was to be said about living in England at the end of history: 'Modern Life is Rubbish.'[29] In May 1993, Coxon spray-painted the same phrase on a wall by the seafront at Clacton, as Albarn explained to *Melody Maker* exactly what these magic words meant to Blur. 'Modern life is the rubbish of the past,' he said. 'We all live on rubbish, and because it's built up over such a time, there's no need for originality anymore. There are so many old things to splice into new permutations that there is absolutely no need to create anything new.'[30]

The nineties had begun with a great spurt of optimism, as artists confronted the rubble of the Cold War and declared that all of history was up for grabs. 'Contemporary culture can only exist as a melting-pot now,' said My Bloody Valentine's Kevin Shields in 1991.[31] Primal Scream declared that 'music is music', and that the segregation of genres was analogous to the segregation of races and cultures — a form of bigotry. British journalists wrote excitedly about the new classless culture of indie-dance, where fashion-conscious club kids, studenty indie types and working-class ravers could happily coexist on the dance floor. In America, Perry Farrell and Calvin Johnson hoped to gather the indie diaspora of the eighties into an alternative nation, and Kurt Cobain dreamed of a new spirit of generational solidarity among the youth of the world. With the worldwide success of *Nevermind* in 1992, this dream seemed to have become a reality: the old borders between the underground and the mainstream were erased, anything was possible.[32]

But the sheer size of the alternative nation made it ungovernable, and its citizens' need to be unique and individual made it difficult for them to reach any meaningful consensus. The centre, as pop theorist Lawrence Grossberg noted, was disappearing. Fans of college-rock bands like Superchunk, Pavement and Stereolab sought to redefine 'indie' as opposed to 'alternative'; riot grrrl declared itself a republic, with a constitution radically different, and in many ways opposed to that of the alternative nation; and a bitter argument erupted over the precise definition of punk, which many of the music's fans felt was incompatible with mass acceptance. As a result, the new culture quickly split into subcultures. 'Identity politics and fashion trends divide us into a nation of small tribes,' wrote Craig Marks in July 1993.[33] By this point, the mood had altered considerably from that of 1990 — the goal was no longer to mix, but to separate, as subcultures sought to define themselves and the values they wished to preserve within the increasingly homogenised world of global youth culture.

No band was more representative of this change than Blur. In 1990 Albarn had happily described Blur as part of a generation that 'can't distinguish one thing from another', and the band had proved it by getting on *Top of the Pops* with a song that owed as much to Def Jam as it did to Dinosaur Jr. Blur knew it was a product of a globalised world, but the band's feeling about this was primarily one of curiosity. 'We want to go to America,' said Albarn in 1991. 'So much of our culture is American now — we want to make the connection.'[34] But Blur did not connect with America, and America did not connect with Blur. The experience had thrown the band back on itself, and by 1992, Blur was no more interested in grafting breakbeats onto rock guitars than it was in having an American producer work on a British pop record. Merging was over. 'It's just that we've done so much travelling,' said Albarn in the summer of 1992. 'I think everyone comes to the same conclusion: that they definitely belong to a culture.'[35]

Fragments of this culture had sustained Blur through the strip-malls and beer-barns of America: the thought of people queuing in shops and presenters saying 'goodnight' on the BBC, the taste of sugary tea and the sound of Ray Davies's voice on the Kinks tape Albarn played in the van.[36] This was the 'rubbish' of the past from which the band built its new music. Blur's project, in 1993, was not unlike the 'montage practice' recommended by Walter Benjamin — the creation of a new world from the fragments of the old. But Albarn's epiphany had come from homesickness, from a wish to return to the past. So when the singer picked over the rubble of history, he was very careful about what he chose. Cherry-coloured Docs, yes; sports trainers, no. The Smiths, the Specials and XTC, absolutely; grunge, G-funk and house music — absolutely not. England, yes; America, no. Blur guitarist Graham Coxon was still quite fond of Dinosaur Jr and Sonic Youth, but after

1993, Albarn more or less forced him to listen to them on headphones in the privacy of his tour bunk bed.[37] If British culture was going to be rebuilt, it had to be done using British material. 'I think it's very naïve,' said Albarn, 'to think that we can all co-exist under some sort of general culture, which is what everything's moving towards these days.'[38] Albarn had discovered that the placeless sense of alienation that came with a merged world could only be dispelled by returning to one's roots — 'paring yourself down', as he put it, 'to what you really are'. In the nineties, the singer realised, where you were from was more relevant than it had ever been, precisely because the stores in the malls were the same wherever you went.

What Pop Stars Are For

'Forget about those Pixies,' said Black Francis, 'it's 1993!' The singer had announced, during a radio interview that the Pixies had come to an end, and was explaining his decision to the *NME*. What it had finally come down to, he said, was that his solo project wasn't getting the attention it deserved. His record company had been treating it as an indulgence, while pestering him constantly with demands for a new Pixies album. 'It's a good record,' he said, 'and all you guys wanna talk about is when I'm gonna do it with the big P-word again. Fuck you! That's when I'm gonna do the next Pixies record. See ya!' Two weeks later, he'd changed his name to Frank Black, and admitted to Richard Kingsmill on triple j that he'd split up the Pixies because he wanted to be the centre of attention. 'Is there a touch of egomania in me?' he asked, answering Kingsmill's question with a question. 'Are you kidding? You're talking to a rock star. If I don't get enough limelight, I shrivel up!'[1]

In August, Kingsmill spoke to Kim Deal, who had only learned about the end of the Pixies after Francis announced it on the radio, but had not been too surprised by the news. The band had long since ceased to be a democracy; her songs had been steadily dropping off the Pixies' set lists since 1990, and her vocals had all but disappeared from the band's last two albums. She had noticed too, the way Francis had been, as she put it, 'going around saying "I am the Pixies, I am the dictator of this band".' But Deal refused to get into a war of words with her former colleague. She had come to understand, as Francis himself had, that Black Francis was a rock star, and prone to rock star behaviour. 'Y'know, it's cool to have an asshole who's a lead singer,' she told Kingsmill, 'I like that.'[2]

Deal was joking of course. Being an asshole rock singer was not the least bit cool in 1993. The rock star had been banished from the alternative nation, his essential need to elevate himself above his audience and his bandmates now seemed undemocratic, his desire for attention somewhat infantile, his appetite for partying wasteful and insensitive. 'Give the finger to the rock and roll singer, as he dances upon your paycheck,'[3] advised Beck, on his 1993 album *Mellow Gold*. The heroes of the nineties were heroic because they were ordinary, and Kim Deal — with her unwashed hair, normal clothes and friendly demeanour — was the living embodiment of the new anti-rock star: humble, sincere and not so different from her fans.

But as the Breeders — Kim Deal's other band — toured their way around America in the summer of 1993, the group's bass player, Josephine Wiggs, began to wonder whether rock's new regime was really that different from the old. It was easy to believe that bands were the same as their fans in the days when Soundgarden slept on people's living room floors. But in this post-Nirvana world, where alternative rock bands filled stadiums, it seemed less and less plausible. 'No matter how much these guys talk about how they're the same as their fans,' she said, 'their fans know they're not — *we* know they're not.' 'But I feel exactly like the audience,' insisted Kelley Deal, Kim's sister and the Breeders' guitarist. 'No, but you're not!' said Wiggs. 'You're the one up onstage playing while they're out there standing in a puddle of beer.'

At this point, Kim Deal joined the conversation. 'You know, a lot of them out there in a puddle of beer have their own bands and they can get up onstage and do what we're doing,' she said. 'Of course they can,' Wiggs replied, 'but only certain people are any good at it.' 'You mean only certain people get lucky,' said Kelley with a laugh. 'No,' sighed Wiggs, slightly exasperated. 'That's not what I mean at all.'[4]

Brett Anderson, twenty-six-year-old lead singer with the British rock group Suede, was certain that rock stars were nothing like ordinary people, and that becoming one had nothing to do with luck. You had to want it, and he had wanted it since he was a schoolboy living with his parents in Hayward's Heath, a town south of London. In 1989, Anderson, his girlfriend Justine Frischmann and Mat Osman began rehearsing and writing songs together as Suede. They found guitarist Bernard Butler through an ad in *Melody Maker*, and replaced their drum machine with a real drummer, Simon Gilbert, not long after. By the time Frischmann left in 1991, Suede had already established its sound — melodramatic, emotional pop songs with glam rock guitars and flyaway choruses. Anderson was finding his voice as a writer too; his songs were poetic, but never abstract, full of unfashionably specific references to the sights and sounds of urban life in England. His romantic odes shifted unexpectedly from the second to the third person, the love object changed sex mid-stream. Onstage, Anderson used his lithe, androgynous good looks to complement the sexual ambiguity in his songs, swivelling his hips and flaunting his chest by wearing suit jackets without shirts and midriff-baring tops.

None of this, at the height of Madchester, was the kind of thing the kids were queuing up to see, and Suede suffered for it during the band's first year in London. But by February the following year, with baggy over and shoegaze already on the nose, Suede's unfashionability was looking more and more like a virtue, and the band knew it. 'Everything you're supposed to be in 1992, we're not,' said Anderson at the time. 'Our music's passionate and uptight instead of laidback and dreamy, we're theatrical when you're supposed to be ordinary blokes.'[5] By March 1993, Suede — without having yet released an album — had featured on no fewer than nineteen magazine covers, and had been hailed by the *NME* as 'the best new band in Britain'.[6]

Anderson, mindful of the fact that this honour had in the past been bestowed on Sigue Sigue Sputnik and the Stone Roses, cast a wary eye over the hype. 'The UK music press are always getting it wrong,' he said, 'because they're just … they're too obsessed with the idea of things.'[7] But the idea of Suede was, from a music journalist's point of view, irresistible. A perennial complaint of the previous twelve months had been the mysterious disappearance of the pop star from Britain's music scene. Where, writers wondered, was the nineties equivalent to Adam Ant or Morrissey or Marc Bolan? Where was the glamour, the sex, the danger in modern music? In a two-page feature published in *Q* magazine in November, Phil Sutcliffe interviewed a handful of industry insiders, artists and journalists in an attempt to find out. 'Currently, the pop star is dead,' offered Dave Bates, Phonogram's head of A&R. 'However, I do believe pop could come back, not with manufactured groups, but with true glamour that gets girls screaming outside bands' hotels, and kids from industrial cities thinking, I want to get paid, get laid, get out of here, and that's the way to do it.'[8]

If Suede hadn't already been on every magazine cover in the land by the time this was printed, one would have to assume that Bates had gone straight back to the office, picked up the phone, and set about manufacturing the kind of truly glamorous, non-manufactured pop band he was describing. As it was, he most likely already had Suede in mind. 'It's not just girls who pack themselves at the front of the stage and try to rip Brett's clothes off,' said one of the band's fans. 'It's boys, too. It's nothing to do with homosexuality ... it's everybody, it's a mania.'[9] Anderson was the kind of star that fans wanted in a very literal sense — they dreamed about him at night and thrust their hands out to touch him as he stomped around the stage. Suede gigs provoked scenes of teenage frenzy not seen at rock shows in Britain since the demise of the Smiths.

For Anderson, all this was exciting, but not too surprising. In fact, by March 1993, it had become almost routine. 'There's been a lot of hysteria at our gigs,' he told *The Independent*, 'but we're quite bored with playing live already. Once you've captivated a couple of thousand people, got them in the palm of your hand and had them salivating ... you don't really know where to go from there.'[10] Suede demanded its audience's undivided attention, and Anderson wanted to be everything to his fans. But their adulation, once he had it, meant nothing to him. Worshipping him, it seemed, was the least they could do.

Anderson's willingness to admit that Suede's relationship with his fans was an unequal one — that they loved and admired him while he scarcely gave them a thought — was refreshing in 1993. 'In the past two years, bands have been very apologetic,' said *Q* magazine's editor, Danny Kelly. 'They've thrived on the attitude that "we're the same as the audience".'[11] In 1990, the Stone Roses' Ian Brown had said that he wasn't interested in making a spectacle of himself, that he would rather participate than perform. Shaun Ryder and Bez of the Happy Mondays didn't even think of themselves as being in a band; on stage, in the studio and meeting journalists, they would simply be themselves. This was the 'Spike Island Spirit' that Tony Wilson spoke of, an equity culture in which fans and bands dressed alike because they were.

But by 1992, it seemed time to admit that pop's new republic had been a failure. Ian Brown's refusal to perform had not sparked a revolution in youth consciousness, it had simply meant that the Stone Roses didn't perform very often, and that when they did, it wasn't very good. And equity culture seemed vastly overrated now that the Happy Mondays had bankrupted their record company to fuel their crack habits, and left their fans standing in a puddle of beer with nothing but a second-rate funk album to console them. By 1993, it seemed that baggy's only real legacy was a bad one, a 'long season of anti-personality', as the *NME*'s John Mulvey put it.[12]

These early-nineties disappointments proved that rock singers were really nothing like their fans, that they lived in another world and reserved the right to play by different rules. But they also suggested that this was perhaps as it ought to be — that fans didn't actually want a 'participatory' experience of rock in any case, and in fact sought stars they could worship and admire. None of this was a surprise to Brett Anderson, who could now with some justification say 'I told you so'. 'That's what pop stars are for,' he said in 1992, 'to give you an idea of living life to the extreme.'[13] For Suede, the idea of rock singers being ordinary blokes was a contradiction in terms, the whole point of being in a band was, as Anderson put it, 'to be extraordinary'.[14] Anderson had long understood that pop music, at its best, was inherently elitist, that rock stars were good at being stars, while ordinary people were not. Now, it seemed, in 1993, Britain was finally coming around to his way of thinking. Indie rock's doomed experiment in mob rule was abandoned by the UK's music press at the start of that year, as journalists and fans alike came to understand that some people were born to lead and others to follow. Suede, the *NME* concluded, represented 'the triumph of decadent aristo-foppery over prole pop'.[15]

Suede's new sense of ambition, and Anderson's willingness to make a spectacle of himself suggested that the band might succeed in

America where so many other English groups had failed. The early signs were good — the single 'Metal Mickey' broke into the Billboard Modern Rock Top 10 in September 1992, and the band's shows in New York were sensational. But in the long term, Suede's appeal didn't really translate in America. Like Blur, they quickly fell foul of the US market's strict segregation of pop from its opposite, rock. 'Alternative people thought we were too pop,' Anderson later explained, 'while pop people hadn't heard of us.'[16] Their significance in the context of UK music — as a corrective to the excesses of baggy and shoegaze — also counted for very little in a country that had barely registered the existence of either. The idea of Suede might be great, but as Anderson himself pointed out, the English press generally made too much of ideas, and many American critics felt the same way. 'Music writing in the British weeklies is a criticism of ideas rather than music,' wrote *Spin*'s Jim Greer in April 1993, 'which is how, for instance, complete nonentities such as the Boo Radleys (!) or The Verve (!?) or Suede (#$!!@*) receive off-the-scale reviews based solely on their supposed newness or freshness or ideological correctness.'[17]

But in the end, the biggest obstacles to Suede's success in America were the very things that had ensured it in Britain: the band's burning ambition, its aristocratic attitude, and Anderson's belief in himself as a star. Success itself was regarded with such suspicion in US rock's new fraternity, that its stars were forced to insist that they didn't have it, even after they did. (Chris Cornell, for example, told Jonathan Poneman late in 1992 that Soundgarden was not 'a commercial band' — despite the fact that its album had just gone platinum — because the group did not write 'accessible pop songs'.[18]) Whether or not they enjoyed playing stadiums and having their videos shown on MTV, grunge singers had to at least pay lip-service to the idea that these things were embarrassing, and that they were in many ways a sign of failure to live up to one's ideals, as they were for Nirvana. For a band to actively seek adulation and stardom, and then admit that the audience meant nothing more to them than that, as Suede did, was very much out of step with the times. And while Suede began with similar subject matter to Nirvana's, the two bands quickly diverged. Suede, according to music critic Jon Savage, wrote about 'a fresh generation, formed by recession, "with sweet F.A. to do today", if you want, the English equivalent of the slackers'.[19] But Suede's goal was to rise above all of this with a vision of a life of risk, pleasure and adventure. Grunge was more realistic and earthbound, insisting on the way things were rather than the way they could be. Grunge was about looking in the mirror; the goal was self-contemplation, not self-projection.

All of this helps to explain why one of the only English rock records to do any real business in America in 1993 was Radiohead's 'Creep', a 'violent belch of self-degradation' (as *Spin* described it) recorded by a group the English music press had barely noticed.[20] Like the season's other big hit, 'Loser' by Beck, 'Creep' was negative to the core, a drifting, down-tempo ballad with a chorus that erupted in jagged guitar noise and a sneering refrain. 'I'm a creep,' sang Thom Yorke, 'I'm a weirdo.'[21] The single had stiffed on its first release, selling 6000 copies in the UK before being deleted. But after being added by influential American radio stations Live 105 and KROQ early the following year, the song went from being a hit to an anthem, the inescapable sound of alt-rock radio during the summer of 1993. 'It's not likely that many Top 40 hits will contain squalls of feedback or a singer screaming like he's exorcising a lifetime of demons,' wrote *Rolling Stone*'s Chris Mundy in January 1992. 'And it's less likely that a check of the charts will reveal titles like "Territorial Pissings" … or a song featuring Cobain shrieking "I'm a negative creep".'[22] Mundy's negative prediction described exactly the state of the Top 40 eighteen months later, and offered an uncanny premonition of Radiohead's breakthrough hit. Thom Yorke wasn't Kurt Cobain, but he looked a lot like him with his bleach-blond mop and stripy shirts, and in the absence of a new Nirvana song, 'Creep' was happily accepted as the next best thing.

UK journalists bemoaned the disappearance of the pop star. But in grunge-obsessed America, stars were seen as a problem — they made people feel inadequate and sabotaged their self-esteem. For this reason, Belly singer Tanya Donelly advised her fans to take their Take That posters down. 'It's self-minimizing to concentrate on someone you don't know,' she said.[23] The only way to relate to your audience as a rock singer in the nineties was to admit you had been similarly oppressed by other, more popular people, and that you were, fundamentally a failure — and Radiohead excelled at this. 'Self-loathing is something we can all relate to,' guitarist Ed O'Brien told *Billboard* magazine. 'Every day we see people who are better looking or richer or more worthy than we feel.'[24] 'You're so fucking special,' sang Thom Yorke, 'I wish I was special.'[25] According to *Beavis and Butt-head*, Radiohead's ability to admit that they sucked made them one of the few British bands that didn't; a series of print ads for the band's debut, *Pablo Honey*, carried an endorsement from Beavis, in which he insisted that Radiohead made 'music that doesn't suck — huh huh huh'.[26] But the duo's support had been purchased by EMI, and this became very clear when people heard the record. With the notable exception of 'Creep', *Pablo Honey* really did suck — and not in a good way

Check Out America

In 1993, Urge Overkill was poised to take over the world. The band's hometown of Chicago had been described in a *Billboard* cover story as 'The Next Seattle', Nirvana's enthusiastic patronage had got the group a deal with Geffen, and the wave of seventies revivalism that Urge had been riding since 1990 now seemed about to break. The band released two perfect singles in a row, 'Sister Havana', a made-for-the-stadium rock anthem with a ridiculously catchy chorus, and 'Positive Bleeding', another tasty stick of seventies bubblegum with 'woo-oo-oo' backing vocals and fun, upbeat lyrics. Onassis struck an old-fashioned rock rebel pose in the verses, 'Guess I'd better go it alone, 'cause baby I'm a Rolling Stone', and boasted about his newfound freedom in the chorus: 'Well, I live my life, remote-controllin' my destiny.'[1]

In a season of creeps and losers, after two years of dirt and grunge, many music critics were starting to wonder what had happened to all the fun in rock and roll, and Urge Overkill seemed ready to bring it back, just in time for the summer vacation. The band's new music spoke of long, hot nights and good tunes on the car stereo; while the title of its Geffen debut, *Saturation*, hinted at a new sense of fun and ambition for the nineties — an impression confirmed by the album cover, which showed a giant 'UO' logo floating over the Chicago skyline like a funky UFO. This blatant populism had prompted their old friend Steve Albini to accuse them of being 'pandering sluts'. But the band had set its sights on something bigger and better than small-time indie politics, it wanted to be Cheap Trick, not Big Black.

Saturation was released in the same month as *Exile in Guyville*, the recording debut of twenty-six-year-old songwriter Liz Phair. Her music was drawn from the same classic-rock archetypes as Urge's, but rendered in a far less bombastic style — most of the songs on *Exile in Guyville* were performed by Phair alone, with extra instruments added by her producer, Brad Wood, and engineer Casey Rice. Phair, like Urge Overkill, was from Chicago, the stories she told on her album's sixteen songs were drawn from the same places and people as the ones on *Saturation*, and many of them were in fact about Blackie Onassis, whom Phair had dated for a year or so. But Phair's point of view was quite different from Urge's. 'Positive Bleeding' presented a picture of the rock singer as powerful and carefree, going it alone, like a Rolling Stone; Phair's 'Fuck and Run' described the same scenario from the other side. 'I can feel it in my bones, I'm gonna spend another year alone,' she sang. 'Fuck and run, fuck and run, ever since I was seventeen.'[2] Onassis had spoken about living like a swinger in the early seventies, but Phair demolished this fantasy with a portrait of the swinger as he really would have been in 1993. 'Check out the thinning hair,' she sang. 'Check out the aftershave / Check out America / You're looking at it babe.'[3] Phair's lyrics were blunt, and deliberately non-poetic, because she wanted very much to be understood. 'It's just unequivocal, you know?' she later said. 'I'm just saying what the hell I'm saying.'[4]

The title of Phair's album referred to Chicago's indie music scene, nicknamed 'Guyville' because it was run by guys: guys in bands who, according to Phair, were not at all comfortable with the idea of a young woman playing rock and roll, and were openly dismissive of the notion that women could be artists, let alone geniuses. To Phair, this was absurd. Feminism had been as much a part of her upbringing as rock and roll, and the critical theory she'd learned during her degree at Oberlin College merely backed up what she already believed: that feminism was, as she put it, 'the "of course" clause. Of course women can do anything men can do'.[5] But Phair's conviction counted for very little in Guyville, with its complex and surprisingly rigid hierarchies of cool, and its casual, institutionalised sexism. Like Kathleen Hanna and Polly Jean Harvey, Phair was confronted with the curious gap between liberal academic life — where the feminist critique of culture was virtually taken for granted by the mid eighties — and rock and roll, which, for all its talk of freedom and liberation, still tended to define those things in exclusively male terms. Freedom in rock, particularly in the heavy, blues-derived seventies variety then in vogue, often meant freedom to do as you liked with women, or freedom from women's demands.

The guys of Guyville believed that women could not be geniuses, and this belief was backed up by the music they listened to and the heroes they worshipped. Guyville was a culture based on collecting and preserving the past, run by 'a little establishment' of men who wore their record collections, according to Phair, 'like a badge of honour … Like, "this is what I'm into, I know a lot about it".'[6] Phair saw that these records had become indie rock's canon, and that the canon was being used to reinforce a myth that kept women out of rock and roll. Of course women can't rock, the guys of Guyville would say — look at the list! Cheap Trick, Led Zeppelin, the Rolling Stones — do you see any girls on there? Phair had the idea of upsetting this hierarchy by destroying the fusty aura that had accumulated around the Great Works. She would commit an act of musical vandalism to prove to herself and her peers that these things were not icons to be worshipped, but found objects, which could be creatively manipulated to tell new stories in new ways. 'I was going to appropriate "guy rock",' she said, 'to turn it on its head a little bit.'[7] She chose, as her template, the Rolling Stones' *Exile on Main St* (roughly equivalent to Milton's *Paradise Lost* in the indie-rock canon), and set about rewriting it from the point of view of Liz Phair. The result was a collection of brutally honest, and achingly sad songs by a woman in her twenties who had been thinking about men and listening to rock and roll all her life, and had suddenly decided to stop thinking and start speaking, to stop listening and start doing. 'I was like, really, you guys are into music?' she said. 'Okay, watch — I can *make* music.'[8]

When Matador Records released *Exile in Guyville* in June 1993, Phair expected it to sell just over a thousand copies, and thought it would be nice if it was heard by 'people within a mile radius of my apartment'.[9] By December, it had sold 20,000, and had been voted Album of the Year by *Spin* and *Village Voice*. Her feelings about this were an odd mixture of delight and disgust — she was thrilled that her music was being heard, but the idea that she had done something out of the ordinary by being a woman and recording an album's worth of honest rock and roll songs about life at the end of the twentieth century was, to her, 'grotesque'. 'You've got to be kidding,' she thought to herself. 'If this is the greatest thing to have happened to a female, where *is* everybody?'[10]

Exile in Guyville was, by Phair's own account, a very 'private' album, in which she'd given voice to thoughts and feelings she'd never shared with anyone. As the album began to take off, and the size of her audiences grew, she was surprised at the extent to which those feelings were shared. Over and over again, fans approached her and said of her songs, 'Yeah, that is true for me, but I would never say it.'[11] At a women-in-rock summit meeting including PJ Harvey, Tori Amos and ex-Sugarcubes singer Björk and hosted by *Q* magazine early in 1994, Amos suggested that the three singers' work had in common a tendency to reflect and amplify the secret fears and desires of those who heard it. 'I sense that our intentions are about exposing things within our being, which become mirrors for other people,' said Amos. 'That's what the poet's job is. I'm only a mirror.'[12] But by this point, Liz Phair had all but made up her mind that if the poet's job was to be a sort of psychic reflector for her audience by exposing her emotions, it was no longer a job she wanted. Phair was unusual among female singers of the early nineties, in that she seemed to have very little trouble with the exploitation of her image (she was more amused than angered by photographers' attempts to turn her into an indie-rock pin-up), but was deeply troubled by the selling-off of her emotional life. 'It's truly frightening,' wrote Nils Bernstein in his review of *Exile*, 'that she can bare her wounds for all to see.'[13] But if Phair's music was frightening for Bernstein or his readers, it was only in the most vicarious way. Phair, on the other hand, was really scared. The confessional quality of the songs on *Exile* made them hard for her to perform on stage, even when she got over her nerves and the show went well, she found herself 'literally horrified' by the effect she had on her audiences.[14]

The terms of the new authenticity dictated that music must be honest, confessional and full of emotional hurt. But Phair quickly realised that the price that had to be paid for success on these terms was, for her, far too high. With *Exile in Guyville*, Phair had approached the edge of a billion-dollar misery industry that had sprung up in the wake of grunge, and decided, for the sake of her own sanity, to back away from it. And yet satisfying this industry was what was required of a rock star in 1993, if such a thing could be said to exist. The American rock star, in the 1990s, could not be an unreconstructed rock pig, an aristocratic superbeing, or an ironic purveyor of good times. The new rock star would have to come from a place of emotional hurt, to be able to express fear and desire and longing, to confess their sins, to admit that they sucked. But they would have to be prepared to do this in a truly spectacular fashion, to bypass the small-minded politics of indie and whatever scruples they might have about sharing their feelings with the masses, to stage Nuremberg rallies of hurt and compose symphonies of suckage.

In the end, neither *Saturation* nor *Exile in Guyville* were the sound of summer in America in 1993. That honour fell to another band from Chicago, fronted by a singer who was capable of doing all these things and more, an artist whose reserves of emotional hurt and talent for expressing it seemed almost limitless, whose naked ambition allowed him to take his therapy-rock out of the ghettos of Guyville and into the stadium, an artist who, as Michael Azerrad put it in *Spin*, was 'unashamed of being that most embarrassing of things. A rock star.'[15]

Alternative to Alternative

The taboo on the tattooed had well and truly been lifted. But a new taboo had already been put in its place. When L7's Jennifer Finch had looked forward to walking into her local 7–11 and hearing something cool, she'd most likely been hoping, as many in the underground had been, that the success of an alternative band on commercial radio had proved to radio programmers that all kinds of alternative music could safely be playlisted. By 1993, it had become clear that this was not the case. Nirvana's success had shown that distorted guitars and gloomy vocals could be played on the radio, but most radio programmers took this as a sign that only distorted guitars and gloomy vocals should be played on the radio. Having found a successful formula, US radio moved quickly toward standardisation. Nirvana had worked, and so had Pearl Jam. Stone Temple Pilots sounded a lot like both, and could be slotted into the new format with ease. The Red Hot Chili Peppers' white-boy guitar funk had gone down a treat with listeners, so the Spin Doctors' white-boy guitar funk probably would too.

Chicago's Smashing Pumpkins fell foul of these new rules. The band shared strong genealogical links with Nirvana: its influences included the Pixies, Black Sabbath and Led Zeppelin, and its debut album, *Gish*, was produced by Butch Vig in a similar style to *Nevermind*. But the Smashing Pumpkins' sound could not be easily classified as grunge. Billy Corgan's lyrics owed more to eighties goth favourites like The Cure and Bauhaus than was fashionable at the time, jazz-trained drummer Jimmy Chamberlin gave the music a prog-rock feel, D'arcy

Wretzky's basslines were straight out of the learn-to-play-me school of New Order's Peter Hook, and guitarist James Iha worshipped at the feet of My Bloody Valentine. Corgan's singing also owed more than a little to shoegaze, his curiously androgynous voice was mixed low under the band's layers of guitar noise in a way that made it hard to hear the lyrics, though Corgan helpfully informed those who might have been interested that they dealt with 'pain and spiritual ascension'.[1]

James Iha was proud of the band's un-pin-downable mixture of styles. 'It's very individual,' he said in 1991. 'We don't really fit into any specific category.'[2] But shortly after Caroline records released *Gish* in May 1991, the music industry began taking steps toward the standardisation of alternative rock, and the Smashing Pumpkins, as Corgan acknowledged later, 'were doing all the wrong things'. 'It was very much this kind of flannel-driven, no guitar solos, three-minute pop songs thing,' he said, 'and we were playing these six-minute songs with solos.'[3] Radio gave some attention to the single 'Rhinoceros', and the band toured with Pearl Jam and the Red Hot Chili Peppers in August 1991. But the Smashing Pumpkins did not break through to the mainstream to anything like the extent that its touring companions did. 'Anybody who heard *Nevermind*, then tried the Pumpkins for more of the same,' observed *Creem* magazine's Dave Thompson, 'was doomed to disappointment.'[4] *Gish* spent only one week on the Billboard chart, and climbed no higher than 195.

Gish was by no means a write-off — the album was well-reviewed and sold steadily, if not spectacularly, into 1992. But it suited Billy Corgan to believe that his band had been rejected by the alternative nation, because he was used to being rejected. He had been rejected by his biological parents, who'd left him in the care of his stepmother, rejected in high school for being a too-tall geek with an ugly birthmark, and rejected in Guyville for being a pop careerist in an indie world. He had, by the age of twenty-six, come to think of himself as an outsider, and saw his band in exactly the same terms. 'We weren't with any of those scenes,' he said of the band's early days in Chicago. 'We weren't cool like the Touch and Go [Records] bands.'[5] The note of pride in Corgan's voice as he said this spoke of the vast talent he had developed for synthesising hurt into ambition. In 1988, the Pumpkins scored an early triumph when they were booked to support Jane's Addiction in Chicago, and one week before the concert, Corgan appeared on WNUR to give away tickets. Noting that the show was going to be filmed, the interviewer asked if he was looking forward to it. 'Yeah,' Corgan replied with a smile, 'it'll be nice for all my old high school pals who didn't like me to see me on TV.'[6]

Corgan's long history of rejection taught him to rely on himself and determine his own goals, and this allowed him to develop the sound of the Smashing Pumpkins in defiance of, rather than in deference to, the demands of scenesters, critics, and even the band's own fans. 'It sounds kind of twisted,' he admitted in 1991. 'But we don't really play for audience reactions. That's for the arena-rock fans.'[7] But if Corgan's words made him sound as though he shared Steve Albini's 'who cares if you listen' philosophy of music, subsequent events would reveal that this was nothing more than a coincidence.

Corgan had no real allegiance to indie rock or its ideals, so when he found himself excluded from the club in 1991, he vowed that the Smashing Pumpkins' next album would be everything indie guitar rock was not. He began to define his music against the prevailing aesthetic: if alt rock was cynical, nihilistic and self-deprecating, the Pumpkins would be sincere, romantic and entirely selfish. If grunge was loose and slack, his band would be uptight and exacting. And if indie was ashamed of success and allergic to hype, Corgan would write for the stadium. He dreamed of making the kind of epic, symphonic art-rock he'd loved as a teenager: Queen, David Bowie, Pink Floyd, and the Electric Light Orchestra.

Late in 1992, Corgan broke a long spell of writer's block with a song called 'Today', a stinging ballad about alienation and suicide that gave Corgan back his confidence, and set the tone for the album, which the singer later defined as 'me versus them, or me versus me'.[8] Corgan's basically adversarial relationship to the world found an outlet in a flood of new songs about those who'd done him wrong: his parents, his friends, his critics. He recorded a demo of 'Today' and played it for the Virgin reps. 'They loved it,' he told Dave Thompson. 'Suddenly, all these people were shooting their mouths off about how great the album was going to be.'[9] Corgan had always felt that the Smashing Pumpkins could make a world-class record. But at the time, the rest of the band was in no state to realise such a project. Wretzky and Iha had ended their long relationship in the middle of an eighteen-month tour and were now barely speaking, and Chamberlain had become addicted to heroin. So when the dilapidated Pumpkins failed to deliver the performances he required of them, he simply erased their parts and played them himself. 'I just have a vision,' he explained in 1992. 'And I can't let them not having a vision stop me.'[10] Working around the clock with Vig and engineer Alan Moulder, Corgan channelled a lifetime's worth of loneliness and resentment into one hour of music that ran the gamut from string-soaked ballads to apocalyptic guitar fury.

Timing, as Thompson noted in his *Creem* piece, is everything — and in this instance, the Pumpkins got it right. Released in July 1993, *Siamese Dream* debuted at number 10 on the Billboard chart, and was still hovering around the Top 30 three months later, by which time it had sold almost a million copies. Michael Snyder of the *San Francisco Chronicle* watched the group, now cleaned up and given a new sense of purpose by the success of the album, play a sold-out show at the Warfield Theatre in October. 'Smashing Pumpkins,' he concluded, 'is the buzz-band of the moment, and a horde of MTV-weaned thrashers pushed and pummelled one another in the pit by the stage.'[11]

Watching the Pumpkins strike their neo-rock star poses on stage, Michael Azerrad suggested that the band's 'avowedly un-indie music has helped force the question of what exactly is "alternative".'[12] The Pumpkins, as Azerrad pointed out, had spent no time on an indie label (apart from one Sub Pop single), had no scruples whatsoever about selling out, and made music that, by this point, owed far more to Queen than the Pixies. There was only one sense, really, in which the Smashing Pumpkins' *Siamese Dream* could be described as alternative, a lunatic possibility hinted at by comedian Todd Snider on his 1994 single, 'Talkin' Seattle Grunge Rock Blues'. 'Now that's alternative,' exclaimed Snider. 'That's alternative to alternative!'[13] Chicago music journalist Bill Wyman seemed to agree with this assessment. In his year-in-review column, Wyman insisted that the Smashing Pumpkins' new direction amounted to 'an explicit rejection of much of the insularity that increasingly characterises underground music and the fringes of alternative music in America'. Like Liz Phair and Urge

Overkill, the Pumpkins had, according to Wyman, cast aside 'the harshness, contrariness and machismo of the underground in favour of a professed desire to sell records'.[14]

There was, as Steve Albini pointed out in a subsequent letter to Wyman, something truly absurd about this argument. 'If I read your heavily parenthetical English correctly,' he wrote, 'you are making the case that Liz Phair, Urge Overkill and the Smashing Pumpkins are somehow unique in rock music because they are brazenly trying to sell records. Genius.'[15] Albini, who had frequently described Corgan in the past as a careerist, now added the singer to his list of 1993's 'pandering sluts' — artists without principles, who served the service industry and left their integrity to rot.[16] There seemed to be some truth to this. Corgan had, by his own admission, sacked the band while recording *Siamese Dream* because they couldn't play up to the standard he needed, and this standard was at least partially determined by what he thought would get played on the radio. 'It's a good song,' he'd ask himself as he listened to the playback of 'Disarm', 'but is it a hit?'[17] When the song was a hit, and the album had raced to the top of the charts, he started 'leaping up and down in an airport somewhere. But it's not something I like talking about,' he quickly added, 'because I don't want people to think that success is all I care about.'[18]

Corgan cut short his victory dance because he knew what the Albinis of the world would say about him if they caught him doing it. But this was the whole point. For Corgan, people like Steve Albini were no different to the cool kids at school who'd looked down their noses at you because you dressed funny or didn't know what was 'in' and what wasn't. It was indie hipsters and ideologues that he'd had partly in mind when he wrote the lyrics to *Siamese Dream*'s ferocious opening number, 'Cherub Rock'. 'Freak out and give in,' he sighed, 'doesn't matter what you believe in / Stay cool, and be somebody's fool this year.'[19] Indie rock said it was cool to stay underground and make deliberately difficult music. But to be cool was to conform, and Corgan was resolved, in all things, to do only what he believed in, which in this case was playing world-class pop-rock for the masses. If the story of the Smashing Pumpkins could be said to have a moral, it was, as far as Corgan was concerned, be yourself.

Corgan's arena rock was not made for arena-rock fans; it was made for himself, because he was a born arena rocker. He had realised, sometime after the release of *Gish*, that he could no longer pretend that he was a cool indie musician. 'Bored by the task of saving face,' as he later put it, he'd admitted to himself that he was, at heart, 'a sappy rock boy' who wanted to write art-pop epics of love and loneliness.[20] This appeal to boyhood became key to the creation of *Siamese Dream*: the abused inner child accusing his parents in 'Quiet', the same child taking his revenge in 'Disarm', the recreated seventies pop wonderland of 'Spaceboy', the subsequent loss of innocence described in 'Geek USA'. And it was to his childhood that he'd turned when he began mixing the album. As he listened to the playback, he wondered whether his fourteen-year-old self would have loved it, and if the answer was yes, he knew he'd done good. If Corgan had 'pandered' to anyone in the making of his new album, it was to himself, and no-one else.

Corgan identified so completely with *Siamese Dream*, was so convinced that it represented his soul laid bare, that it became, as far as he was concerned, critic-proof. 'To hammer it because I made a deliberate attempt to beautify it, because I didn't just release some backroom demo with the guitars mixed too high, that's like criticizing me for the way I walk,' he said.[21] Criticism, for Corgan, was synonymous with personal abuse, and he'd put up with enough of that in his life already. The Smashing Pumpkins seldom played a bad show in 1993, but on those occasions when the band wasn't up to scratch, Corgan's temper got the better of him, and the gig deteriorated into an on-stage fight; Corgan claimed that this too was beyond the scope of criticism. 'Look,' he told Azerrad, 'I'm saying what I'm saying, and if you don't like it, too fucking bad. It's me, it comes from my heart, I'm not making it up. I think, in the long run, that kind of honesty is more important than sacrificing your integrity to being Gerry and the Pacemakers and putting on a good show.'[22] For Corgan to insist that it was better for him to preserve his self-esteem than to give his fans what they paid for might seem inconsiderate, but it was exactly this kind of self-assertion that they admired in him.

In the Shade

Having observed the spectacular rise of the Smashing Pumpkins in 1993, music writer Charles Aaron began to formulate a theory that alternative rock in the nineties amounted to a real-life *Revenge of the Nerds*, 'a group therapy session for kids who fancy themselves misunderstood'. But the Breeders' Kim and Kelley Deal were having none of it. 'High school is over,' declared Kelley, having heard out Aaron's hypothesis. 'Right,' agreed Kim, taking a drag of her cigarette as the band's tour bus sped down the interstate. 'Like we started this band to get back at all those people who were mean to us when we were kids. Sorry, it doesn't work that way.'[1] In an industry where victim status had become so desirable that even the oppressors wanted a piece of it, the idea that someone might have it and give it up was virtually unthinkable, but this was exactly what Kim Deal did in 1993.

Deal's story up to this point — talented female bass player and songwriter in seminal band, increasingly sidelined by egotistical male frontperson — had the makings of a perfect nineties drama. Her stoic silence as her songs disappeared from the Pixies albums would get the audience on side, the release of her own band's utterly brilliant second album, an album that eclipsed her former colleague's solo debut in every respect, would give Deal her triumphant final act. But the singer turned down the starring role in the story of her life, because the notion that she had been oppressed in the Pixies and deserved sympathy left her with what she described as 'a mixture of feelings'. On the one hand she felt it was nice that journalists and fans loved her and supported her career. On the other hand it sometimes gave her the feeling that she was in a school musical and her audience had turned into her mother. 'You know,' she joked, launching into a spot-on impression of Mrs Deal, 'Kim, you should be singing on this song. Why does that guy have the microphone all the time?'[2] The idea that she'd spent every night of the last two Pixies tours waiting eagerly for the set list to appear, only to slump back, crestfallen at the non-appearance of 'Gigantic' ('none of my songs *again*') was, she insisted, untrue, and gave her very little credit. The Pixies, Deal said, was a band. She had simply come to understand that Black Francis's increasing egomania would not allow for that band to have two lead singers, and as a result, she'd focused her creative energy on her own group, the Breeders.

The Breeders had existed since 1988, but the group's line-up had changed significantly in the intervening years. Tanya Donelly had left to start a new band called Belly; drummer Britt Walford, who also played in the Chicago group Slint, decided he couldn't commit to the Breeders, and left to pursue other projects (including the Palace Brothers). By the time Deal convened the band to record an EP in April 1992, the rollcall included ex-Perfect Disaster bassist Josephine Wiggs, new drummer Jim Macpherson, and Kim's twin sister, Kelley Deal. Kim had originally asked her if she could play drums. 'No,' said Kelley. 'I want to play lead guitar.' 'But Kelley, you can't play lead guitar,' Kim protested — to no avail.[3] She eventually relented. The Deal sisters had a history of making music together that went back to their teenage years in Dayton, Ohio. Whatever this curious new arrangement turned out to be, Kim felt sure it would at least be interesting.

When *Last Splash* was released in August 1993, it was clear that the experiment had paid off. Kelley didn't play guitar the way it was meant to be played, she'd never learned blues scales or chord progressions. But her lack of chops forced her to keep things simple, and what Kelley lacked in technique she more than made up for in imagination; her outbursts of noise and off-kilter lead melodies pushed the Breeders' songs into strange new territory. No muso would have thought to play the scrunched-up clusters of notes Kelley dropped between Kim's verses in 'New Year', but hearing the result, few would disagree that they served a song about cockroaches surviving the apocalypse better than anything Clapton could have come up with.

The guitar melody of 'Saints', Kim Deal explained, was a cross between 'When the Saints Go Marching In', and the opening riff of Black Sabbath's proto-metal classic 'Paranoid'.[4] This was no ironic joke — the Deal sisters had an abiding love for early seventies hard rock that went back to their youth. Both twins got heavily into music in 1975, when the radio was ruled by groups like Sabbath, Led Zeppelin, Aerosmith, Free and Deep Purple. But 'Saints' combined elements of this music with ideas drawn from the post punk bands the Deal sisters heard later in the decade. The song's minimalist structure and sparse use of language could be traced back to the deconstructed rock of Wire and Gang of Four; Kelley's lead playing came straight out of the tradition that those artists had sought to discredit and destroy. As far as the Breeders were concerned, there was no contradiction in this. The long-haired heroes of the seventies had made them want to be in a rock and roll band, post-punk had brought the music down to earth and allowed intelligent people to play it with a straight face. For the Breeders — as for other bands of their generation such as Soundgarden and the Flaming Lips — the task was to broker a reconciliation between the two approaches, to 'play Black Sabbath songs without the parts that suck' as Kim Thayil put it. But the goal was still to rock, to be in a band, to play big riffs, to drive around the country in a van and blow people away. Kim Deal had been doing this without a break since she joined the Pixies in 1987, Kelley — who had been working as a computer analyst until she joined the Breeders — embraced it all with the zeal of the newly converted. 'She's a rock and roll animal,' said a slightly awestruck Jim MacPherson after a show in Montreal in November 1993. 'She's way worse than Kim. She parties so hard, you wouldn't believe it.'[5]

The idea of a mostly female post-punk band living and playing like they were Led Zeppelin seemed designed to fulfill the wildest fantasies of rock critics in 1993, an act of feminist revenge on a par with Liz Phair's *Exile in Guyville* or PJ Harvey's cover of 'Highway 61 Revisited'. 'For the most part,' wrote music critic Mark Kates, '*Last Splash* is caught up in what it means to be the subject — the voice of rock and roll — and what it means to be female … The sisters Deal are lined up with Polly Harvey, questioning whether the rock and roll that's made an outsider of their gender can be trusted to get across their love, and their

161

dissatisfaction.'[6] But Kim Deal had about as much interest in playing the lead in this postmodern revenge tragedy as she did in acting out the part of the wronged woman in the Pixies. Deal dismissed as ridiculous the notion that she had been made an outsider by rock music. To her, the idea that women had been 'disempowered' by a chauvinistic rock culture was simply a cop-out. 'Really, a lot of women don't have the interest,' she told *Hot Press* magazine's Andy Darlington in October. 'You gotta go to the music store, you gotta find a guitar, you gotta learn it. Then you gotta carry it everywhere, and that fucker is heavy. It's hard, but that's what you gotta do.'[7] The Deal sisters' attitude to rock's macho culture hadn't changed much since they were a singing duo in Dayton, Ohio. They didn't see rock sexism as a power structure they had to define themselves against. They'd realised early on that rock was stupid, but more fun than anything else, and had always believed that they could do it better anyway. 'We played in bars and ignored what people said,' Kelley later recalled. 'After all, we knew that the people who thought they were badass didn't rock *at all*.'[8]

In the summer of 1992, the Breeders toured Europe with Nirvana, and Kelley kept herself amused in the tour van by reading a biography of the Marquis de Sade, the notorious eighteenth-century sex criminal and author of violent pornographic novels such as *Justine* and *The 120 Days of Sodom*. Leafing through it one day, Kim decided that she was unimpressed — she'd read enough of the marquis' fevered imaginings to know she could think of worse — and began writing a song in which she challenged him, as she later put it, to 'an immoral duel'. 'I was like, okay, you little libertine,' she explained to Richard Kingsmill in a mocking singsong. 'You know, "You're a real cuckoo".'[9] There was, to Kim Deal, something pathetic about de Sade. He seemed to her like a kid at a party, determined to show off by doing a cannonball into the pool and making the biggest splash. In her playground ode to the divine Marquis, Deal dismissed the whole game as childish, and knew she could afford to since she could easily win it if she chose to, that she could think the filthiest thoughts, make the loudest noise, be the biggest badass. 'You wanna go to hell?' she thought, as she tossed Kelley's book into the back of the van. 'Go ahead, do a cannonball. I'll be the last splash.'[10]

Family Values

Reviewing *Last Splash* in *Hot Press* magazine, Niall Crumlish remarked on how much more fun it was than the Breeders' first album, *Pod*. He attributed this not to Kelley Deal's discovery of her inner rock pig, Kim's newfound love for surf music or Jim MacPherson's southern-fried funk, but to the fact that *Pod*'s producer, Steve Albini, had not been invited back for *Last Splash*. 'Albini's absence from the producer chair contributes handsomely to this record,' he wrote. 'Several of these songs would no doubt have been rendered unlistenable by him.'[1] But this lucky break was offset by a potential disaster on the horizon. In four weeks, Geffen would release Nirvana's new Albini-produced album, *In Utero*. Nirvana had been talking for six months about how they wanted to lose most of their audience so they could go back to playing clubs, how they wanted to scare the pants off MTV viewers with an abrasive lo-fi punk album, and how they'd specifically sought Albini's help in making the new record sound as much like the Breeders' *Pod* as possible. Reviewers, fans and industry folk braced themselves for the very real possibility that Steve Albini had taken the band that had made rock music fun again, and made it no fun at all.

The release of *In Utero*'s first single was accompanied by a worldwide sigh of relief. 'Heart-Shaped Box' was no alienating noise-fest. It was a haunted love song for Courtney Love with a pleasurably noisy chorus in the much loved quiet/loud/quiet style of *Nevermind*. The song had been recorded at Pachyderm Studios during the sessions with Albini, but had been remixed and overdubbed by another producer — Scott Litt, best known for his work with R.E.M. Albini was predictably angry about his work being vandalised after the fact, and gave a series of interviews in which he explained how Geffen had put pressure on the band to make the album sound more commercial. And yet, as Cobain was careful to point out, this was not exactly what had happened. The Geffen execs had hated Albini's work, but they were always going to. What had surprised the singer was that he found himself agreeing with them. 'The first time I played it at home, I knew something was wrong,' he told *Melody Maker* in August. 'I got no emotion from it.'[2] This first draft of *In Utero* had, in a sense, turned out exactly the way Cobain had hoped it would — it was brutal, alienating and cold as the grave. 'Typical Steve Albini,' as he later put it, 'the sound we wanted really bad.'[3]

But almost nine months had passed since the singer had decided this was the kind of album he'd wanted to make, and his outlook had changed considerably in the meantime. He'd fallen in love, got married and had become a father, and these things had made him happier than he'd been at any time in his adult life. He became, as he later explained, 'a lot more optimistic about everything', and as a result the outsider stance he'd been maintaining over the past eighteen months started to look as though it came more from paranoia than principles. He realised that his constant complaints were turning him into a crank and a bore, Seattle's answer to Sinéad O'Connor, whom he poked gentle fun at in 'Radio Friendly Unit Shifter' with the line 'I do not want what I have got'.[4] This, he felt, was how the public was starting to see him — as an ungrateful rock brat. The new album's projected title, 'I hate myself and want to die', was a joke about what he thought his audience thought he was like, as was the chorus of 'Heart-Shaped Box'. Just when you thought the young rock star, having got everything he wanted, had settled down, he popped up again like a depressing jack-in-the-box. 'Hey! Wait! I've got a new complaint!'[5]

Cobain made a resolution to be less of a grunge cliché. 'For the most part,' he said of the new album, 'I made sure not to complain. I really tried not to.'[6] There were outbursts on *In Utero*, of course, most notably on 'Rape Me', a last ditch attempt to make himself heard on the subject of women's treatment at the hands of men ('It's like, how obvious do I have to be?').[7] But even this had an ironic quality about it. After a year of playing anti-rape songs for date rapists with no discernable effect on their behaviour, Cobain had lost much of his faith in the idea of music as a form of communication, and had decided that it was a far more effective use of the band's time and money to play fundraisers and benefits than to preach at people with song lyrics. 'We're not a PC band,' he told a reporter in October. 'I mean, we're entertainers! That's what music is about.'[8] *In Utero* was, in the end, still a long way from most people's idea of entertainment — its eruptions of post-punk fury were as terrifying as its pop tunes were pretty. But by the time the band got around to remixing the album, Cobain had decided that he was more interested in pleasing his fans than pissing them off, that he wanted to give them something they'd love, not something they'd hate. Having accepted this, the decision to have Scott Litt add some harmonies and overdubs to 'Heart-Shaped Box' was an easy one to make. Fixing the rest of the album was not that hard either. Albini's horror-movie mix had made the record sound disturbingly uneven. Litt simply turned the vocals up, gave Novoselic's bass some much-needed definition, and added some compression to the final mix to smooth things out. 'That did it,' said Cobain.[9]

It had been an article of faith in the non-service industries for over fifty years that what most people called normal life, the daily routine of working, shopping and consuming entertainment, was sick and absurd, and that artists, by dint of being liberated from the social bullshit of their societies, were the only ones who could see that this was the case. If the modern rock star's job was — as most modern rock stars believed — to tell ugly home truths about modern life, then the ability to complain effectively was as important to a rock career as the ability to play guitar. 'You always write about what isn't fixed in your day-to-day life,' said Liz Phair, 'those parts of you that feel like: "Hey, wait a minute!".'[10] Phair saw the artist's role as being permanently unsettled, standing outside of society, pointing out its shortcomings and demanding change. In 4 Non Blondes' 1993 hit 'What's Up?', singer Linda Perry made this seem a very noble pursuit indeed. Perry sang about stepping out into the street in the morning and asking, 'What's going on?', and insisted that she would keep repeating this question until America was made fair once again. 'I pray every single day,' she sang, 'for revolution.'[11]

But by the end of 1993, Kurt Cobain had begun to wonder whether this idea might be a lie — a self-serving fantasy designed to make artists feel special and privileged, when in fact they were the ones whose lives had become sick and absurd. Cobain suspected that the artist's complaint, his incessant need to ask 'What's going on?', was not a brilliant insight, but a symptom of neurosis, which he hoped medical science would soon be able to cure. 'I wish there was a pill that would allow me to be amused by television and just enjoy simple things instead of being so judgemental,' he said in August.[12] Chatting with Everett True and the Breeders' Kim Deal on Christmas Eve, he told True that he admired Deal for being 'upbeat and happy and friendly', while he was 'pissy and mean'.[13] To Cobain, Deal was one of the very few rock stars in 1993 who didn't confuse art with therapy, who saw music not as a way to get back at a world that never understood her, but as a good job where you get to play guitar, smoke pot and make kids dance.

True talked to them about Christmas, and went on a lengthy rant about how Christmas sucked because it reinforced the false values of Western society and its patriarchal family structure. Deal puffed on her joint and laughed, Kurt remarked that it sounded like something he'd told the journalist in 1992. 'I don't see anything good in the family structure,' said True. 'I do,' Cobain protested, 'if it's a good family.' True asked Deal and Cobain what they wanted for Christmas. 'You know those reindeers that you can hang on shower stalls and you have the radio on while you're taking a shower?' said Deal. 'That's what I want.' Cobain thought of his wife, who would soon be returning home from Atlanta, where she'd been mixing the new Hole album with Scott Litt. 'I just want to have a nice, quiet casual Christmas with Frances and Courtney,' he said.[14] The values True had been so strenuously denouncing were exactly the ones Cobain had recently learned to embrace. He was tired of standing outside the world and pouring scorn on it, he wanted to do what everybody else did — to work and get paid, watch TV and buy Christmas presents, to love and be loved. It might make him dumb, but it did make him happy.

1994

The Job We Never Wanted

'Fuck these fucking people,' said Eddie Vedder in November 1993. The singer threw the music paper he'd been reading into a corner, stood up and looked Q magazine's Matt Snow directly in the eye. 'Fuck you,' he growled. 'Fuck 'em all. Fuck the whole thing. Because it's totally fucked. Totally ridiculous.' Vedder stomped out of the room.[1] His outburst had been prompted by a review of Pearl Jam's recent London show, in which he was described as a 'sensitive, overblown, preening gibbering pretence of a poet', who suffered from 'a messiah complex' backed by a band of 'cock-rock strutters extraordinaire'.[2] Even for the British music press, which tended to look down its nose at Pearl Jam, this was harsh. But Vedder didn't need a bad review to send him over the edge in 1993. Even the good things about being in a band were starting to piss him off. Pearl Jam's second LP, *Vs*, had sold over a million copies in its first week of release, making it the fastest-selling album in chart history. This had catapulted Pearl Jam into the upper echelons of rock fame; Vedder's face and voice were everywhere, and the *Vs* tour played to stadiums. But this state of affairs did not suit Vedder at all. 'I don't like rock stars,' he said, 'and here I am being turned into one.'[3] The singer who'd happily mingled with his fans at Lollapalooza in 1992 now wore monster masks in public so that nobody would recognise him or try to take his picture, and when he found out Pearl Jam had been booked to play a 10,000 seat sports arena in Rotterdam, he dashed the cup of herbal tea he'd been drinking to the floor in a fit of rage. 'How can you have a religious experience in a venue this size?' he asked *Spin's* Jim Greer. 'I feel like someone has to stick up for the music.'[4]

Vedder felt betrayed by the music business, suspicious toward his fans, and was losing his faith in rock and roll itself. He was in dire need of some perspective, and a book he'd started reading while on tour in the UK seemed to offer exactly that. Shortly before the paper-throwing outburst in London, Matt Snow had remarked on the copy of Kurt Vonnegut's *God Bless You, Mr Rosewater* sticking out of the singer's bag. 'His sense of ironicism is unparalleled,' said Vedder. 'I'm inspired by this kind of thing. Irony. It's a good way to look at the world, you know, a sense of irony. Seems a good way to get out of it without feeling suicidal, to get a laugh out of it. Seems like the English are pretty ironic.'[5] Here, Vedder hit on one of the main reasons why English critics disliked his band. Pearl Jam, it was felt, had no sense of irony, and this was agreed to be a problem common to many of the new US bands, including Soundgarden, the Smashing Pumpkins and Alice in Chains. 'American rock,' said Pulp singer Jarvis Cocker in April 1993, 'takes itself far too seriously.'[6] Cocker was being interviewed by *Select* magazine for a cover story called 'Who Do You Think You Are Kidding, Mr Cobain?', the second major offensive in British music's war of emancipation, following the release of Blur's *Modern Life is Rubbish* in March. 'What makes British pop great is that there is some sense of dryness or wryness, I suppose what you'd have to call irony,' said Luke Haines of the Auteurs. 'It's something American music totally lacks.'[7] Vedder's musings on 'ironicism' would have confirmed what most British critics and indie-pop pundits already believed — that American songwriters could not use irony because they hadn't quite grasped the concept.

In writing up his interview with Vedder, Matt Snow had great fun at the singer's expense by portraying him as having unwittingly confirmed his own theory about himself by mispronouncing the word at the centre of his argument, which was itself very ironic. What was even more ironic was that America's irony deficiency was vastly overrated by the British, who only managed to convince themselves that they could do it while the Americans couldn't, because they failed to grasp the subtler permutations of American irony. But this was an easy mistake to make. Irony — as Winona Ryder discovered in *Reality Bites* — is notoriously difficult to define, and comes in several different varieties.[8] Vedder had become a victim of situational or cosmic irony, which is the kind that happens to you whether you like it or not. What he longed for was an ironic point of view on the world, a semi-detached position somewhere outside of his own predicament, from which he imagined he might be able to greet the demise of his generation's ideals with a shrug.

This is romantic irony — so-called because it began with German Romantics like Schlegel, Heine and Holderlin in the early part of the nineteenth century. Romantic irony evolved as a response to disappointment and failure. It was developed and perfected by poets born during or after the French Revolution — who grew up on stories of the Terror and the Napoleonic wars, but came of age in far less interesting times — a politically conservative climate in which bourgeois values held sway. For obvious reasons, romantic irony turned out to be ideally suited to American indie rock, a style invented by losers in a decade of winners, a genre whose history was, as Bruce Pavitt insisted in 1995, 'the history of failure'.[9] It was first adopted by the Replacements, embraced by Seattle groups like Mudhoney and Nirvana (whose 'Smells Like Teen Spirit' was, after all, heavily ironic), taken to fresh heights of absurdity by Urge Overkill and the Jon Spencer Blues Explosion, and refined to perfection by Pavement.

Pavement's second album, 1994's *Crooked Rain, Crooked Rain*, offered a frequently hilarious insect's eye view on the process that was then driving Eddie Vedder to the edge of a nervous breakdown: the commercialisation of indie rock. 'Music seems crazy, bands start up each and every day,' sang Stephen Malkmus on the album's first single, 'Cut Your Hair'. Malkmus cheerfully described the industry's need for special new bands with 'advertisin' looks and chops', and erupted in unexpected fury as he set down the new rules for grunge photo shoots: 'No big hair!'[10] In his cracked croon, the singer condensed the careers of countless early nineties hopefuls into a series of tiny vignettes. 'Face right down to the practice room,' he yelped. 'Tension and things, a career, career, career.'[11] Other songs described the indie music fan's secret craving for nostalgia, the speedy proliferation of subcultures in alternative rock, and the sad inability of eighties guitar heroes to keep up with the new authenticity.

'A lot of the lyrics and sound of the new record was because of where we recorded in New York City,' explained guitarist Scott Kannberg. 'It was a music building with all these struggling bands. Had all these rehearsal spaces in the place, and we'd see these people every day. Just kinda made us a little sad.'[12] Steve Albini had noted late in 1993 the way that many people in the indie rock community were trying to turn their bands into small businesses and had ended up hating their bands the way they used to hate their jobs. 'It's almost turned into the job we never wanted,' said Pearl Jam's Stone Gossard in 1992.[13] And groups like Gossard's, who'd since upscaled their operations into big business whether by accident or design, hated being rock CEOs even more than their less-successful peers disliked their jobs in sales and marketing. By 1993, the sense of disillusionment had, for many, soured into despair. 'Up until about two weeks ago, I thought being in a band was all I needed,' said Juliana Hatfield, 'it was the best thing. But now something's missing.' 'Oh God, I know,' replied her friend Evan Dando. 'It's that hollow feeling, that creepy, hollow, existentialist sort of Sunday kind of yikes.'[14] It was easy to see the tragedy in all of this, in the sorry tales of indie rockers who'd sold out their ideals for money and fame, and the even sadder spectacle of a hundred flannel-clad hopefuls rushing, lemming-like to do the same. But only Pavement seemed able to see the funny side, to stand back and view the whole thing as an ironic joke rather than a painful disaster.

Of course it helped that Pavement had, by 1994, experienced nothing like the level of fame and exposure that Pearl Jam, Alice in Chains and Nirvana had. But it was the group's inability to take indie rock too seriously in the first place that had allowed it to avoid the industry's temptations. Pavement had begun its career with what the *NME* described as 'the non-career move to end them all' of having its membership split between two different cities on opposite sides of the country. 'Photo shoots featuring the whole band are rare,' observed the magazine's Keith Cameron.[15] And if Pavement sometimes seemed like an awkward amalgam of two completely different groups, its drummer, a forty-something studio owner named Gary Young, gave the impression that he was in a third. He never really sounded as though he'd learned the songs, and openly admitted in interviews that he

171

neither liked nor understood Pavement's music. Young quit the group at the end of 1993 because he couldn't comprehend why his bandmates didn't want to sign to a major label and become MTV stars.

Irony had afforded Malkmus some much-needed perspective on life in general and music in particular. He'd been aware since he'd started the band that rock and roll was slightly ridiculous, and was clearly bemused by much of the new earnestness. He once compared 'Alive' to Gloria Gaynor's 'I Will Survive', which he said was 'like that Pearl Jam guy, but without flannel, and moshers',[16] and poked fun at the Smashing Pumpkins and Stone Temple Pilots in 'Range Life'. Malkmus had trouble taking these bands seriously because he saw seriousness itself as a problem in rock, and believed that the kind of 'religious experience' that Vedder attached so much importance to should be done away with as soon as possible. The rituals of rock, he explained to Richard Kingsmill in 1993, were there to maintain 'the Gothic aura, the sort of separateness that dates back to Roman times'. But the singer was quick to dispel the idea that his detachment made Pavement's music dispassionate. 'There is some distance,' he acknowledged. 'Our goal is to have some throwaway humour, like [French Art Brut painter] Jean Dubuffet, and then to kick in with something we really feel.'[17] Pavement was, fundamentally, a rock and roll band rather than an essay or an arty joke, and could be enjoyed on a simple rock and roll level. 'There are some good riffs and some good shalalas,' he insisted.[18]

Malkmus also disputed the idea that irony had made Pavement permanently jaded, as though the band's Olympian view of the music scene had left it without the will to rock. 'People tend to think our band is defeatist,' he said, 'but it's not true.'[19] The idea that Pavement suffered from existential laziness came partly from the lo-fi sound of its early recordings, partly from the band's apparent determination to sabotage its own success, but mostly from the coincidence of its arrival along with Richard Linklater's *Slacker* and other manifestations of the 'pathetic aesthetic' in the early nineties. The association had helped Pavement at the time, but by 1994, 'slacker' was over, run into the ground by the ubiquity of Beck's 'Loser' and Radiohead's 'Creep', and finally reduced to a pop cartoon by Ethan Hawke's character in *Reality Bites*, a goateed singer-songwriter with a disaffected manner and a grungy theme tune called 'I'm Nuthin'. Linklater himself had long since moved away from the subject of slackers, and had turned his attention to a drama set in an American high school in the mid seventies. The least Pavement could do, according to Scott Kannberg, was to keep up with the director. 'This new album is more influenced by [Linklater's] second film, *Dazed and Confused*,' the guitarist explained. 'So we don't really like being called "slacker rock" anymore because we feel like we've gone beyond our "slacker" stage and into our *Dazed and Confused* stage.'[20]

The *Dazed and Confused* soundtrack had been one of 1993's supreme guilty pleasures, an immaculate collection of pre-punk classics by Alice Cooper, Nazareth, Black Oak Arkansas, Deep Purple and Black Sabbath. The album was perfectly matched to the alt-rock zeitgeist in a year when the Breeders covered Aerosmith, the Stone Temple Pilots swiped Zeppelin riffs, and Soundgarden finally made it cool for people to admit that they liked Sabbath. Most of the grunge bands were influenced by seventies hard rock to some extent, and the mere fact that long-haired guitar groups were filling stadiums full of teenagers made the connection even more obvious. 'With all the lighters out there it felt like we were doing Aerosmith "Dream On",' remarked Krist Novoselic after a Nirvana show in 1993.[21]

But there was a stark contrast between seventies stadium rock and its nineties variant. Nirvana, Pearl Jam, Soundgarden, Stone Temple Pilots and Alice in Chains sang about alienation, parental abuse, depression, date rape, the corporate exploitation of youth culture, heroin addiction, and suicide. The music on the *Dazed and Confused* soundtrack seemed to come from a more innocent time, when bands and their fans didn't have to worry about these things, since it was mostly about getting high and rocking out. This, Malkmus insisted, was as it should be. 'Rock and roll should be about cigarettes and alcohol and fun and shagging and making out and stuff like that,' he said.[22] The music on *Crooked Rain, Crooked Rain* was influenced as much by Led Zeppelin, Kiss and Aerosmith as it was by earlier Pavement favourites such as The Fall and Swell Maps, from the loud and proud cowbell in 'Silence Kit' to the stately feel of 'Fillmore Jive', an elegy for the golden age of stadium rock, wherein Malkmus bade 'goodnight to the rock and roll era' and observed the appearance of new faces on the seventies music scene: 'Jam kids on their Vespas, with glum looks on their faces.' By the end of the song 'the street is full of punks', and the long-haired rockers fade out of sight.[23]

Dazed and Confused's final act takes place at a keg party in the forest. At one point, Cynthia, played by Marissa Ribisi, entertains a small audience of stoners with a theory designed to explain the strange sense of disappointment that had overtaken youth culture since Woodstock. Pop time, she explains, is not a slippery slope, but a turning cycle. 'It's like the every other decade theory,' she explains. 'The fifties were boring, the sixties rocked, the seventies — oh my God, they obviously suck. Maybe the nineteen-eighties will be radical, y'know?'[24] The joke, of course, was that Cynthia had no idea that she was living in a golden age full of 'Gold Soundz'; that the junk lying around her bedroom was exactly the kind of stuff nineties hipsters like Janeane Garofalo's Vicki in *Reality Bites* would be obsessing over in twenty years' time; that the Thin Lizzy and Black Oak Arkansas records in the box by her bed would one day become hip-hop fetish objects. Linklater's joke raised a hopeful possibility too. Most smart high school kids in 1993 felt exactly as Cynthia did in 1976, that they were living in a disappointing decade full of used-up ideas. Might they be as wrong as she obviously was? Was it possible that the nineties was a great era in the making, and that the music of Nirvana, Pearl Jam and even Pavement might one day be considered classic? Stephen Malkmus, in 1994, declared it too close to call. 'You have to wait,' he warned.[25] In the meantime, the band, having successfully surfed the zeitgeist by following indie movie trends, waited to see what their next move should be. 'I just hope Richard Linklater makes a great third film,' said Kannberg.[26]

There were other signs that American irony was alive and well in 1994, not the least of which was the release of the self-titled debut album by Weezer in May. Weezer's litany of ironic failure began with its cover, which showed the four band members wearing ordinary clothes and standing up straight in front of a plain blue background. Singer Rivers Cuomo insisted that this no-frills packaging was not, as it was for other alternative bands, a victory of truth over style, but the result of the group's failure to dress itself correctly. Cuomo had long since cut off his big hair and hidden the eighties metal clothes he'd worn when he first moved to LA at the back of the closet, but he and the band didn't really identify with grunge, so there was no question of them donning flannel and growing goatees. As a result, the band had no style to speak of, and the cover image, Cuomo said, ended up being 'just a boring old picture of the four of us standing there like idiots'.[27] The awkward vibe carried over to the album's first single, 'Buddy Holly', a new wave-ish pop song, which began with an assortment of inappropriate borrowings from nineties gangsta rap. 'What's with these homies dissin' my girl?' Cuomo wailed. 'Why do they gotta front?'[28]

The song's scenario — a nervous nerd in spectacles who gets beaten on by tough guys, awkwardly declaring his love for a girl who looks like Mary Tyler Moore — evoked the fifties, as did the title. But for the twenty-something members of Weezer and their MTV-watching teen audience, memories of the fifties could only be memories of *Happy Days,* the long-running seventies sitcom that catered to the nostalgic remorse of baby boomers while inadvertently worming its way into the subconscious of their children. In the 'Buddy Holly' video, director Spike Jonze magically inserted the band onto the set of Happy Days — dressed in matching suits, they performed their song while Al looked on approvingly and Arthur 'the Fonz' Fonzarelli busted a move on the dance floor. Jonze's video suited the song to a tee, but the band, it seemed, were no more comfortable in the fifties than they were in the nineties. Bass player Matt Sharp deferred to the superior style of the Fonz. 'He is the essence of cool,' he explained in an interview with Public Access TV in Long Beach, California. 'Just like you guys, right?' asked the reporter. 'Yeah,' replied Sharp with a sarcastic laugh. 'Right.'[29]

I'm in the Band

In March 1994, Pamela Des Barres interviewed Courtney Love at the singer's home in Seattle. 'In some ways, I'm really excited to do this interview with you,' said Love. 'In other ways, I don't want to identify myself with you, even though I totally do identify with so much of your life. But you know, it's that word.' 'The G-word?' offered Des Barres.[1] Hole's frontwoman, like any good student of rock history, had read Des Barres's memoir of the sixties, *I'm with the Band: The Confessions of a Groupie* from cover to cover. She related to it, in the sense that she'd always been attracted by the sexual energy of rock, 'watching guys that make you want to fuck them' as she put it. But she despised groupies. 'It's such a waste of female energy,' she said. Love told Des Barres a story about going to the after-party for a Billy Idol concert with Faith No More's Roddy Bottum in the late eighties, watching the girls in the bathroom adjusting their tube-tops and make-up in the hope that tonight they might finally get past the road manager and sleep with Idol's drummer. 'If I gave each one of you a guitar and taught you how to play,' she thought to herself, 'you'd be repulsed. You wouldn't even want the power.'[2] Love believed that the future of rock belonged to women, but only if they stopped pouting into the mirror and started practising. 'Get some guitars!' she told MTV's female viewers in February. 'This is the nineties — empower yourself!'[3]

Love told Des Barres how she had trained herself, over the years, to reroute the effort she might otherwise have put into sleeping with rock stars into becoming a rock star. Riding the Greyhound bus into Seattle, she'd dreamed of conquering Mark Arm in a professional, rather than a romantic sense, of having Mudhoney open for Hole before the year was out. Twelve months later, the two bands toured the UK together. Hole's name appeared below Mudhoney's on the marquee, but Love was still determined to beat the boys on their own terms, or at least match them, to scream just as loud, to trash just as much gear, if not more, than the headline band. This spirit of one-upmanship led to one of the most notorious episodes of Love's career. On tour, she watched Arm dive into the crowd and surf to the back of the room every night. 'Why can't I have the same level of contact with the audience that these guys do?' she wondered. Love decided to give it a try one night in London. 'I was wearing a dress and I didn't realize what I was engendering in the audience,' she told Des Barres. 'It was a huge audience and they were kind of going ape-shit. So I just dove off the stage, and suddenly, it was like my dress was being torn off of me, my underwear was being torn off of me, people were putting their fingers inside of me and grabbing my breasts really hard, screaming things in my ears like "pussy-whore-cunt". When I got back onstage I was naked.'[4]

No story more clearly demonstrated the ideological divide between Courtney Love and her contemporaries. At the same time Love was diving into the pit, Bikini Kill was reorganising the social structure of the mosh so as to make it safe for girls. But Love wasn't interested in creating a separate space for women in rock, either literally or metaphorically, on stage or in the reviews columns of the music magazines — to her, riot grrrl's rejection of rock standards was little more than a cop-out, where girls win the game by rewriting the rules. 'As supportive as I am of them,' she told Des Barres, 'there's a faction that says, "We don't know how to play, but we're not going to follow your male-measured idea of what good is." Look, good is *Led Zeppelin II*. That's fucking good.'[5] Love had no interest in what *Beavis and Butt-Head* called 'sucking on purpose'; she wanted Hole to compete in the same league as Led Zeppelin, Van Halen or Nirvana, because she was, and always had been, intensely competitive. When Tatum O'Neal won an Oscar at the age of ten in 1973, Love was furious that she hadn't got it herself. When Joe Strummer told her, in 1987, that she was the worst guitarist he'd ever heard, it made her more determined than ever to be the female Jimi Hendrix. When Guns N' Roses ruled hard rock in the late eighties, she formed a band called Hole in order to destroy them. 'All I wanted to do,' she later explained, 'was to fuck them up.'[6] Now, in 1994, she was married to the most famous rock singer in the world. 'Do you feel competitive with him?' asked Des Barres. 'I just wish that his band was smaller,' Love replied.[7]

Cobain, of course, had often wished for the same thing over the past year, as his family life turned into a soap opera and his privacy disappeared. Nirvana's ballooning fame, his own wish for peace and quiet, the press's insatiable appetite for scandal, his addiction to heroin, Love's almost pathological need for attention, and the couple's fierce determination to protect their daughter proved a volatile mix in 1993. 'I hadn't punched anyone since the third grade,' Love told a music TV program in England. 'But I hit two people this year.'[8] In February 1994, Love appeared on the cover of *Melody Maker* with a cigarette in her hand and a rueful smile on her face, under a quote from the interview she'd given Caitlin Moran. 'One thing this last terrible year has proved: if you lie about us, I will hit you, Kurt will shoot you, and we will sue.'[9]

The chaos of Love and Cobain's personal life inevitably found its way into the new Hole songs Love was writing, and lent a strangely premonitory quality to some older ones. 'Doll Parts' was a song she and guitarist Eric Erlandson had begun working on not long after the release of *Pretty on the Inside* in 1991. It was written about Cobain before the two became a couple, and described the mixture of desire, admiration and envy Love felt toward the nascent rock star, and toward male rock stars in general. 'I want to be the girl with the most cake,' she sang. 'I love him so much it just turns to hate.' 'Doll Parts' put Love in one corner of a love triangle between the star and his fans, and insisted that she be entitled to more of his attention than the rest of them put together. 'Yeah, they really want you,' she taunted, 'but I do too.'[10] If this line was affecting in 1991, it was positively chilling in 1993, when the number of people who wanted Kurt Cobain had grown from hundreds to millions.

'Doll Parts' was recorded for Hole's new album with Love playing the song on a warm-sounding acoustic guitar, her tough voice sweetened by multi-tracked harmonies. The album as a whole saw the group move away from the confrontational racket of *Pretty on the Inside*; songs like 'Softer, Softest' and 'Miss World' owed more to Fleetwood Mac than they did to Big Black, and Love's new wave fetishes were proudly on display: the windswept atmosphere of 'Plump' recalled Bauhaus, the skipping hi-hats and heartracing bassline of 'Jennifer's Body' betrayed the influence of New Order's 'Temptation'. Love explained to a reporter backstage at the VMAs that the new Hole album would be different because 'I write better songs now'.[11] But she'd also made a conscious decision to make an album people would love. She took great care over the songs' arrangements, and spent hours with producer Paul Q Kolderie finessing the sound. Her philosophy of pop, in 1993, was analogous to her approach to beauty and style. 'I have to be pretty if I'm going to get over,' she told zine writer Lisa Carver in November. 'And I have to get over if I'm going to fuck up the system. And I'm going to fuck it up.'[12]

By the time Love met Des Barres in March, Hole was getting over. The single, 'Miss World', was already on high rotation on MTV, and the music industry was buzzing with talk of Hole having fashioned something magical out of Courtney Love's annus horribilis. '*Live Through This* is about to come out, and everyone is expecting it to be really big,' said Des Barres, making small talk with drummer Patty Schemel and bass player Kristen Pfaff while she waited for Love to wake up from her afternoon nap. 'I'm afraid to think like that,' said Pfaff. 'Yeah,' said Schemel, 'we don't want to jinx it.'[13]

Usual Torments

In theory, 1994 should have got off to a good start for Eddie Vedder. The new year was supposed to have seen the singer make a public reconciliation with Kurt Cobain, as Nirvana and Pearl Jam shared the stage at a televised MTV spectacular. But when it came time to film the event on 24 December 1993, Vedder was nowhere to be found. The official explanation given was that he was sick and had lost his voice. But rumours had begun to circulate: that the singer was scared of his arch-nemesis, that he had refused to play unless Pearl Jam's name appeared at the top of the bill, or that he had simply decided to go surfing instead. 'I heard that Eddie Vedder escaped,' said Kurt Cobain as he sat backstage, talking with Kim Deal and Everett True. 'He ran away, they can't find him.'[1]

Vedder was, in truth, extremely ill. The pent-up stress and exhaustion of the *Vs* tour had hit him like a ton of bricks the moment he'd got home to Seattle. 'I was really fucked up,' he explained to *Melody Maker*'s Allan Jones. 'And then they were calling, saying, "Well, can you be better by Tuesday? Can you do this? Can you do that? Can you play the show?" And I was feeling like shit.'[2] But while the story that Vedder had walked into Seattle's Pier 48, seen the lights, cameras and rows of empty seats, turned on his heel and run as far from the place as possible was untrue, Vedder admitted it was plausible. There were many times, toward the end of the *Vs* tour, when he'd contemplated doing exactly that.

Over the previous six months, the singer had found himself in show business, and by the end of the year had come to the firm conclusion that it was not the kind of business he wanted to be in. The golden rule of show business, after all, was 'the show must go on'. But Vedder could not go on with the show at the expense of his integrity — and this was what he felt was at stake that particular night, as it had been on many other nights of the *Vs* tour. Vedder was admired by critics and loved by fans because he seemed able to connect on an emotional level with every audience he met. And yet this was not an easy thing for the singer to do. 'The songs, in order for me to sing them, have to be felt,' he said.[3] Some nights he just didn't feel it. But since he had to give the audience what they expected of him, he had been forced — more times than he would have liked — to fabricate little details of emotional expression on stage so that his performance would register with the crowd as sincere. Vedder now had to be fake in order to seem real, and the cruel irony of this situation kept him up many nights during the early months of 1994. In the wee hours of the morning on the 3 April, Vedder called a friend and spilled his guts. 'If you go out and do three shows, it's great,' he explained. 'If you do sixty, somewhere along the line, you're going to become an actor.'[4]

The next day, Kurt Cobain pulled a disappearing act of his own. Having not seen or heard from the singer in several days, his mother filed a missing persons report with the Seattle police, and Cobain's friends began to worry for him. They had every reason to do so. Early in March, shortly after Nirvana had finished a tour of Germany, Cobain had overdosed on pills and champagne in a hotel in Rome, and no-one — least of all Courtney Love — believed this had been an accident. When Love walked into the room and found her husband on the floor, she was certain he'd killed himself. Cobain had been discharged from the hospital in reasonably good physical and mental health, but two weeks later had spun out of control again, locking himself in his room with a gun and a bottle of pills. Love had organised an intervention, which seemed to turn him around somewhat, and the singer checked into a Los Angeles rehab clinic on 30 March. But he escaped the following day, and had hardly been seen since.

Five days later, Seattle's KSTW news opened with an extraordinary story. 'The voice of grunge music takes his own life. Seattle's Kurt Cobain is dead.'[5] The report told of how an electrician had come to Cobain and Love's house to do some repairs at around 8.30 in the morning, and had found the singer lying on the floor of the living room with his head blown apart by a shotgun blast. 'There was a note on the counter on a full-sized sheet of paper,' the man explained. 'I only read the bottom line. It said, "I love you, I love you".'[6] 'Details of the suicide note,' said the news anchor, 'have not been released.' The screen showed Nirvana fans gathering in gloomy clusters outside the house, holding one another and crying, and footage of a local DJ, playing one of hundreds of requests for Nirvana songs he'd received since the news broke. The news anchor promised that when the show returned from a commercial break, they would talk to Nirvana fans and try to find out 'why this talented millionaire took his own life'.[7]

The contents of the letter were finally revealed two days later, when over 7,000 mourners gathered at the Seattle Center to hear a recording of Courtney Love reading the note in full. Love, who sounded as though she'd been crying for hours, provided a live commentary on her husband's words as she read, poking fun at him, cursing him, pleading with him and calling his bluff, as she did with the letter's closing paragraph. '"And remember …"' she read. Then, seeing what was coming next, she addressed the audience, saying, 'And don't remember this 'cause it's a fuckin' lie.' She went on, with a heavy sigh. '"And remember, it's better to burn out than to fade away."'[8] Love was fighting history, and she knew it. The power of the myth Cobain was invoking by quoting Neil Young's elegy for punk rock was too strong to be dispelled by any disclaimer. Before she'd even read the note, the world had made up its mind about what her husband's death meant. Adulthood, it seemed to say, means lies and compromises, money and boredom. Die young, and you'll always smell like teen spirit. By sacrificing his life for his art, Cobain had guaranteed himself a place in rock's pantheon. Or, as his mother put it on learning of his death, 'joined that stupid club'.[9] 'I guess you gotta go out in a blaze of glory,' offered one of the Nirvana fans gathered outside Cobain's house on the afternoon of his death.[10] Cobain himself would never use a word like 'glory' to describe anything he did, but his suicide note revealed that rock's first law of thermodynamics was not too far from his mind when he pulled the trigger of his shotgun.

The *NME* marked Cobain's death by running a sombre black and white photo of the singer on its cover. Cobain stared soulfully from behind his stringy hair, wearing heavy black eyeliner and a five-o'clock shadow. The paper's designers cleared away the usual clutter of the front page to make way for a simple typographic tombstone: 'Kurt Cobain (1967–1994)'.[11] The image seemed ready made for rock's gallery of martyrs, as did *Melody Maker*'s cover shot of a worried-looking Cobain in sunglasses standing on a New York street.[12] But as David Stubbs pointed out in his two-page tribute to the singer, Kurt Cobain could not be admitted to the Stupid Club quite so easily. 'Rock and roll mythology dictates that heroes die because they wanted to live too much,' wrote Stubbs. 'Kurt Cobain, however, didn't want to live. He wanted to die.'[13] Stubbs reminded his readers that there was no real precedent for this in rock and roll. Cobain's death had very little in common with those of Hendrix, Morrison and Joplin, all of whom — despite their undoubtedly self-destructive tendencies — died accidentally as a result of excess, rather than intentionally as a result of despair, as Cobain had. Nirvana's singer was, in the end, too smart for the stupid club. His death was not a spontaneous act of self-destruction, but a self-conscious one, informed by knowledge of rock history. Even the tone of his suicide note suggested that Cobain knew he was playing a role. It read less like a last goodbye and more, as Love succinctly put it, 'like a letter to the fuckin' editor'.[14]

Cobain's influences in death were much the same as his influences in life, an unstable mixture of classic rock, personal pain and questionable lifestyle choices — Beatles, divorces and drugs, as he put it in Nirvana's first band bio. Cobain's problems with heroin and painkillers had played their part in his demise, and his parents' divorce and its crippling effect on his emotional life were given considerable space in his suicide note. He also returned several times to the theme of 'empathy', insisting that his decision to end his life was at least partly a result of his extreme sensitivity. Cobain assumed the familiar role of the romantic artist who, because he feels too intensely, cannot simply 'get along' like everybody else. 'I think I simply love people too much, so much that it makes me feel too fucking sad,' he wrote. Many of those who commented on Cobain's death after the fact echoed this, even before the contents of the letter were revealed. 'Only guys like the one in the song "Dumb" from *In Utero* are naturally anaesthetised to the stable mediocrity of everyday existence,' wrote Stubbs in his *Melody Maker* piece.[15] Nirvana biographer Michael Azerrad told MTV that Cobain was 'sweet and sensitive … Perhaps a little too sensitive for the business he was in.'[16]

According to *Time* magazine, Cobain 'suffered the usual torments of the underground poet entering the mainstream'.[17] But then, underground poets do not usually make a habit of comparing themselves to the lead singer of Queen, and this was exactly what Cobain did in his suicide note's most surprising passage. 'When we're back stage and the lights go out and the manic roar of the crowds begins,' he wrote, 'it doesn't affect me the way in which it did for Freddie Mercury, who seemed to love, relish in the love and adoration from the crowd which is something I totally admire and envy.' Mercury, who had died in 1992 of an AIDS-related illness, was a performer of the old school, a singer whose basically showbiz approach to rock and roll allowed his band to negotiate the spectacular eighties with consummate ease. Leftist rock critics and punk ideologues accused Queen of everything from insincerity to fascism. But Mercury, like the rock idols he'd admired as a boy, just loved being popular, and saw Queen's popularity as the measure of the band's success.

However much he tried to emulate this model, to accept that he was a new wave entertainer, or that Nirvana was 'the nineties version of Cheap Trick', Cobain had absorbed too much of punk to be able to do so. 'Kurt had an ethic toward his fans rooted in the punk rock way of thinking,' said Krist Novoselic, in his own pre-recorded address to the fans. 'No band is special, no player royalty. That's the level Kurt spoke to us on.'[18] Punk rock, especially the American variant that had provided Cobain with his musical education, insisted that there was no essential difference between the band on stage and the kids standing in a puddle of beer in the crowd; the goal was to break down the gothic aura that separated rock from life. Cobain had been to just enough arena-rock concerts as a kid to know how it felt to be on the wrong end of the aura. 'It was entertaining, I suppose,' he said of an Iron Maiden concert he'd once seen, 'but I felt alienated.'[19]

But by the end of 1993, stadium rock and MTV had turned Nirvana into Iron Maiden. The fans no longer saw Cobain as one of them;

they regarded him as a hero to be worshipped on the one hand, and a commodity to be grabbed on the other, like some cross between the Dalai Lama and a KFC dinner for five thousand. He'd stopped crowd surfing long before the *In Utero* tour, fearing for his life. 'These kids,' he told *Melody Maker*, 'all they know how to do is tear people apart.'[20] But while the fans worshipped and wanted him, there were some nights when he scarcely gave them a thought; what was a magic moment of communion for the kids was, for him, just another night in front of a thousand screaming mouths he'd never see again. 'Sometimes,' he confessed in his final message to the world, 'I feel as if I should have a punch-in time clock before I walk out on stage.'[21]

Clocking on and off with a guitar in hand was not, in itself, such a bad thing — it was, on a very simple level, the life Cobain had chosen for himself. 'I can't work among people,' he'd said around the time of *Bleach* in 1989, 'I might as well try to make a career out of this.'[22] If Cobain was Cliff Richard or David Lee Roth or Paula Abdul he might easily have kept doing it too. But those performers had never really promised their fans anything other than vicarious good times. Cobain had promised reality. 'Nirvana replaced the prefab sentiments of pop with hard, unreconstituted emotions,' wrote *Newsweek*'s Jeff Giles. Their music, he insisted, 'appealed to a mass of young fans who were tired of false idols like Madonna and Michael Jackson'.[23] It thus became Cobain's job to deliver the real thing, and yet this was the one thing he no longer felt capable of doing. Kids, as Cobain well knew, were smart; they could spot phonies. And there were many nights, standing on stage, screaming himself hoarse so as to give his fans a convincing facsimile of the emotions they wanted to hear, that Cobain felt phoney to his core. 'The fact is, I can't fool any of you,' he wrote, shortly before taking his own life. 'It simply isn't fair to you or me. The worst crime I can think of would be to rip people off by faking it.'[24]

Nine days later, in a concrete-walled dressing-room somewhere in the bowels of the Paramount Theatre, *Melody Maker*'s Steve Kulick talked to Eddie Vedder about the last days of Kurt Cobain. 'People like him and me, we can't be real,' he explained. 'It's a contradiction. We can't just be these people who write these real songs. We have to live up to the expectations of a million people.'[25] Vedder, like everybody else, had watched Cobain's death being announced on the TV news. He saw the fans hugging each other, watched rock journalists and social commentators speculate about what it all meant, and felt a chill go down his spine. The singer had no need to wait until after the commercial to find out why this talented millionaire had decided to blow his head off. Instead, he threw the TV against the wall, and proceeded to do the same with everything else in his hotel room that wasn't nailed to the floor. Later, when he'd calmed down a little, he thought about the conversation he'd had less than a week ago with a friend, in which he'd described at length the way that money and mass media had robbed his art of its meaning, alienated him from his fans, destroyed the integrity of his own personality, and made him want to kill himself. 'I felt like calling that person,' he told *Spin* magazine, 'and just saying, "Do you see? Do you see what it does? Do you see?"'[26]

The Kingdom of the Pleasing

On 8 April 1994, James Brown, editor of the British men's magazine *Loaded*, received a phone call from a reporter at the *Daily Express*. Could he confirm, the journalist wanted to know, that Kurt Cobain was dead? It was a strange moment. Brown had spent most of the morning listening to Blur's new record, *Parklife*, and had in fact been dancing around the *Loaded* office with the album on the stereo, cranked up as loud as it would go, when the phone rang. In March 1993, Blur had declared war on grunge and *Select* magazine had run its 'Who Do You Think You Are Kidding, Mr Cobain?' feature. Now, a little over a year later, Blur was about to release what many were hoping would be the definitive statement of the new British pop, and Kurt Cobain was dead.[1]

The imminent arrival of *Parklife* had been heralded by a single, released in March, called 'Girls and Boys', a shamelessly populist new wave disco anthem about English kids on holidays in southern Europe. The tune merged oompah fairground organ with Eurotrash disco so as to simultaneously evoke Englishness and cheap package tours. It also left room for some of Graham Coxon's most inventive playing — the guitarist cut the song's sweetness with rhythmic blasts of art-rock dissonance, which betrayed his abiding (and unfashionable) love for King Crimson's Robert Fripp. But 'Girls and Boys' wasn't written with art-rock aficionados in mind, nor was it meant to cater to the retro aesthetic of London clubs like Syndrome; it was made for the suburban kids described in the lyrics, and when they subsequently embraced the song as an anthem in the spring of 1994, Albarn was not the least bit surprised. 'The chorus is "girls", "boys" and "love",' he pointed out with a smile. 'It's quite a universal message really, isn't it?'[2] *Modern Life is Rubbish* had been the first indie album in five years to acknowledge the existence of the suburbs; *Parklife* was designed to be played there, to be heard at school discos, barbecues and twenty-first birthday parties.

The last-ditch effort of *Modern Life is Rubbish* had turned Blur's fortunes around. Albarn, it seemed, had been right — after two years of grunge, British kids wanted British pop again, and Blur was in exactly the right place at the right time. Over the course of 1993, as its audience grew in proportion to its music press column-inches, the group that had spent most of the previous year being alternately laughed at in England and ignored in America embraced popularity with a vengeance. 'It's amazing,' reflected Alex James, 'how a little bit of success can make everything all right.'[3] Their confidence bolstered, the band members went back into the studio with Stephen Street to begin work on a new album. Blur took risks, widening its stylistic palette to take in everything from snot-nosed punk ('Bank Holiday') to chanson ('To the End'), experimenting with synths, sequencers, strings, horn sections and duck calls, and working in cameos from guest vocalists including Stereolab's Laetitia Sadier and actor Phil Daniels, best known to pop fans for his role in The Who's *Quadrophenia*. Albarn, meanwhile, explored his range as a songwriter. He produced at least one honest-to-goodness masterpiece in 'This is a Low', and a host of other minor miracles, including 'End of a Century', 'Trouble in the Message Centre' and 'London Loves'.

The first five songs on *Parklife* were linked by the fact that they described ordinary people on the middle-to-lower rungs of society who had broken out of the pattern of normal life. Some chose to do so, others were pushed. Some quickly reinserted themselves into the normal world, others decided to stay permanently outside of it. 'Tracy Jacks' was an account of a civil service employee who one day snapped, caught the first train to the seaside, took off his clothes and ran around naked. 'Bank Holiday' caught the manic edge of the annual public holiday, as suburban families tried desperately to cram all the fun they couldn't have in everyday life into a single day off. And 'Parklife' was written in the voice of a man who had left all of this behind, an unemployed layabout who watched the lunchtime joggers go 'round and round' while he fed the pigeons and the sparrows. All of these stories were told at one remove — the word 'I' appeared only in 'Parklife', (a song which was written from the point of view of a character who was clearly not Damon Albarn); the others were written in the third ('Tracy Jacks') or second person ('Girls and Boys').

'I am part of a tradition,' Albarn wrote in 1994. 'I am part of a music-hall clown entertainer tradition that's been in this country since the beginning of the century.'[4] Albarn had realised that it was no good writing about the people if the people weren't listening, and Blur affirmed its wish to be associated with proletarian entertainment by launching *Parklife* at the Walthamstow dog track. 'What's the appeal?' asked Zoe Ball. 'It's just another aspect of Parklife, really,' said Albarn. 'It's a night out. You can have a drink and watch dogs goin' round in a circle.'[5] The new Damon Albarn was no tortured, lonely artist, but a man of the people, dressed in casual sportswear, drinking lager and talking about making 'music your gran would like'.

Blur made themselves so much at home in what radical playwright Bertolt Brecht once described as 'the Kingdom of the Pleasing' that, in April 1994, Albarn became the first Brechtian satirist to be voted 'Most Fanciable' by *Just Seventeen* magazine. The schoolgirl scrawl Danny Kelly had observed at his local bus stop in 1991 turned out to have been a sign of things to come — James, Coxon, Rowntree and Albarn were now teen idols, and their shows were full of young girls with short haircuts and Doc Martens, arguing over which one was cutest and singing along to all the words. 'The audiences have been a lot more ecstatic,' said Coxon, 'and there's been a lot more of them as well.'[6] Coxon looked slightly freaked out by Blur's new pop-star status, but Albarn appeared to have eased into it like it was the most natural thing in the world. 'Does it annoy you that you're a heart-throb?' asked *The O-Zone*'s reporter in June. This was a grunge question in a Britpop world, a question that carried the assumption that rock singers were serious artists whose precious solitude was threatened by what Henry Rollins had recently referred to as 'the brutality of mass acceptance'.[7] Albarn was having none of it. 'It's not something you get annoyed about really, is it?' he asked with a cheeky smile.[8]

The discourse of pop stardom suited the newly democratised Blur. Serious music mags like *Q* and *Vox* discussed bands in terms of subjective unmeasurables like art, integrity, authenticity and significance. *Smash Hits* and *Just Seventeen* reduced music to very simple concepts: Who's the most fanciable? Who has the best hair? Who's had the most hits and whose song will get to the top of the charts first? In the increasingly fragmented indie music world of the nineties, with its conflicting standards and endlessly proliferating subcultures, there was something soothing about this return to the values of the early sixties, the days when popularity could be used as a measure of success. It was fun, this new spirit of competition — it made music more like sport, a game with rules, winners and losers. The music weeklies, with writers who had always enjoyed this kind of intellectual slumming ('Are They the Best Band in Britain?') eagerly embraced the trend, and other media outlets quickly followed suit. At the Walthamstow dog track, Albarn placed his bet in his newly acquired cockney accent, while ITV's reporter assessed Blur's prospects. 'As far as the sweepstake on who's the king of the world of British pop music goes,' she said, 'the only contenders are Pulp, Suede and Blur, in a Britpop three-dog race.'[9] But there were already signs that Britpop's bookies might have to adjust their tip sheets. One week earlier, Granada TV had run a profile on a group from Manchester called Oasis, and its songwriter Noel Gallagher seemed supernaturally confident that he could beat any other band in Britain. 'This is our year, without a shadow of a doubt,' he said. 'No one can touch us.'[10]

A New Smell

If there was a sense in which Cobain's suffering, and the similar trials endured by Eddie Vedder, could be seen as instructive — a warning to future punks about the real cost of selling out — there was very little sign, in 1994, that anyone had understood it as such. On the contrary, punk bands were now defecting to the mainstream in record numbers. The year had so far seen the release of major-label debuts by the Offspring, and Green Day, who graduated in no time at all from playing clubs to stadiums. The band was scheduled to appear at both Lollapalooza and Woodstock '94, and had been seen on the cover of *Rolling Stone* and *Spin*, which declared 1994 to be 'The Year Punk Broke'.[1]

According to Sonic Youth's Thurston Moore, The Year Punk Broke had been 1991, 'when punk rock finally [broke] through to the mainstream'.[2] Moore's point at the time had been that Sonic Youth and the bands it was touring with, Nirvana and Dinosaur Jr, represented the punk diaspora, groups who had their minds blown by the music in 1977, and had spent fifteen years waiting for punk to take its rightful place in popular culture. But the process had taken so long that the music had changed beyond all recognition by the time it broke through. In 1991, Sonic Youth resembled the Grateful Dead far more than it did the Sex Pistols, and Dinosaur Jr seemed to have more to do with Creedence than it did with Minor Threat. The bands that broke in 1994 seemed, by contrast, to be far closer to what most music fans would think of as punk. They had short, spiky haircuts and played short, fast songs. They wore vacant stares and sang about boredom, parents and TV. 'I relate to everything Billie Joe is saying up there,' said one Green Day fan, interviewed by MTV after the band's performance at Lollapalooza.[3] Because its concerns were defiantly high school and proudly immature, Green Day now seemed to embody teen spirit to a far greater degree than grunge, which had grown up rather too quickly. The new punk quickly joined the new new wave (Weezer) and the new stadium rock (Smashing Pumpkins) as one of the various alternatives to alternative. 'It's good to have a fresh smell,' said triple j's Helen Razer when she met the band backstage at Lollapalooza. 'It's good to see a band that don't wear flannelette shirts.'[4]

The new smell was, however, strongly reminiscent of an old one — the heady mixture of cheap hairspray and week-old rubbish that had wafted through London in the summer of 1976. Razer, like most journalists who met Green Day, was struck by how closely its music resembled that of the first wave of British punk bands — The Clash, The Damned, Stiff Little Fingers and the Buzzcocks. But the group's singer Billie Joe Armstrong explained to her that he'd never really listened to those groups, and by the time he had, Green Day already sounded like Green Day. His real influences, he implied, were the same things that influenced the Buzzcocks — youth and boredom. 'We've been listening to bad radio for half of our lives, and watching bad television for the other half.'[5] Green Day *had* been influenced by other punk bands, but they were bands that most radio and TV presenters were unlikely to have heard of in 1994. The host of MTV's *120 minutes* wondered if Green Day might have been weaned on LA punk like X and the Germs. 'No, it wasn't even that,' replied Billie Joe. 'It was more of the community that we were surrounded with, the bands around us.'[6]

The members of Green Day hailed from Pinole, California, and had gravitated toward the thriving punk scene in nearby Berkeley and its leading light, Operation Ivy, in the late eighties. Green Day played one of its first shows at Operation Ivy's last — a farewell gig that, in retrospect, seemed more like a passing of the baton. Armstrong inherited a number of important ideas from Op Ivy's Jesse Michaels, including the notion that punk could address personal as well as political concerns, that it could be melodic and even poppy, and that the music was, fundamentally, about thinking for yourself. The venue was significant too. Operation Ivy's final show took place at a legendary share house on Berkeley's Gilman Street, which served as a headquarters for the city's punk community. Gilman Street, according to Kaya Oakes, was 'a kind of idyllic communist fantasy: collectively run, all ages, with people pitching in voluntarily to build the place, do sound, run the door and take out the garbage'.[7] Here, the members of Green Day saw a functioning version of punk's communal ideal, an ideal that remained important to them long after they moved out of the commune itself. Punk, Armstrong explained in a 1994 interview, is 'a real subculture of people that are dedicated to creating something of their own that goes against the mainstream'.[8]

Green Day slowly built a following, and put out two albums on the small Berkeley-based label Lookout Records before signing with Warner Reprise, which released 1994's *Dookie*. Warner's promotional muscle helped the album sell almost three million copies by September. This meant that *Dookie* was in the American Top 40, more or less requiring the host of that venerable institution to pronounce its name at some point, a name that, the band helpfully informed the public, meant 'shit'. 'We made Casey Kasem say "dookie",' said a beaming Tre Cool, clearly pleased with himself.[9] But while the band liked to play dumb, nothing could have been further from the truth than the idea that Armstrong, Cool and Mike Dirnt were clueless kids or shallow trend-hoppers. The band had real roots in punk, and a commitment to the movement's egalitarian ideals that showed no signs of eroding as the group's popularity skyrocketed. In September, the band set out on a national tour and succeeded where Pearl Jam had failed in keeping its ticket prices low. 'Everybody was breathing down our necks, "keep the prices high",' said Armstrong. 'Why? Because of money, you know, everybody wants a lot of money.'[10] Green Day kept their overheads low by sleeping in the tour bus instead of hotels, and passed the savings on to their fans, who paid no more than fifteen dollars for their concert tickets, and sometimes as little as seven dollars. The gesture was typical of Green Day, a realistic, post-*Nevermind* version of Fugazi's famous 'five dollar' policy.

Green Day's attitude to its fans once they got through the gate also shared much in common with punk's pioneers. Fugazi's Guy Picciotto had started wearing dresses on stage to deliberately confuse and confront hardcore's macho contingent, and the band had complicated its music with tricky rhythms so as to discourage slam-dancing. Likewise, when Green Day noticed that their new star status had attracted 'meatheads' and 'dicks that jump on people', they took steps to defuse the audience's testosterone levels. The band chose, as tour support, a queercore group named Pansy Division, which had signed to Lookout just as Green Day switched to Warner. 'Suddenly,' said Pansy Division's frontman, John Ginoli, 'this band that had been formed to play music for openly gay guys our age ... was playing in front of swarms of predominantly straight teenagers. A lot of them weren't too happy about it.'[11] Pansy Division was booed and given the finger by shirtless boys in the mosh pit everywhere the tour went. But Green Day had long understood that punks were their own worst enemies, that they had a strong tendency to rebel against 'mainstream conformity' into something just as bad, punk conformity. 'How many stupid people are here tonight?' asked Armstrong onstage. 'Yeah!' replied the crowd, en masse.[12] It was exactly this kind of herd mentality that Green Day hoped to discourage by taking Pansy Division with them on tour. Once the word got out that Green Day was touring with an openly gay punk band, many venue promoters tried to stop Pansy Division from performing. But Green Day always insisted that if their support band couldn't play, neither would they. After a while, Pansy Division began to get letters from kids all across the country, 'expressing gratitude that finally a band had spoken for them'.[13]

But there was a price to be paid for the mainstream success of bands like Green Day, Offspring and Pennywise. It seemed that, for every newly converted young fan, an older punk was left feeling disgruntled and alienated.'In March, I saw the Offspring open up for Pennywise,' wrote one. 'None of Epitaph [Record]'s bands were on the radio, but the small club was still packed. In July, at the same club, the crowd was almost entirely high schoolers who watch too much MTV. Now, the Offspring are playing a live show, and the local alternative station is giving away free tickets if you call in at the right time. Does any of this sound like punk rock to you? It bothers me that something as pure as punk is being treated like grunge and no one seems to care.'[14] Nowhere in this letter to *Spin* did the writer mention a decline in the quality of punk music. His complaint was that the music had been made impure by being shown on MTV and liked by high school kids, a complaint that reflected one of the maddening contradictions at the heart of punk rock. On the one hand, the music was built on what music critic Simon Frith calls 'a people's version of consumerism',[15] which said that mainstream media manipulated public taste by force-feeding its audience pop, and that punk offered a genuine, and superior, alternative to mass-produced trash. But when the public realised that they'd been hoodwinked, and embraced real music — as they had in 1994 — punks saw this not as a victory, but as a disaster. Their objections seemed to rest on the idea that the masses didn't really get it, that they liked the music in the wrong way, and for the wrong reasons.

The public, from the point of view of those who were interested in preserving culture, had long been an enemy in this regard. In his 1958 book *Culture and Society*, Raymond Williams described the first appearance of the 'masses' in the late nineteenth century, characterised by their 'gullibility, fickleness, lowness of taste and habit. The masses, on this evidence, formed the perpetual threat to culture. Mass-thinking, mass-suggestion, mass-prejudice would threaten to swamp considered individual thinking and feeling. Even democracy would lose its savour in becoming mass-democracy.'[16] In the same way, people's consumerism could be ruined when too many people liked it. This had been a concern within punk since the days when suburban thugs started showing up to Black Flag concerts in the early eighties, and the fate of grunge in 1993 merely confirmed what many punks already believed — that underground music must stay underground. Since 1985 — if not 1991 — punk fans had got in the habit of defining culture in reverse: if only a small number of people like and understand it, it must be good; if it's embraced by the masses, it's not. Thus punk, like the high culture that preceded it, began to resemble a bizarre parody of the entertainment industry, in which popularity had become the measure of failure.

Problems, Traumas, Whatever

In September 1994, during an interview at triple j's studios in Sydney, Pavement singer Stephen Malkmus played a track from Kraftwerk's 1979 album *The Man Machine*, and talked at length about the admiration he had for the group. There was, at the time, something very incongruous about the leader of the famously shambolic indie rock band enthusing over the pioneers of robot pop. 'Could you ever see yourself dabbling with machines and computers?' asked Richard Kingsmill. 'That's hard,' replied Malkmus, 'because I missed out on computers.' The singer explained that when he was in high school, his father had discouraged him from spending too much time with the kids in the computer lab. 'My dad was like, "That's square, you gotta play sports".' But Malkmus didn't write off the possibility of electronics playing a part in indie rock's future. 'As long as you have good personalities like Eddie Vedder and Kurt Cobain,' he explained. 'Eddie Vedder, if he was playing a keyboard, it would work just the same way.' The lasting appeal of the guitar, he believed, was mostly due to the instrument's accessibility. 'The guitar is still the proletarian instrument that anyone can play,' he said, 'and it's cheap to learn.'[1]

Malkmus's use of the word 'proletarian' reflected a long association between the guitar and The People in the public imagination, which dated back to the folk movement during the post-war period. Because of the strong links forged between folk and rock in the mid-sixties, the idea that the guitar was a working-class instrument came to occupy an important place in rock culture. Images of performers like Dylan (in his

196

early years), Bruce Springsteen, Neil Young, The Clash, the Ramones and Nirvana encouraged the notion that guitar music was people's music. On the other hand, the legacy of genres like art rock, disco, new romantic, and synth pop — all of which, to some extent, embraced non-working class ideals like art, luxury, and decadence — left rock fans with the idea that keyboards, sequencers and computers were bourgeois. Punk had been founded on this distinction — the tale of street-level garage bands toppling the costly spectacles of art rock in 1976 was one of the music's oft-repeated fables. And when punk broke in 1991, the idea of a working-class revolt against corporate rock was underwritten by the new groups' no-frills set-ups. Sub Pop's Bruce Pavitt deliberately appealed to the music press's class fantasies by presenting Kurt Cobain as a 'suburban grease monkey' and Tad as 'blue-collar mountain men', and reviewers wrote off the over-technologised rock of eighties heroes like Def Leppard as music made by 'studio computer geeks' — in other words, for squares. But Malkmus suggested that these stereotypes might need to be revised as the nineties wore on. 'With technology getting so cheap now and accessible to everyone,' he said, 'maybe that's gonna change. Because if you can mix an album on a computer, that's gonna be even easier and more direct and less expensive than going to a studio.'[2]

The case of Nine Inch Nails had already demonstrated how it might be done. Though it had always been, in theory, a band, Nine Inch Nails initially consisted of just one person — songwriter, arranger and vocalist Trent Reznor, who produced much of the group's first album using little more than an outdated Macintosh computer and a sampler. 'I didn't have a band,' he explained, 'so the only means was electronics.'[3] Reznor, in 1994, was one of the few alt-rock stars to grasp and promote the potential computers offered for musicians to produce and distribute their own work. The singer had grown up with comic books and science fiction novels, and had subsequently inherited the sci-fi buff's characteristic blend of optimism and paranoia with regards to new technology. 'Did you hear about this new device they have, but you won't see it anywhere?' he asked Joshua Berger in 1994. 'Imagine walking into a record store, and there's a database of everything that's ever been put out — from obscure imports to Bon Jovi. You tell them which one you want, you pay with credit card, and with high speed it downloads onto a digital cassette.' Reznor, who had recently been through corporate hell in his dealings with his record company, TVT, was very excited by the potential this new device had to put power back into the hands of musicians. 'The main thing record companies have been holding over people is distribution,' he said. 'This takes them out.'[4]

The first Nine Inch Nails album, *Pretty Hate Machine*, became an underground hit and a firm college radio favourite in 1990, and Reznor toured the record relentlessly over the next two years. The band's live show was an unusual mix of guitars and samplers, which might have fallen foul of alt rock's ban on technology if it weren't for the fact that it was very difficult to see exactly what was going on at a Nine Inch Nails gig. 'There's so much smoke it's impossible to tell whether or not the group actually play,' observed *Melody Maker*'s Jon Wiederhorn, reviewing a show in Boston in August 1990. But by the end of the set, Wiederhorn didn't care much. Regardless of how 'live' the music was, it sounded impressive, and Reznor was riveting to watch: whispering like a crank caller one minute, screaming like a lunatic the next; crouching in the shadows or flinging himself across the stage. In Boston, he smashed up the drum kit halfway through the band's hit 'Head like a Hole' and stalked offstage, never to return. 'The smoke clears,' wrote Wiederhorn, 'but the sampled percussion track continues.'[5]

Kurt Cobain told Courtney Love he'd probably like Nine Inch Nails' songs if they were made using guitars rather than computers.[6] John Frusciante sniffed that Reznor's music did not contain enough 'air molecules',[7] and macho moshers at Lollapalooza jeered him for playing 'faggotty synth music'.[8] But by and large, Reznor got away with this kind of thing in America where EMF did not because the conceptual framework of his music made it clear that he was battling against technology rather than relying on it. 'It's almost like there's a contest going on between humanity and the machine,' said *Spin*'s Eric Weisbard. 'Yes,' agreed Reznor, '*Pretty Hate Machine* was about juxtaposing human imperfections against very cold, sterile arrangements.'[9] Much of the rock fan's paranoia about synths and computers came from a fear that technology was taking over music in the same way that skilled factory workers had already been replaced by machines. This paranoia was deliberately exploited by Kraftwerk and the English synth bands that followed them, but Reznor rejected the ironic pose of this first wave of techno-pop in favour of a much simpler set-up. By identifying himself very clearly as a suffering human being in an over-technologised world, Reznor could appeal to the rock audience's basic need to hear its humanity affirmed, while playing alienating electronic noise.

'I'm not the happiest guy in the world,' Reznor admitted in 1990. 'I'm not sure why, but I can't say, "It's because someone stole my bike."'[10] By 1993, *Pretty Hate Machine* had sold over two million copies, and Reznor was now in a position to buy any number of bikes, or anything else he thought might make him happy. But nothing did. Instead, he found his muse leading him toward even darker stuff than he'd explored on his first album — Nine Inch Nails' 1992 EP *Broken* was so relentlessly bleak that even its creator seemed slightly alarmed by it. Reznor began to wonder where all this anger was coming from, and where it might be going. 'I was seeing that the energy Nine Inch Nails was drawing on had a definite negative vibe, and that although it was powerful, it was not the end of the road,' he said in 1994. 'It leads toward something else.' The singer had a feeling that whatever this something else might be, the journey there would be 'pretty harrowing'.[11] But he was determined to push on. Sitting in a hotel room, Reznor came up with the idea of a song cycle in which he would attempt to solve the case of himself, to determine the precise reasons why — despite his growing level of material comfort — his life felt empty.

Seeking a cure for his own postmodern blues in 1992, Blur's Damon Albarn had spoken of 'paring yourself back to what you really are'. But Albarn had only removed a single layer — unzipped his blue jeans to discover a pair of Union Jack briefs. Reznor, like a man picking at a scab, would not stop until he drew blood. 'Take the skin and peel it back,' he sang, 'now doesn't it make you feel better?'[12] Nine Inch Nails' journey to the centre of the self, *The Downward Spiral*, was released in March 1994, and the album's opening song gave a good indication of where the spiral might lead. 'I am the sex that you deny,' hissed Reznor, 'I am the hate you try to hide.'[13] Here, in 'Mr Self Destruct', Reznor warned of the heavy price to be paid for repressing one's desires, and dramatised his imminent emotional ketchup burst by contrasting synth-pop interludes with blasts of distorted noise. Reznor made no attempt to hide his hate or deny his sex: the former was proudly on display in 'Big Man with a Gun'; the latter was the subject of 'Closer'. But neither sex nor violence seemed to satisfy him because neither could provide his life with meaning in a world where, as he sang in 'Heresy', 'God is dead and no-one cares'.[14]

In 1991, Jane's Addiction — one of Reznor's favourite bands — had suggested that the collapse of all values meant it was time to party. 'Ain't no wrong now there ain't no right,' sang Perry Farrell, 'there's only pleasure and pain.'[15] *The Downward Spiral* showed what might happen to this philosophy after a two-year bender, when the pursuit of kicks for their own sakes had started to yield diminishing returns, and the prospect of more exotic distractions seemed unlikely to compensate for the death of God. Not that Nine Inch Nails didn't explore this option. In 'Closer' — the closest thing to a love song on the album — the singer tried to fuck his way to faith, to fill the God-shaped hole in his life with pleasure. But he fell a long way short. By the end of the album, Reznor had downgraded his expectations to an alarming degree. Society, culture, love, religion, sex, violence and mindless kicks had all let him down, and the singer was left with nothing but himself. In 'Hurt', Reznor described a man who cut his skin just to prove that something exists outside of his mind. 'I focus on the pain,' he sang, 'the only thing that's real.'[16]

Reznor's art was therapeutic — an attempt, as he put it, 'to deal with my own thoughts and recycle them into something that I feel better about myself for expressing'.[17] Nine Inch Nails, Reznor insisted, was a means to release his most antisocial impulses in a harmless way, he made music so he wouldn't have to hurt himself — or others. In 'Burn', a song recorded especially for the soundtrack to Oliver Stone's *Natural Born Killers*, Reznor drew explicit parallels between the mass-murderer's motivations and his own, suggesting that they were both victims of alienation and neglect, but that Mickey Knox had chosen to do in reality what Reznor did through symbols and representations. 'This world rejects me,' he sang, 'this world gonna have to pay.'[18] Reznor's suspicion that the desire to rock and the desire to kill were closely related was confirmed by L7, who agreed to donate their song

'Shitlist' to the *Natural Born Killers* soundtrack because Mallory Knox was 'a female character we could really get into'.[19]

By the mid nineties, the public's fascination with real-life murderers like the Menendez Brothers and OJ Simpson had fostered the idea that killers could be stars. To believe that the reverse was also true — that stars could be killers — required very little imagination. The *NME* described L7's Donita Sparks as 'like Travis Bickle with PMT',[20] and Nirvana, on its first tour of the UK, as 'The Sweet fronted by Jeffrey Dahmer'.[21] Talking to Jon Savage in 1993, Cobain seemed to confirm this assessment. 'I always felt they would vote me "Most Likely to Kill Everyone" at a high school dance,' he said.[22] When the singer died, *Interview*'s Howard Hampton eulogised him as 'the self-assassinating rock star, John Lennon and Mark Chapman as a one-man band'.[23] Hampton's disturbing image anticipated the pose later adopted by Marilyn Manson, an artist Reznor signed to his Nothing Records label in 1995. Like the Portland-based sixties revivalists the Brian Jonestown Massacre, Manson's name suggested a strange new hybrid of superstar and murderer, sex and violence incarnate.

Reznor plunged headlong into evil in his art so that he wouldn't be consumed by it in his life. But if this was — as he admitted — a bit like going through therapy in public, it wasn't entirely selfish. The real measure of his success, he believed, was the healing effect his music had for his fans. He knew he'd done well when audience members came up to him after a show and told him that he had spoken for them, that he had said onstage what they could never admit to themselves. 'That's the best,' he said.[24] Music theorist Lawrence Grossberg suggested in 1993 that this might be the only serviceable definition of authenticity in the fragmented music scene of the mid nineties. When all the arguments about guitars vs samplers were laid aside, 'authentic rock', Grossberg wrote, 'depends on its ability to articulate private but common desires, feelings and experiences in a shared public language'.[25] Thus, Reznor saw that it was necessary for him to stay alive, because it had become his job to confront and describe psychic horror for his audience. 'I'm a public servant,' he explained.[26]

This Year Sucked

'So, uh, this year sucked,' said Beavis, as he looked back on 1994 in music. 'It seemed like there were all these new bands this year and they all looked the same,' offered Butt-head, 'and they all had the same kind of clothes and stuff and they all had lead singers that sucked and then they tried to sound like they were sucking on purpose.'[1] The exciting new style minted by the first wave of alternative rock bands in 1991 had, three years later, become a formula — the radio was now flooded with songs that sounded a bit like Pearl Jam, a bit like Nirvana, but not quite as good as either. A mere two years earlier, grunge had seemed like an endlessly renewable source of new musical ideas. Now it had run out of steam, and suckage was to blame.

'Histories of popular music routinely employ a model derived from nineteenth-century physical science in order to describe the process of popularisation,' wrote Michael Jarrett in 1992. 'Energy tends toward a state of equilibrium.' This model seemed to hold true in 1994: alt rock had simply succumbed to the golden rule of music history — that anything that starts out full of promise will, in time, begin to suck. 'Hot jazz turns to swing, bop turns cool, eroticism becomes lassitude, black bleaches to white, the dirty gets laundered, the uneven is worn smooth: the structure of this apocalyptic sequence reproduces itself.'[2] This model, as Jarrett pointed out, left no room for innovation — once the rot set in, the decline would be relentless. MTV's couch potato critics had no doubt that this was the case. 'Next year will probably be worse,' Beavis predicted. 'Time sucks. Huh huh huh huh.'[3]

It was a little too convenient, however, for Beavis and Butt-head to blame history itself for the death of grunge, since many believed that the duo's own TV network was responsible for the music's demise. 'I think that something like a music channel can be very powerful,' said Eddie Vedder in November. 'Sometimes they think they're the ones who decide what's seen and what's heard.'[4] Vedder's hatred for MTV had grown to the point where he was now unwilling to speak its name in public. But his slightly tortured syntax betrayed an undeniable fact: MTV was not *like* a music channel, it was *the* music channel — an international franchise with over four billion viewers and no competition to speak of. In an unsent letter to the network written during the making of *In Utero*, Kurt Cobain had denounced 'Empty TV' as 'the entity of all corporate Gods',[5] equivalent, in the singer's estimation, to William Burroughs's Mayan Priests, the one per cent of the population who 'make with one-way telepathic broadcasts, telling the workers what to feel and when'.[6] In their mid-nineties summary of alternative culture, *Alt. Culture* authors Steven Daly and Nathaniel Wice observed that MTV in America played a unique role: 'a central pop medium in a country without a coherent music press or a national radio station'.[7] If the network picked up a song, radio stations and magazines quickly fell in line; if they didn't, it was a safe bet that no-one would ever hear it. Early in 1994, for example, MTV had aired a clip by a group called Angelfish at two in the morning. Following this brief experiment, the network's music programmer decided that the song didn't really work in the playlist, and Angelfish's video was shelved. There was no reason to think that anyone would hear from Angelfish or its singer, Shirley Manson, ever again. MTV *did* decide what was seen and what was heard — therefore, if music was in decline in 1994, it was most likely MTV's fault. Daly and Wice went so far as to argue that the degeneration of rock music had been part of the music channel's hidden agenda since its debut in 1981. 'MTV's deepest concern was cleansing pop music of any remaining unseemly, rough elements,' they wrote. 'In short, it wanted to eradicate youth culture.'[8]

'What I think could have been a unique new art form has become a series of three-minute commercials for products,' said Trent Reznor in 1994. 'This one might be for Bon Jovi and that one for Pearl Jam and that one for Close-Up tooth polish or whatever. It's interchangeable.'[9] Reznor believed that MTV had a deadening effect on musical art, draining it of its soul and significance by intercutting it with banal advertisements and hyperactive station promos. It was exactly this kind of thing that convinced Eddie Vedder, in 1993, that Pearl Jam should stop making videos for MTV altogether. 'I don't want to be the travelling medicine show where we go out and do the song and dance and someone else drops the back of the wagon and starts selling crap,' he told the *LA Times*. 'I don't want our music to sell anything.'[10]

But the fact that MTV played ads wasn't the only reason musicians like Vedder had come to see it as an enemy. It could be argued that rock music could be used to sell toothpaste with or without MTV's help — radio stations had always used rock hits as a way of delivering consumers to advertisers. But Pearl Jam made no attempt to get its songs off KROQ. There was something qualitatively different about MTV's effect on music, a difference Reznor hinted at in his use of the word 'interchangeable'. Soundgarden had noticed it in the summer of 1992, when the band was supporting Guns N' Roses, around the same time that MTV began playing the video for 'Outshined'. Kim Thayil observed that the audience looked completely bored and unmoved until Soundgarden played 'Outshined', at which point they sprang to life, moshing furiously, until the song ended, when they went back to being bored. 'We could have been anyone up there,' said Thayil, 'a completely interchangeable band.'[11] This was the most disturbing thing about MTV, the way it seemed to remove the essential differences between discrete styles of music, reducing everything to the same low level. Reznor's assertion that MTV had made it difficult to tell the difference between Pearl Jam and Bon Jovi was very much to the point.

The group that performed 'Blaze of Glory' in 1991 was nothing like the one that recorded 'Jeremy' that same year. Jon Bon Jovi was a grinning rock superstar with a feather-cut hairdo; Eddie Vedder was a normal guy in normal clothes who liked to surf and hang out. Bon Jovi soared above the stadium on a trapeze; Vedder mingled with the crowd and jumped into the mosh. Bon Jovi's hits were escapist fantasies of power and romance; Pearl Jam's were brutally honest confessionals, straight from the singer's heart. For all these reasons and more, Pearl Jam was proof that MTV had not yet succeeded in killing youth culture, and Vedder was a hero of the musical revolution *Newsweek* had referred to in its obituary for Kurt Cobain — the fresh generation of angry young men who hated the 'slick MTV-driven establishment' so much that they 'took it over'.[12] The establishment certainly appeared chastened. Following the success of Sam Beyer's murky 'Smells Like Teen Spirit' clip, and the even more surprising popularity of Pearl Jam's bleak 'Jeremy', the tone of MTV changed, as Daly and Wice put it, from 'garish to downbeat', as the pop-metal videos of six months before were quickly consigned to the scrapheap.[13] Former Van Halen singer David Lee Roth grumbled that MTV was now 'mainlining moroseness', but Jon Bon Jovi himself insisted that grunge had injected some much-needed reality into the music world. Vedder and Kurt Cobain, he said in 1994, were 'real guys with real problems that wanted to talk about them'. Pearl Jam's singer in particular was, he said, 'a real, real dude'.[14]

And yet this was exactly the point at which Vedder felt his own real-ness disappearing. MTV's whole-hearted embrace of Pearl Jam's music had robbed it of the authenticity that made it significant in the first place. By playing the videos for 'Jeremy' and 'Alive', and running constant updates on the band's activity, the network was turning Pearl Jam into an advertisement for itself. The millions of people who watched the group on MTV began turning up to Pearl Jam's shows expecting more of the 'real' behaviour they'd seen on the screen, and people who ran into Eddie Vedder in the street now wanted him to be 'real' for them too. Vedder quickly saw that, for the sake of his own sanity, he would have to put some distance between himself and this new audience by carefully rationing his appearances in public. The result of this was that the communion between Vedder and his fans that took place in Pearl Jam's videos became a fantasy. The singer was in no sense a part of his fans' world; he was rich, famous, adored by millions and forever out of reach. By 1993, it could be said that Vedder was unlike Jon Bon Jovi in only one important respect — he hated being Jon Bon Jovi. 'Paint Ed Big,' he sang in 1993's 'Blood'. 'Turn Ed into one of his enemies …'[15] Vedder's persecution complex may have had some basis in fact. Daly and Wice believed that MTV's agenda in the nineties was really no different from the one it had pursued in the eighties. 'By so eagerly embracing absolutely anything reeking of authenticity,' they argued, 'the channel devalues anything it touches. Nineties MTV has still got it in for youth culture — only this time it's killing it with kindness.'[16]

Vedder believed that MTV had successfully erased its audience's ability to distinguish between authenticity and its opposite. 'They don't know what's real and what isn't,' he told Steve Kulick in May 1994. 'And when someone comes along who's real, they don't know the fucking difference.'[17] This was bad news for Vedder, but good news for the music industry. If it was no longer possible to tell the difference between Pearl Jam and Bon Jovi, then consumers would have no hope of distinguishing Pearl Jam from bands that actually looked and sounded like Pearl Jam.

In the video for the Stone Temple Pilots' 1994 single 'Interstate Love Song', Scott Weiland looked and sounded so much like Eddie Vedder that the singer told Weiland to 'get your own trip, man'.[18] The seemingly unstoppable rise of the 'Clone Temple Pilots' had caused a great deal of consternation among critics and music fans, who liked to point out that despite their flannel shirts, goatee beards and down-tuned guitars, the band were not from Seattle or even the northwest, and had, up until 1991, been a hair-metal band. But while he admitted that the Stone Temple Pilots were 'Seattle-sounding', Tom Carolyn, the A&R representative who signed the band to Atlantic, was not overly concerned with where they came from or who they might have ripped off along the way. 'Whether you break a window with a hammer or pound on it with a rock,' he said, 'it still sounds like breaking glass.'[19]

By 'breaking glass' Carolyn meant 'breaking bands', and MTV's whole-hearted support for grunge was helping the industry do plenty of that. Bush, Candlebox, Collective Soul and Silverchair were just a few of the Seattle-sounding bands that scored hits in 1994. None of them were from anywhere near Washington state, but they were by no means all grunge Monkees. Candlebox were cynical opportunists who flattened their hair and moved in on the northwest gold rush, but Silverchair was nothing if not real — a trio of teenagers from Newcastle, Australia, who loved Pearl Jam, took a sincere stab at writing a Pearl Jam song, won a TV competition to have it produced in a studio and ended up with the most-played single on American radio in 1995. But while Silverchair itself was not cynical, the selling of the band in America certainly was. Like all of the second-wave grunge groups who emerged in 1994, Silverchair was marketed to fit a formula, and the formula — ironically — was one that Vedder had invented. Pearl Jam had defined the reality indicators of the nineties — gruff vocals, heavy guitars, proletarian work-wear, long hair, real problems, sucking on purpose — and these things had turned out to be quite easy to replicate. The market was being flooded with cheap reality copies, and the value of the real thing was collapsing.

In 1993, music theorist Lawrence Grossberg warned of the coming 'end of authenticity', and urged rock performers to get out of the reality business before it was too late. 'The only authenticity,' he said, 'is to know and even admit that you are not being authentic, to fake it without faking the fact that you are faking it.' Grossberg insisted that audiences in the post-MTV world were looking for 'salvation without authenticity'.[20] But for Eddie Vedder, this was no salvation at all. While he kept his copy of *God Bless You, Mr Rosewater* close to his heart, Vedder would not be satisfied with 'ironicism'. He yearned for soul and significance, and knew all too well that his audience — despite Grossberg's assertions to the contrary — did too. He felt strongly that he'd been robbed of his innocence, that music, which was once a sacred thing for him, had become debased by experience. But Vedder did not believe there was anything inevitable about this. Music's decline, the singer believed, was not due to the passage of time, or any pseudo-scientific law of music history, but to MTV. This gave him some measure of hope: if the process was material rather than predestined, he could fight against it. 'The common rule,' he sang on Pearl Jam's 'Not For You', was 'If you hate something don't you do it too.'[21] In interviews, Vedder made it very clear that 'Not For You' was addressed to MTV, that its intention was to inform the network that Pearl Jam was no longer prepared to help them sell airtime to advertisers.

By the time the song was released in November 1994, Pearl Jam had long since stopped making videos. And yet the singer had discovered that restoring the purity of his art was not going to be as simple as that. MTV had turned him into a rock star, and this, it seemed, had been the easiest thing in the world to do — Vedder had barely noticed the process taking place. Effecting the reverse transformation, turning himself from a media monster back into a human being, was going to take every ounce of his strength. 'Cleaning teenagers of all their dough because they like your band — that's easy, that's playing the game,' he told the *LA Times*. 'What's hard is to stop playing the game.'[22] Vedder was referring here to the way his struggle to distance his band and himself from an exploitative industry was itself being exploited — in the absence of any new Pearl Jam videos to play, The Trials of Eddie Vedder was becoming an MTV hit. 'If you say, I'm not playing your game, I want out … they still think you're part of it,' he told Steve Kulick. 'They just can't accept that you don't want to be a part of it, that you were never a part of it. They think it's just an angle.'[23]

At the end of 1994, as Pearl Jam's third album *Vitalogy* began to sell in the millions, and the band faced the prospect of another stadium tour, Vedder confronted a disturbing new possibility. 'Music was the thing that always helped me,' he said, 'and now a lot of the problems seem tied to the music.'[24] Vedder had already lost an argument over whether 'Betterman' — a slightly mawkish ballad about an abusive husband — should be included on *Vitalogy*. He'd fought to have it left on the shelf, not because he thought it was bad, but because he knew it was good, because he knew it would be a big hit, knew it would win the band more fans and make him more famous. That Vedder should have tried to scrap 'Betterman' while fighting just as hard to save 'Bugs' — an almost unlistenable experiment played on a broken accordion — gave some indication of where his thinking was headed. Vedder had come to realise that the only way to stop being a rock star might be to stop making rock music.

My So-Called Life

One week after *Vitalogy* was released, on 30 November 1994, Guy Debord — philosopher, filmmaker and flâneur — shot himself in the heart after a long battle with alcoholism. It had been three decades since Debord and the movement he led — the Situationist International — had first called on artists to stop making art and start making trouble, four since Debord himself had come to the realisation that art was part of the problem, rather than part of the solution. 'In 1953, I wrote in chalk on a wall in the Rue de Seine, blackened with the patina of years, the redoubtable slogan *Never work!*' recalled Debord, one year before he took his own life. 'It was originally thought that I was joking.'[1]

As a student, Debord had been profoundly influenced by early twentieth-century movements like Dada and Surrealism, which had suggested that art might transform everyday life. But by the time he was in his twenties, the Surrealists seemed to Debord as Pete Townshend and David Crosby had to Kurt Cobain in 1990 — like sellouts. Debord could see that the angry young men of the 1920s had become the bourgeois careerists of the 1950s, and their once-revolutionary artworks now adorned the walls of boardrooms and the private homes of millionaires. The new post-war artists seemed to be eagerly preparing their works for the same fate, 'the acceptance and decoration of the present world'.[2]

This, Debord felt, was unacceptable. The failure of Surrealism to liberate humanity was in no way compensated for by the Dalís in the museums and the surrealist-influenced photo layouts in the pages of *Vogue* magazine. Art, it seemed, had simply become a sector of the commercial entertainment industry, which was itself a subsidiary of what Debord called 'the society of the spectacle'. Debord saw that the creation of art objects had become counter-productive — by being transformed into commodities, the artist's refusals became meaningless, sealed-off representations of the freedom they promised. Therefore, he concluded, the creation of art objects must stop. Debord, as Simon Ford put it, hoped to see 'the artist metamorphosed into a theorist of revolution'.[3] In place of painting and sculpting, he advocated un-sellable activities such as walking around, writing on walls, vandalising other artworks, getting into fights and starting riots. 'The arts of the future,' he wrote in 1961, 'will be upheavals of situations, or they will not be.'[4]

What was at stake here, Debord felt, was nothing less than the future of real life itself. 'All that was once directly lived, has become mere representation,' he wrote in his 1967 book, *The Society of the Spectacle*.[5] Debord believed that capitalism and communications media had conspired to bring about a state of permanent unreality in the post-war world. The transformation of everything into a representation of itself had made it impossible for anyone to know what was real and what was not. 'For one to whom the real world becomes real images,' he argued, 'mere images are transformed into real beings — tangible figments, which are the efficient motor of trancelike behaviour.'[6] Debord's words spread like wildfire through the universities of Paris, and became a catalyst for the student uprising of 1968, 'The first true holiday,' according to the Situationists, in which 'millions of people cast off the weight of alienating conditions and the inverted world of the spectacle'.[7] With hindsight, however, it became possible to see that 1968 marked not the return of real life, but its final disappearance. When the second edition of *The Society of the Spectacle* was published in 1988, Debord observed that 'in all that has happened in the last twenty years, the most important change lies in the very continuity of the Spectacle. Quite simply, the Spectacle's domination has succeeded in raising a whole generation moulded to its laws.'[8]

This generation — still unnamed at the time Debord wrote his new preface — was the very same one Damon Albarn would describe in 1991 as being unable to tell one thing from another, a generation that had learned about love from television, a generation grown so used to the spectacle that it could no longer conceive of any other way of life, and had — as Debord predicted — lost the ability to distinguish reality from representation. Linklater's characters in *Slacker* argued that travel was no longer worth the effort — it was expensive and time-consuming, but most importantly, it wouldn't look as good as it did on TV. Kurt Cobain observed in 1990 that TV had turned scenarios into sitcoms and conversations into clichés. Beck Hansen never watched the stuff, but after catching a glimpse at a friend's place later that same year, it became very clear to him why life in LA seemed so empty and alienating. 'Oh my god,' he said to himself. 'Everyone I know is imitating a sitcom. That's why I couldn't relate to them.'[9] Macaulay Culkin tried to cut through the confusion in a TV commercial aired in 1994. 'I'm not really your boyfriend,' he said, breaking the fourth wall and looking the viewer directly in the eye, 'and this house isn't real, it's just a set.' But this wasn't a public service announcement on behalf of real life, it was a soft drink ad. Thus, with his next sentence, Culkin promptly undid whatever good he had done, and sunk his viewers still further into the postmodern mire. 'The only things that are real,' he said, 'are you, me and Sprite.'[10]

By the early nineties, the thirteenth generation had lost its faith in the existence of a real world to such an extent that it promoted the word 'like' from an obscure piece of Valley Girl dialect to an essential part of everyday speech, and carefully appended the word 'thing' to any noun or phrase that sounded as though it might have been uttered by a character on TV at some point in the past. Thus the Lemonheads' Evan Dando decided to drop out of Skidmore after a semester because he was tired of 'the college thing',[11] L7 moved from an indie to a major label for 'the distribution thing',[12] Courtney Love qualified her admiration for Pamela Des Barres because she was worried about being associated with 'the groupie thing',[13] and Justine Frischmann, asked on MTV how she felt about being 'the next big thing', replied that she didn't really believe in 'the whole "next big thing" thing'.[14] Sammy in *Reality Bites* told Leilani that his goal in life was to have 'maybe, like, a career or something',[15] *Spin* praised Radiohead's 'Creep' as being 'like, cathartic',[16] Beck told triple j's Helen Razer he bought his clothes at thrift stores, 'where you buy, like, junk and stuff',[17] and a mourner interviewed on the day of Kurt Cobain's death told interviewers he'd come to the house because 'It's like, he's gone, and I just came to, like, say goodbye'. It was a fitting epitaph for Cobain, born the year Debord pronounced real life dead. It was *like* he was gone, but his face appeared so often on MTV in 1994 that it was hard to tell.

Cobain's so-called death was quickly followed by the television debut of *My So-Called Life*, a drama series about a high school girl named Angela Chase, whose teenage insecurity is exacerbated by her fear that she might be about to utter a cliché to the point where she is, at times, virtually mute, 'too cynical to speak', as Radiohead's Thom Yorke put it in 'My Iron Lung'.[18] Angela obsesses over her emotions because they seem convincing to her in a way that other things do not — for reasons Christian Slater, in his role as Hard Harry in *Pump Up the Volume*, understood all too well. 'You look around and nothing is real,' he says to his devoted teen followers, 'but at least pain is real.'[19] In 1991, Richey Edwards had cut his arm with a razor blade to prove to a journalist that the Manic Street Preachers were a real band; by 1994 he had started doing it routinely, just to prove he was a human being. The masochistic protagonist of Nine Inch Nails' 'Hurt' clings to pain as a solace for the same reason — it is, he says, 'the only thing that's real'.[20]

In the third episode of *My So-Called Life*, aired in September 1994, Angela watches newsreel footage of President Kennedy's famous 'Ask not' speech, and reflects that people of her parents' generation love to talk about where they were when he was shot. 'Which makes me kind of jealous,' she says. 'I wish I'd lived through something important enough to know where I was when it happened.'[21] It could be argued that Angela has already lived through the LA Riots, the fall of the Berlin Wall and the death of Kurt Cobain. But none of those things seem as real to her as the things that happened in the sixties, when the development of the spectacle was at an earlier stage. She pines for a time when things really happened, when America was not imitating itself, when America was really America. Of course, America was not the only country to suffer a reality crisis after 1968 — Damon Albarn had already observed that England was becoming less like England as the days went by, and New Zealand was fast disappearing too. Radiohead visited the country as part of its seemingly never-ending *Pablo Honey* tour early in 1994. 'We were taken to one of the most beautiful places I've ever seen in my life,' said Thom Yorke. 'And suddenly it occurred to me that the only reason we were there was because … I can't put my finger on it. Something to do with the industry, and a lot to do with MTV. And wherever you see MTV, there's a Coca-Cola machine right next to it. And all of a sudden, the view lost its meaning.'[22] Yorke felt himself being drawn toward the centre of the Spectacle, his band becoming enmeshed in the process by which the real is transformed into a representation of itself, emotions into sitcoms, forests into fake plastic trees. Toward the end of 1994, the band added to its set a new song, written on tour, called 'The Bends'. 'I wish it was the sixties, I wish we could be happy,' sang Yorke. 'I wish, I wish, I wish something would happen.'[23]

The Best Year

According to Noel Gallagher of Oasis, most English bands, when trying to break into the American market, made a simple blunder. 'They're too English, for a start,' he told 2FM in June 1994, 'so some kid from Boston or wherever isn't gonna understand what Brett Anderson's talking about.' Blur was about to embark on a nine-date tour of America's more cosmopolitan cities with Pulp as support, and Gallagher didn't think they stood much of a chance either. 'No-one's gonna understand *Parklife* outside of, y'know, Putney,' he said.[1] The guitarist's theory seemed to be confirmed by Beavis and Butt-head's review of *Parklife* in August. 'What the hell language is he speaking?' asked Butt-head. 'Yeah!' said Beavis. 'I can hear some American words in there, but it's like, I can't really tell what he's saying.' The two watched in silence for a few more moments as Blur's cockney fantasia unfolded on the screen. 'England sucks,' said Butt-head.[2]

Oasis, meanwhile, was having its own difficulties overseas. 'This lad,' said Noel Gallagher, waving his G&T in the direction of his brother as the *NME*'s tape recorder rolled in April 1994, 'thinks it's rock 'n' roll to get thrown off a fuckin' ferry.'[3] Noel was referring to an incident that had occurred when Oasis was on its way to Amsterdam for a show supporting The Verve in May. The band had got through five bottles of Jack Daniels on the short bus trip to the port, and by the time they got on the ferry, Liam was completely out of control — shouting, swearing and terrorising the passengers. Security caught him stealing from the on-board duty-free store, locked him in the brig, and told Oasis's tour manager that the singer would on no account be allowed into Holland. Two weeks later, Liam was unrepentant about his behaviour. 'That's rock and roll!' he said. But Noel wasn't having it. 'Nah,' he said, 'rock and roll is going to Amsterdam, doing your gig, playing your music and saying you blew 'em away.' 'Rock and roll is about being yourself!' Liam retorted. 'No it's not,' said Noel, like an impatient teacher talking to a slow student. 'Rock and roll is about music. Music, music, music.'[4]

'The reason we started this band,' said Noel, in an interview with Manchester's Granada TV in June, 'was because, above all else, I love music.'[5] The guitarist had grown up listening to the Rolling Stones and the Beatles, and worshipping at the feet of the Smiths' Johnny Marr. Later, he was swept up in the excitement of Madchester, 'goin' down the Hacienda', as he put it in an interview with 2FM's Mark Kates.[6] He saw the Stone Roses play at Spike Island in 1990, and while he was under no illusions about the quality of the gig, the idea that an indie guitar band with the right songs and the right attitude could take on the world would see him through the next four years of his life. Noel took the aspirational patter of the Manchester groups — believe in yourself, make it happen — very seriously. Unlike the Mondays' more 'studenty' fans, he saw the success of Shaun Ryder as exemplary, symbolic of rock's eternal promise to the working-class youth of Britain: that rock and roll could get you paid, laid, and out of wherever you were. In 1991, Noel began writing songs in earnest, songs about getting out of the city and making some money; songs, as he later put it, about 'escaping and being free'.[7]

In spring 1992, Noel took a job as a roadie with the Inspiral Carpets. 'The worst thing,' he said, 'was knowing that I was miles better than the Inspirals. Miles better. But I needed the money.'[8] Thankfully, the gig turned out to be fairly short-lived. As one of the most hyped British bands of the early nineties, the Inspiral Carpets' fortunes were inextricably tied up with the fate of baggy, and when the music press lost interest and moved on to shoegaze, the group's star fell dramatically. The Inspiral Carpets downsized their operation toward the end of 1992, and their roadie was laid off and sent back to Manchester, where he was astonished to find that his younger brother had joined a band. Not a very good band, but a band, Noel thought, that had potential.

The Rain had a solid rhythm section, and Liam was a surprisingly good frontman. But the group was missing something, and that something, Noel felt, was himself, and the songs he'd written. He made Liam, bassist Paul 'Bonehead' Arthurs, Paul McGuigan and drummer Tony McCarroll an offer. 'If I join this band,' said Noel, 'you fuckin' belong to me seven days a week, and we're going for it big time.'[9]

Twelve shows later, the band — which had since been renamed Oasis, at Noel's suggestion — was signed to Creation Records by Alan McGee, who had caught their act quite accidentally at a show in Glasgow in the summer of 1993. 'He walked in, saw us onstage, and said, "Who's this band?",' explained Noel Gallagher. 'They said, "Oh, it's just this bunch of guys who threatened to smash up the stage if we didn't let them play."' McGee, according to Noel, 'bought a drink, watched us do the gig. We came offstage, and he gave us a six-album deal — just like that.'[10] Noel laughed, recalling the moment at which his rock and roll dream began to come true. A few months later, he found himself standing behind Johnny Marr in a Manchester music store. 'This is what it's about,' he thought to himself, as he watched his childhood hero drop nine thousand pounds on the counter. 'Sooner or later, this is what I've got to be!' As it turned out, he wouldn't have to wait long. Oasis recorded its first album, *Definitely Maybe*, early in 1994. Released in July, it became the fastest-selling debut in UK chart history, while the single 'Live Forever' went to number one. In no time at all, Oasis seemed to have gone, as *Q* magazine's Stuart Maconie put it, 'from roadies and no-hopers to the future of Western art'.[11]

Noel Gallagher was pleased, but not especially surprised by the band's success. 'I just don't think there's anybody else doing anything at the moment which is really saying anything,' he said. 'People who write songs are getting a bit too self-centred. They tend to sing about themselves, their childhood and their past, and how crap their life is. That's just boring. So you had a rough childhood — join the club.'[12] Noel began, as Kurt Cobain had, with Beatles, drugs and divorces. He was a child of the sixties, whose life had been shaped by economic decline, the early separation of his parents, and the tantalising possibility that rock and roll could allow him to transcend both. But where the freedom offered by music was, for Cobain, fatally ill-defined, Gallagher had no doubt about what it meant — the freedom to work hard, seize opportunities, make something of yourself and, with a bit of luck, never have to work a day in your life again. The 'whatever' in Nirvana's 'Smells Like Teen Spirit' betrayed the ennui that crippled Cobain's optimism: whatever, nevermind. But when Noel Gallagher used the word, it spoke of possibilities. 'I'm free to do whatever I choose,' went the lyrics to 'Whatever'. Like many of the verses Noel wrote during his purple patch of the early nineties, these seemed to predict in advance the state of grace he would later achieve as a successful rock star with records in the charts, and money in the bank. 'Whatever' was released as a stand-alone single in November 1994, Liam Gallagher delivering his brother's lyric with all the rock star cheek it demanded. 'I'm free to do whatever I like,' he sneered, 'whatever I like if it's wrong or right, it's all right.'[13]

Like Noel, Liam saw rock and roll as being fundamentally about escaping from limitations and being all that you could be. 'We just wanna be the biggest band in the world,' he told Zoe Ball. 'And we want all the things that go with it. I wanna be a big pop star and do loads of people's heads in.' Ball, like most UK music journalists in 1994, seemed relieved and overjoyed to hear guitar bands spouting such stuff after the long, slow season of shoegaze. 'You're being hyped as the best band around at the moment,' she said. 'Is the hype true?' 'Yeah,' said Liam, scratching his chin. 'Best band on the planet — it's a fact.'[14] Oasis hastened the death of indie-rock-as-art, and embraced the new spirit of competition — in which chart placement, audience sizes and big, bold claims to greatness had replaced the confusing and pretentious waffle of the old indie. 'A lot of people get all embarrassed about the success they get,' said Liam, not naming any names. 'Oh,' he whined, in a mocking imitation of the unhappy rock star, 'I didn't really want it.' Liam scoffed. 'Of course you wanted it!'[15]

But when it came to the crunch, Liam's idea of freedom differed from Noel's in one important respect. Noel saw freedom as being somewhat like retirement — work hard, pay your dues, and you can make enough money to not have anybody tell you what to do. For Liam, on the other hand, rock and roll meant doing whatever you liked, whenever you liked. Where Noel viewed the episode on the ferry as a disaster — his brother sabotaging an important gig with stupid behaviour — Liam saw it as exemplary, the stuff rock legends are made of. 'It's like what fuckin' Bobby Gillespie said,' he reminded Noel. 'He said, "I'm sick of all these bands who don't get into situations no more." The last band that did it was the Pistols — they'd go out and, like, something would *happen*.' This was what Liam had enjoyed about the fight on the ferry — in that moment, Oasis wasn't just a band standing on stage and singing about being free and not giving a fuck, it was a band going out into the world and actually *being* free and not giving a fuck. 'It happened, right?' he said. 'That was reality, it *happened*.' As the argument wore on, Liam grew increasingly frustrated with his brother's professionalised view of rock and roll, which seemed to reduce the music to a series of obligations and appointments. Noel might be content to sit in his hotel room and practise his fretwork, but Liam would be out on the street causing trouble, getting in a fight with 'some crazy fucking crackhead bird', another example, he said, of 'a situation that just arose. That is *life*.' 'How often do you have arguments like this?' asked the *NME*'s reporter. 'Every fuckin' day,' replied Liam, exasperated.[16] But it was the argument that made Oasis exciting — the constant tug-of-war between Noel's need for control and Liam's lust for life meant that Oasis ended up with the best of both worlds. The songs were incredible, and the band was real. When they played, they blew people away, and when they went out, things happened to them.

By living the life they sang about, the Gallaghers seemed, at one stroke, to have removed the quotation marks that had haunted rock and roll over the past four years. Oasis was sublimely unselfconscious, and this, as the Stone Roses' Ian Brown pointed out, was more than could be said for some of Britpop's other great white hopes in 1994. 'Suede seemed like a step backwards to me,' he said. 'Like, when us and the Mondays were written about a lot of things seemed to be getting more and more real. But Suede doing their seventies' Bowie imitations took it back again.'[17] Oasis, Brown insisted, was a sign that things were moving forward. This might have seemed an odd thing to say, considering how proudly the Gallaghers wore their Beatles influences on *Definitely Maybe*. Oasis, after all, had just become the first band formed in the nineties to appear on the cover of *Mojo* — a magazine invented to cater to a new demographic of past-worshipping, boxed-set collecting music fans. 'You've got the band you've always wanted,' said the headline of the January 1995 issue.[18] But Oasis didn't just copy the music of the sixties. It seemed to have re-connected with that decade's optimism, before the world lost its faith in the future. They were non-retro in a way that no band had been since 1968. This was perhaps the reason why Maconie felt moved to describe Oasis as the future of Western art. It had been accepted for the last two decades that Western art had no future but Oasis made it look as though postmodernism might be nothing more than a nervous complaint of the overeducated. 'Oasis just aren't … drama students,' explained Brown. 'Oasis are real. *Proper* real,' added the Stone Roses' bass player, Mani. 'That always shines through.'[19]

The band took all of this in its stride. 'We deserve all the praise we get at the moment, because we write the best songs,' said Noel. 'Because we mean it, you know what I mean?' added Liam.[20] But despite their earlier stated reservations about Suede and Blur, the Gallaghers had decided, by the end of 1994, not to get into a slanging match with other British bands. 'Music is not a contest,' said Noel, in an interview with Donna Matthews of Elastica at the Brit Awards in November. 'You can't come here and slag other bands off,' he said. 'Why not?' asked Matthews, obviously disappointed. 'Because,' Noel replied, 'we're all trying to take America, America, America.' Noel insisted that it was important for British bands to stick together, to keep their eyes on the prize. 'We're gonna go and break America,' he said, 'and we're gonna say to 'em, who invented your language? We did. Who made you realise what your music was? We did.' The healthy state of Britpop, the sheer quantity and quality of great music coming out of England suggested that the dark days of 1992 were long gone. '1994 has been the best year,' Noel declared. 'What about '95?' asked Matthews. 'Ninety-five is gonna be even better. And '96 is where we just take over.' England had stopped sucking, the decline had been arrested; now, the only way was up.[21]

1995

Classic Rock Now

'We didn't intend to be in a pop band,' said Thom Yorke in 1995, 'we just happen to be in one.'[1] Throughout 1994, Radiohead had been faced with the difficult task of trying to repeat something it had done accidentally. 'Creep' had become a hit without Yorke ever once thinking that it might get played on the radio. Now, as he set about recording a batch of new songs with producer John Leckie, it sometimes felt to Yorke as though he could think of nothing else. By June, he and the band — Jonny Greenwood, Colin Greenwood, Ed O'Brien and Phil Selway — were routinely second-guessing themselves and suffering from an acute case of cabin fever. They decided to take their record company's advice and embark on a short tour to rebuild their confidence, and this seemed to do the trick: a reinvigorated Radiohead went back into the studio with Leckie and recorded a handful of new songs, five of which were released as an EP — entitled *My Iron Lung* — in October.

On first hearing, the title track seemed a curious release from a group that had spent the better part of a year trying to distance itself from the perception that it was a poor man's Nirvana at best and a one-hit wonder at worst. 'My Iron Lung' stuck closely to the quiet/loud/quiet formula of Nirvana and the Pixies — a formula Radiohead had already successfully exploited with 'Creep'. The *NME* described it as 'Dear Prudence' with a bomb strapped to its body. But this could just as easily describe Nirvana's 'Heart-Shaped Box', the song 'My Iron Lung' most closely resembled. The lyrics revealed that Yorke was all too aware that he was running out of ideas. 'This is our new song, just like the last one,' he sang, 'a total waste of time.'[2] And yet somehow, Yorke had managed to turn his sense of frustration with the demands of the industry and his own shortage of ideas into a real source of inspiration. Yorke's apoplectic ranting in the chorus, fed through a distortion pedal and almost drowned out by the band's noise, was as terrifying as anything on *In Utero*, and the song as a whole was far more convincing than anything Radiohead had released since 'Creep'. Reviewing that single in 1992, comedian Sean Hughes had complained that it simply wasn't angry enough. 'It should go *mad*,' he said. Now, with 'My Iron Lung', Hughes had got his wish.[3]

The impression the EP had given of a band with a new sense of purpose was confirmed by Radiohead's live shows early in 1995. Watching Radiohead at the Oxford Apollo in February, *Melody Maker*'s David Bennun could scarcely believe he was looking at the same group that had reluctantly slumped across the stage at Reading in July 1994. 'Fuck me,' he wrote, 'the fervour of them.'[4] In some small but crucial way, the sense of disgust that had motivated 'Creep' had been amplified and redirected. Yorke had stopped beating himself up in public and had raised a skinny fist to the world. 'Thom has a guitar-free mic pose that sums it up,' wrote Bennun, 'part sulk, part hunch, part poisoned defiance. Look at me. Please don't look at me.'[5] Yorke had spent the better part of the past two years standing on stages and being stared at by people, and the experience had changed him profoundly. 'The stuff we've been going through is mind-altering,' he told the Stud Brothers shortly after the release of *My Iron Lung*.[6] The new songs Radiohead had recorded with Leckie had seen the band try to give form to this experience. As its title suggested, Radiohead's second album, *The Bends*, was about what can happen to the human body when it rises to the surface too quickly.

As a song cycle about the pressures of unexpected fame, *The Bends* ought to have been terrible. But when the album was released in March 1995, it soon became apparent that Radiohead had somehow found a loophole in one of rock music's irrefutable laws. The usual course of events saw a young band with a swag of great songs sell a million records, spend twelve months touring the world, and go back into the studio to record a follow-up, only to find that they'd run out of ideas and had nothing to write about except what they'd been doing over the last twelve months — playing stadiums, sleeping in hotels and watching their own faces on TV. Radiohead had reversed the paradigm. *Pablo Honey* had been uninspired — the work of talented musicians who had nothing much to say about anything. But the album had spawned a hit, and had gone on to sell one and a half million copies worldwide; and the feeling of sharing your feelings with one and a half million strangers by playing your songs every night of the week for over a year in twenty different countries had finally given Thom Yorke something to write about. Yorke took the specific indignities of the music industry — the distant faces in the crowd, the identikit hotel rooms, the banal, repetitive TV interviews — and linked them to the wider feelings of boredom and alienation experienced by ordinary people in the last decade of the twentieth century. Yorke's paranoid streak allowed him to see that the two were related — that the band's problems were connected to the problems of the whole world; that the disappearance of New Zealand was connected to the ubiquity of Coke machines, that Coke was in business with MTV, and that MTV was in business with Radiohead. This, according to Jon Savage and Hanif Kureshi, was what it meant to be in a pop group in the mid nineties. 'Pop has become a principal motor of the Western consumer machine,' wrote the pair in their 1995 anthology, *The Faber Book of Pop*. 'It is in the vanguard of the spread of Western values into new markets.'[7]

The Bends, while gloomy, offered listeners release from its grim scenarios in satisfying outbursts of stadium rock. The *NME*'s Andrew Mueller described 'High and Dry' and 'The Bends' as 'shameless fists-aloft crowd pleasers, the former a rewrite of U2's "Stay", the latter lurching on a riff that more recalls Lynyrd Skynyrd or Boston'.[8] It was the band's newfound ability to recycle alienation into classic rock riffs and singalong choruses that convinced Mueller that Radiohead might recover from the misstep of *Pablo Honey* and conquer America. 'They'll do it the way Nine Inch Nails have,' he wrote, 'by bringing the world's self-described outsiders to sing along in vast throngs to the same words to the record they all own. Nice work if you can get it, but one wonders how happy Radiohead, grimly determined misfits that they are, will be to do it.'[9] Here, Mueller hit on the conundrum Radiohead faced in 1995: how could the band consolidate the success of *The Bends* without going further down the spiral of madness that had inspired its creation? Bennun wrote that Radiohead's new songs were 'so marvellously radio-friendly that the group will undoubtedly spend the next three years traipsing around EMI's most lucrative target zones selling them'.[10] But considering what the band had been though in 1993, this sounded more like a premonition of disaster than a prediction of success. After all, Yorke — as several writers observed — shared more than just a love of R.E.M. and striped sweaters with the lead singer of Nirvana. Like Cobain, Yorke suffered from an empathy surplus; the same hypersensitivity that made him a great songwriter made it hard enough for him to deal with normal life, let alone the relentless crush of celebrity culture. 'If there's anyone who's stared harder into the deluxe fly-dive holidays of fame,' wrote Jennifer Nine, in her *NME* review of *The Bends*, 'he sleeps with angels now.'[11]

Bored-Furious,
Stop-Start

In 1993, Elastica's Justine Frischmann placed an ad in the classifieds pages of *Melody Maker*. 'Guitarist wanted,' read the copy. 'Influences: The Fall, the Stranglers, Wire.'[1] The successful applicant was Donna Matthews, who joined drummer Justin Welch, bass player Annie Holland and songwriter Frischmann to record a series of near-perfect singles over the course of the next twelve months, two of which — 'Line Up' and 'Connection' — charted in the UK Top 20. By 1995, Elastica had become a regular fixture in the music press, and Frischmann's name and face had begun to appear in the unlikely context of the *Sun* and the *Daily Mail* — her relationship with Britpop's favourite son, Damon Albarn, had made her the subject of tabloid gossip. This upset Frischmann, who'd always aspired to be in a cult band rather than a pop group, but it didn't hurt the band's profile. In Britpop terms, the appearance of a sharp-witted indie band like Elastica in the gossip rags was a victory, one of a growing number of signs that indie rock was the new pop, that Elastica, Blur and Oasis had usurped the position once occupied by Take That and Peter Andre in the national consciousness. Like the post-punk bands Frischmann had listed in her wanted ad, Elastica played smart, literate guitar pop with a sense of humour and a subversive edge. But they seemed to have succeeded where those groups had not by becoming household names — a feat which put them closer to the orbit of arty pop stars like Adam Ant or Duran Duran. As Elastica talked to MTV's Kennedy after a blinding performance at the 1995's KROQ Weenie Roast, this was a comparison Frischmann seemed happy to embrace. 'Adam Ant and the guys from Duran Duran were at the show yesterday,' said Kennedy, 'and all they could talk about was your band. Does that feel all right?' Frischmann smiled. 'It's totally great for us,' she said, 'because they were big heroes when we were growing up.'[2]

But not all of Frischmann's heroes saw her band in such glowing terms. By the time Elastica's eponymous debut album was released in March 1995, two of the three groups listed in the ad Matthews had answered had taken legal action against the band for copyright infringement. Wire alleged that Elastica had stolen the melody of 'I Am the Fly' for 'Line Up' and the riff from 'Three Girl Rhumba' for 'Connection'. Meanwhile, the Stranglers, noting the strong similarity between 'Waking Up' and 'No More Heroes', had also sued. These legal troubles gave credence to the band's critics — the argument that Elastica was derivative and retro had now been upheld in a court of law. And yet, as music writer Jon Savage observed, there was a subtext to these accusations that went beyond one band stealing a riff from another. 'A whole world of dismissal is enshrined in the sound-alike argument,' wrote Savage. 'Implicit is the idea that pop no longer has any vigour, that it has all been done before, that it and we are adrift in a postmodernist squall of emotion-free irony, referencing and pastiche.'[3]

Savage believed that Elastica, like most musicians of their generation, had given up on the search for true originality as a wild goose chase, but had nevertheless fashioned something from their second-hand materials that spoke of their own experiences and their own epoch. 'This is not nostalgia,' he wrote, 'more a perception that the past cannot be beaten; rather, why not take all this stuff and engage with it physically and emotionally, moulding and pummelling it into something that works for you?'[4] Justine Frischmann saw Elastica's music in similar terms. 'I think in the nineties it's very hard to make music that isn't self-referential if you're making music with a classic line-up,' she said. 'I think probably by the time I was born, the Beatles and the Stones had done everything that could truly be done with rock and roll so, in a way, I think it's impossible to be truly ground-breaking now.' But Frischmann didn't really believe this was a problem. Rather, she saw pop history as an inheritance, and was determined to make the best use of it. 'The thing is,' she went on, 'this is the first time the nineties has existed. It's the first time the chemistry of Elastica has existed. I think what we're doing is definitely a different combination of people and influences to anything before.'[5]

Savage observed that older critics, 'brought up on a linear cultural model', had trouble accepting the idea that the past could be used creatively.[6] They pined for the days when music was dynamic and original, and cried 'gotcha' whenever they caught new bands recycling old sounds. Postmodernism had existed as an idea for at least three decades when Savage wrote his piece on Elastica, but the linear model he referred to was still the guiding principle of mainstream rock criticism. This model maintained that rock music moved from a dark past to a brighter future, that it must progress in order to survive, and that every generation must reinvent the form to suit the times. Its presence in the world of pop attested to the fact that rock music had been born as modernism came to an end, in the last decade during which it was possible for people in Western Europe and North America to believe in progress in a wider sense. Its durability in England had a great deal to do with the role played by British art schools in fostering new rock and roll talent — musicians and critics with art educations inherited modernism's mania for progress, and applied the same standards to music. They saw innovation as a mark of greatness and repetition as a form of decadence and a symptom of decline. According to this model, rock music seemed to have suffered a colossal failure of nerve at some point in the mid eighties, after which new bands began to recycle the past at an exponential rate. The generation born in the sixties, it seemed, had betrayed the tradition — unable or unwilling to invent a new style of its own, it had resorted to stealing from the past. 'In making a clean break from their parentage, hippies built the cultural arena in which we still live,' observed Julian Dibbell in *Details* magazine in 1991. 'Their perverse insistence that we both occupy that arena and tear it down fuels the dilemma of our generation.'[7]

The baby boomers' 'ideology of permanent revolution' — as Dibbell called it — was not only exhausted, it also failed to take account of the important role that collage, quotation and outright theft had always played in rock music. But even the more astute critics, who understood how this process worked, felt that Britpop had crossed the line from reference into outright pastiche. In May 1994, *The Wire* published a piece by Simon Reynolds called 'Post-Rock' — a round-up of half-a-dozen British groups who, Reynolds argued, were pushing the form of rock music into radical new shapes by crossbreeding it with electronic music. Reynolds observed that Seefeel, Bark Psychosis, Main, Papa Sprain, Stereolab and Pram had explicitly defined their studio science against grunge, with its luddite insistence on real bands playing real guitars in real time. But he also noted that post-rock futurism was a timely antidote to Britpop's wholesale plundering of the past. Not that Reynolds was against plundering — the writer championed post-rock's use of the sampler precisely because it allowed the groups to creatively recycle the entire history of music. But where Seefeel and Bark Psychosis had made modernist junk-sculpture out of old sounds, Blur, Suede and Oasis seemed to him to be nothing more than knock-off artists. 'In 1994, just six short years from the new millennium,' he complained, 'this is where the money is at: in the musical equivalent of reproduction antiques.'[8]

Money — as Reynolds implied — was part of the problem. When Belgian rock group Deus visited England in 1994, singer Tom Barman found himself astonished by 'the cynicism and careerism' of the musicians he met. 'Everyone is desperate to get signed and be famous,' he told *Mojo* magazine. 'That's cool, in a way, but it means there are very few original bands around.'[9] By 1995, record companies were prepared to offer unheard-of amounts of cash to bands who played in an identifiably Britpop style, and the reasons not to take the money were fast disappearing. Blur had trashed the indie argument about selling out as elitist nonsense, and Oasis had given aspiration and ambition a fresh shot of working-class cool. Critics could complain that Britpop bands had abandoned the difficult quest for new forms in favour of easy money, but the idea that music had to move forward required a belief that there was somewhere to go, and those who had been seduced by Britpop's shiny surfaces were starting to believe they'd never had it so good. Radio 1 rang with chirpy pop odes to fun and freedom like Oasis's 'Whatever', Supergrass's 'Alright' ('We are young, we run green'[10]), and the Boo Radleys' 'Wake Up Boo' ('Twenty-five, don't recall a time I felt this alive'[11]). 'I think everyone like Blur and Oasis just realised at the same time that pop music was about being brash and in-your-face,' said the Boo Radleys' Martin Carr in *Ray Gun* magazine. 'It wasn't just moping around in your bedroom, it was music for getting ready to go out on a Friday night. It was supposed to be a celebration, almost.'[12] Britpop was a party, and no-one wanted it to stop.

With this in mind, Peter Shapiro argued in *Spin* early in 1995 that the term 'post-rock' might more properly be applied to Blur and Oasis than Stereolab. 'That's post-rock in the sense of Francis Fukuyama's notion of Post-History,' he wrote, 'in which dialectic is dead because capitalist democracy has won.'[13] Here, Shapiro summed up the logic of late Britpop neatly; by this point, the music had no real need for critical discourse. The proof of its success as art lay in its popularity, its future depended on nothing more than the industry's ability to match supply to demand. 'Zeitgeist my arse,' wrote the *NME's* Jennifer Nine in February. 'The question is not whether it's too soon to have an Elastica tribute band, but how fast the reserve sides can line up next to the pitch.'[14]

Nine was reviewing a show at Dublin Castle in London's Camden Town — the favourite stomping-ground of Blur's Alex James, and the epicentre of the Britpop boom. The band was Powder, a London-based three-piece whose distinctly English brand of speedball pop was, Nine concluded, very Now. 'It might seem arbitrary that Now is currently this lurching, drum-heavy, fist-tight, bored-furious, stop-start, Brit-new wave, Stranglers-sneering-cockney-relentless pop thing,' she wrote, 'but fashion's tyrannical, babe.'[15] Britain's music scene had always been fast, its rate of change dictated by the weekly publication of its music press. But the success of Britpop had sped things up still further. Now that Blur and Oasis had proven that indie rock could be big business, speculative money was transforming the scene beyond all recognition. Where, in 1992, groups like Powder might have had a year or more to toil in relative obscurity before attracting the attention of labels, now they were being signed for large advances after playing only a handful of shows — or, in the case of Powder's labelmates, Menswear, before the band was even formed. According to songwriter Chris Gentry, Menswear's first show had to be a secret gig so that A&R people *wouldn't* turn up. The speed of the new pop economy left bands with little time to do anything other than keep up, and none at all for the kind of experiments that led to innovation. 'Face facts,' wrote Nine. 'This is Camden. You wanna play in these leagues, you don't come slouching around here with your half-arsed ideas of last year's pop, or God forbid, *one you thought up yourself.*[16] New ideas were out of the question, and even new derivative ideas — the careful synthesis of new wave that Frischmann and Albarn had perfected over the course of 1993, for example — would most likely take too long to pull off. When Nine complained that Powder was derivative, her point was not that the band sounded like the Stranglers, but that it sounded like Elastica sounding like the Stranglers — a reproduction of a reproduction.

The Future of Rock

In 1995, the man who produced *Nevermind* threw his flannel shirt in the bin, and declared that grunge was officially dead, and may have been for some time. 'Grunge died before it was ever really born,' Butch Vig told *Volume* magazine. 'May it rest in peace.'[1] Since 1994, Vig had turned down countless offers to make Nirvana-sounding rock records, and had instead devoted his time and the resources of Smart — the studio he owned in Madison, Wisconsin — to a project that owed far more to hip-hop than it did to alt rock. Vig and his partners Steve Marker and Duke Erikson had been experimenting with samplers, building instrumental tracks using found sounds and recycled outtakes, making 'weird sonic things with guitars and loops'.[2]

Vig and Marker had planned to create music of their own ever since they first built Smart in the mid eighties, but the financial demands of running the studio meant that paid work always took precedence, and the personal project was repeatedly put on the back burner. Oddly enough, it was paid work that got them back into it. Vig had become much sought after as a remixer for hire, and a series of commissions from Nine Inch Nails, House of Pain and Depeche Mode gave him the opportunity to refine his hip-hop-rock hybrid on the record company dime. 'Typically, we would erase and rearrange the song,' he explained, 'and then we would record new noise loops, put new drum loops down, add new guitars, drums, keyboards, make it into a whole different thing.'[3] Remix work gave Vig and Marker's project a direction, and also provided it with a name. 'This friend came to the studio to play some percussion on a remix of a Nine Inch Nails track,' said Vig, 'and when he saw all the loops that I had going around the desk he said, "Man, this fuckin' shit looks like garbage to me. Are you sure you know what you're doing?"' Vig wasn't at all sure that he did — but he knew right away that he'd found a handle for his virtual band: Garbage. 'We liked the name,' he explained, 'because it could just be a blend of all sorts of trash and stuff.'[4]

Much of the music for Garbage's first album had taken shape by the spring of 1994. But over the past twelve months, Vig had become convinced that the group was making songs rather than beats, that they would soon need a singer, and that the singer should be a woman. 'I really liked working with L7,' explained Vig. 'There's a different kind of psychology going on in the studio when you're working with women.'[5] Vig, Marker and Erikson began writing lyrics 'from a female point of view', and started looking around for a performer who could bring them to life. As it turned out, they didn't have to look far — Marker found Garbage's singer on his couch. One night in March 1994, the producer was watching MTV at two in the morning, when he happened to catch a video by a band called Angelfish. He knew, as soon as he laid eyes on the group's singer, Shirley Manson, that she was perfect for Garbage. Marker's timing was just right. If he'd been watching MTV at any other moment on any other night he wouldn't have seen Manson at all — Angelfish's video had bypassed the Buzz Bin and was headed straight for the real bin, and the night in question was the one and only time it was shown on the network. But the clip's failure to get traction on MTV was, at that point, probably a blessing in disguise. Angelfish was on its last legs; the group's members were fighting amongst themselves, and Manson — who'd never really felt comfortable in the band — was looking for an out.

On the day Kurt Cobain died, the three founding members of Garbage met Shirley Manson at a London hotel and, a few weeks later, she flew to Madison for some trial recordings at Marker's home studio. The session was a disaster. Marker set the nervous singer up in front of a microphone, played her some Garbage instrumentals, and asked her to improvise. 'There were just these little blasts of music, and one of them humming a tune,' Manson told *Rolling Stone*, 'and they were like "make up some words."'[6] Manson — who had never written a song in her life, let alone made one up on the spot — was terrified, and managed only the most tentative bits of scat singing. But a few weeks later, Manson, as Vig put it, 'had the balls' to call him back and ask for another shot, and this time everything worked. Slowly, she made her way through the songs Marker, Erickson and Vig had drafted, rewriting lyrics, suggesting melodic ideas and turning the trio's audio junk-sculptures into real songs. None of this came easily to Manson — the singer was nervous in front of the microphone, unsure of her abilities as a writer and deeply insecure about her role in the group. But on songs like 'Queer', 'Vow', and 'Only Happy When It Rains', she managed to turn her frustration and self-doubt into the motor of her performance, if not the actual subject of the songs.

In January 1995, Vig played some rough mixes for Billy Corgan. The Smashing Pumpkins singer remarked that it sounded 'pretty poppy'. But as Vig pointed out, this couldn't have surprised him too much. 'He knows that I'm a pop geek. I love hooks messed up with noise, and if you listen to the Pumpkins or Nirvana or even Sonic Youth you can hear that dichotomy of noise and melody blended together. That's the kind of thing I hope we're doing in Garbage.'[7] But there was a world of difference between the pop structures deployed on songs like 'Come As You Are', and the pop process that Vig had now embraced with Garbage. Nirvana, Sonic Youth, Smashing Pumpkins and L7 were all guitar bands that wrote pop songs. Garbage was three studio-bound boffins with samplers and computers fronted by a flown-in female singer; exactly the kind of thing that alternative rock had been put on earth to destroy. Vig was quite aware that he was committing indie-rock heresy. 'If it was me, and I'd heard about three producers hooking up with some woman singer from Scotland, I'd look at it cynically,' he admitted to *Rolling Stone*'s Eric Schumacher.[8]

Over the past four years, rock critics and audiences had been given an intensive crash course in musical authenticity. Thanks to Nirvana, Pearl Jam and Soundgarden, they'd learned the difference between real alternative rock bands and fake metal made by studio computer geeks, and were not about to be fooled again. Now, Garbage was asking them to grasp the concept of real alternative rock made by studio computer geeks, and the transition was not an easy one for them to make. 'Cynics might argue that Shirley's being used as a puppet the way Phil Spector used his female singers,' offered a reporter from *Ray Gun* magazine. 'Nothing could be further from the truth,' replied Vig. 'We're a band.'[9] Garbage, as far as Vig was concerned, was just as much a rock group as Nirvana was. But its existence demanded a much-needed redefinition of what a rock group could be.

Grunge's reassuringly humanist vision of long-haired dudes playing proletarian rock had been necessary in 1991 as an antidote to the excesses of the eighties. But by 1995, it had become a problem. Grunge's luddite tendencies had locked bands into a sound-alike formula as deathly, in its way, as that of the pop-metal groups they had sought to replace. 'I've gotten really bored with most bands,' Steve Marker told *Alternative Press*. 'Two guitars, bass, drums and a guy yelling over the top. It's boring, conservative and reactionary.'[10] Reviewing Nirvana's MTV *Unplugged in New York* album, Rob Sheffield wrote that alt-rock's ban on 'fake music' had 'done more to bleed the humour and spontaneity out of music than samplers ever did'.[11]

'Some musicians live in an acoustically sealed vacuum, a world that consists only of bass, guitars and drums,' wrote Filter's guitarist Brian Liesegang in November 1995.[12] In a *Spin* feature on 'The Future of Rock', Liesegang sneered at the practitioners of 'so-called alternative rock' for driving music down a retro cul-de-sac, and promoted a new technology-assisted form of rock made possible by sampling. Liesegang and his musical partner, Richard Patrick, had been members of Nine Inch Nails, but had left to form their own group before the release of *The Downward Spiral*. They shared with Reznor an almost evangelical belief in the need for rock to evolve beyond 'flannel revivalism', a line Reznor continued to push as *The Downward Spiral* edged its way toward multi-platinum status in the summer of 1995.[13] It was appropriate that Vig had found the name for his new project while working on a Nine Inch Nails remix, since both groups represented, in slightly different ways, the first stirrings of a new cyborg rock, part human, part machine, which seemed, by mid decade, to offer the most promising escape route from the dead end of grunge. In a year when Bill Gates denied that there was 'anything unique about human intelligence', alternative rock began to abandon its humanist fantasies, and admitted that it might have something to learn from machines.

The Future's Been Sold

In August 1995, BBC TV screened a special music program called *Britpop Now*, a survey of new UK bands featuring live performances by Elastica, Pulp, PJ Harvey, the Boo Radleys, Powder and Blur. At the start of the show, Damon Albarn appeared seated in a large, antique chair, telling the story of how England had won the music wars. He invited viewers to cast their minds back to the dark days of 1992, when American rock bands stormed the UK charts, and all seemed lost for British pop. 'If you weren't Nirvana, or a diet Nirvana, you were nothing.' Albarn let a satisfied smile break over his face as he went on with the tale. 'Well,' he said, 'I think all that's changed now. British bands are no longer embarrassed to sing about where they're from. They've found their voice. So for the next forty-five minutes, sit back and enjoy some of the best music in the world — the new Britpop.'[1]

The Gallagher brothers were conspicuous by their absence, but no-one watching the show would have been surprised not to see them. A state of war had existed between Blur and Oasis since May, when the latter band's new single 'Some Might Say' had entered the national chart at number one. Albarn had decided to pop in to Oasis's victory party. 'You know, just to say, "Well done",' as he later put it. Music, after all, was not a contest. But someone forgot to tell Liam Gallagher who, on seeing Albarn walk through the door, went right up to him, looked him in the eye and said, 'Fookin' number *one*.' Albarn, taken aback, decided two could play at that game. 'I thought, "Okay, we'll see.""[2] When he learned that Oasis was about to release its next single a week before Blur's, thus sabotaging his band's chances of hitting the number one spot, Albarn had no doubt as to what should be done. Delaying the release would make it look as though Blur was backing out of a fight, and neither the band nor its record company wanted to be called chicken. Blur and Food Records' Andy Ross quickly came to a decision — the new Blur single, 'Country House', would be released on 14 August, the same day as Oasis's 'Roll With It'.

'Country House' was, as Albarn later admitted, the kind of song he wrote in his sleep — a catchy pop tune with clever lyrics built around a club-footed rhythm that Alex James had started referring to as 'the Blur stomp'.[3] The lyrics were in the updated music-hall tradition of 'Tracy Jacks' — a cockeyed look at a deluded English gent who decides to spend his way out of his mid-life crisis by buying himself a big old house in the country. It sounded no more like a hit single than a lot of the other clever, catchy pop tunes Blur had recorded for its new album. But when the band played it at the Mile End sports stadium in June, Albarn saw 36,000 arms swaying in time to the song's jaunty beat and 18,000 mouths singing along to the chorus, and realised in a flash what kind of song he had on his hands. Plans were quickly made to have 'Country House' released as a single, and Damien Hirst was commissioned to make a video.

Anyone who imagined, upon hearing that the brightest star of Britain's contemporary art scene had made a music video, that the result might go over the average *Top of the Pops* viewers' head, was in for a surprise; 'Country House' was so defiantly lowbrow it made Warrant's 'Cherry Pie' look like *In the Realm of the Senses*. Hirst cast Keith Allen as the 'successful fella' described in the song, and filmed him in a series of bawdy set-pieces with the members of Blur, comedian Matt Lucas, *Loaded* pin-up Jo Guest, an assortment of page three models, a marching band and a couple of pigs. The video was, in its own terms, a success — Allen was wickedly funny as the rat-race refugee, and Hirst threw in enough comic inventions to keep things interesting. But the impression it gave of Blur as a gang of madcap funsters — the Beatles in *A Hard Day's Night* let loose on the set of a Benny Hill movie — belied the fact that it came close to breaking up the band.

'Country House' became a sticking point in an ongoing argument within Blur. On one side were Alex James — playboy pop star and unabashed womaniser — and Damon Albarn — knockabout man of the people. On the other stood Graham Coxon — indie stalwart and political idealist. The video's casually sexist scenario was bound to appeal to Albarn, with his newfound love of lads, lager and *Loaded*. It was also, as music writer John Harris has observed, exactly the kind of thing James, Damien Hirst and Keith Allen would have come up with during the course of a big night out at the Groucho Club. But for all these reasons, it stood for everything Coxon disliked about Blur in 1995. As a fan of smart indie-rock bands like Pavement and Sebadoh, Coxon found the video's shameless populism embarrassing. And as a feminist, he saw nothing funny or ironic in the idea of his band being associated with page three girls and *Carry On* antics. The fact that he was, at the time, in a serious relationship with Jo Johnson of the riot grrrl group Huggy Bear made him even less inclined to do so. 'How did Graham take it?' asked the *NME*'s Steve Sutherland. 'His life must have been hell.' 'Yeah,' replied Damon Albarn, 'I think it was.'[4]

But Coxon's right-on attitude, like the hardline political correctness of his girlfriend's band, seemed to Albarn like a leftover from a bygone era, the 'reclusive indie thing' of the late eighties. Albarn believed that this outsider stance had more to do with cowardice and lack of ambition than principles, and a growing number of his contemporaries — from the Gallagher brothers to Pulp's Jarvis Cocker — seemed to agree. By 1993, this idea had been enshrined in music-weekly law, and indie bands that adhered to ideals at the expense of their popularity were routinely ridiculed by press and peers alike. 'The underground in London just deteriorated totally,' said Johnson in 1995, reflecting on Huggy Bear's beginnings. 'Indie just became an abstract term for a style of music, not ideas or values, 'cause they were all signing to major labels. The reasons for being independent were snorted at.'[5]

Huggy Bear had made itself briefly notorious in February 1993, when the band appeared on Channel 4's *The Word* shortly before the start of a UK tour with Bikini Kill. After their interview was finished, the band hung around backstage, and watched a pre-recorded piece about a pair of supermodels called the Barbi Twins as it went to air. The members of Huggy Bear began heckling presenter Terry Christian from the side of the stage, which prompted Christian to refer to them on air as a 'garbage-y band' and eventually got them kicked out of the studio.[6] The contrast between this and Blur's appearance on *Britpop Now* two years later, in 1997, could not have been starker. Albarn didn't sit on the sidelines and heckle the presenter — he *was* the presenter, and this suited him just fine, as did the sight of Pulp's Jarvis Cocker hosting *Top of the Pops*. 'Between us all,' he said, 'we run the pop culture in this country.'[7] Britpop had made rebellion redundant. It was no longer a counterculture, but the culture. Its stars were equally at home presenting on the BBC, standing on stage at Glastonbury, running from the *Daily Star*'s photographers or smiling from the cover of *Smash Hits*; its hits were just as likely to be whistled by milkmen as shouted by indie kids at Mile End. This, Albarn felt, was as it should be. He didn't want to be in the kind of band that set up camp on the outskirts of society and poured scorn on normal people and the things they liked. He wanted Blur to be in society, and to give normal people exactly what they wanted. The trick to this, he felt, was to become normal himself, to let go of the idea that his job as an artist was to be a sort of professional complainer, and to learn to love the things that everyone else did — TV, pop music, page three girls, Jo Guest and football. 'I just want to be a simple person,' he told Sutherland. 'I just want to be normal.'[8]

Albarn's slightly overzealous embrace of working-class culture meant that the subject of class was never far from any discussion of Blur. Now, the band's chart war with Oasis brought it dramatically to the fore. When 'Country House' beat 'Roll With It' to the number one spot on 20 August, the *Daily Mail*'s headline described it as 'the pop victory that makes it hip to be middle class'. One week later, nursing a pint in the Mars Bar, Albarn was approached by a woman who wanted his autograph. She described herself as a 'Blur girl' and dismissed Oasis as 'northern louts'.[9] In September, when Blur appeared on MTV to perform their new single, they warmed up with a mocking, music-hall rendition of 'Roll With It'. 'It's not as complex as your music is it?' remarked the host.[10] His comment pointed to a strong subtext of the Blur vs Oasis argument: Blur supporters felt that 'Country House' was better because it was smarter and more refined; Oasis fans loved 'Roll With It' because it was honest and unpretentious. The Gallagher brothers, as the Stone Roses put it, were proper real; Albarn was a drama student, whose working-class props were part of an act.

Blur's new material did nothing to dispel this impression. For all its populist sing-along appeal, 'Country House' had a cold, detached quality to it that, once the first flush of excitement had worn off, made its victory seem hollow. Sutherland joined a small but growing number of music critics who wondered whether Albarn's fondness for the third person had more to do with a lack of commitment than a passion for objectivity. 'You never climb off the fence,' he complained. 'It's a cop-out.' Albarn admitted he was reluctant to let on what he thought of his sea-changers and wife-swappers, but insisted that this was only a cop-out 'if you, as a listener, demand some sort of judgement'.[11] Albarn, it seemed, was a modern-day music-hall satirist who felt no need to form an opinion about his subjects. This curious admission revealed the fatal contradiction at the heart of Blur's music. David Sprague's *Rolling Stone* review claimed that *The Great Escape* 'solidifies Albarn's position as sole heir to a tradition of pop as social commentary'.[12] But while the album *sounded* like satire, it confined its critique to cheap shots at easy targets because its author had no real wish to change the state of affairs. He wished, rather, to change himself and his songs to suit the state of affairs: to lead a normal life and not care about the problems of the world, and to write songs to provide the soundtrack to such a life.

Albarn had realised while touring *Modern Life is Rubbish* in 1993 that the Americanisation of the world was unstoppable, and had resigned himself to making a living from 'having an occasional rant about it'. In *Parklife*, he was still complaining, although he admitted to the *NME*'s Keith Cameron that he wasn't really sure why: 'I just wish I could understand what I was really upset about.'[13] But the singer soon answered his own question. Discussing 'End of a Century', a song which gave voice to his feeling that the coming of the year 2000 would be a huge disappointment, Albarn admitted that he had no real hope for the future, and that he saw no sign that anyone else did either. 'We've stopped being optimistic, as a species,' he told Cameron.[14] This would explain why the songs in Blur's catalogue that rang truest were not the perky music-hall satires, but the admissions of defeat and hopelessness. Albarn's strongest lyrics were those that reflected his belief that the world could not be saved, but that music might offer a pleasant distraction along the way. 'There are a few important things in life,' said Damien Hirst in 1994, 'religion, love, art and science. At their best, they're all just tools to help you find a path through the darkness. None of them really work that well, but they help.' Albarn had come to see Blur songs in the same terms in which Hirst saw his 'pharmaceutical' paintings — as a consolation for hopelessness.[15]

This strain of Albarn's work began in 1991 with two songs on *Leisure*: 'There's No Other Way', and the startling album track 'Sing' ('I can't feel / 'cause I'm numb / sing to me').[16] It continued with 'For Tomorrow' and 'This is a Low', and reached a gloomy crescendo with 'The Universal', the third single from Blur's 1995 album *The Great Escape*. The song offered a vision of the third millennium in which people pass their time singing karaoke songs and dreaming of winning the lottery without ever wondering what their lives might mean, since The Universal — a cross between Prozac, MTV and Orwell's Big Brother — has removed the bug in the programming of the human brain that allows it to ask questions. He admitted to the *NME* that the song was 'probably very negative'. But while 'The Universal' was a nightmare, it was also a seductive one, since it grew from a sincere wish on Albarn's part to be relieved of the burden of thought, 'to just allow myself to become a complete ... what's the word? Ghost.'[17] This was what the Blur singer meant when he talked about wanting to be normal. He imagined a world full of people whose lives passed in a happy stupor of TV, shopping and football, and longed to dissolve himself in this vast ocean of thoughtlessness. 'If the days just seem to fall through you well just let them go,' sang Albarn, as 'The Universal's achingly beautiful chorus surged up on a wave of strings and brass. It sounded joyous, but it was the joy of giving up.

241

What You Want, if That's What You Want

On the first day of the 1995 Lollapalooza tour, at The Gorge natural amphitheatre in Washington, an unprecedented event took place. 'All moshing stopped,' reported MTV's Alison Stewart, in a tone of voice journalists usually reserved for earthquakes and death tolls in foreign wars. The crowd had been stilled by Sinéad O'Connor, performing a set of songs taken from her new album, *Universal Mother*. The singer was very pleased with the response. 'I wanted to calm people down,' she told Stewart. 'So if I did that, I'm happy.' For the festival's organiser, Perry Farrell, the secret was in the way the singer held her notes. 'When you sing,' he told O'Connor, 'you don't use a lot of vibrato. It was so nice to hear that.' Gesticulating wildly to illustrate his point, Farrell explained that most singers duck and weave around the note because they're insecure, not just about their singing, but about themselves. 'The note,' he insisted, 'is you.'[1]

When Farrell had called O'Connor earlier in the year to ask if she wanted to play at Lollapalooza, the first thing she'd asked was, 'Who's on the bill?' As soon as she heard the word 'Hole', the singer decided she was in. 'I think they're amazing,' she said.[2] Hole was co-headlining the tour with Sonic Youth, whose fourth album for Geffen, *Washing Machine*, was being released in September. Other bands on the ticket included Cypress Hill, Beck, Elastica and Pavement, who had in fact been scheduled to play Lollapalooza the previous year, but had had to pull out due to an unfortunate run-in with the Smashing Pumpkins' Billy Corgan. Sometime between the announcement of the tour and the first show, Corgan had got wind of Pavement's song 'Range Life', with its obscure allusion to his band, and subsequently declared that if Pavement was going to play, the Pumpkins would pull out. Stephen Malkmus explained later that year that he would often build 'little trap doors and stuff for people to fall into' in Pavement songs, and suggested to triple j's Richard Kingsmill that Corgan had simply taken a bad step. The singer tried, not very hard or very successfully, to play down the animosity between the two bands. 'What do you think of the Smashing Pumpkins?' asked Kingsmill. 'They're really good. For, you know, histrionic rock,' said Malkmus.[3] The Pavement frontman went on to restate Steve Albini's 1993 assessment of the Pumpkins — that they were pandering sluts playing fake stadium rock — but in less vituperative and more concise terms. 'They give you what you want,' he said, 'if that's what you want.'[4]

For his part, Billy Corgan believed that Malkmus resented the Pumpkins' failure to conform to accepted standards of ironic indie cool. He lumped the Pavement singer's jibes in with a remark made by Kim Deal after Lollapalooza '94. 'I want the pill he has, the one that makes him so fucking important,' said Deal. Corgan insisted that the Breeders' singer was simply threatened by his honesty. 'Kim Deal, genius that she is, does not write emotional, personal music,' he explained. 'Pavement does not write emotional, personal music. See what I'm saying? The criticisms tend to come from people who hide behind a veneer or persona of coolness or an aesthetic of indieness. When you see me, I'm not hiding anything.'[5]

Corgan maintained, as he had from the beginning, that his music was great because it laid his soul bare. He didn't hide, and he didn't pretend. He put all of himself into his art, and this distinguished the Smashing Pumpkins not only from their less sincere indie-rock peers, but also from the 'syntho music about nothing' on the radio. But because he defined musical excellence as emotional realism, Corgan — like Eddie Vedder — was hit very hard by the Reality Crash of 1994, when the market was flooded with fake reality bands, and real bands found themselves having to fake it just to get over. 'There just doesn't seem to be any room to be real,' he complained.[6] The extent of the problem became clear to both Corgan and the band during the course of Lollapalooza, as they struggled to reconcile their artistic principles with the demands of a large-scale arena tour. 'You're on tour and you're constantly having to provide a product for people to ingest,' explained Jimmy Chamberlin. 'It jades you.' Corgan had the curious feeling that the band's music, the very thing that ought to have guaranteed his freedom, had somehow turned on him. 'We were part of a movement, to bring "alternative rock music" to the world,' he told 2FM's Mark Cates. 'Now it's kind of closing in on us to the point where we feel constrained by that.'[7] Chamberlin agreed. 'Sometimes,' he said, 'the music can be the enemy.' Chamberlin's choice of words — 'product', 'ingest' — gave the impression that he'd come to see working in the Smashing Pumpkins as being not too dissimilar to working at Burger King, as though there was no essential difference between playing in a rock band and doing the kind of McJob people joined rock bands in order to avoid. By the end of a three-month tour, the Smashing Pumpkins had come to hate their hits the way Dante hated the Quick Stop in *Clerks*.

If the band's music was — as Billy Corgan believed — the literal embodiment of its author's soul, the implications of this were truly frightening. When the note is you, what happens to you when the note is sold? By 1995, many alternative rock artists had realised that the mass-marketing of self-expression had turned their personalities into cheap commodities, and had decided, as a result, that they would no longer be taking their feelings to market. The songs on Liz Phair's 1995 album *Whip-Smart* represented only a fraction of the hundreds she'd demo-ed while making the record, most of which she rejected because they were too honest. 'I was trying to keep control,' she explained. 'Because I really didn't want to share my emotions any more. Every time I tried to write a song, I found the discipline was no longer my outlet; it was a product that I knew was going to be used in some way. It really fucked up my songwriting for a while.'[8] Dave Grohl, when writing lyrics for the first Foo Fighters album, also put a ban on self-expression.[9] He insisted that he'd worked hard to make sure the band's first single, 'This is a Call', was about nothing, so that it could be about anything, and that this was true of most of the songs on the album. 'You could read a million things into any one of those songs,' he said.

'It's kind of fun to see what people get out of them.' Trying to figure out what they were *really* about, he said, was a fool's game. 'It's just sort of a little puzzle that gets you nowhere,' he said of 'This is a Call'. 'It's a labyrinth, and you come to a dead end, and you're extremely disappointed.'[10] Even Courtney Love, alt rock's most notorious over-sharer, told *The Face*'s Amy Raphael that she gave away far less in her songs than she did in interviews. 'My personal world is my personal world,' she said. 'When I wrote *Live Through This*, I didn't write one word that had anything to do with my inner life. That's my gift, my gimmick. If it's not worth anything, then it's fine.'[11]

Corgan, too, felt that his confessions were being cheapened in the marketplace — but he saw this as the fault of journalists who twisted his words and took them out of context, and so confined his emotional lockout to the interview circuit. 'I've just ceased talking about those things in public,' he said, 'because it cheapens them, and I'm not going to cheapen what's real.' Corgan maintained that his songs were *him*, and that critics and listeners had no right to pick them apart, since this threatened to unravel his self-esteem. He backed up his stance with an appeal to art history. 'If I write songs, I'm as much of an artist as someone who paints a picture,' he said, 'and I choose to express whatever I want to express. Nobody questions an artist's emotional attitude with a painting. But somehow, musically, we have to dissect where it comes from.'[12]

This was not exactly true — painting, like music, had its critics, and visual artists were still called upon to explain and justify their work. Nevertheless, many modern painters had come to adopt a stance like the one Corgan described, in which the artwork was said to speak for itself, and to obey no law other than its own. Marxist critics saw this 'art for art's sake' as a result of the artist's alienation. 'Like the factory worker, he sends his product out into an unfriendly void,' wrote feminist literary critic Meredith Tax in 1972. 'The use of his product, if any, is conjectural; he probably thinks it has none to anyone but himself. How can he be other than alienated from his work?' In the late twentieth century, artists could no longer imagine a social function for their art, because they no longer had any meaningful connection with their audience. 'The artist has been put in the position of producing for a market, for strangers far away, whose lifestyles and beliefs and needs are completely unknown to him, and who will either buy his works or ignore them for reasons that are equally inscrutable and out of his control,' wrote Tax.[13] This was exactly the position Billy Corgan found himself in. He'd declared shortly before the release of *Gish* that he wrote and played primarily for his own gratification, and told his fans at Lollapalooza '94 that he believed in nothing but himself. Now he joked bitterly that the Smashing Pumpkins had chosen their new single by 'conducting a survey of Kmart shoppers between the ages of thirty and thirty-five'.[14] With his audience reduced to a sea of anonymous faces in the stadium at best, and a horde of fickle shoppers at worst, the singer turned in on himself, and insisted that he was producing his work for nobody but himself. 'I disconnect the act,' sang Corgan in 'Fuck You (An Ode to No-One)'. 'I disconnect the me in me / And you're mistaken, it's you that's faking.'[15]

Corgan told MTV's Kurt Loder in 1995 that the commercialisation of alternative rock had forced him 'to make even more determined statements'; to ignore, as far as possible, the words of his critics, the wisdom of the industry and the demands of the Pumpkins' millions of fans, and to push the band's music to new extremes of emotional intensity, technical perfection, and sheer length. The group had just released its third album, a two-hour epic entitled *Mellon Collie and the Infinite Sadness,* along with a fierce single, 'Bullet With Butterfly Wings', in which Corgan described how stadium rock had stolen his soul in 1994. 'The world is a vampire,' he sang, 'sent to drain.' The singer told of how his angst had been consumed as entertainment, and how the demands of showbiz had forced him to turn great songs into bad cabaret. 'Can you fake it for just one more show?' he sneered, in mocking imitation of the festival promoter.[16] Alison Stewart interviewed the band on the set of the 'Bullet With Butterfly Wings' video, a nightmarish reimagining of Lollapalooza, in which the Pumpkins could be seen performing their song in a dirt pit in front of a surging mass of angry troglodytes. These were in fact real Pumpkins fans, recruited as extras by director Samuel Bayer, who, as Stewart put it, were 'such fans of the band that they were willing to cover themselves with mud for the entire day'. Bayer's images were deeply disturbing. By reducing each member of the mosh pit army to the same grunge-coloured hue, the director transformed his extras from a mass of individuals into an individualised mass, a powerful symbol of the extent to which stadium rock had alienated Corgan from his fans. 'The youth of America continues to frighten me,' said Corgan, as he supervised the work from the shade of a tarpaulin.[17]

Meanwhile, at the real Lollapalooza, a strange inversion of this scene was taking place, as Pavement faced its own horde of frightening American youth at a show in West Virginia. Here, instead of covering themselves in mud to prove how much they loved the band, the fans threw mud at the band to let them know they hated them. 'Whoo, what a rough show that was,' said Bob Nastanovich, as he scraped the mud off his Moog.[18] Pavement's problem at Lollapalooza had less to do with alienation than stubbornness — the kids knew what they wanted, but Pavement was not about to give it to them. They'd come to mosh, and Pavement, as Thurston Moore observed, did not play 'instantly recognisable mosh riffs'.[19] This reflected a wider problem with Lollapalooza '95: despite being, as Nastanovich later put it, 'a much cooler year' than '94, the line-up failed to appeal to the wider audience. The opening date at The Gorge didn't sell out until the day of the show, and a number of other dates didn't sell out at all. 'Blue plastic seats,' said Beck, when asked to give his impression of the tour. 'Empty, very empty. And it's 105 degrees. And there's a small cluster of youngsters who are displaying their energetic support, but they're about a mile and a half away.'[20]

Some felt the festival in '95 lacked a strong headlining act — the each-way bet of booking Hole and Sonic Youth had failed to compensate for the lack of a Smashing Pumpkins or a Pearl Jam on the bill. Hole was too divisive, and Sonic Youth more well respected than widely loved. Thurston Moore had the feeling that his band was slightly at odds with both the promoters' and the audience's expectations — as did Justine Frischmann. Elastica was in extraordinarily good form for a band that had been touring almost non-stop for six months by the time they got to The Gorge. But Frischmann found they had to work very hard to move the crowd, and wondered whether they weren't slightly out of place. Beck, too, had trouble making a connection. 'I spent the whole summer out in these incredibly, hideously, devil-adjective-hot intolerably humid outdoor facilities playing at two in the afternoon, watching the half-baked youth of the summer of '95, [and] desperately trying to connect with them,' he said. 'It was futile.'[21] Bob Nastanovich concluded that Pavement was 'a misplaced band on a failing bill'. But the keyboardist insisted that if 1995 was the year all moshing stopped, then his band could feel justifiably proud of its part in having brought it to an end. 'Pavement's the band that effectively did in Lollapalooza,' he said. 'So anyone that disses us for our participation should be happy that we actually played a significant role in the demise of that ridiculous summer event.'[22]

Intergalactic Pop Megastar

In the middle of the afternoon, in the middle month of the middle year of the 1990s, Jarvis Cocker sat in a small tent at Glastonbury and waited for his moment. His band, Pulp, was to headline the festival later that evening, playing to over 100,000 people, and Cocker was more nervous than he'd ever been in his life. He tried to tune out the noise of the crowd he knew he'd have to entertain in six hours' time, and to gather his thoughts. 'It got nearer and nearer to zero hour,' he later wrote, 'and I spread out all my little jobs: at half ten I got changed, at quarter to eleven I put my contact lenses in, at five to eleven I put my make-up on. Lots of little jobs so I didn't have to sit there pondering the awfulness of existence.' A brief respite from existential angst came in the unexpected form of Robbie Williams from Take That, who stuck his head into Cocker's fortress of solitude to wish him luck. 'Robbie read us some of his poetry,' said Cocker. 'I was dubious at first, because sometimes poetry can be embarrassing, but it was really good.'[1]

Pulp had been offered the headline slot after the Stone Roses had cancelled at the last minute. The long-lost hopes of British indie had been planning to use Glastonbury to herald the release of their second album — titled, with characteristic modesty, *Second Coming* — but had to pull out after guitarist John Squire broke his collarbone. While Cocker had mixed feelings about replacing the Roses, there was an undeniable symmetry to the way things had worked out, which clearly pleased the singer. Glastonbury would see Pulp's first live performance of a new song called 'Sorted for E's and Wizz'. 'I'm not that into fate,' he said, 'but the title came from me talking to this girl about when she went to Spike Island. That was her main memory, all these blokes walking around saying: "Is everybody sorted for E's and Wizz?" It just seemed like a totally appropriate place to play it for the first time.'[2]

'Sorted for E's and Wizz' would be the second single released from Pulp's forthcoming album, *Different Class*. The first, 'Common People', was the reason they were headlining Glastonbury. Written around a sparkling keyboard riff, and pushed into overdrive by Russell Senior's siren-like guitar, 'Common People' seemed at first to be a breathless tale of art-school romance, but soon revealed itself as something more. The girl, it transpires, loves Jarvis not for his looks, or for his mind, but for his ineffable aura of working-class authenticity. Her attraction to him is mingled with a certain amount of envy, because — while she is rich and popular and good looking — she wants, more than anything, to be real. 'I wanna live like common people,' she tells him. 'I wanna do whatever common people do. I wanna sleep with common people, I wanna sleep with common people like you.' Cocker manfully obliges ('I'll see what I can do'), but warns the girl from Greece that working-class chic is not so easily acquired.[3]

Cocker wrote the song as a response to a mid-nineties trend, 'A certain voyeurism on the part of the middle classes,' he said, 'a certain romanticism of working-class culture and a desire to slum it a bit.'[4] Talking to *The Face*, he mentioned the new fashion for football and the popularity of Mike Leigh box sets. But the singer surely had Britpop in mind as well — he couldn't fail to have noticed the hungry look South London journalists got in their eyes when they talked to Oasis, or Damon ('I've lived in Essex all me life') Albarn's increasingly strained attempts to prove that he was the salt of the earth.[5] These were just the more obvious signs of a cultural craze for downward mobility, which saw middle-class youth embracing 'good, wholesome things' like football, lager, pool and pop music with a vengeance; trying to live like common people, to do whatever common people do. Pulp's record company, Island, had originally planned to put the single out in July. But as 1995 got underway, Cocker began to get the feeling that, for the first time in Pulp's long history, he had written a song that captured the mood of the nation at precisely the right time. Not wanting to miss the moment, he persuaded

Island to release 'Common People' in the last week of February. By the end of the month, it had gone to number two in the national chart.

Cocker's portrait subsequently appeared on the cover of over a dozen magazines, including the *NME, Melody Maker, Smash Hits, The Face, Vox* and *Select*. He looked supremely comfortable on all of them, as though he'd been practising to be on the cover of magazines his whole life. This, it transpired, was not too far from the truth. The singer had always imagined that, in the moment before he died, he would have to watch the reruns of The Jarvis Cocker Story as they flashed before his eyes, and he felt he owed it to himself to make sure they were entertaining. 'If you've got these long boring bits of sitting in watching telly doing really crap things, they're the bits that come back to you,' he told *Select*. 'So you have to work on your life and make it worth replaying.'[6] 'Did you always want to be famous, Jarvis?' asked Andrew Smith. 'Yeah, I was desperate to be famous,' replied the singer. 'Did you care what for?' 'I always wanted to be in a pop group.'[7] Cocker felt he had been faced, quite early in life, with a simple choice: pop stardom or oblivion. 'It's like this,' he explained to Smith. 'There's something freakish about you, so you either consign yourself to the margins of society, or think of it as unique.'[8]

Cocker learned, over the years, to cultivate his essential oddity, and to accept the burden of loneliness in exchange for the rare gifts it bestows upon the nascent pop singer. In 1972 he was a sickly child with coke-bottle glasses, sitting alone in his bedroom with the radio on. In 1983 he was fronting an oddball post-punk group called Pulp, trying desperately to maintain the momentum of playing the band's first BBC Peel Session to very little success. In 1989 he almost gave up on music, moving to London to study photography at St Martins College, a decision that only served to make him more painfully aware than ever that he was from Sheffield. By 1991 he'd reconvened the group, and found himself struggling to bring disco back in a baggy world. Now, in 1995, he was the nation's favourite pop star, with a Top Ten hit and a legion of fans. Andrew Smith watched him being chased by a gang of teenage admirers on the way to an appearance at HMV's Oxford Street megastore. After taking a quick survey, the reporter found that Cocker's fans loved him for exactly the same reason kids used to ignore him at school, the same reason he couldn't get arrested in the eighties and couldn't get laid at St Martins, the very same reason the *NME* described him, in 1991, as 'looking like one of the Good Lord's genetic mishaps': 'The one thing they all agree on,' wrote Smith, 'is that he's different.'[9]

The right to be different was asserted in the first thirty seconds of Pulp's new album with 'Mis-shapes', a stirring anthem for the dispossessed set to a sprightly, Hit Factory beat. 'Oh, we don't look the same as you, and we don't do the things you do,' sang Cocker, 'but we live 'round here too.' But the song moved speedily from a plea for understanding to a declaration of war: 'Brothers, sisters, can't you see? The future's owned by you and me.' Cocker went on to explain that, as an act of revenge undertaken by smart, poor people against rich, stupid people, the war would be fought by intellectual, rather than physical means. And yet it was a war, nonetheless. 'We want your homes, we want your lives,' he sang, 'we want the things you won't allow us.'[10]

Cocker had a strong sense, by the end of 1995, that this future might have arrived — or at least be not too far away. 'There is a battle going on,' he told the *NME*'s Roger Morton. 'But I think it's won, or about to be won.'[11] The singer was referring to pop rather than politics — but the two seemed very closely connected at the time. When Oasis — the band that had announced its arrival with the words 'You're the outcasts / You're the underclass'[12] — had its first number one hit with 'Some Might Say' in May, the effect was comparable to that of Nirvana beating Michael Jackson to the top of the charts in 1991 — a victory for 'proletarian guitar rock' over conservative pop. Jon Savage, watching the band perform on *Top of the Pops*, noted the fact that Oasis had triumphed in the same week that the Conservative Party had been beaten in a council election, and had the feeling that 'something was really happening', a feeling Noel Gallagher appeared to share.[13] At the 1994 *Q* Awards he'd bounced out of the bathroom, having hoovered up a few little white lines, and been surprised to find himself face to face with Tony Blair, the recently appointed leader of Britain's Labour Party. 'Fuckin' hell,' said Gallagher, as he threw his arm around the somewhat flummoxed Blair. 'Fuckin' do it for us, man!'[14]

Over the course of the next year, Blair and his entourage had made a concerted effort to garner the support of the music industry, and of Blur in particular. Albarn went to a meeting with Blair and Alistair

Campbell at the Houses of Parliament, and New Labour's Darren Kalynuk worked hard to get Alex James on side as well, by introducing him to Labour MPs and top-shelf whiskey in exclusive after-hours clubs in Soho. Six months later, Noel Gallagher made his own support for New Labour public when he took the stage at the Brit Awards to accept Oasis's award for Best Group from Pete Townshend. 'There are seven people in this room who are giving a little bit of hope to young people in this country,' he said. 'That is, me, our kid, Bonehead, Guigs, Alan White, Alan McGee and Tony Blair. And if you've all got anything about you, you'll go up there and you'll shake Tony Blair's hand, man. He's the man! Power to the people!'[15] Margaret Thatcher's successor, John Major, had resigned on the same day Oasis played Glastonbury. The next general election would not be held until 1997, but Blair, as John Harris noted, was looking more like the prime minister every day.

For Jarvis Cocker, pop had always been somewhat political. Older by some years than his Britpop contemporaries, Cocker had fond memories of punk, and very few of the 1980s. 'It was like, "Right, you've had your fun, that's enough permissiveness, back to Victorian values."'[16] Cocker saw the decade's conservative, materialistic politics mirrored by conservative, materialistic music. Eighties idols like Simon Le Bon and Mick Hucknall seemed to him too much like the popular, good-looking, well-off people who had made his everyday life miserable to be proper pop stars. 'That's when music went wrong,' he told *The Face*. 'That's when it lost it.'[17] He felt shut out of pop, a loser in a decade of winners. But he also grew to hate, with a passion, the indie culture that grew up in new pop's shadow, a culture that defined itself in opposition and grew far too comfortable with its outsider role. Cocker felt that the eighties indie scene allowed bands to get away with bad ideas and bad music far too easily because its goals were small to the point of being non-existent. 'I always felt it was important to be doing things in the proper world,' he explained. 'I never liked the idea of "alternative music", I wanted to make the mainstream better.'[18]

After 'Country House' went to number one in 1995, Cocker went out drinking with Blur until six in the morning. Three hours later he was at the *Smash Hits* offices, wearing a cheap silver spacesuit and having his picture taken for a cover story with the headline 'Intergalactic Pop Megastar'. Cocker felt like he was going to die, and die looking like an idiot, to boot. But he resisted the temptation to throw a rock star wobbly and refuse to do the shoot, out of what he described as 'a sense of duty'.[19] Cocker felt he owed it to his thirteen-year-old self, to the Jarvis Cocker who used to get kebabs shoved in his face up the back of the bus, to be the kind of pop star he'd always wanted to be, and to enjoy every ridiculous moment of it. Having grown up odd in a suburb of a northern industrial town, Cocker had always seen pop as his one means of escape from normality. Pop music was a hole in the fence, through which society's mis-shapes might find their way into places they weren't supposed to be, into the 'proper world' that had once been the exclusive domain of the Marti Pellows and Simon Le Bons. Now that he had found a way in, Cocker had no immediate plans to leave. 'The Cranberries have complained that being pop stars has deprived them of the ability to lead a normal life,' said *Melody Maker*'s David Stubbs. 'Sod that,' replied Cocker. 'Why did they join a group in the first place? Who wants a normal life?'[20]

1996

These People are Losers

In 1996, after five years of real guys with real problems, a long-repressed craving for unreal bands and real fun began to make itself known. 'If I want despair, anger and sorrow,' wrote one music fan, 'I'll tune in to Jerry Springer. For a good time, I'll rock and roll all night, and party every day.'[1] This may well have been the first time the word 'party' had been used as a verb since 1990, when a group of Faith No More fans had accosted Mike Patton backstage, asked him if he was going to party after the show, and were rewarded with a look that suggested he'd rather stick a fork in his own eye. The writer was registering his approval of the fact that Kiss, the hard rock band formed by Gene Simmons and Paul Stanley in 1973, had finally reformed, and would be touring the world, in full make-up, for the first time since 1979.

Gene Simmons believed that alternative bands had a lot to learn from Kiss, and was full of advice for rock's new miserablists. Simmons had spoken to Kurt Cobain on the phone about the possibility of Nirvana recording a song for *Kiss My Ass*, a Kiss tribute album, only weeks before he died, and he was still baffled by the encounter. What on earth did Cobain have to worry about? 'If you're black or Hispanic, or another minority, you could complain,' he said. 'But a blond white boy? The centre. You *are* popular culture. You're in a famous rock and roll band. You have no right to be upset — about anything. You were molested as a child — I don't give a shit. You're now the idol of millions. The American dream really does exist, it really paid off.'[2] Kiss's no-

nonsense view of rock as entertainment seemed very refreshing after five years of bellyaching over 'selling out'. 'This is rock and roll,' said Paul Stanley, for the benefit of those who might still be under the mistaken impression that they were painting frescoes or appearing as a guest on an episode of *Oprah*. 'Get up there, play your music, and thank the audience for giving you everything you've got from them.' Richard Kingsmill asked Stanley if he saw his band as an antidote to the gloomy preoccupations of grunge, when 'depression was popular'. 'It still is,' said Stanley. 'People singing about drugs and heroin and miserable lives — to me, these people are losers. If you fight, you can win.'[3]

Stanley raged against what he saw as a pop world turned upside down, where the loser drug addicts whose audiences and girlfriends he used to steal had somehow become winners — and then had the gall to claim they didn't enjoy it. Grunge had turned losers into winners, and winners into losers, as many of Stanley's eighties progeny had already discovered. In 1991, Skid Row's *Slave to the Grind* had debuted at number one; twelve months later it had gone platinum. The band toured the world for the next eighteen months, taking with them the two enormous walk-in wardrobes with built-in mirrors they used to transport their stage outfits. Everywhere they went, they drove into town in limousines and stayed in luxury hotels. But when music writer Lynn Snowden caught up with Skid Row on their 1996 tour, she found the band sleeping on the tour bus and carrying their own clothes in backpacks. What had happened, singer Sebastian Bach explained, was 'the revenge of the college people'. Bach, like Stanley, saw the culture of alt rock as a bizarre reversal of real values, where the strong are punished and the weak are rewarded. 'I'm sorry I didn't do heroin when I was pregnant,' he said, before launching into an impression of Eddie Vedder. 'Cancel the tour!' he yelled. 'I don't feel well … I've done eight shows!'[4]

A Mutually Exploitative Situation

'How does it feel to be part of the grunge scene?' Beck boggled at the music journalist who had just asked him this question, unsure of how to respond. 'Yeah,' he thought to himself. 'I think I'm really gonna go with this "grunge" thing you know? It seems like it has a lot of potential.'[1] The question was absurd, because in 1996 grunge had been dead for over a year. It was dead enough to have its history told, as it did in November when Doug Pray's documentary *Hype!* was released in cinemas. By showing how the music industry's embrace of the Seattle sound had come close to ruining Seattle itself, Pray hoped to shed some light on the bands' anxieties over 'selling out', which he admitted could seem baffling to outsiders. 'It seems sort of whiny if you didn't really see it or if you're not really there,' he explained. 'You kind of wonder, What are they complaining about? Wouldn't anybody want to be the Capital of Hip? It is a different perspective when you're really there and you realise how much history there is.'[2] The film spared the viewer none of the heartache that results from a thriving cultural ecosystem being strip-mined for profit.

At the end of the film, Eddie Vedder delivered a speech. 'If all this influence that this part of the country has and this musical scene has … if it doesn't do anything with it, that would be the tragedy,' he said. 'If it doesn't do something with it, like make some kind of change or make some kind of difference … This group of people who feels this certain way. This group of people who thinks these things that the underdogs we've all met think. If they finally get to the forefront, and nothing comes of it, that would be the tragedy.'[3] Here, Vedder reached toward a vision of the future — a new, compassionate society, in which the non-values of capitalism are finally replaced by a philosophy of the underdog. And yet, for all the passion in his delivery and the sincerity with which he spoke, there was — as Naomi Klein has observed — something troubling about the vagueness of Vedder's terms. When he spoke of bands making 'some kind of change' or 'some kind of difference', one got the impression he wasn't quite sure what he meant, let alone how it might be brought about.[4]

This, as Klein pointed out, had been a problem for alternative rock from the beginning. Grunge tapped the collective energy of the thirteenth generation, but never really seemed to know what to do with it. In November 1991, as the requests for 'Smells Like Teen Spirit' started flooding in to MTV, Krist Novoselic had railed against what he saw as the uselessness of LA metal. 'What does Axl Rose stand for?' he asked. 'What is his platform?'[5] But Novoselic, with his savvy grasp of politics and his heartfelt sense of outrage at the Gulf War, was a special case. Most grunge bands — Pearl Jam included — were, in the last analysis, not so different from Axl Rose. They expressed their audience's rage and disaffection, and assumed that the rest would take care of itself. 'When the world's cameras were turned on Seattle,' Klein wrote, 'all we got were a few anti-establishment fuck-yous, a handful of overdoses, and Kurt Cobain's suicide.'[6] As Damon Albarn pointed out in 1993, 'I'm fucked up' is not a revolutionary statement — it's too easily re-routed into solipsism and romantic despair, and the 'establishment' has no reason to be troubled by either. Teenage angst, as Geffen, Sony, Universal, Atlantic, Time Warner, Viacom and Coca-Cola Amatil quickly learned in 1992, is harmless at worst, and lucrative at best.

Alternative bands soon realised they were being exploited, and that they were, themselves, involved in the exploitation of youth. Some tried to stall the process by problematising their music, as Nirvana did. Others, like L7, decided to accept it as unavoidable, but to use the money and attention to do something constructive — the traditional rock star round of benefit gigs and endorsements. Still others — the Smashing Pumpkins being the most obvious example — simply recycled their fury at having been sold out into even more furious music, which led to even more furious moshing, but not much else. Their treatment of the basic problem was either symptomatic or therapeutic — an actual cure seemed like too much to hope for. Thus, the decline of grunge came to be seen as inevitable, and artists and critics alike sank further into romantic gloom. Their view of history became cyclical and tragic — everything underground gets swallowed by the mainstream, everything good turns bad; this year sucked, next year will be worse. 'Face the muzak,' wrote media critic Andrew Hultkrans in 1995, 'if you don't sell your "counterculture" image, someone else will. Within six months, you'll find your cherished "individual" lifestyle plastered on billboards, pushing blue jeans and wine coolers.'[7]

For Zack de la Rocha of Rage Against the Machine, this fatalistic view was not acceptable. 'The musical community,' he told MTV, 'is a community that I refuse to believe is part of this disparate, Generation X inactive community. I think they can become a force.'[8] De la Rocha was speaking one month after the release of the band's second LP, *Evil Empire* — which *Rolling Stone* described as 'maybe the most political album ever to hit the number one spot on the pop charts.'[9] The band's popular appeal was easily explained — Rage was an extraordinarily powerful rock band, a group that took the aggression and intensity of seventies rock and eighties hardcore, and stretched it tight over hip-hop beats. But the band's commitment to political activism made it unique; de la Rocha would not be satisfied by merely moving the crowd — he wanted to move them to act. The album's first single, 'Bulls On Parade' — a furious swipe at US foreign policy — came with a video, which, according to guitarist Tom Morello, explored 'the causal relationship between revolutionary culture and revolutionary action'.[10] For Morello, there was nothing incongruous about juxtaposing images of Rage rocking onstage with others of protesters fighting cops in the street. A rock band, he insisted, was a potential means to a revolutionary end, the band's deal with Sony was 'a mutually exploitative situation', in which the band used the label to spread its insurrectionary message.

The album's title was borrowed from a phrase Ronald Reagan used to describe the Soviet Union during his presidency. Reagan's skillful deployment of comic-book imagery in the field of foreign policy allowed him to justify his government's military spending by making it seem as though the United States was on the right side of a war between good and evil. But it also helped push his more radical economic agenda. Reagan sought to give business a freer hand while divesting his government of public responsibility — he achieved both aims by convincing the electorate that he was trying to get 'big government' out of citizens' lives. Thus, taxpayer-funded healthcare was made to seem like evidence of what Robert Hughes called 'creeping Marxism', and those who opposed free trade could easily be made to seem like enemies of freedom.

Reagan's success in these initiatives prepared the ground for the spectacular corporate triumphs of the late eighties, and the even more impressive, though less well-publicised, victories of the nineties. The idea that the corporate world had been chastened by the recession was mostly sleight of hand. Bush simply picked up where Reagan had left off, bailing out the banks while sticking to the line that what was good for business was good for the country. Thus, in the first half of the nineties, the power and reach of corporations expanded at a terrific rate. With very few restrictions on global trade still extant, and communism in Eastern Europe gone, the world was transformed by the arrival of the truly global corporation.

'It's time for everybody to lighten up,' said Kiss's Paul Stanley in 1996. 'There are no more world wars, there is no more communist menace.'[11] But to some, it seemed as though a new menace had already appeared in place of the old one. In the nineties, world powers and developing nations alike courted the interest of global corporations and found themselves increasingly at their mercy, while the brands themselves were answerable to no-one but their shareholders. Communities and ecosystems disappeared in the race for profit as the world was remade in the image of big business, American-style. This, Rage Against the Machine felt, was the real Evil Empire. 'The Reagan administration tried to breed this fear in the American public by referring to the Soviet Union as the Evil Empire,' de la Rocha explained. 'You can flip that on its head to see that the US has been responsible for many of the atrocities of the late twentieth century.'[12]

Many alternative rock bands, when asked in interviews about their political views, admitted that they felt disenfranchised from politics, and espoused some variation of the 'it doesn't really seem to matter who's president — they're all the same' line offered by Sonic Youth in 1990. Morello and de la Rocha saw that this was true, but seemed uniquely aware of the reasons why the two-party system had become a sideshow. Rage was the first group of its kind to publicly acknowledge that power was now wielded in the corporate, rather than in the political, world. It was not enough, they believed, to vote one president out and replace him with another, or to lobby governments on single issues. 'There are lots of bands who support some very noble causes,' Morello told the *LA Times*. 'But we're talking about a bigger overhauling of society.'[13] For Morello, a committed Marxist, the goal was to rock the state, and not just the vote.

As the group's most confident speaker, Morello's point of view tended to dominate in interviews. This sometimes gave the impression that the band presented a unified front, an impression that quickly fell apart when the other members were given the opportunity to speak — or, in de la Rocha's case, when they could be persuaded to do so. 'Convincing Zack to talk is as difficult as making Courtney Love shut up,' said Amy Raphael, describing the singer as 'a highly strung individual whose past is shrouded in mystery and who refuses to discuss his lyrics'.[14] De la Rocha believed that Rage could be a political force in its own right, but saw no sense in 'talking shit' in interviews when he could be involving himself in community projects and activist groups. Drummer Brad Wilk shared some of Morello's and de la Rocha's political goals, but very little of their faith in rock and roll as a means of bringing them to fruition. When the band played their 1992 hit 'Killing in the Name' at New York's Roseland Ballroom, and the largely male, white, teen audience bounced up and down and shouted along to the chorus while giving the finger, Wilk saw far more evidence of mass stupidity than revolutionary potential. 'When you get a lot of people in a room, the intelligence level kind of goes down to the lowest common denominator,' he told *Ray Gun* magazine. 'I just think that a lot of times when people go to a show — this sounds really stupid and basic — people just want to be rocked, you know?'[15] Bassist Tim Bob Commerford, on the other hand, did not believe rock and politics should be mixed in the first place. The jazz musicians he worked with outside of Rage told him in no uncertain terms that music with political lyrics was not music at all, but propaganda — and the bass player had come to agree with them.

In July, Rage Against the Machine set off on a world tour, which included a stop in Moscow — the heart of the former Evil Empire. Here, Morello faced a challenge: how to sell Marx to people who had waited seventy years to get rid of him. In America, Marxism had been a dead duck in political and cultural life since the sixties, when intellectuals and economists alike began to understand just how badly communism had failed in Eastern Europe. For Rage Against the Machine to openly embrace Marxism in mid-nineties America was so old-fashioned it was positively exotic, and the 'commie' cap Morello wore onstage was more confusing than confrontational. In Moscow, on the other hand, it was quite a different matter. In a radio interview, Morello urged his Russian fans to approach American-style democracy with extreme caution. 'I would warn all your listeners to closely watch Boris Yeltsin and his masters on Wall Street,' he said. But as music writer R. J. Smith pointed out, the band was preaching anti-capitalism in a place where capitalism had just got started, to a young audience still basking in the glow of its new-found freedom from totalitarian rule. This, to many of the band's Russian fans, was insensitive, if not actually stupid. 'Do they really like communism?' one of the fans asked Smith. 'If they lived here for seventy years, they would not play this kind of music — only patriotic songs.' Rage Against the Machine's Russian tour promoter told Morello, in no uncertain terms, to leave his 'commie' cap backstage.[16]

I Am My Own Scene

On a warm spring night in May 1996, Gwen Stefani was driving toward her home in Orange County from a meeting in Los Angeles. She'd drunk a cup of coffee to keep herself awake, which had given her a pressing need to use the bathroom by the time she reached Artesia. Stefani pulled into a gas station, ran in, relieved herself, and made to get back in her car when she was stopped by a guy in a Metallica T-shirt. 'Hey,' he said. 'Aren't you that chick … ?' Stefani, whose band No Doubt had an album in the Billboard Top Ten and two videos in high rotation on MTV, was getting used to this kind of thing. She acknowledged that she was, indeed, that chick. 'You know,' said the man, as she signed an autograph for him, 'I don't really like that "Spiderwebs" song. But I *really* like that other one, the one that's in the Top 20.'

'Spiderwebs' was No Doubt's new single — an up-tempo pop song that, like much of the band's material, showed the influence of the British ska groups Stefani had loved as a teenager. The other song, the one the guy liked, was 'Don't Speak', a magnificent ballad written about the end of Stefani's relationship with No Doubt bassist Tony Kanal, which had already spent six weeks at number one in the US charts. 'Wow, thanks!' said Stefani, as she hopped back in her car and continued her journey home. The next day, she talked to her manager, who told her that a friend of his had called him that morning and asked if she might really have seen Gwen Stefani running into a gas station in Artesia at ten o'clock at night. 'You know,' she exclaimed, telling the story a week later, 'like someone knew that I went to the bathroom at some gas station!' Stefani laughed, and hung her head slightly. *'That's* when I realised,' she said, 'that I was *really* famous.'[1]

No Doubt had formed in 1987, when Stefani and her brother Eric had met Kanal — a soul and funk fan — and introduced him to UK bands like Madness, the Specials and the Selecter. The group fused these formative influences with the sound of new bands they all liked, including Fishbone and the Red Hot Chili Peppers. They made contact with Flea, who helped them record a demo (which Stefani later described as 'terrible'), and eventually signed to Interscope, which released the band's self-titled debut in 1991. Unfortunately, *No Doubt* was buried under the avalanche of grunge, and the band had to wait another five years for the music world to come around to its particular way of thinking. When it did, it was with no small amount of relief. 'I forgot — and after the onslaught of rock's funereal last five years, who could blame me? — that groups could be fun,' wrote *Spin*'s Jonathan Bernstein, 'and if they were fun, that didn't automatically make them pariahs or confidence tricksters.'[2] No Doubt's 1995 single, 'Just a Girl', effected a perfect transition from the old alt rock to the new. The theme (women's oppression at the hands of men) and the guitars (loud) would not be out of place on a Hole album. But the lilting ska beat was quite new, as was the band's bright, cartoonish image.

Stefani's distinctive look was an important part of the band's appeal — and another case of No Doubt having waited five years to be in exactly the right place at the right time. Grunge fashion, like grunge music, had become a bore by 1995. Its palette was too limited, and its overall look too drab. In April 1994, Kim Gordon and stylist Daisy von Furth minted a fresh nineties look when they launched their fashion label X-Girl with a guerrilla-style catwalk show on the streets of New York's Soho. X-Girl combined elements of preppy sportswear — polo shirts and tennis shoes — with a dash of hip-hop style to effect what Nathaniel Wice described at the time as 'a stylistic clearing-of-the-decks after the mess of grunge'.[3] Stefani, with her preference for tiny midriff tops worn with track pants and fur-lined parkas, had managed a similar turnabout from slack to sporty. Like Gordon, she wasn't so much a designer as a thrift-store aficionado who'd got in the habit of mending and adjusting her clothes to suit her own particular tastes, and to avoid the possibility of another disaster like the one that took place at a 1995 show, when Stefani looked out into the crowd and discovered, to her horror, that there was a girl in the front row wearing the same off-the-rack dress as she was. 'Fashion is an extension of your personality,' she told *Access Hollywood*, 'and I've always been crazy about having things no-one else has.' Stefani caught herself slightly as she said this, screwing up her nose. 'I don't know why I think that's so important. I guess being an individual is what fashion's all about,' she added, as she showed off the bright-green fur-lined bomber jacket she'd found on a recent trip to Japan. 'You know, being an individual and trying not to be like everyone else.'[4]

The alternative nation had, as Donita Sparks predicted in 1992, made being unique and individual popular — and more importantly, practical. To be a punk in a small town in the American south in 1985 was literally to put one's life at risk. Ten years later, the same crazy hair dyes and piercings that the Butthole Surfers used to get beaten up for wearing were available at the shopping mall. For kids who felt different, and wanted to express their individuality, it was now as simple — as Ben Folds Five put it — as clicking one's heels. Folds' 1995 hit, 'Underground', was a joyous, piano-driven romp through this new alternative wonderland, a mini-musical that reminded the lunchroom loners of America that 'there's a place to go'. 'Show me the mosh pit,' sang Folds. 'Hand me my nose-ring!'[5]

But some worried that the point had been lost — that in their rush to express their difference from mainstream society, alternative music fans had ended up looking exactly like one another. 'My name is Chip, and I'm different,' sang Frank Black in 1995's *Teenager of the Year*. 'I don't conform, I wear a different uniform.'[6] As he gazed out at the Lollapalooza-goers of 1995, Beck saw a homogenous sea of flannel, dotted with spots of colour chosen from the new range of Manic Panic hair dyes, available at all good drugstores. 'It was inverted hegemony,' he complained. 'Everyone was trying so hard to be different, but they all ended up looking the same.'[7] Artists like Beck and Frank Black asserted a genuine non-conformism against the mass non-conformity of the alternative nation. 'How has the scene changed since you were playing with the Pixies?' asked a TV interviewer. 'Well,' replied Black, idly strumming his guitar and staring into the distance behind his beatnik shades, 'I am my own scene — so it's basically just me and my guitar.'[8] Beck, too, rejected the idea that he was part of any kind of alternative trend. 'Labels? Slap, 'em on,' he said. 'They'll fall off if the breeze is blowin' hard enough.'[9]

'I used to at least feel comfortable with my place as an outsider,' mused the grouchy protagonist of Daniel Clowes's comic book series *Eightball*. 'But now *everybody* seems to be an outsider. How can I like something when creeps like this also like it?'[10] To place oneself outside of these bogus outsiders, to be truly unique, free of labels, in a scene of one's own — this became the new ideal in 1995, and advertisers quickly caught on. To the girl who complained, in a letter to *Spin*, that 'alternativeness being a fashion show' was the 'trend that should die in 1996',[11] the makers of Simple shoes could offer a simple solution, 'a clean, trendless alternative, without all the usual fashion problems'. 'If you're searching for meaning or just avoiding fashion trends,' read the company's press ads, 'you need to: 1. Avoid the common path; 2. Counter peer pressure; 3. Project classic design sense.'[12] Advertising to a jaded demographic, eternally suspicious of trends and hypes, involved new challenges for marketers. Gen X consumers, as one exec put it, 'have a much more cynical outlook — you got to hit them with a little more irreverence for the system'.[13]

In an essay on Gen-X philosophy published in an online bulletin board, Mark Saltveit claimed that 'boomers always look to their peer groups for identity and direction. When faced with a trend, slackers are more likely to shrug and dismiss it with one word: "whatever".'[14] But the needs of the alternative nation were, fundamentally, not so different from those of their parents. In reality, X-ers combined a desire to express their individuality in a homogenised world with a longing to belong. Individuality was important enough to Gwen Stefani for her to have devoted an entire song to it on *Tragic Kingdom*. In 'Different People' Stefani reflected that the only way for her to cope with the sheer size of the planet and the number of people on it was to remind herself that no two of those people were alike, that they all had different thoughts and different ways of expressing them — herself included. 'Look at me,' she sang, 'I'm my own person.'[15] But the happy chorus of Ben Folds' 'Underground' spoke of the secret wish at the heart of alternative music and fashion, that the lonely and disaffected might find salvation in community, a community defined by shared tastes. This wish was all the more powerful for the fact that it could not be admitted, as MTV's marketing strategists knew all too well. The network flattered its viewers by telling them that they were all very special individuals, but its trade advertising told a different story. 'Buy this 24-year-old and get all his friends absolutely free,' read the copy of an ad the network placed in *Advertising Age* in 1993. 'He heads up a pack. What he eats, his friends eat. What he wears, they wear. And he's never heard of ... well, you get the idea.'[16]

Learning from Las Vegas

In 1996, Weezer released its second album, *Pinkerton*, to very little acclaim. The record was a more difficult affair than the band's debut; the pop hooks were buried in a noisier mix, and the material was darker. But if Weezer no longer sounded like the band that had given the world 'Buddy Holly', the good news was that there were now plenty of others that did. By 1996, the influence of Weezer's first album had percolated through the music world, and post-Weezer records were beginning to emerge. Nada Surf's 'Popular', for example, was exactly the kind of post-grunge MTV hit Rivers Cuomo no longer felt capable of writing. On *Pinkerton*, the dash of bitterness that had given Weezer's first album its edge was served straight up, and many found the result hard to swallow. 'Popular' was a much more appealing concoction, a nerd-rock screed about all the good-looking kids with easy lives and fashionable clothes who made the singer's high school life hell, served over a piece of music that sounded almost but not exactly like Weezer's 'Say It Ain't So'. That the single was produced by Ric Ocasek, the man who had guided Weezer toward pop perfection two years earlier, only added to the impression that Nada Surf had picked up where Weezer left off.

In July, Nada Surf was booked to appear on MTV's *Beach House*, performing their hit in front of an audience of good-looking kids with easy lives and fashionable clothes. But on the day of the shoot, as the bussed-in football jocks and cheerleaders wearing their off-the-rack grungewear took up their positions, Daniel Lorca started to feel as though he'd made a big mistake, and by the time the cameras were ready to roll, the bass player was nowhere to be seen. Singer Matthew Caws found him ten minutes later, standing alone on a nearby cliff, staring out to sea, refusing to go back and play 'Popular' for the entertainment of popular people. The singer worked hard to coax his colleague off the edge. He told Lorca that the band should do what they came to do and play *Beach House* — not for the money, not for the kids or even for the music — but for the irony. 'Look at it as a giant performance-art piece,' he said. 'People smart enough to understand the song are going to be smart enough to realise that this is the ultimate postmodern thing.'[1]

Caws' advice was sound. 'Popular' wished for a world without popular kids, a world where their football pennants and cheerleader trophies meant nothing, a better, fairer world where those born with perfect bone structure did not automatically inherit the earth. Now the members of Nada Surf were about to perform the song for the amusement of the very same people it railed against, on a show which simply reinforced the values of the brutal high school pecking order it described. Since the band couldn't possibly be happy about this, they faced the accusation that they must be doing the spot for the money — or to fulfil a contractual obligation, which amounted to the same thing. The only way for the band to admit to this litany of failure and still walk away from *Beach House* with some semblance of dignity would be to appeal to postmodernism, which had, by 1996, been helping artists to rationalise failure for almost thirty years.

Postmodernism was the catch-all term for a range of strategies invented by artists in the mid sixties in order to address the failure of modernism to change everyday life. Its clearest demonstration could be found in the world of architecture. By the 1960s, American architects had begun to realise that their adherence to the tenets of modern design had failed to create liveable housing for low-income workers. The result was a crisis of faith among architects, and many began looking again at all that they had sought to avoid. They learned to accept that modernism's white-cube ideal might be impractical, if not impossible for ordinary people to live in, and started to study Vegas casinos, roadside attractions, and kitsch retro furniture in an attempt to come to terms with the tastes of the masses for whom they were ostensibly designing. Painfully aware that they were slumming it, they learned to do these things with a wink and a nudge.

In the world of painting, a similar reversal took place. The abstract painters of the 1940s had taken modernism's war against mass culture as far as it could go. In 1963, Andy Warhol's soup cans and detergent boxes served notice that their island of resistance could no longer be maintained, that artists must learn to accept the world of money and advertising or perish. Warhol, with his bland demeanour and permanent attitude of cheerful open-mindedness made this look very easy. His pop art was often described as a 'celebration' of mass culture, though his attitude toward it was probably better summed up by his own phrase: 'I like boring things.' He never claimed that mass culture had any great intellectual significance — he simply trashed the debate by insisting that intellectual significance was overrated and unrealistic. 'Buying,' he once said, 'is much more American than thinking.'[2] This attitude served Warhol very well over the next two decades. In the 1996 film *Basquiat*, Warhol — played by a silver-wigged David Bowie — could be seen making his way through the money-hungry 1980s art world with supernatural ease, just as he had in real life. Many of the younger artists portrayed in the film cling to the notion that art is separate from or opposed to the world of money and business, and suffer as a result. Director Julian Schnabel showed how Warhol's semi-ironic habit of thinking and talking about art only in terms of money, fame or popularity made him immune to such dramas.

Warhol seemed ahead of his time in 1996, because the semi-detached attitude he took toward mass culture had, for most intelligent people, become an essential means of psychic survival by the mid nineties. In a 1993 interview, author Douglas Coupland spoke of the huge sense of excitement mingled with relief that came over him when he first discovered pop art, as he realised that artists like Warhol and Lichtenstein had invented a way for him to understand and critique the mediascape without having to fight against it.[3] In the nineties, 'thinking pop', as Warhol termed it, became necessary, because in a media-dominated world, it was simply no longer possible to stay angry about everything all the time, as L7's Jennifer Finch realised.

'You have to have a sense of humour to survive here,' she said of her native LA. As an idealistic punk in a city of freeways, strip-malls and bad heavy metal bands, Finch had lived in a near-permanent state of outrage until she met her bandmate Donita Sparks, who helped her see the funny side. 'A lot of people are like, "LA is so fake and phoney",' she explained. 'That's why we like it here!'[4]

Surviving the nineties was no different from surviving LA; one had to learn to laugh at banality, and to see the depth in surfaces, to learn to like bad things — as Mike Patton said of Vanilla Ice — for 'wrong reasons'. In September 1994, 350,000 visitors attended Woodstock '94, a music festival held on the 25th anniversary of the original event, featuring appearances by the Red Hot Chili Peppers, Green Day, Blind Melon and Nine Inch Nails. This new Woodstock retained some of the attractions of the old one, including Crosby, Stills and Nash, Joe Cocker, and a great deal of mud. But the Vietnam War was conspicuous by its absence — as was the feeling that the event meant anything at all besides a multimillion dollar profit for its organisers and a lucrative sponsorship deal for Pepsi. To music writer Jim De Rogatis, the event seemed less like a music festival and more like a gigantic outdoor shopping mall.[5] But when one visitor to Woodstock '94, writing in an online forum, complained that the festival had been 'purely manufactured for commercialism', another suggested that having fun in the midst of, and despite, such blatant exploitation was 'the ultimate form of rebellion'.[6]

In 1995, the editors of a zine called *Hermenaut* advocated precisely this kind of ironic attitude as the only kind of intellectual freedom available in a commercialised world. 'Let us then be in-between,' they wrote. 'Let us revel in *Baywatch*, Joe Camel, *Wired* magazine … but let's never succumb to the glamorous allure of these things.'[7] To be in mass culture, but not of it — this is the strategy employed by Brodie, the smartass protagonist of Kevin Smith's 1995 film *Mallrats*, who responds to the corporate takeover of public life by wasting time in the mall, shopping with no perceptible shopping agenda. 'I love the smell of commerce in the morning!' he exclaims, throwing his arms in the air.[8] Being far too smart to blindly accept the air-conditioned nightmare, Brodie has learned to love the mall the way modern architects learned to love Vegas — ironically. Brodie's gesture was exactly the kind of postmodern 'performance art piece' Caws suggested Nada Surf might pull off on MTV's *Beach House*. The singer knew that MTV — like the mall — was banal, exploitative and possibly evil. But since he felt that the effort involved in opposing evil would most likely be wasted, he hoped instead to appear to be cooperating with it, while at the same time making it clear — to those who had an interest in such things — that he was not; to do the show, while letting his fans know that he knew that they knew that he should not be doing the show.

Gestures of this kind had become commonplace in alternative music by 1996, from the matching suits and stuck-on smiles worn by Nirvana in the video for 'In Bloom', to the album cover of No Doubt's *Tragic Kingdom*. Here, Gwen Stefani was pictured wearing a short red dress, smiling and holding aloft an orange — which on closer inspection turned out to be riddled with holes and buzzing with flies. The band's name was spelled out in big showbiz-style chrome letters over her head, while the band itself stood glumly under a barren tree in a field of corn. 'Bought and sold out in the USA' read the guarantee printed on the bottom left corner of the label.[9] In its own way, the image was as loaded with disgust as the baby swimming toward the dollar bill on a fish hook on the cover of *Nevermind*. But it was also, after all, a picture of a girl in a short dress with a big shiny sign over her head. In this way, No Doubt got to have their corn and eat it too — as did many other groups in the mid nineties. By this point, the sense of 'ironicism' Eddie Vedder admired in Kurt Vonnegut, but couldn't quite get the hang of himself, had become as essential for artists trying to negotiate the treacherous terrain of the music industry as it was for fans trying to buy their CDs at the mall.

An interview with Bruce Pavitt and Jonathan Poneman in *Hype!* suggested that irony had been essential to the breakthrough of alternative rock from the beginning. The pair described how they'd created Sub Pop to be an indie-rock 'hit factory' that might compete with major labels on an international level.[10] But since they knew that these ambitions would be frowned upon in the indie community, they turned the label's business aspirations into an ironic joke about the music business. Sub Pop advertised its wares with knowingly crass corporate slogans, and joked in its press releases about the lengths it would go to exploit its artists and rip off their fans. Stunts like these allowed the label and its artists, as Michael Azerrad put it, to 'quest for ever-higher levels of money and exposure while laughing it off as a joke about questing for ever-higher levels of money and exposure'.[11] 'We went along with it' said Tad Danielsen, speaking of Sub Pop's late eighties marketing pitch. 'It seemed kind of funny at the time.'[12]

'Irony,' wrote *Mondo 2000* scribe Andrew Hultkrans, 'is the X-er's true birthright.'[13] Certainly, irony seemed to be everywhere in 1996, an impression heightened by the ubiquity of Alanis Morissette's second single, 'Ironic'. In an online essay published at the height of the song's popularity, Matt Sturges concluded that of the eleven scenarios presented in the song, only two could be properly considered ironic (though Sturges awarded a half-point for 'it's the good advice that you just didn't take').[14] But most people knew what irony was when they saw it, even if Morissette and her songwriting partner Glen Ballard appeared not to. As he watched Tom Morello eat McDonald's French fries within sight of the monument to the 1907 uprising in Moscow, Rage Against the Machine bassist Tim Bob Commerford was fairly sure he'd seen a prime example. 'Isn't it ironic?' he sang, doing his best Alanis impersonation. 'Don't you think?'[15] In October, music writer Elizabeth Gilbert went to Las Vegas to do a story on the newly opened Hard Rock Hotel and Casino. The building was a typical Vegas folly — a luxury hotel complex the size of three city blocks with a twenty-storey high Fender Strat sticking out the top. The inside was a riot of autographed guitars, rock-themed cocktail bars and 'Anarchy in the USA' slot machines. But Gilbert barely made it through the lobby. 'I am momentarily paralysed by what I see when checking in at the Hard Rock,' she wrote. 'Right above the front desk, big cheerful brass letters spell out, "Here we are now, entertain us". Underneath, smaller letters note, almost parenthetically, "Kurt Cobain".'[16] As the desk clerk beamed at her and told her to have a nice day, Gilbert wondered whether there was any room for 'in-betweening' in a place like the Hard Rock, whether, in 1996, alternative rock had anything more to learn from Las Vegas.

Flux and Chaos

Beck's November 1996 single, 'Devil's Haircut', was inspired by a phrase, 'electric music and the summer people', which the singer found on the back cover of an album in a thrift store. 'A terrible record,' he said, 'I can't remember what it's called — some easy listening thing from the sixties.'[1] The cheap utopia described in the phrase had an irresistible irony to it. On the Lollapalooza tour, Beck had played enough electric music and seen enough of 1995's summer people to know that neither were all they were cracked up to be. He'd tried his hardest to connect with the youth of America, but soon learned that they wanted nothing more from him than the hit they'd seen on MTV. Once he'd got that out of the way, they quickly lost interest. With visions of empty blue plastic seats and bored, distant faces still fresh in his mind, Beck wrote what he later described as a 'very cynical' set of verses about the alternative nation and its prefab nonconformists. But by the end of the year, the song's lyrics had changed a great deal, as Beck took the alienating experience of a rock singer on the festival circuit and gave it a more mythic dimension. He now sang in the voice of a stranger coming to town with the 'briefcase blues', a thousand-year-old traveller landing in modern America and observing the mess humanity had gotten itself into: 'love machines on sympathy crutches / discount orgies on dropout buses'.[2] Beck renamed the song 'Devil's Haircut', in accordance with a lesson he'd learned during his early folksinging days in LA. Back when no-one knew or cared who he was, the singer would often appear — unannounced and uninvited — on the stage of a club while the featured entertainment was still being set up. Beck figured he had about thirty seconds to get the crowd's attention before he got escorted from the premises, and quickly learned that the best way to do that was to sing about the devil.

In those days, Beck would have completed a tune like 'Devil's Haircut' with an acoustic guitar in hand, building the melody around folksinger chords. He still wrote songs like this occasionally, but the disorientating experience of the past twelve months seemed to demand a more disoriented method of songwriting. Beck had sought a way of composing by cutting rather than writing, and had found it in hip-hop, where sampling technology and turntable trickery allowed artists to jump between musical worlds at the flick of a fader. That it was hip-hop production, rather than rapping, that appealed to Beck at this juncture was significant — up until this point, rock bands or songwriters who ventured into hip-hop's storehouse of ideas tended to walk away with the raps and leave the samples on the shelf. From *Blood Sugar Sex Magik* to the Offspring's 'Come Out and Play', the results of the rap-rock crossover to date gave the impression that the white contribution to contemporary black music would be to add 'real instruments', as though hip-hop groups used loops and samples from old records because they couldn't afford a band. For Beck, who got into Grandmaster Flash well before he heard Pussy Galore or Lead Belly, hip-hop's magpie approach to composition had always been part of the fun. 'Loser' had been one of the first alternative rock hits to incorporate hip-hop's production methods as opposed to just its rhyme schemes — the song was built around a loop from a Dr John record and featured sampled sitar and drums, turntable scratching and fragments of film dialogue. The songs that Beck was writing in 1995, 'Devil's Haircut', 'Novacane', 'Hotwax', 'High 5 (Rock the Catskills)', demanded that this approach be taken even further.

Beck had found the means to do this when he made contact with John King and Mike Simpson — known to the world as the Dust Brothers — in January. Like most hip-hop producers, the Dust Brothers built their music up from looped samples and drum breaks, but their short-attention-span aesthetic meant that the loops never looped for very long without being interrupted by something else, while the duo's encyclopaedic knowledge of music ensured that, whatever it was, it worked. 'Modern records are very predictable,' said Simpson in 1996. 'Usually, if you listen to a song for thirty seconds, you get it — you know where it's going, you know what's gonna happen, you know what to expect. We wanted to try to keep the music exciting so you have to listen to the whole song, otherwise you're gonna miss the best part.'[3] At the time, the music world was still catching up with the duo's staggering work on the Beastie Boys' 1989 album *Paul's Boutique*. Now, the brothers would apply the same knack for juxtaposition that led them to mix the Commodores into The Sweet on that album to bring Beck's schizophrenic vision to life.

King and Simpson worked from the living room of a house they rented in Silver Lake in LA, recording straight from a pair of old microphones into a simple mixing console. This cosy environment suited the slightly studio-phobic Beck perfectly. 'Studios are too antiseptic, like a laboratory,' he complained. 'Laboratories don't have much to do with music.'[4] The Dust Brothers' low-key set-up facilitated exactly the kind of spontaneous invention Beck's new music required; because the control room was also the live room, any inspired moment of goofing off could immediately be captured for posterity, without the often fatal delay that falls between an idea and the proper recording of an idea. Beck would play a riff on a guitar or a keyboard, and Simpson and King would sample it and play it back as a loop, over which the three would add more sounds — harmonica, turntable scratching, Moog synthesiser and drums. The first song they tackled in this fashion, 'Hotwax', became a honky-tonk blues piece built around a lopsided guitar riff, interrupted at various points by a scratched-up funk chorus, a moment from the *Car Wash* soundtrack and a smooth wizard explaining 'the rhythms of the universe' for a couple of wide-eyed kids. 'Novacane' started out like a forgotten Isaac Hayes soundtrack album, with a sinister bass rumbling away under a laid-back groove, but its chorus descended into pure New York noise, and the coda sounded like Thurston Moore jamming over Kraftwerk's 'Pocket Calculator'.

Recording was postponed over the summer of 1995, while Beck fulfilled his touring commitments. He came back to the studio somewhat altered by the double-whammy of Lollapalooza and the unexpected death of his grandfather, Al Hansen, an artist who was part of the Fluxus movement. Beck wanted to honour his grandfather's spirit with music that was more 'celebratory', and to neutralise the 'neutral experience' of Lollapalooza by pursuing his new aesthetic of surprise and random association. Both of these resolutions would inform the recording of 'Where It's At', which began with a laid-back riff Beck came up with while noodling around on a Wurlitzer keyboard one afternoon. The song's 'party in the studio' atmosphere — all handclaps and shout-along choruses — belied the fact that it was a party for one, since Beck played every member of the crowd himself. As the chorus came to an end, the carefully built-up illusion of a southern-style soul party was abruptly shattered by the arrival of an anachronistic disco robot.

'High 5 (Rock the Catskills)' was another song produced during this second sitting; a sample-adelic odyssey that took Beck's new montage practice to its limits. The verses picked up where 'Novacane' left off, riding a robotic eighties groove before exploding into an unspeakably noisy chorus, all screaming and detuned guitars. When the racket was abruptly replaced by the soothing sounds of Schubert's 'Unfinished Symphony' halfway through the song, it seemed as though the Dust Brothers, feeling that Beck was becoming annoying, had tried to placate the listener with a selection from their light classical repertoire. This 'party malfunction' as Beck described it, was followed by an even more serious blunder later in the song, when the digital beats were hijacked by a blast of bad eighties metal. 'Turn that shit off man!' yelled a rapper. 'What's wrong with you, man? Get the other record. Damn.'[5]

When *Odelay* was finally released in June 1996, *Rolling Stone* declared the album a classic, and its composer a musical saviour. 'Could the future of rock and roll be a snot-nosed slacker with a bad haircut, an absurdly eclectic record collection, two turntables and a microphone?' Certainly, *Odelay* was timely — the record appeared at the precise moment when alt rock, having failed to evolve, began to *devolve*, rock in general became tainted by association, and many indie music fans and critics began keeping a more open ear to hip-hop — in particular the sample-happy approach of producers like Bomb Squad, Prince Paul and the Dust Brothers. Beck's new collage approach also offered a tantalising alternative to the post-Nirvana cult of 'real bands'. When punk rock noise appeared on *Odelay*, its claims to authenticity were always undermined by an absurdly unnatural edit, as in 'High 5 (Rock the Catskills)', where the guitar frenzy suddenly gave way to a funky computer, or 'Lord Only Knows', which began with a brief snatch of the kind of racket Nirvana might have pursued for the length of a whole song, but proceeded in a completely unrelated country-funk style. Bands appeared and disappeared, the album put the listener in a place, but the place turned out to be nowhere. 'Where It's At', according to Beck, was 'a party, but a party without a specific location'.[6]

Odelay trashed the documentary fiction of indie and the carefully maintained artifice of mainstream rock, in favour of what Beck called 'pure deconstruction' — the singer tried to leave things unfinished so that listening became an active rather than passive pursuit. 'I wanted to create songs somebody could enter,' he explained, 'a scenario exists and you kind of go in and create your own story within it.'[7] This approach applied to his lyrics as much as his music. When triple j's Michael Tunn pointed out that a lot of his words were hard to understand, Beck said, 'It's not really about understanding.' 'Right,' replied Tunn, 'so you don't write them to have a meaning.' The singer corrected him: 'I didn't say that. They're there if you need 'em.'[8]

Ever since 'Loser', music journalists had developed the habit of portraying Beck as a noble savage for the nineties, an archetypal couch-surfing slacker whose addled lyrics and abrupt changes of style could be explained by the short attention span he shared with most members of his generation. In fact, his method had more in common with the book that inspired this cliché — Douglas Coupland's 1991 novel, *Generation X* — than with the cliché itself. By 1996, 'Gen X' had become synonymous with a certain bored, ironic attitude toward media and popular culture, a tendency to relate to the world at one remove. But Coupland had never thought this was the point of the book. *Generation X* was not an indulgence in end-of-the-century decadence, but an expression of longing, a wish for an escape from the society of the spectacle. After Dag attacks an expensive car that has a bumper sticker on the back that reads 'SPENDING OUR CHILDREN'S INHERITANCE', he wonders out loud whether his anger might have been slightly misplaced. 'I don't know, Andy,' he says, 'whether I feel more that I want to punish some aging crock for frittering away my

world, or whether I'm just upset that the world has gotten too big —
way beyond our capacity to tell stories about it — and so all we're left
with are these blips and chunks and snippets on bumpers.'[9] Foremost in
Coupland's mind as he wrote the book was the notion that the means
to transcend this fragmented world might lie in our ability to connect
its dots. In the end, his characters redeem themselves by doing the very
thing Dag regards as impossible — telling stories.

Despite his best attempts to avoid the world of blips and chunks,
Beck knew all too well that, as a child of the seventies, his imagination
had been colonised by mass-media and mass-culture; the Spanish
chorus of 'Hot Wax' translated as 'I am a broken record / I have
bubblegum in my brain',[10] and much of his music was written to give
a sense of what this felt like. *Odelay*, he said, was about 'disorientation
in modern life and culture', and the album's abrupt edits and pop-
art lyrics ensured that the listener felt disoriented, instead of merely
hearing its effects described.[11] But Beck deconstructed in order to
reconstruct; he collected thrift-store records, outdated keyboards,
second-hand slogans and words from faded billboards and assembled
them into a musical language with a purpose that was not to confuse,
but to communicate. 'Devil's Haircut' was not, he insisted, 'a bunch
of gibberish' but 'a blues song'; an old-fashioned story about the wages
of sin told in the voice of a man who's seen it all, who knows that our
shiny summer rock spectacular is nothing but a 'rotten oasis', that
spiking one's hair up and dyeing it green is no cure for alienation, but
a fast-track to purgatory from a Faustian bargain-bin. 'People say what
I'm doing is like switching channels on the TV,' he said. 'But I don't
see it like that: I look at it like it's integrating the flux and chaos and
making something substantial from it.'[12]

This is How I Feel, This is Who I Am

Fiona Apple was only nineteen years old in 1996, but she had done a lot of learning in her short life; she'd had piano lessons since she was eight, been singing since she was ten, and — most importantly — she'd been in therapy since she was twelve. She had learned, as Peter Weir put it in his profile on the singer, 'to talk about her feelings early and often', and — like most teenagers — she had no shortage of feelings to talk about.[1] 'Everything that happens to me I feel very deeply,' she told MTV's Kurt Loder. 'And when you feel things deeply and think a lot about how you feel, you learn a lot about yourself. And when you know yourself, you know life.'[2]

Therapy had helped Apple find her voice, and had also prepared her well for the interview circuit. Journalists who met her after her album's release were surprised by how unguarded she was, the ease with which her conversation could turn from a list of her upcoming live shows to an account of the time she was raped when she was twelve. They soon discovered that her lack of guile in interviews was consistent with her honesty on stage — watching Apple perform was a little like accidentally reading a stranger's diary, as one interviewer told her after seeing her show in Paris. 'She said she felt guilty watching me on stage because she felt like she was hearing something she wasn't supposed to be hearing,' said Apple. 'And that really said to me that I'm doing what I want to be doing.' Apple's emotional exhibitionism came off as tough rather than pathetic, because her audience watched her fall apart by her own invitation, and bore witness to her torments by her own decree. The first single from *Tidal*, 'Criminal', was a perfect introduction to her own peculiar theatre of cruelty. Producer Andy Slater set up a sinister piano blues pinned down by a hip-hop beat, and Apple introduced herself with the words 'I've been a bad, bad girl'. She went on to give an account of her selfish and destructive behaviour, which sounded more like a threat than a confession, and warned that she would continue to suffer in public whether the listener liked it or not. 'Don't you tell me to deny it,' she sang, 'I've done wrong and I'm gonna suffer for my sins.'[3]

Apple's record label, Sony, hired Mark Romanek to make a video for 'Criminal' early in 1996. Romanek was a stylish director with a knack for matching avant-garde photography and cinema techniques to alternative rock hits: he drew on the work of surrealist photographers and filmmakers for Nine Inch Nails' 'Closer', and crossed French new wave cinema with *Midnight Cowboy* for Beck's 'Devil's Haircut'. For 'Criminal', Romanek came up with a treatment inspired by the work of Nan Goldin, an American photographer whose career was being celebrated at the time with a retrospective at the Whitney Museum of American Art. This institutional recognition had been a long time coming for Goldin, whose work had been invisible in the eighties because it seemed the very opposite of photography-as-art: Goldin used too much flash, payed little attention to composition, and treated her negatives and prints with extreme neglect. But Goldin saw her work less as art than reportage, a series of stolen moments from desperate lives, not the least of which was her own. In an interview conducted as part of the exhibition, she explained that she'd started taking pictures not because she wanted to be a photographer, but because she wanted other people to know what was going in her life. 'My photography has come out of emotional need rather than aesthetic choice,' she said.[4] Once again, Romanek had perfectly matched style to idea: the phrase could as easily have come from Apple's mouth as Goldin's. 'I think I just use music as a vehicle so I can sing what I'm saying,' the singer told Scott Frampton. 'It's the act of actually saying it; actually performing it to people that gives me the satisfaction that I needed for my whole life. Just being able to be, "This is how I feel, this is who I am. You heard it, that's it."'[5]

Romanek's treatment for 'Criminal' was loosely based on Goldin's *The Ballad of Sexual Dependency*, a series of photos she took between 1976 and 1995, and named after a song from Bertolt Brecht's *The Threepenny Opera*. The pictures were snapshots of Goldin's friends and lovers living their lives — sleeping, waking up, smoking cigarettes, taking drugs, dressing up, going to parties, getting in fights, having sex, falling in love and passing out on the floor. For 'Criminal', Romanek compressed the *Ballad* into three hot MTV minutes, as though Goldin had been hired to direct an instalment of *Beach House*, or its sordid aftermath. The video was set in a seventies-style tract house, on the morning after a wild party. Romanek cleverly translated Goldin's stills into a moving format by having his extras stay completely still while Apple moved around the house, and he evoked her snapshot style by lighting his subjects from the front with a cold, chemical flash. Some shots — like the one of Apple surfacing from the bath — were explicit homages to Goldin's photos. But the video's real achievement was in the way Romanek matched the photographer's conceptual world to the singer's. Nudity in Goldin's pictures was a form of confession, as it was in 'Criminal', where Apple was shown shedding her clothes as she unburdened herself of her sins. Apple later said she was 'horrified' by this idea, and refused to do it until Romanek explained that it would be 'tongue in cheek' — though what he meant by this was hard to say. There was nothing funny or ironic in Apple's emotional striptease. The effect was, in the end, the same one she created on stage or in interviews; the same effect Nan Goldin's subjects had on the visitors to her show at the Whitney. By the time the last shot faded to black, viewers were left feeling that their own privacy had been invaded, rather than that of the girl on the screen.

Junkie's Promise

'More and more fashion photography looks like my work,' Nan Goldin observed in 1996, 'and has this larger expanse of possibilities of who can be beautiful.'[1] Goldin's subjects were often social outcasts of some variety — gay men, lesbians, transvestites, or drug addicts, and her lens, while always sympathetic, was rarely flattering; her subjects' flaws were clearly on display. As a result, neither Goldin's pictures nor her subjects were 'beautiful' in the sense that a mid eighties magazine editor or video director would have understood. That decade's aesthetic equated beauty with artifice — immaculately applied make-up, perfectly coiffed hair — but also with health and abundance. Its ideal was represented by supermodels like Elle Macpherson, Cindy Crawford and Claudia Schiffer. But as Goldin pointed out, this had begun to change in the nineties. The fashion for long hair, large breasts and rows of white teeth had given way to a more ambiguous aesthetic, typified by models like Kate Moss and Jaime King, who appeared in campaigns for CK and Guess?, photographed in a snapshot style against bad, cheap interiors, looking skinny and unhealthy. Goldin saw this as a victory of sorts, the fashion industry relaxing its rules to allow for more realistic and varied ideas of physical beauty.

But as in music, the reality revolt in fashion had some unfortunate side effects. Naomi Wolf had warned, in her 1990 book, *The Beauty Myth*, that working to expand the mass media's 'index of possibilities' was a waste of time. 'Let's abandon this hope of looking to the index to fully include us,' she wrote. 'It won't, because if it does, it has lost its function.'[2] Advertising, she reminded her readers, works by making people feel bad about themselves — by inventing an ideal, and then telling you that it can be yours for a price. Sure enough, by the mid nineties, instead of promoting health, wealth and physical perfection, the fashion industry had begun advertising sadness, sickness and addiction. A fashion shoot published in *Ray Gun* magazine in 1995 showed sweaty, skinny models posed against bare walls, smoking cigarettes. Stylist Tara St Hill made George's hair look stringy and dirty, and photographer Corrine Day zeroed in on Emma's chipped nail polish and pale, sallow skin.[3] The feature was called 'Goths on Acid', but the models didn't really look like goths, and acid was most likely not what they were on — the piece was a prime example of what was being described in the media as 'heroin chic'. Day's photos of a deathly looking Kate Moss made headlines, as did Davide Sorrenti's pictures of his then-girlfriend (and heroin addict) Jaime King in a series of obviously junk-inspired scenarios — waiting for her man at a train station, nodding off on the couch in a pair of ripped tights under posters of Sid Vicious and Kurt Cobain. Heroin chic dovetailed neatly with the fashion industry's new downward mobility, but its popularity also reflected a surge in the popularity of the drug itself. In the nineties, heroin, as Eric Stoltz put it in *Pulp Fiction*, was 'coming back in a big fuckin' way',[4] with the *Washington Post* reporting that imports of the drug had risen from four to six tons a year in the early 1980s to twenty in 1994. According to an essay by Mark Ehrman, the junk boom could be explained by a changing drug market, as the usual suppliers in South-East Asia faced competition from growers in Mexico and South America. 'There, cocaine drug cartels eagerly diversified into heroin, a less exacting crop with longer-term customers,' he wrote. This more competitive market had led to lower prices and improved merchandise; in 1994, heroin in the US was five times as pure as it had been in 1985, for exactly the same price. 'At this purity,' wrote Ehrman, 'it was no longer necessary to inject the drug to get high — smoking heroin off tinfoil ("chasing the dragon") became a socially acceptable activity in many influential circles, as did snorting.'[5]

In his 1993 interview with Alice In Chains, *Q* magazine's Mark Cooper noted the growing popularity of heroin in alternative rock circles, and quoted the band's song 'Junkman' in which singer Layne Staley described himself as belonging to 'that elite race' of 'stoners, junkies and freaks' as evidence of the trend.[6] Later that year cartoonist Peter Bagge lampooned the grunge stars' fondness for the stuff with his drawing of a flannel-clad doofus singing 'I scream, you scream, we all scream for HEROIN!' But twelve months later, alt rock's dalliance with heroin no longer seemed like a laughing matter. Kurt Cobain's death was inextricably tied up with his addiction, and Courtney Love told Amy Raphael that one of the reasons it had been so hard to keep her husband off heroin was because in Seattle, at the time, it seemed as though everyone they knew was either doing or selling it.[7] By this point, Love had also witnessed the demise of Kristen Pfaff, the bass player in her own band, from a heroin overdose.

March 1995 saw the death of the Smashing Pumpkins' tour keyboardist Jonathan Melvoin and the sacking of Jimmy Chamberlin, whose own heroin addiction had grown to the point where Billy Corgan felt he could no longer function in the band. Not long after, the career trajectory of the Breeders came to a crashing halt when Kelley Deal was arrested for possession of heroin and subsequently checked into rehab. And the Stone Temple Pilots imploded spectacularly in May that same year when police caught Scott Weiland buying drugs at a motel in Pasadena. His wife bailed him out, but as they drove away from the courthouse, Weiland insisted that they stop by his dealer's place. When his wife refused, the singer bailed on her — straight out of the moving car and onto the street. Weiland picked up where he left off at the Chateau Marmont, doing drugs with Courtney Love for about two weeks before Weiland decided he'd had enough and needed to get straight. Just before checking himself into the Betty Ford clinic, he handed Love an apology note to his fans, which she read live on air in a KROQ interview. 'I have a disease,' it said, 'it's called drug addiction, and I want to say that I'm sorry.'[8] By this point, Weiland's heroin habit had cost him every cent of the considerable royalties he'd made from the band's hit, 'Interstate Love Song', along with the last of whatever trust and goodwill his bandmates had felt toward him.

In 1991, Perry Farrell had told Kurt Loder that he admired heroin users for their honesty. 'What they believe in, they stick with,' he said. 'Most people these days, they're full of shit — they'll do anything to get along.'[9] Here, Farrell had hit on a major factor in heroin's newfound fashionability. The selling-off of alternative music and culture would proceed at an exponential rate over the next five years. One by one, every subversive movement from riot grrrl to Cali-punk would be recuperated and turned into a consumable version of itself. But while heroin chic makeovers were now available at the mall, heroin itself could not be adopted or discarded so easily. One couldn't simply take it up for a summer and then drop it when it became lame, as one might with green hair or Green Day. 'The drug emerged as an authentic commitment in a time of mass-dabbling in transgressive styles such as body-piercing and tattooing,' wrote Ehrman. 'The solemnity of heroin use seemed to mock the luxury of consumer choice.'[10]

This idea was explored at length in Irvine Welsh's 1993 novel, *Trainspotting*, a collection of interrelated stories about a group of heroin addicts living in Edinburgh in the late eighties. 'They were like vampires,' Welsh wrote of his protagonists, 'living a largely nocturnal existence, completely out of synchronisation with most of the other people who inhabited the tenements and lived by a rota of sleep and work. It was good to be different.'[11] Welsh never imagined his book would even be published, let alone made into a film. But this was exactly what happened in 1996, when screenwriter John Hodge and director Danny Boyle decided to adapt *Trainspotting* for the big screen. Boyle's hyperkinetic film opened with a shot of Renton, Sick Boy and Spud running from the cops down an Edinburgh street. On the soundtrack, Iggy Pop's 'Lust For Life' played while Renton reeled off a litany of consumer desire. 'Choose life, choose a job, choose a career, choose a family, choose a fuckin' big television, choose washing machines, cars, compact disc players and electrical tin openers, choose DIY and wondering who the fuck you are on a Sunday morning, choose sitting on the couch watching mind-numbing, spirit-crushing game shows.'[12]

Here, Renton paused for effect. In the world he grew up in, Thatcher's eighties, consumer choice was advocated as the motor of economic growth and the path to personal freedom. Thatcher, like Reagan, conflated capitalism with democracy to the point where the two were indistinguishable from one another; freedom was defined as the freedom to choose between a wide range of goods and services, the freedom to create a life by assembling a lifestyle, the freedom to make money and spend it however one liked. But this definition of liberty may have been somewhat overrated. In 1964's *One-Dimensional Man*, philosopher Herbert Marcuse insisted that 'the disappearance of this kind of freedom would be one of the greatest achievements of civilisation'. Marcuse proposed a world where people could be free from meaningless choices, where they could choose not to choose — and in *Trainspotting*, Renton declared that he'd found such a place. Choose life? 'Why would I want to do a thing like that? I chose not to choose life: I chose something else. And the reasons? There are no reasons. Who needs reasons when you've got heroin?'[13]

1997

Dan Abnormal

Trainspotting was released in tandem with an immaculately hip soundtrack album, which connected the dots between the artists Welsh's characters loved (Bowie, Iggy, Lou Reed), the music they might have danced to while off their heads (Underworld, Primal Scream, Leftfield), and Britpop. Pulp contributed a priceless piece of kitchen-sink drama called 'Mile End', Sleeper covered Blondie's 'Atomic', Elastica was represented by '2:1', and Blur's 'Sing' finally had its moment to shine — its fin de siècle hopelessness made far more sense next to Lou Reed's 'Perfect Day' than it had on *Leisure*. The album might have been a perfect Britpop primer had it not been for the omission of Oasis, but if Noel Gallagher was miffed about being excluded from Boyle's art-school party, he didn't show it. At the film's premiere in February, a reporter asked Gallagher if he saw any similarities between *Trainspotting* and Oasis. 'Well,' Gallagher replied, 'our group's all about being honest and being real, and that's what this film is about. I mean there's a lot of swearing and shit and shooting up. But that's real life, you know what I mean? Stuff happens.'[1]

The stuff was happening more and more in Noel's vicinity, as the cocaine craze that had fuelled Britpop during 1996 gave way to a new sensation. Annie Holland and Donna Matthews had begun taking heroin out of Justine Frischmann's sight on Elastica's 1995 tour. But by the time they came home, nobody was hiding it anymore — there was no longer any need. Heroin, as Frischmann later told John Harris, became fashionable.[2] The drug's social stigma had been circumvented by dint of it being smoked rather than injected, and by 1996 it was not unusual for a party to end with a piece of tinfoil and a lighter being passed around the room, a ritual affectionately known as 'chasing the beetle'. Later that year, Damon Albarn wrote an ode to Britpop's latest behind-closed-doors craze called 'Beetlebum'. The title did double duty as a drug reference and an allusion to the Beatles — Albarn had become annoyed at the way Oasis were so often compared to the band despite, in his opinion, sounding nothing like them. 'Beetlebum', with its lazy *White Album* atmosphere, surreal lyrics and hypnotic guitar figure, was Albarn's way of saying to the Gallaghers, this is how it's done. But when the tune was released as a single in January 1997, the singer didn't mention any of this. 'I have no explanation for it,' he said. 'It just sounded good.'[3]

One month later, an album appeared, simply titled *Blur*. In the round of interviews to promote the record, Albarn maintained his silence on the subject of 'Beetlebum', and refused to offer any clues as to what the other lyrics might be about. 'They'll be forever shrouded in mystery,' he said.[4] Fans who'd looked forward to finding the lyrics printed on the album's inner sleeve — as was customary on Blur releases — would have been disappointed, since the insert revealed nothing but a photo of the band at work in the studio. After hearing the record, they would have noticed a few other things missing too: the spiky strings and perky brass, so prominently featured on *Parklife* and *The Great Escape* were gone, as was the cast of characters — no more suburban perverts or students on holiday, no more Bill Baron, Tracy Jacks or Ernold Same. The last three Blur albums had been a riot of detail, of people, places and products. This one barely had nouns. No names, no title, no lyrics, no strings or horns, no explanation forthcoming from the author. *Blur* offered Blur fans a lot less of everything, everything but one — Graham Coxon.

Over the past four years, Blur's pursuit of the English ideal had demanded that its guitarist's taste for American college rock — the Pixies, Sonic Youth and Dinosaur Jr — be pushed to the side. There hadn't been much room for shambolic indie noise in the perfect pop world of *The Great Escape*. But by 1996, Albarn had come to realise that this was a problem for Blur, and a problem with Britpop generally. The bored-furious, stop-start, Brit new wave sound, which had seemed so exciting in 1995, had begun to yield diminishing returns, an endless succession of sarky pop tunes sung in fake cockney accents over oompah music. 'I'd like it if the bigger bands in Britain took a few more risks,' he said. 'I wouldn't like another year like last year.'[5] At the precise moment when Britpop peaked in the media — Liam Gallagher on the cover of *Vanity Fair*, the *Trainspotting* soundtrack racing up the charts — Albarn was already looking for a way out of it, and so began to take a new interest in his guitarist's CD collection — the very same albums Coxon had been compelled to listen to on headphones in the privacy of his bunk bed over the past four years. In the dissociative jumps of Beck's *Odelay*, the fragmented syntax and off-kilter melodies of Pavement's *Crooked Rain, Crooked Rain*, and the expansive noise-scapes of Sonic Youth, Yo La Tengo and Sunny Day Real Estate, the singer discovered the means by which Blur, having perfected the English ideal, might begin to tear it down.

Blur's reconciliation with its guitarist spoke of a more fundamental shift in the band's philosophy. Coxon, after all, was not just the band's token Pavement fan, he was also its indie-rock conscience. As such, his presence within the group had been incongruous in 1993, when Albarn began to steer Blur in a more populist direction, and virtually intolerable by the end of 1994, the point at which the group became a household name. Albarn didn't mind being snapped by paparazzi and screamed at by teenagers, because he'd come to see fame as a measure of success. Coxon, meanwhile, clung fast to the old-fashioned idea that great music should be challenging and even somewhat frightening at first. By his standards, Blur's popularity was virtually proof that the band had stopped making interesting music. 'Pop makes me very sick,' he told the *NME*. In the midst of the frantic fun of 1995, Coxon's right-on attitude and riot grrrl girlfriend had made him look, to the rest of the band, like a party pooper. But by the end of 1996, Britpop's party was well and truly pooped in any case, and Albarn, Alex James and Dave Rowntree were starting to feel a little pop-sick themselves. 'It's not healthy to sell too many records,' Albarn told Matt Pinfield. The MTV host had just provided a demonstration of why this was so, when he'd described the band's last three albums as 'a celebration of English life'. The singer corrected him, as the band squirmed uncomfortably in their seats. 'That got really misunderstood,' he said. 'It got turned into this sort of banal celebration of Britishness.'[6] Albarn, like so many of his generation, had proceeded from the assumption that his band could make pop smarter, and had subsequently discovered, to his horror, that pop had made his band stupid.

Somehow Blur had become the kind of band whose album was bought by the kind of people who only buy one album a year, the album which has the song on it that everybody likes. Albarn had always hated those bands, now he was in one of them, and intelligent people whose opinions he'd always respected had begun to hate him the way he hated Jon Bon Jovi or Eddie Vedder. For Blur to become the kind of band he liked, it would have to make itself less popular. So when Graham Coxon wrote Albarn a letter saying, 'I want to make music that scares people again,' the singer was all ears.[7]

Blur was scarier, noisier, and more confusing than anything the band had done since 'Sing', and better than the best moments on *The Great Escape* by a mile. The music had a loose, spontaneous quality, and more open-ended structures, within which Coxon was free to invent in a way that the tightly wound genre pastiche of songs such as 'Country House' had not allowed. 'MOR's insistent morse-code guitar riff was interrupted by outbursts of controlled chaos that Thurston Moore would have been proud to call his own; 'I'm Just a Killer for Your Love' crawled along on a trip-hop beat, accentuated with amplified pick-scrapes and a sleazy glam riff; and 'Essex Dogs' conjured a nightmare atmosphere from a varispeed feedback loop, fractured bits of post-punk funk and volleys of pure noise.

Albarn, meanwhile, had finally figured out how to stop making sense, and his lyrics were much better for it. His earlier need to distance himself from the murky introspection of grunge had led him into the even more treacherous world of the infallible author for whom the suffering of mere mortals is a bit of a laugh. But by 1996, for a variety of reasons, Albarn had decided he could no longer afford to take this Olympian point of view. 'I've given up trying to write about the ordinary man,' he told Richard Kingsmill, 'because I've realised that I'm not an ordinary man anymore.'[8] On *Blur*, Albarn found a way to cut out the middleman without sinking into subjectivity, by emulating the last-second, mix-and-match method of Pavement's

Stephen Malkmus, or the fractured roadside poetry of Beck, whose influence could clearly be heard on 'Country Sad Ballad Man'. These techniques suited Albarn's muse like a glove, which only went to show that — despite all the 'England vs America' posturing of 1993 — the singer's view of the world was actually much closer to that of Frank Black, Thurston Moore and Kurt Cobain than it was to Ray Davies'. Albarn had long ago realised that modern life is rubbish — songs like 'MOR' and 'Essex Dogs' showed him learning, as his American counterparts had already done, to tell new stories with the fragments, instead of trying to put the old ones back together.

All in all, *Blur* seemed to have been a success — it had saved the band's life, left Britpop in the dust, and transformed Blur, at one stroke, from a frothy pop act into something harder to chew, but ultimately more satisfying. But one month after the album was released, the plan came unstuck. In April 1997, Blur released a second single from its self-titled album. Clocking in at just over two minutes, 'Song 2' was a miniature masterpiece, a rattletrap drum kit beating out a 'Sgt Peppers' rhythm, a trebly guitar playing something that sounded more than a little like the opening riff from 'Smells Like Teen Spirit', an avalanche of guitar noise and a lyric that sounded as though it could have been made up on the spot — which it was. Albarn told Kingsmill that he came up with the lyrics for 'Song 2' by shouting out whatever 'subconscious stuff' came into his head as the tape rolled.[9] But he delivered the song's nonsense with such conviction that it was hard to let go of the idea that it was about something.

Various interpretations of 'Song 2' were put forward, for example, that it was a parody of grunge, or an ode to Pavement's Bob Nastanovich. But in the end, nobody really knew what it meant, so it could mean anything you liked. It became a screen onto which listeners could project themselves, an anthem for whatever. As such, it recognised no national or cultural borders, and so gleefully stormed past the barrier at LAX that read 'No English Bands Allowed' to become Blur's first US Top Ten hit. In England, it went to number two. Advertisers quickly figured out that its atmosphere of unspecified excitement meant it could be used to sell anything from cars to premium intel, and TV promo producers realised they finally had a song from the nineties that wasn't 'Unbelievable' by EMF to put under their extreme sports highlights montages. Considering that the point of the album had been to de-popularise the band, this was potentially disastrous — not to mention ironic. But the really surprising thing about 'Song 2' was the way it allowed Blur to have their cake and eat it too. It pushed them as far away as possible from Britpop's sinking ship, restored their indie credibility, *and* made them all rich. It was as though, having abandoned his career-long goal to make music for the masses, Damon Albarn had finally written a song that *everybody* loved.

Even Stephen Malkmus seemed impressed. Pavement's new album, *Brighten the Corners*, had been released in the same week as *Blur*, and in the round of interviews to promote the record, Malkmus mentioned Damon Albarn almost as often as Albarn talked about him. 'I like the way he can sing in lots of different ways,' Malkmus told *Mojo*'s Ben Thompson. 'One minute it's David Bowie, and then it's the Kinks guy, and then it's just yelling … and he can play the piano and stuff, which I think is cool.'[10] If this mutual admiration society appeared a little too cosy to be true, that was because it was. As Thompson later learned, a deal between the two groups had been brokered as far back as 1995, when Justine Frischmann met Pavement on the Lollapalooza tour. The following year, Malkmus flew to London to collaborate with Elastica on a song for the soundtrack to Richard Linklater's *SubUrbia* and Frischmann introduced him to Albarn. According to Thompson, 'Damon proposed a deal whereby if Pavement talked up Blur in America (where they'd not, as yet, made it quite as big as they'd hoped) he would talk them up in Europe (ditto).' Malkmus accepted. 'He's looking for an out,' the Pavement singer explained. 'He's all, "Oh, it's terrible, I've created this Britpop monster".'[11] By 1997, thanks in no small part to Malkmus's own efforts, the monster appeared to be breathing its last. 'Britpop is played out,' said Frischmann. 'Our next album will be influenced by the likes of Beck and Pavement.'[12] The trick now was to avoid turning the antidote to the cliché into a cliché itself. 'Sonic Youth, Beck and Pavement,' grumbled Coxon in an interview, having heard this litany of indie cool reeled off for the tenth time that morning. 'As if they're the only bloody American bands.'[13]

The Year of the Women

Fiona Apple was often asked in 1997 about how it felt to be part of 'this new phenomenon of lady rockers'.[1] The question always made her laugh — she felt as though she'd been hearing about a new wave of women in rock for as long as she'd been listening to music, which most likely she had. In 1993, when Apple was fifteen years old, Kim Deal pointed out that she'd been hearing about it since *Doolittle* came out in 1989. 'When I first got this "is there a resurgence of women in rock" question, I pondered it,' she said. 'But then you start to *catch on*. And then somebody else says, "This year is the year of the women!" And then the next year is the year of "the resurgence of women in rock". And then a few years later, you can do another interview. "This is the time of the resurgence of women in rock." So I have a sneaking suspicion,' said Deal with a chuckle, 'that there is no "resurgence of women in rock". They're just *in* it.'[2]

But if 1997 was no different in kind from 1989, or 1993, it was at least different in scale. *Exile in Guyville*, *Last Splash* and *Rid of Me* had sold in the hundreds of thousands, but *Tidal* and *Tragic Kingdom* had gone platinum in a matter of months, and *Jagged Little Pill* had sold nine million copies by the end of 1996.[3] In a much talked-about feature article titled 'Rockin', Ragin' and Female', *Cosmopolitan*'s Jen Salvato claimed that 'a revolution of rage and passion is spreading among the female ranks of guitar-wielding warriors. Storming past the eager-to-please Mariah songbirds, they're fronting bands, winning awards, conquering the charts.'[4] Women also conquered the festival circuit in 1997. Singer Sarah McLachlan organised a touring festival with an all-female line-up called Lilith Fair, which went on to outsell that year's Lollapalooza by a considerable margin. Lilith Fair's main stage saw performances by McLachlan, Fiona Apple, Jewel, Tracy Bonham and Meredith Brooks, whose single, 'Bitch', had reached the number one spot on the Billboard charts earlier that year. 'Bitch' was the perfect song for the summer of 1997, a rootsy rock tune grafted onto a shuffling *Odelay* drum loop, with a stereotype-busting lyric about female empowerment ('take me as I am …') delivered in a voice that sounded enough like Alanis Morissette's to be familiar, but not enough like her to annoy people who were annoyed by Alanis Morissette.[5]

Brooks told *Rolling Stone* that the point of the song was to 'reclaim a word that had taken on a really derogatory meaning'. Hearing this, and seeing her perform the song on MTV, guitar in hand, wearing a dyed-black slip dress and combat boots, one could almost imagine that 1997 was the year riot grrrl broke — Brooks appeared to have taken the Olympia crew's blend of punk attitude, thrift-store chic, guitar-as-empowerment ethos and semiotic deconstruction to the masses. There were other signs, too, that revolution grrrl-style might finally be underway. Instead of having to eke out a 'safe space' in the mosh pit, girls now had a whole safe festival to call their own. 'There's too much moshing, it's dangerous,' said one festival-goer, explaining why she'd decided to give her money to Lilith rather than Lollapalooza. Lilith was also impressively democratic ('No-one here acts like a star,' said Bonham) and blessedly free of the 'beer-gut boy-rock' clichés riot grrrl had worked so hard to discredit and destroy. *Spin*'s reporter grumbled that the festival was as 'safe and non-offensive as it gets. There's no sex, drugs or Courtney Love.'[6] But riot grrrl had always known that 'sex' in this context was usually code for 'sexism', that drugs were a means to dissipate your dissent, and that the lead singer of Hole was a sex-traitor and a sellout. Any lingering admiration the movement may have had for Love had been swept away sometime between the release of *Live Through This* (with its epic riot grrrl put-down, 'Olympia') and the moment when Love punched Kathleen Hanna in the face backstage at Lollapalooza in 1995.

But riot grrrl's pioneers refused to recognise their heirs, for one very important reason. Riot grrrl had always insisted that its activity take place outside corporate control — it saw the appearance of its bands in the pages of *Rolling Stone* and *Spin* as a sign of failure, rather than success, because the corporately owned media would distort and even disregard its radical message. None of the new 'women-in-rock' appeared to be troubled by this possibility, but where some saw this as proof of a less didactic, more open-minded spirit, music writer Ann Powers wondered whether it might be because the movement had nothing much to say beyond 'this year is the year of the women'. 'Girl culture's impulse to make no distinctions (a reaction against the hardline seventies brand of feminism) produces the sense that any choice is a good one,' she wrote.[7] In this sense, 'Bitch' was the epitome of women-in-rock, 1997 style. Brooks insists, in the song, that she will not be pinned down by definitions. 'I'm a bitch, I'm a lover, I'm a child, I'm a mother, I'm a sinner, I'm a saint, I do not feel ashamed.'[8] This is the opposite of ideology, and as such, very easily co-opted. 'Thus a genuine movement devolves into a giant shopping spree,' wrote Powers, 'where girls are encouraged to buy whatever identity fits them best off the rack.'[9]

Whether or not women-in-rock was ever, as Powers put it, 'a genuine movement' was debatable. In fact, riot grrrl may have been the last time such a thing could be said to have existed in rock and roll; the tenacity with which its members clung to their independence and resisted the media's attempts to 'expose' them gave a sense of how difficult it would soon be to create and maintain a subculture in a post-Nirvana world. Since then, corporate America had refined the art of youth trendspotting to the point where scenes were commercialised from the outset. Lilith Fair's press releases talked of 'community' and 'empowerment', but its stars only met each other because they'd all had hits, so the festival's community was shaped by a corporate agenda over which its participants had no control. And while sub-editors still liked to haul out the jargon of rock-as-revolution, this was as meaningless now as it had been at any time since 1991. Jen Salvato might write of 'guitar-wielding warriors … taking on the male-dominated establishment', but the male-dominated establishment was no more threatened by Meredith Brooks than it had been by Green Day or Pearl Jam.[10] Fiona Apple, for one, did not believe the hype. 'It's not a phenomenon,' she said, 'it's just business.'[11]

While girl power was coming up, riot grrrl was going down. Allison Wolfe blamed the movement's demise on corporate exploitation, arguing that riot grrrl had been tainted by association with girl power hype. 'It got co-opted by the mainstream,' she said. 'Our aesthetics or ideas, but watered down and kind of sold back at a higher price to the mass market. You know, you'd go to Urban Outfitters and there'd be all these fake riot grrrl bands playing over the loudspeaker, all these clothes that were just like what we would wear … we ended up just kind of abandoning it, because it became so trendy, and it wasn't our fault.' There was no surer sign of the assimilation of riot grrrl into the mainstream than the appearance, in 1997, of a Bikini Kill song in an episode of *Roseanne*. The song plays on Roseanne's car stereo as Jenna Elfman — who gave her the tape — smacks her gum and rocks out in the back seat. 'You have no idea what riot grrrls are out there screamin' about,' she says. 'See, we're about takin' control. Chicks — who *rock*!' As Bikini Kill's trebly thrash fills the car, and Elfman flops back into her seat with a satisfied smirk, Laurie Metcalf — as Jackie — can barely conceal her disgust. 'What happened to *music*?' she asks.[12]

The question was very apropos of riot grrrl in 1997. Jackie's outburst is a sudden attack of baby-boomer nostalgia — the kind that plays easily into the hands of conservatives, as Roseanne is quick to point out. 'Who are you?' she shoots back. 'Tipper Gore?' But the activities of some of the movement's members in the mid nineties amounted to an admission that riot grrrl may have neglected music at the expense of ideology, that the scene may have fallen apart not because it was exploited, but because in trying too hard to resist exploitation, it had made its music unlovable. Zine writer Justine Fateman felt that riot grrrl ideology had hardened into dogma, and that the movement had died from a lack of art rather than a surfeit of money. 'It got pretty fucked up,' she said. 'It became this kind of basic training/consciousness-raising thing. It didn't seem like art, it felt like some kind of counselling.'[13]

At the time, Fateman was sharing a house in Portland with Kathleen Hanna, and the two had begun playing together in a band called the Troublemakers. Hanna had also begun to rethink her musical approach in the wake of riot grrrl's demise, and had come to a similar conclusion to Fateman. There must be a way, she felt, to reconcile pleasure with revolt — to have fun, and fuck shit up. In Bikini Kill, Hanna had worked hard to make herself understood. 'I was writing in this dogmatic straightforward way for a long while,' she explained. 'I would write essays and take lines and put them into songs.'[14] Now, she sought a more open-ended form of expression. When she moved back to Olympia in the summer of 1997, she bought herself an 8-track recorder and a sampler, created an alter ego for herself called 'Julie Ruin', and began recording pop songs in her closet.

'Learning to be a little less self-righteous, to not always be writing a slogan, is an important thing for a songwriter,' said Corin Tucker in 1996.[15] Tucker had been a founding member of Heavens to Betsy — one of the original core of riot grrrl bands that appeared at the IPU's Girl Night in 1991. Three years later, at the height of the great arena-rock revival of 1994, Tucker and guitarist Carrie Brownstein bonded over a cover of Boston's 'More than a Feeling', and formed a new group called Sleater-Kinney. When Heavens to Betsy and Brownstein's band Excuse 17 came to an end in 1995, Sleater-Kinney continued. Tucker's strident vocals and Brownstein's trebly guitar sound gave the group audible links to riot grrrl, but the music they made together was something else entirely. Sleater-Kinney played infectious rock and roll that could evoke, from one moment to the next, Bob Dylan, Talking Heads or Sonic Youth. But they did so without a hint of irony or nostalgia — a minor miracle in the late nineties. Like the Jon Spencer Blues Explosion, Sleater-Kinney's return to the tradition was all the more heartfelt for being hard won. Tucker and Brownstein had taken part in riot grrrl's gleeful — and necessary — destruction of rock and roll at the end of the 1980s. Then, having come to the conclusion that rock, after all, offered them the best chance of saying what it was they wanted to say, they had begun to put it back together. 'Hear my voice / in your favourite song / it's enough, it's enough if you want it that much.'[16] In 1996, 'It's Enough' was Sleater-Kinney's 'More than a Feeling', an unabashed ode to the pleasure of rock with music that easily matched the feelings its words described. It ended with an unequivocal statement of intent: 'I play rock and roll.'

Happy Thoughts for Your Next Album

Despite what the music papers said, Radiohead — according to its guitarist Ed O'Brien — was not big in America. '"Fake Plastic Trees" was played to a radio station,' he explained. 'They did a survey of their listeners — eighteen to twenty-five-year-old males who drive jeeps — and it came bottom of the list. We had one hit there ...' Thom Yorke interrupted him. 'And they don't remember it anyway 'cause they've got the attention span of insects!'[1] But while Radiohead hadn't managed to match the success of 'Creep' in America, they appeared, by 1996, to have acquired something far more valuable there — respect. *The Bends* had rescued the group's critical reputation, and the tour with R.E.M. had turned Radiohead into the kind of band other bands talked about. Alanis Morissette took them on as support for a thirteen-date tour in August, and could often be seen wearing a Radiohead T-shirt onstage.[2] Considering that Morissette was, at the time, playing 17,000-seat venues in support of an album that had sold close to ten million copies, this was a considerable leg-up for Radiohead. But if any of this pleased Thom Yorke, he wasn't letting on. When the tour stopped in San Francisco, Yorke and Jonny Greenwood were interviewed by music writer Clare Kleinedler. 'I read somewhere that you've been writing down happy thoughts for the next album,' she said to Yorke. 'Have you written down anything so far?' Yorke thought for a moment while Greenwood stared down at his hands. 'The nearest I got,' the singer replied, 'was writing about the sky above LA.'[3]

That Yorke had managed only one halfway happy thought in the previous three months would not have been too surprising to anyone who'd heard the new songs the band had been playing onstage. 'No Surprises Please' sounded pretty enough, with its music-box melody. But Yorke's lyrics described 'a heart that's full up like a landfill / a job that slowly kills you / bruises that won't heal'.[4] 'Airbag' warned of a coming world war, and in 'Electioneering' the singer ranted like a preacher in a pulpit about 'riot shields / voodoo economics … cattle prods and the IMF'.[5] When Kleinedler asked Yorke about his influences, his answer — 'books about politics' — revealed the source of his bad mood. Having just finished Will Hutton's *The State We're In*, Yorke had begun to feel that even the good things about life in 1996 were tainted by what he called 'global hideousness' — the sky above LA was one of the few places he could look without seeing a Starbucks logo or some other sign that the world was being bought and sold from under his nose. Later in the interview, he went on a lengthy rant about garbage ('where does it all go?') and described his hobby as 'trying to sit in front of the television for more than twenty minutes without shouting at it'.[6] Radiohead's singer was, as Ed O'Brien put it, 'a bit of a worrier'.[7]

With its revolting images of vomit and burning swine flesh, 'Paranoid Android' — the first single from the band's new album — gave no indication that Yorke had added anything to his list of happy thoughts since leaving LA. His disgust at the state of the world was as palpable there, as it was on 'Climbing Up The Walls' and 'Exit Music (For a Film)'. Other songs were equally disturbing, for less obvious reasons: the man in 'Karma Police' who 'buzzes like a fridge;'[8] the 'pig in a cage on antibiotics' in 'Fitter Happier;'[9] the promise of 'a quiet life … a handshake, some carbon monoxide' in 'No Surprises'.[10] This last song's chiming guitar part was, according to Greenwood, inspired by the Beach Boys' 'Wouldn't It Be Nice', the closest thing to an ironic joke that Radiohead would currently allow itself. Like Nirvana's 'Dumb' and Blur's 'The Universal', 'No Surprises' expressed a profound wish to not know, to believe what the TV says, to stop worrying about where all the garbage goes. But the sleep its lullaby melody promised was all the more tempting for the fact that the singer knew he couldn't afford to fall into it. This, Yorke explained, was the meaning of the album's title, which offered the seductive idea that he might stop raging against the machine and acquiesce to modernity with a simple 'OK computer' — a phrase he later described as 'terrifying'.

Despite all this, the singer refused to accept the notion that Radiohead's music was depressing. 'It's not, because those are just the words,' he said. 'The point is I put the words to music which I think is incredibly uplifting. Otherwise there'd be no point doing it at all.' Yorke had intentionally mismatched his claustrophobic concerns to the band's new widescreen soundscapes; the search for a clearing, for a world without logos or landfill, was realised in music. Tellingly, the only truly happy moment Yorke described on *OK Computer*, the only point at which uplifting music was met by an optimistic thought, was the one in which he imagined himself leaving the planet. In 'Subterranean Homesick Alien', Yorke dreamed of being abducted by a UFO while walking down a quiet road. 'They'd take me on board their beautiful ship,' he sang, 'and show me the world as I'd love to see it.'[11]

The mostly ecstatic reviews that greeted *OK Computer* upon its release in June 1997 suggested that the album had arrived just in time for another profound shift in British music. Burned out by Britpop and its unhealthy obsession with celebrity, success, and inner-city style, music writers in the UK had started yearning for wide-open spaces, song cycles and big themes. There was talk, too, of a prog revival — although this reflected not so much a wish to hear Genesis or Emerson, Lake and Palmer again, but a desire to see music progress, to see it go somewhere beyond the top of the charts. Nothing summed up the dead end Britpop had reached in 1997 quite so succinctly as the title Oasis gave to its third album: *Be Here Now*. The songs on Oasis's first two records had been about making it — becoming a rock and roll star, living the dream, buying a house by the sea — and about what it would take to get there: 'You gotta say what you say, don't let anybody get in your way.'[12] Now that the band was there, and no-one was standing in their way, there was nothing to say except 'we're here'. Likewise, now that the indie tradition had become the centre of popular culture, Britpop, as Peter Shapiro had predicted back in 1995, became post-history; it had no need for progress, because it had nowhere to go, nothing into which it could develop. As a result, Britpop's rebellious gestures became rhetorical and its satire unconvincing. The forced smile behind 'Country House' was a symptom of the same malaise that crippled *Be Here Now*. Musically, too, Britpop had reached a standstill. Having established popularity as the measure of success, it could only produce more of what it knew people liked; when Britpop bands talked about writing more 'ambitious' music, it usually just meant more strings, or more sales.

Radiohead had always been out of step with Britpop. As an English band with a grunge hit, they'd been ideologically suspect from the start — the obvious Nirvana pastiche of 'My Iron Lung' had simply confirmed that Radiohead was too gloomy and too American to participate in the new British cheerfulness of 1995. But the band had no real desire to be invited to the party. 'We don't really like cocaine that much,' Yorke explained.[13] More importantly, Radiohead had achieved megastardom a good two years before Blur and Oasis, and as early as 1995, the buzz was beginning to wear off. By the time they came to record *OK Computer*, the band was no longer interested in writing hits for guys in jeeps; its interests now lay in quite a different direction. Radiohead's search for a world beyond pop had led the band to reconnect with an assortment of modernist traditions — jazz, modern composition, Krautrock, electronic music — all of which were founded on the idea that music had a future beyond the playlist or the hit parade. Releasing a six-minute single in three different time signatures, playing echoplexed keys over drifting chords, chopping up beats and swapping instruments — these were hardly radical acts in 1997. But in the late-Britpop context, *OK Computer* felt like a window being opened in an airless room. *Top of the Pops*, the album seemed to say, was not the top of the world. There was, after all, the sky, and beyond that — space.

Veganistic Views

In March 1998, *Q* magazine's Phil Sutcliffe asked his readers to imagine a world without CDs and record shops. 'Smart music speeds through space from artist to listener, and some of the world's most powerful businesses are rendered instantly obsolete.'[1] Sutcliffe was referring here to the very same technology Trent Reznor had hopefully looked forward to in 1994 — music available via the internet. But what had seemed like science fiction back in the mid nineties was now, Sutcliffe insisted, a reality, and the 'device you won't see anywhere' was now everywhere. This, as Reznor had predicted, spelled good news for artists and bad news for business. 1997 had seen a group called Purity become the first British band to secure a record deal on the strength of a track posted on their website, and the following year, singer-songwriter Ani DiFranco sold over 100,000 copies of her album *Little Plastic Castle* from righteousbaberecords.com. Meanwhile, Sutcliffe reported that piracy had cost the music industry an estimated $6.25 billion in 1997. Record companies tried to recoup their losses by prosecuting the operators of digital jukeboxes and unofficial fan sites, and nervous retailers crossed their fingers and hoped downloading would go away. HMV spokesman Gennaro Castaldo told Sutcliffe his company had 'no plans' to get into cyber-sales.[2]

In 1996, *Rolling Stone* network launched a cable TV segment called *Wild Wild Web*, whose purpose was to cover the new phenomenon of bands on the internet. In October 1997, the show did a story on Blink-182, the Californian punk group whose catchy new single, 'Dammit', was on its way to becoming a hit, thanks to a generous flogging on KROQ. The band's members were not, as the presenters put it, 'web-savvy'. But Blink's fans had picked up the slack, building tribute pages with tour information, song lyrics and photos of the band. Following a hyperactive station sting — featuring the sound of a dial-up modem playing over an ersatz Aphex Twin beat — the camera cut to a shot of Blink's guitarist and bass player, Mark Hoppus and Tom DeLonge respectively, sitting on a couch talking about what the internet meant for the future of humanity. 'For us, as a society,' said Hoppus, 'I think that the internet offers us a great way to just waste a lot of time.' Hoppus sounded sceptical about the net in general, and the live 'cybercast' the band were scheduled to perform later that evening in particular. 'The technology really needs to catch up,' he said. 'It sounds rad. But if you tried to watch it on my computer at home, you'd get like a second of crappy noise, and then everything freezes.' Later, DeLonge unravelled a lengthy spiel about the internet being a government plot to brainwash the world using recovered UFO technology. 'Oh lord,' said Hoppus, rolling his eyes.[3]

All in all, the members of Blink-182 proved themselves to be disappointing as spokesmen for the information superhighway. But Blink's inability to take the internet too seriously reflected their more general refusal to take life too seriously, and this, as the host of *Wild Wild Web* explained, was part of their appeal. 'They're a punk band minus the punk attitude,' he said. 'Just a couple of guys hangin' out and having a good time.'[4] A few weeks later, in an interview with the Canadian TV show *MuchMusic*, Hoppus explained that it was all part of the band's 'high school mentality'. 'Which is what?' asked the host. 'Having fun with your friends and making fun of people less fortunate than us,' DeLonge replied, deadpan. 'We mock what we don't understand,' Hoppus added.[5] Despite their boyish looks and teen-themed videos, the two were not quite as young as they seemed — Hoppus was twenty-two, DeLonge twenty-three. But Hoppus had known since he left high school that the future of the band would depend, to a large extent, on its ability to maintain a high school attitude. 'It's just that we haven't grown up yet,' he told music writer Steve Tauschke in 1995. 'We're still trying to act young and not grow into the mature adult stage where everyone gets boring.'[6]

For Calvin Johnson, Kurt Cobain and Bikini Kill, 'Teen Spirit' had been code for revolution — it stood for idealism undefiled by adult compromise. For Blink, it meant fun uncomplicated by ideals. Bands with 'messages and purposes', said Hoppus, 'just get too preachy and they don't concentrate on writing good songs'.[7] Blink were reacting against a tendency toward didacticism in late-eighties, early-nineties US Punk; post-Bad Religion bands whose need to ram home a message about the state of the world seemed to short-circuit their ability to write a catchy tune. The result had been a glut of would-be anthems with worthy lyrics and shout-along choruses, which, in the end, felt more like poorly written essays than great songs. These had a tendency to alienate younger punk fans, who felt as though they were being lectured at rather than spoken to. Blink-182, with their 'songs about zits and girls not liking me' (as DeLonge succinctly put it), spoke a language their audience could understand, and their songs were much better for it.[8]

'Dammit' began like an overheard phone conversation ('It's alright / to tell me / what you think / about me') and ended with a heartbreaking scene at the local multiplex ('you'll show up / and walk by / on the arm / of that guy').[9] The tune had more emotional ups and downs than a rom-com, packed into less than four minutes, and Hoppus sang it like he'd been there. This was, admittedly, much easier to do when you were singing about girls than it was if you were trying to start a proletarian revolt, but it was hard to argue with the results. 'We write songs about things that happen to us and our friends and we try to keep a sense of humour about everything,' said Hoppus, by way of explaining Blink's appeal. 'A lot of bands just get way down on trying to act really self-important and have a really strong message, and there's definitely a place for that. But there's also a time to have fun with your friends and just say "fuck everything".'[10]

Because they'd livened up punk rock by writing fun songs about feelings instead of angry ones about politics, Blink came to see non-fun things like feminism and anti-corporatism as contrary to the spirit of punk. The band's videos were directed like eighties screwball comedies, with all manner of high jinks involving mega-babes, meathead jocks and gross cafeteria food. Both 'Dammit' and 'Josie' — the second single from *Dude Ranch* — contained borderline homophobic 'Dude, I'm not gay' comic set pieces: the first had Hoppus accidentally pull DeLonge's pants down in a fight at exactly the point that the former's ex-girlfriend walks into the scene; the second saw an 'I Love You' note intended for Alyssa Milano accidentally land on a fat kid's desk — with predictable results. The *Porky*'s-style antics continued at the band's shows, which sometimes included wet T-shirt contests, or DeLonge yelling, 'Show us your tits!' from the stage.

For older punk fans, with fond memories of Fugazi, queercore or riot grrrl, this kind of thing seemed a betrayal of punk's highest ideals, and barely worthy of the name. 'Every time I hear the word "punk" in connection to Blink-182,' said Jessica Hopper in an interview with *Spin*, 'the word dies a little death.'[11] But for DeLonge and Hoppus, punk meant having fun with your friends, doing what you liked, and saying 'fuck everything'. Furthermore, punk — as any shout-along post-hardcore band could tell you — was about not conforming and standing up to authority figures. According to these definitions, critics like Hopper could easily be dismissed as Old People Making Rules. DeLonge argued that the fact that Blink annoyed such people constituted proof that they were staying true to the movement's ideals. 'I think it's much more punk to piss people off than to conform to all those veganistic views,' he said. Hoppus agreed. 'For someone to say we're sexist just shows that they have, like, two brain cells and they're living in their own little PC world.'[12]

The band's contempt for 'PC' — political correctness — reflected their age, and the age of their audience. Blink and its fans had grown up in a high school and college environment where leftist ideologues seemed to have ruined teenage fun more thoroughly and more successfully than Tipper Gore or Jerry Falwell ever could. In the eighties, for bands like Bad Religion, the enemies of youth culture were firmly entrenched on the right. In the new world of campus dating rules, they appeared to be coming from both sides, but most often from the left. By the mid nineties, the reaction against PC had developed to the point where the term had become a form of abuse, which could be used to discredit anyone or anything that stopped people from having fun — or making money. When Blink signed with MCA in January 1998, and the fanzines and message boards erupted in fury over the band's corporate sell-out, Hoppus came to the conclusion that these were the same blinkered bores who told the band they shouldn't hold wet T-shirt contests, or told their fans they shouldn't be enjoying them when they did. 'We assume that the punk scene is a place where kids want to be different and do their own thing,' he told Steve Tauschke, 'and yet as soon as a punk band gets on the radio the fanzines will say those bands are selling out just to get the money.' This, Hoppus argued, was narrow-minded, and contrary to punk's original spirit. 'When punk first started, no-one cared about getting on the radio or selling albums, and all of a sudden it's about how to be politically correct and being true to your fans — which is not the true punk philosophy.'[13]

Again, Ian MacKaye, Kathleen Hanna or Kurt Cobain would all no doubt have argued that not being a sexist, a racist or a homophobe, resisting corporate control and treating your fans with respect was exactly what was meant by 'true punk spirit'. But in a sense, Hoppus was correct. Punk and hardcore in the US had quickly developed into a politicised movement with ideals — social justice, independence and anti-corporatism — that were derived from the counterculture of the sixties via figures like MacKaye or Calvin Johnson. As such, it marked a significant departure from the event that sparked its creation — the arrival of the Sex Pistols in 1976, and their ill-fated American tour two years later. As Greil Marcus demonstrated in his 1990 book, *Lipstick Traces*, the Sex Pistols were in no sense down for the cause; rather, they were heirs to a tradition of destructive nihilism that rendered all causes obsolete. 'Anarchy in the UK' was not a demand that people rise up to change the world, but a statement of a negativity so complete it threatened to destroy it.[14] Cobain had sensed this after reading Marcus's book in 1991, and had taken care to step back from the abyss. 'The only problem I've ever had with the Situationist punk rock,' he wrote in his journal, 'is the absolute denial of anything sacred.'[15] Cobain had too much sympathy for women and racial minorities to be able to say 'fuck everything'. Blink — for whom this statement was a guiding principle — had no such scruples. To those who said they weren't punk because their videos were sexist or because they were making too much money, the band could always reply, 'Fuck you', which, of course, was the most punk thing of all. Later, when they got tired of arguing with such people about whether or not they were punk, the band simply shrugged off the term. 'We don't really go around saying we're punk,' said DeLonge, 'because then you constantly have to prove yourself to everybody.' 'We're just Blink-182,' said Hoppus, 'we'll do whatever we want.'[16]

The trouble with nihilists — as John Goodman observed in the Coen Brothers' 1998 movie *The Big Lebowski*, is that you never know what they're going to do next. In the film, Goodman's character, Walter, and his best friend, The Dude, have a number of run-ins with a gang of violent kidnappers, who repeatedly threaten to cut off The Dude's 'johnson'. Because of their sadistic behaviour and German accents, Walter had earlier leapt to the conclusion that they were Nazis. But in a scene at the pair's favourite bowling alley, about halfway through the movie, The Dude sets him straight. 'They kept saying they were nihilists,' he says. *'Nihilists!'* exclaims Walter, in a 'now-I've-seen-everything' tone of voice. 'I mean, say what you will about the tenets of national socialism — at least it's an ethos!'[17] Nihilists, as the nihilists remind The Dude, believe in nothing, therefore, they can do anything. And this non-philosophy of theirs is in no way incompatible with making money — their lack of principles makes them more effective as kidnappers and more ruthless as extortionists. Likewise, for the Sex Pistols — as opposed to say, Fugazi — there was no contradiction in playing punk rock while making money. Malcolm McLaren had branded the group's first assault on the charts with the slogan 'Cash from Chaos'. The band's 1997 reunion tour went out under the slogan 'Filthy Lucre'. 'What's wrong with me making money?' asked John Lydon, mock incredulously, at the band's Australian press conference.[18] It was hard to think of a reason. Rock critics tended to see nostalgia reunions as a betrayal of youthful ideals for commercial interests. But if your youthful ideals could be summed up in the phrase 'we don't care', there was no reason not to take the money.

1998

Watching This World

John Rzeznik hadn't worked a day job since his band, the Goo Goo Dolls, had scored a US Top Ten hit with 'Name' in 1995. But that didn't mean he didn't have to work. Rzeznik's job now was to write hits — and this, he'd discovered, was not as easy as it had first seemed. Shortly after the release of the band's fifth album, *A Boy Named Goo*, the singer came down with a case of writer's block that lasted almost two years — by 1997, Rzeznik had accumulated only the barest scraps of music and lyrics, none of which suggested they had the potential to become hits. When the drought finally broke, in November, it was with a song the band had been commissioned to write for a new Nicolas Cage movie called *City of Angels*. Rzeznik later said the tune simply fell in his lap — a lovely chord sequence suggested a yearning melody that suited the singer's whiskey-and-cigarettes voice down to the ground. The idea for the lyrics, meanwhile, came from the screenplay — Rzeznik wrote them in the voice of the film's protagonist, an angel who wants to be human. Fleshed out in the studio with a mandolin and a string arrangement, and christened 'Iris' by the band's guitarist (after a country singer he'd been listening to), the song was released as a single in April 1998, and went on to spend eighteen weeks at number one on the Billboard charts.

In 1987, the German director Wim Wenders made a film called *Der Himmel über Berlin* which was released internationally the following year as *Wings of Desire*. Wenders' subject — an angel named Damiel watching over a broken city, observing human beings but unable to intervene in their lives — was partly inspired by the ninth of Walter Benjamin's 'Theses on the Philosophy of History'. In one of the film's most moving scenes, Damiel — played by Bruno Ganz — approaches Peter Falk at a *currywurst* stand. Falk is playing himself, Peter Falk, an American actor in Berlin, shooting a film about World War Two. Damiel can't usually be seen or heard by humans, but Falk, for some reason, knows he is there. 'I wish I could talk to you,' he says, 'to tell you how good it is to *be* here.' This makes no sense, until the viewer realises that Falk himself was once an angel too — an angel who grew tired of experiencing life at one remove, always observing, never touching or feeling, smoking or drinking coffee — which he now loves to do. He wants Damiel to know how good all these things are. 'But you're not here,' he says. 'I'm here. I *wish* you were here.' Slowly, Damiel begins to wish this for himself, and after he falls in love with a trapeze artist, his decision is made. Damiel jumps from Berlin's famous Victory Column, shedding his wings on the way down. When he hits the street, he bleeds. Later, when he drinks a cup of coffee, he can taste it.[1]

In 1998, Brad Silberling was hired to direct a remake of *Wings of Desire*, with the film's action moved to Los Angeles. *City of Angels* differed markedly from Wenders' original in most respects, but its premise was essentially the same — an angel falls in love, and decides to become human. At the start of the film, Seth (Nicolas Cage) meets a woman named Maggie (Meg Ryan). Unlike most other people, Maggie can see Seth, and the two begin to fall in love. But they can't really be together, because Seth is not really there. Eventually, it is explained to Seth that if he wants to feel real love, he will have to live in the real world, and if he chooses to do this, he will have to give up his divine privileges. The question that now faces him is expressed on the film's soundtrack by the Goo Goo Dolls' 'Iris'. 'And I'd give up forever to touch you,' sings Rzeznik. ''Cause I know that you feel me somehow.' In the song's video, scenes from the film are intercut with shots of Rzeznik on top of a skyscraper, observing the film's action through a battery of telescopes. As the singer wheels around his lonely laboratory on an antique swivel-chair, he sings a line that expresses Seth's deepest wish — to stop being a spectator, to live in the world, to be, as Falk put it, *here*. 'When everything feels like the movies / yeah you bleed just to know you're alive.'[2]

Both the film and its soundtrack hit expressed a profound late-twentieth-century problem: the unconvincing nature of everyday life. The easiest character to relate to in *City of Angels* was not the human Maggie, but the otherworldly Seth — just as in *Wings of Desire* it was Damiel, and not his circus love, with whom the audience was encouraged to identify. The plight of the angel, who must watch human life unfolding before him as on a screen, at one remove, was closer to most people's everyday experience than that of the 'real' people in the film, whose ability to be *in* their lives seemed almost supernatural. This, according to Damon Albarn, had been the normal state of affairs for most people since 1990. 'We started looking at our lives instead of living them,' he told the *NME*'s Steve Sutherland. 'That's the extraordinary thing about the nineties — we feel separate from the rest of existence.'[3] The Eels gave form to this feeling on their 1996 single, 'Susan's House'. Singer Mark Oliver Everett, known to the world as 'E', described a litany of everyday urban horror over a soundtrack of canned sitcom laughter and applause. The narrator sees suffering everywhere, but it seems no more real to him than a TV show, so he keeps walking.[4]

Beck, in an interview with *Rolling Stone*, suggested that nineties people found it hard to take reality seriously, 'because they see so much of the world as a cliché'. The singer said his goal was to transcend this second-hand experience of life, 'to embrace the world', as he put it.[5] But his words suggested another possibility. If everyday life seemed a poor imitation of the movies, might one become real by crossing over onto the screen? In 1993, critic Robert Hughes argued that this, for many Americans, was now the most reliable form of redemption available. 'To be on TV, if you believe in TV,' he wrote in 1993, 'is to break through the ceiling — to become realer than real.'[6]

MTV had already confirmed Hughes's observation one year earlier, by naming its groundbreaking reality TV show *The Real World*. Author Dave Eggers later recalled one of his friends, David Milton, writing a letter to the network, begging it to cast him in the show. 'Only there, burning brightly in front of a million dazzled eyes,' wrote Milton, 'will my as-yet-uncontoured self assume the beauteous forms that are not just its own, but an entire market niche's due ...'[7] On Pavement's 1997 album, *Brighten the Corners*, Stephen Malkmus offered his listeners the ultimate form of modern day wish fulfilment. 'Freeze,' he sang, 'don't move / you've been chosen as an extra in the movie adaptation / of the sequel to your life.'[8] When everything seems like the movies, your best hope is that, with practice, you'll get so good at playing the part of yourself that you'll one day get to do it for real — on TV.

But in 1997, a message from one of the lucky few who managed to cross over suggested that the trip was not worth the effort. In *Wings of Desire*, Damiel is tempted into the real world by Peter Falk's report from the other side. Falk has been a spectator, and now he's in it — and he assures Damiel it's better. At the 1997 MTV Video Music Awards, the message from Fiona Apple was: stay where you are. Apple had just beaten Meredith Brooks and Jamiroquai in the category for 'Best New Artist'. Having accepted her statuette, she began her speech with a warning. 'I'm not gonna do this like everybody else,' she said. This was true — the speeches so far, like all speeches at all awards ceremonies, had said, 'I'm here — I wish you were here. Be here now.' What Apple had to say was the exact opposite. 'So, what I want to say is: everybody out there that's watching, everybody that's watching this world — this world is bullshit. And you shouldn't model your life about what you think that we think is cool and what we're wearing and what we're saying and everything.' As the audience whooped like she was on *Oprah*, Apple delivered her final message. 'Go with yourself,' she said. 'Go with yourself.'[9]

The Eye of the Storm

As a teenager, Jarvis Cocker had got into the habit of seeing his day-to-day existence as a rehearsal for his real life — a life that could only begin once he broke into what he described in 1995 as 'the proper world'.[1] Cocker's band, Pulp, did not really exist, as far as he was concerned, until it was on TV. Being nominated for the Mercury Music Prize at the end of 1994 told him that 'this group is real', performing in front of one hundred thousand people at Glastonbury six months later made it realer still.[2] When Cocker crashed the stage during Michael Jackson's performance at the 1996 BRIT Awards, the last remaining hurdle that stood between himself and the proper world had been crossed — the outsider had broken in. Now, in 1998, he wanted out again. 'The situation I've been in,' he told *Mojo*'s Ben Thompson, 'is like watching a film, seeing what's on the screen and then suddenly being inside it.' Cocker paused. 'To be honest,' he said with a rueful smile, 'I think it's better to be in the audience.'[3]

Because Pulp had existed for over a decade before 'Common People' became a hit, journalists often asked Cocker whether the band's long period of waiting in the wings had better prepared him for the disorienting effects of superstardom. The singer would always set them straight. 'Nothing prepares you for it,' he said. During Britpop's ascendant phase, Cocker had done a lot of cocaine, and a lot of the kind of aggressively optimistic talk that goes along with it. The subtext of this was usually — as he later put it — 'Yes! We're inventing the future!'[4] But when the future arrived, so did the inevitable comedown. Britpop had triumphed, but it couldn't just go on celebrating its triumph. 'At a certain point the party peaks,' Cocker said, 'and you can't remember what you're celebrating anymore. That's when you get casualties.' In theory, he could have gone back to work and started writing new songs, but he and the band were so busy touring and doing interviews and going to parties that there was no time to write. As a result, Cocker became 'one of those people who are just known for being known — a real celebrity'.[5] This turned out to be a lot less fun than he'd thought it would be: Cocker suffered from panic attacks and depression, and became increasingly paranoid. 'You start to question people's motivations for wanting to talk to you,' he explained. 'You think, "Why are they being so nice?"' After twelve months of this, he experienced what Graham Coxon described as a 'mid pop-life crisis'. 'Why are we in this position?' he asked himself. 'What is my *job?*'

Until 1996, Cocker had a pretty clear idea what this was. His job was to observe, recall and describe the lives of human beings; to extrapolate wider truths from small moments, overheard conversations and chance encounters. 'I get all my best ideas from just wandering around and seeing random little things,' he told Thompson. The problem now was that celebrity life had made this impossible. 'Inevitably in my situation you tend to lead a less random existence, everything gets mapped out for you. If you're not careful, you end up scouring the newspapers looking for something to write about, which is something I swore I'd never do.'[6] The only other option available to him was to write about what it was like to become famous — something else he'd always considered off-limits. 'I'd hope never to write a song about being on the road or being in a hotel room,' he'd said in September 1995. 'I don't consider it valid subject matter.'[7] But by the end of that year, having accepted that he might soon have nothing else to write about, Cocker had begun to change his mind. 'I may yet go against my instincts,' he told *Vox* magazine, 'and write about the fame process itself.'[8]

Having insinuated himself into the 'proper' world, Cocker had eventually been granted access to its innermost sanctum — the room beyond the velvet rope. What he found there had surprised him. 'I went to this Versace and Elton John party, so you thought you were at an exclusive thing, right? But then there was a VIP area, and another level after that, and another level after that, and another level after that, and finally, at the end of the night, you find yourself alone in a brightly lit closet with Simon Le Bon eating off a paper plate! That's the celebrity inner sanctum! Honestly, the further up these levels you go, the worse it gets.' The thick of things, it seemed, was a little thin. 'There's no final reward. You're just tricked into thinking you're getting somewhere.'[9] The whole experience reminded Cocker of nothing so much as watching porn in a hotel room — something else he'd done an awful lot of in the past year. At first, he'd been excited to discover that European porn was far more explicit than the English variety. But the thrill soon wore off. The eternal promise of porn, he realised, was that somewhere beyond what you'd just seen was something better, dirtier, more explicit, more hardcore. But the promise was an empty one. The search led nowhere, or always to the same place, and the hardcore was hollow.

This idea — porn as a metaphor for celebrity culture — would give Cocker the theme of Pulp's post-Britpop masterpiece, 'This is Hardcore', released as a single from the album of the same name in March 1998. The song begins with a looped sample of the Peter Thomas Sound Orchestra's 'Bolero on the Moon Rocks' — taken out of its melodic context, the orchestra plays six short stabs at a single note. This sets up a tension that is never really resolved, a counterpoint to the never-realised happiness the song describes. The sample also establishes a sinister, spy-movie atmosphere, which the band builds on with siren-like guitars, moody keyboards and — for Pulp — surprisingly heavy drums. This goes on for a long time before any words appear in the song. Finally, after a minute and a half, Cocker emerges, barely recognisable as the loveable rogue who charmed a nation in 1995. 'You are hardcore, you make me hard,' he sings in a flat, faraway voice. 'You name the drama and I'll play the part / It seems I saw you in some teenage wet dream / I like your get-up if you know what I mean.'[10] These lyrics, written during what Cocker would later describe as the worst period of his life, tell of the singer's infatuation with the world on the screen, and his desire to one day break through — to live the hardcore life. 'I've seen all the pictures, I've studied them forever / I wanna make a movie so let's star in it together.' The chorus is a wall of shrieking guitars and pounding drums and the sheer din forces Cocker to abandon the last of his lounge-lizard cool. 'Oh this is hardcore,' he wails, 'there is no way back for you.'[11]

'This is Hardcore' denounced false happiness in very clear terms, but it also suggested that the real thing might still exist. 'You can't be a spectator,' sang Cocker, 'you've gotta take these dreams and make them whole.'[12] This could have been the voice that led him, as a teenager, to press his face up against the screen and dream of breaking through; but it sounded more like the voice of a man who, having got there and realised that it wasn't that great, had now decided to warn others not to waste their time, to realise their dreams in everyday life instead of imagining that happiness lay somewhere beyond the glass. The need to have real experiences, instead of those that are second-hand or mediated, was a major theme running through Pulp's new album. 'Seductive Barry' was a piece of lush, seventies-style ambience over which Cocker delivered a disarmingly straight come-on. 'Sometimes in the past I have been guilty of creating a seductive mood and then undercutting it by making an ironic or sarcastic comment towards the end or something,' he told Richard Kingsmill. 'The man in this song really, really wants to get off with this woman.'[13] Likewise 'Party Hard' demanded that the quotation marks be removed, once and for all, from 'partying'; and 'Dishes' hymned the pleasure of small moments with a directness that was almost shocking: 'I'm not worried that I will never touch the stars,' sang Cocker, ''cause stars belong up in heaven / and the earth is where we are.'[14]

'A pox on irony!' In April 1998, a month after the release of *This is Hardcore*, film critic David Denby called time on the decade's dominant mode of expression. 'At the end of the twentieth century,' he wrote, 'irony has become the refuge of the gutless and the accommodating.'[15] Denby saw irony as a destructive force in the cinema, as the artist John Currin did in the world of painting. Critics saw Currin's 1995 series of paintings of women lying in bed as pop parodies of pin-up clichés, or as self-reflexive comments on his status as a male artist painting the female form. It didn't seem to occur to anyone that he might have simply painted the women because he liked the way they looked, because the images made him laugh, or moved him, or turned him on. 'One of my main missions,' said Currin, 'has been to try to get my work to be less ironic. ... I think about things that are not ironic, like sexual desire, fear of death, basic things that are by no means new concepts.' Currin forced himself not to be ironic so that he would have to commit to a position — or face the fact that he didn't have one. 'I would rather that my work turn into a cliché than be a kind of artfully dodged, ironic critique,' he said. 'I'd rather that my work be truly a cliché than a critique of clichés.'[16]

Jarvis Cocker met Currin the following year, and used one of his paintings for the cover of *This is Hardcore* — by which point his own stance on irony had converged with the painter's. Back in 1993, Cocker had bemoaned the lack of irony in grunge, and told *Select* that he preferred British pop because it was smarter. But it had always annoyed him when critics described his lyrics as ironic, since it implied that he wasn't emotionally committed to his characters. Now, in 1998, he felt that irony was a luxury humanity in general — and artists in particular — could no longer afford. The ironic attitude, the habit of taking life at one remove that nineties people had learned as a way of coping with information overload, had become a means to justify every kind of stupid behaviour, including his own descent into celebrity drug hell, which he'd told himself he was doing for anthropological reasons. 'Not wanting to get hung up on the millennium or anything,' he told the *NME*, 'but I think there's no room for irony when you're entering a new era. There's a kind of desperate need for people to sort themselves out so they're going into a new era with their lives in place.'[17] *This is Hardcore* closed with a song called 'The Day After the Revolution', a note from Cocker to himself and his generation to stop mucking about before it was too late. 'I love the way you do it,' he sang. 'I love the way you put them on / You know the answers but you get it wrong.' All very clever, very ironic. 'Why did it seem so difficult to realise a simple truth?' He went on, 'The revolution begins and ends with you.' As the tune resolved itself into a sparkling keyboard drone, Cocker recited a list of things that would not survive the millennium. 'Perfection is over, Sheffield is over, the fear is over,' he murmured. 'Breakdown is over, irony is over. Bye bye.'[18]

Meanwhile, across the Atlantic, Wayne Coyne had reached a similar conclusion, as he and his band the Flaming Lips worked around the clock on a song called 'Race for the Prize'. The tune had been written around the time of the band's hit 'She Don't Use Jelly' in 1994, but left on the shelf because it sounded too corny. Now, the Lips treated the song like the pop epic it had always threatened to be. With drums heavier than Bonham and strings sweeter than Disney, the tune was flung far beyond the field of corn into the realm of the sublime.

Hearing 'Race for the Prize', it wasn't hard to see why the Flaming Lips had baulked at the prospect of recording it in 1994. Back then, universal suckage seemed to be the rule, the careful use of irony the singer's best hope for circumventing it. For a singer to stand in front of a microphone and demand that his generation get it together and save the world before it was too late — and to do this with a straight face — must have seemed impossible. But in 1998, Coyne felt that it was the least he could do. 'We act like this music is the biggest deal ever,' he said. 'But it's all self-serving: none of it helps the world. Our generation never cared about these things; it was always about us. Like with cancer, we think, "Someone is going to find a cure." Not us, but someone, and in fact it's never going to get done if we don't do it.'[19]

Rap, Metal, Rap, Metal

Faith No More disappeared off the face of the earth at the exact point that rap-metal — the style of music they helped to invent in 1990 and subsequently left for dead — became the soundtrack of choice for teenage America. The band played its final show in Lisbon, Portugal on 20 April 1998. By August, Korn's third album *Follow the Leader* debuted at number one on the Billboard charts. One month later, Korn, Limp Bizkit, Ice Cube, Rammstein, Orgy and Incubus played on the Family Values tour — which outsold both Lollapalooza and Lilith Fair to become the highest-grossing travelling festival of 1998. Limp Bizkit singer Fred Durst saw the event's success as a sign of a new movement in rock. 'It's a new family,' he told *Kerrang!* 'There's less than ten bands with this mixture of music: Korn, Deftones, Sepultura, Coal Chamber and us.'[1] While by no means homogenous, the groups Durst listed shared a few important elements in common: dropped tunings, heavy bass riffs, loud guitars, vocals that turned on a dime from high-powered raps to blood-curdling screams, turntables, samples and hip-hop drums. 'They got the heaviest beat,' said one fan, interviewed at 1998's Korn Konference. 'And I do *not* like the soft shit!'[2] Nu metal, as it had come to be called, was dark, heavy and aggressive, but it was also popular — and it had become so in a way that most would have thought impossible in the late 1990s. The music received no support whatsoever from MTV and commercial radio, both of which ignored nu metal until it became impossible to do so. Instead, the bands built their audiences by combining a very old approach — touring — with a very new one — the internet. Nu metal's success had been created at a grass-roots level by bands and their fans, and this made it very hard for rock critics — who generally disliked the stuff — to write it off as an industry hype, however much they would have liked to.

The reason music writers had so much trouble coming to terms with nu metal went back to the start of the decade. As John Doran observed in the *NME*, alternative rock had seemed, at the dawn of the nineties, 'to be firmly set upon the path to righteousness'.[3] Faith No More, according to *Spin*, played 'metal without the sleaze',[4] *Melody Maker* described Jane's Addiction as 'a thinking person's heavy metal band'.[5] Nirvana could be bleak, the Chili Peppers hedonistic, Soundgarden slightly boorish, but all seemed like Gandhi compared to Guns N' Roses or Skid Row, whose singer was seen more than once wearing an 'AIDS Kills Fags Dead' T-shirt on stage. Most alternative bands seemed committed, in some form or another, to liberal ideals within rock. They supported worthy political causes, eschewed the trappings of fame and success, and rejected out of hand the misogynistic culture of 1980s metal. Thus, when alt rock dreamed of a fusion of rock and hip-hop, it imagined the best of both worlds. Early signs suggested that this might be on the cards: the musical adventurousness of Sonic Youth met the radical politics of Public Enemy in 'Kool Thing'; L7's feminist grunge was successfully crossbred with Bomb Squad production techniques on *Garbage*; and Beck mixed anti-folk and hip-hop science on 'Loser'. 'It's a new music,' said Stephen Malkmus in 1993, 'and it's something everyone can learn from whether you're into grunge-rock or heavy metal.'[6] Malkmus was a fan of groups like De La Soul and Digable Planets and even rapped a little himself on Pavement's *Crooked Rain, Crooked Rain*. Over the next few years, Lou Barlow matched his brainy indie rock to beats on the soundtrack to Larry Clark's movie *Kids*, the Dust Brothers produced Mark Everett's junk-shop ballads in a trip-hop style, and Rage Against the Machine set Noam Chomsky's politics to EPMD's grooves.

But when 'Epic' was released in 1990, progressive politics and digable planets were a long way from Mike Patton's mind. 'You actually mix hard rock — heavy metal — and rap music,' said *Billboard Top 20* host Bella Shaw at the time. 'What's the connection?' Patton smiled. 'They can both be really aggressive,' he replied. 'They can both be really stupid too.'[7] Patton, with his usual perversity, suggested that the aspects of metal and hip-hop *least* loved by indie intellectuals might be brought together in a form of music that combined the *worst* of both worlds — the mindless aggression of Megadeth with the casual misogyny of N.W.A, the morbid preoccupations of metal with the materialism of gangsta. This, in many ways, was the alternative nation's worst nightmare. In Allan Moyle's 1995 comedy, *Empire Records*, Lucas — a turtlenecked indie connoisseur — sits down with the much younger Warren and looks at the pile of CDs he'd earlier tried to steal from the store. 'Look what you took,' says Lucas. 'Rap, metal, rap, metal.' Lucas believes Warren's musical diet is magnifying his criminal impulses, and suggests he listen to something more morally uplifting. 'Maybe some jazz, or some classical,' he says. 'Maybe you bite me!' sneers Warren, imitating Lucas's superior tone.[8] Warren loves rap and metal for precisely the reasons Lucas doesn't — because they're aggressive, irresponsible and profoundly antisocial.

At the Korn Konference earlier that year, a group of fans described the effect the band's music had on them. 'We can relate to every single lyric, every single beat,' said one. 'It's like it comes from our heart — it's like stuff *we'd* write'. 'It's just raw emotion, you know?' said another, wearing a red baseball cap backwards on his head and a gold chain around his neck. 'And you can relate a lot more than, like, Metallica or Megadeth — what the hell are *they* talkin' about?'[9] The fans' words suggested that nu metal was not so much a betrayal of alt rock's promise as its continuation by other means. The reason Nirvana and Pearl Jam crossed over in 1991 had far less to do with their politics than with the emotional realism of their music, the way Vedder and Cobain seemed to be able to say things that couldn't be said, on behalf of kids who felt they didn't have a voice. By 1998, the Smashing Pumpkins' Billy Corgan had come to believe that this had been alternative rock's most important innovation — honesty. 'Rock and roll pretty much up until the nineties was about being someone else,' he said. 'And we were probably one of the first bands to go, "We're just going to be ourselves," and if it hurts us, it hurts us.'[10] This vision of rock-as-therapy, in which the singer, by honestly (and painfully) revealing his feelings, redeems himself and his audience, was the distinctly nineties element in nu metal's alloy. Rappers and metal groups in the eighties constructed their identities around images of strength and power, but nu metal bands showed they were real by admitting they were weak. 'I am not afraid to explore myself and dig deep in my songs,' said Korn's Jonathan Davis. 'I'm a human being and every human being has problems. I just choose to deal with the dark things in my life in music.'[11]

Korn began in 1993 in Davis's hometown of Bakersfield, California. 'It's the armpit of the world and I hate it,' the singer told *Kerrang!*. 'The only things to do there are get fucked up on drugs, join gangs, get arrested, fuck and have a kid. There's no music scene.' Davis worked at a funeral home by day and at the local coroner's office by night, both of which he loved. 'All I did back then was watch horror movies, and I wanted to see the real shit,' he explained. 'I could do things that serial killers did and get paid for it. I could hack up bodies.' But while working up to his arms in gore was fun, finding people he'd seen walking down the street one day turn up on the slab the next gave him pause for thought — and ultimately, inspired him to start writing about his life and his feelings. 'I didn't want to keep stuff buried because I knew I could die anytime,' he said.[12] Davis joined a Huntington Beach-based group called Creep, which was changed to Korn not long after. The band signed to Epic and released its first self-titled album and a single, 'Blind', in 1994. The first impression was of a slightly freaked-out Rage Against the Machine. 'Blind' begins like an exercise in Morello-style minimalism — a riff that sounds like a robot stuck in a rut, a single ride cymbal beating out a steady tattoo, and then, out of nowhere, Davis appears. 'Are you READY?' he howls, as the band drops into the song. But when Davis next opens his mouth, the resemblance to Rage Against the Machine ends. 'This place inside my mind, this place I like to hide,' he sings. 'You don't know the chances. What if I should die?' Rage Against the Machine traced the roots of alienation back to the real world — to the movement of money and the machinations of power. In 'Blind', Davis is no longer sure such a world even exists. 'Living a life that seems to be a lost reality,' he screams. 'That can never find a way to reach / my inner self / I stand alone!'[13]

Billy Corgan would later say that exploring this kind of 'deep material' was, in the nineties, the only way for rock and roll to move forward. 'The only place left to go was into such emotionally explosive material that it's almost hard to listen to,' he said.[14] If this was the case, then *Korn* represented the end of rock's progress: the album's secret track, 'Daddy', was so emotionally raw that even the man who sang it couldn't bear to hear it more than once. 'You raped / I feel dirty,' screamed Davis. 'It hurt / as a child ... / My God! / Saw you watching / Mommy why? / Your own child!'[15] Davis knew there could be no further progress down this road. The first album, he later said, was about 'getting some shit out ... Now it's time for me to move on.' By 1998, the singer had stopped picking over his childhood and started writing about his day-to-day life, which seemed to be no less weird, if a lot more fun. Korn were now rock stars living a semi-charmed rock star life — buying expensive homes and $15,000 watches, and drinking and partying to their heart's content. Except that Davis's heart wasn't content — not by a long shot. 'It's about how you get everything and it seems like you want more but you don't,' he said of the single, 'Got the Life'. 'Like getting all this stuff, all the cars and stuff. You have all this stuff and I just scream to God telling him I want more.'[16]

The Bums Will Always Lose

'I see it as a hugely more commercial record,' said Courtney Love of Hole's new album, *Celebrity Skin*. 'And it has a lot more sheen.'[1] By July 1998, Love had adopted Britpop's favourite form of doublethink, insisting that alternative rock's anti-commercial stance was in fact a screen to hide a sorry lack of musical ambition. Alt-rock bands, she insisted, just didn't want it that bad, or they were afraid to admit they did. 'The problem is that people between the ages of twenty-three to thirty-three, and certainly amongst my peers in songwriting, tend not to be ambitious because then they're somehow selling out,' she said. Love worried that posterity would not look kindly on this slack approach. When it came time to write the history of rock and roll in 2010, indie's scratchy noise, she argued, would not hold up next to the works of Led Zeppelin or Fleetwood Mac. Already there were signs that this might be the case. 'Weezer will walk into eternity hand in hand with Warrant,' wrote *Spin* writer Mark Schone, 'both emblems of forgotten eras of rock.'[2] For the most competitive woman in music, this was unacceptable. 'To me it's sort of ridiculous,' she said, 'because now we're coming to the end of the millennium and there aren't that many classic records by people in my age group.'[3] As an attempt to make up for lost time, the first two singles from Hole's third album very nearly succeeded. 'Celebrity Skin' was a made-for-the-stadium anthem with a razor-sharp riff and a killer chorus; 'Malibu' a gorgeous summery ballad with a dark undertow — '*Rumours* from hell,' as Love herself put it. '*Hotel California* on fire.'[4] Photos of the band printed in *Rolling Stone* showed the group in a rural setting bathed in sunset light, with Love dressed in hippie-ish brocaded silks and Erlandson in a white suit.[5] Only a year earlier, when *Spin* had asked Veruca Salt's Nina Gordon whether she'd rather listen to 'Heart or Hole', the question had seemed loaded with significance. Now, it was getting hard to tell the difference.

Pearl Jam, too, had embraced the new classicism — though for slightly different reasons. In promoting the group's 1998 album, *Yield*, Stone Gossard repudiated the avant-garde sound of *Vitalogy*, which he now admitted he wasn't at all happy with. 'I just stepped back and let Ed finish it,' he said. 'I think we all did. I was just hoping it wasn't going to be our last record.' The guitarist was troubled by the idea that Pearl Jam's final message to the world might be a schizophrenic smash-up of hardcore noise, devotional chants and broken accordions. 'Experimenting is great,' he said, 'but let's make sure we do what comes naturally too. Let's write four-minute rock songs with good hooks and a great vocal melody that tell cool stories about being alive right now.'[6] Gossard saw the rock process — write songs, record, have hits, tour — as natural, and that in trying to resist or subvert it, Pearl Jam had attempted the impossible and suffered as a result. 'It's just business as usual now,' he said. Vedder confirmed this, though he seemed far less happy about it. *Yield*, he said, was 'a good mainstream record'. He explained that the title — which Gossard had suggested — summed up the band's new attitude; Pearl Jam's oppositional stance had 'given way' to one of acceptance. 'Things have changed,' he said. 'You go from *Vs.* to *Yield*.' But where Gossard saw this as the group making peace with itself, Vedder saw it as a capitulation to forces he no longer felt he could fight. 'I don't know if it's just age, but I'm just getting tired of complaining,' he sighed. 'All this energy going absolutely nowhere.'[7]

Billy Corgan had seen this coming in 1996. Alternative rock, he said, would fail, because its task was impossible. 'So what's seen as disaffection was a failure meant to be a failure,' he explained. 'Alternative music can never be completely co-opted because at its core, it stands against what most mainstream things stand for.'[8] By 1998, he too had given up fighting a war he'd always known he couldn't win, and embraced the art for art's sake philosophy he'd begun to develop during the recording of *Mellon Collie*. The band's fourth album, *Adore*, he said, 'represents a band who's reached a kind of peacefulness, and just wants to make music, and doesn't want to get caught up in the politics of the world or the politics of "you use synthesisers" or "you use guitars". We don't care anymore. We just wanna make music, and we think we make better music than anybody else. And that's what the Smashing Pumpkins is about.'[9]

The release of *Adore*, *Celebrity Skin* and *Yield* in 1998 marked a turning point in alternative rock. Behind Corgan's aestheticism, Love's appeal to posterity, and Vedder's decision to 'yield' lay an admission that alternative rock had failed to do what it had set out to do. 'You know,' said Billy Corgan, 'we're supposed to be the castaways of society, who found something inside of themselves and revolutionised ...' The singer paused, unsure of what exactly had changed as a result of his generation's revolt. There had been no improvement in everyday life, no victory for the underdogs. Capitalism remained intact; the 'establishment' had not been taken over. One thing, however, had changed a great deal. '... the music business, at least,' said Corgan, finishing his sentence. This was undeniable — alternative rock had given the music industry a much-needed shot of adrenaline at the start of the decade by creating a whole new market for youth culture. But this, as Perry Farrell had pointed out in 1992, was the bad news. After Nirvana, every scene became a market, every sub-genre a mini-demographic. By 1998, the corporate exploitation of youth culture had become so routine as to seem inevitable — what had seemed, to bands like the Butthole Surfers in the eighties, like a completely unrealistic fantasy had now become alternative rock's most basic physical law: what comes up, must sell out. Fighting against the flow now seemed to be not only unreasonable, but unnatural — as it did to Stone Gossard. Meanwhile, alt rock's dream of a mediasphere improved by real music seemed further out of reach than it had ever been. Radio in America was now dominated by third-wave grunge bands, teen-pop and nu metal. In 1998, L7's Jennifer Finch was far less likely to hear something cool when she walked into a 7-11 than in 1988 — when radio stations might still have played R.E.M., or The Cars.

Faced with the fact that the music industry, youth culture and the world at large were in significantly worse shape in 1998 than they had been in 1990, that it had not only failed to improve the world but had very likely made things worse, alt rock's view of itself became tragic and pre-destined — 'a failure meant to be a failure'. The idea that music could change life disappeared, the status quo was accepted as permanent — natural, even. With its social function abandoned, alternative rock became simply a matter of 'making good music'. Thus, its goal was no longer to improve the present, but to look good for posterity — or at the very least sidestep oblivion. Bands began to fret over their legacies: have we made a 'classic' record? The hope now was that alternative rock might be afforded a place in the rock and roll hall of fame, alongside punk rock and Woodstock rock and all the other rock movements that failed to improve everyday life, but left behind music of such quality and distinction that nobody could afford to complain too much. 'Malibu', 'Bullet with Butterfly Wings' and 'Even Flow' would be offered as compensation for the disappearance of the dreams they represented, just as 'Hotel California' had become the baby boomer's consolation for the failure of the youth movement to change the world for the better.

1999

Fields Outside

The last year of the nineties saw the re-establishment of cordial relations between indie rock in England and America. Britpop's flag waving had become a bore; 'Cool Britannia' a cliché, and finally, a brand. The orgy of national pride that had gripped the UK music scene between 1994 and 1996 had created an atmosphere redolent of the 1950s, when Keith Richards and Pete Townshend, bored by British pop, had tuned their wirelesses to pirate radio stations or armed forces networks, hoping to hear an American voice singing the blues.

'I love this city, man, but this city's killin' me,' sang Ben Ottewell on Gomez's 1998 debut, *Bring it On*. 'Sittin' here in all this noise, man, I don't get no peace.' As the band brooded over a New Orleans gumbo, Ottewell told, in his bluesy bark, of his plan to leave the metropolis, and eventually, the planet. 'Get miles away / Get miles,' he crooned, while drummer Olly Peacock hit a lazy cowbell.[1] It had been a long time since any British band had pursued such an obviously American sound and got away with it. Radiohead's early resemblance to Nirvana had been a millstone around the band's neck at home for years; Primal Scream's country-blues album *Give Out But Don't Give Up* had turned the group into a laughing-stock; Bush's proximity to grunge had made them music-press pariahs. Now, Gomez's agreeable mishmash of Beck, Dr John, Neil Young and Little Feat sounded positively hip. Guitarist and vocalist Ian Ball's admission that Nirvana's *Unplugged in New York* album changed his life — unthinkable from a British musician two years earlier — seemed perfectly acceptable now.[2] Even the accidental resemblance of Ottewell's singing voice to Eddie Vedder's seemed somehow right for 1998 in a way that it could never have been in 1994.

'Get Miles' was Gomez's 'Subterranean Homesick Alien' — a wish for escape from a too-complex world, or for a vantage point that would allow the singer to make sense of it. This search for space — in both a literal and metaphorical sense — set the agenda for British music in 1998–9. Britpop's urban milieu had become claustrophobic. Now, like the rat-race refugee in Blur's 'Country House', listeners were pining for the great outdoors, and journalists went looking for it in America — which had always had more of the stuff. In May 1998, the *NME*'s John Mulvey interviewed Jason Lytle of the American group Grandaddy: 'an amiably befuddled, sensitive guy, a little out of step with America, more comfortable observing life from a distance — from the fields outside the cities — rather than being in the thick of the action, choking on the smog'. 'I feel completely bombarded and frustrated and unable to do anything about the state of things,' said Lytle. 'It's just really sad to be so slow in the midst of everything that's so … *fast*.'[3] London's music press fell almost as hard for this stuff as it had for Sub Pop's trailer-trash romance ten years earlier. 'The idea of coming from somewhere,' noted music writer Ben Thompson, 'is very alluring to people who don't.'[4]

The flight from the city could also take the form of a flight back in time — to an age when the world was less complex and less interconnected, its traditions still intact. In December 1998, Mojo's Barney Hoskyns wrote of 'urban nerds who have for one reason or another gone scurrying back to America's musical past for succour and perhaps comfort: who've survived punk, hardcore, goth, grunge and industrial music and now just want to quieten down a little, get out into the country and reconnect with the traditions and myths of what Greil Marcus calls "the old weird America".'[5] The 1997 CD reissue of Harry Smith's *Anthology of American Folk Music* sparked a new wave of interest in the folk tradition, and struck a chord with what Ben Thompson described as 'The Woodchuck Nation'; groups like Tarwater, Smog, Palace Brothers, Lambchop and Wilco, who were 'retreating from the arid and unwelcoming US "alternative" rock landscape'.[6] The corporate raid on America's regional indie scenes had destroyed the peace and quiet that made those scenes flourish in the first place, in much the same way that global tourism threatened to destroy the cultural differences that made travel interesting. By the end of the 1990s, musicians had come to realise — as protagonist Richard eventually does in Alex Garland's 1996 novel, *The Beach* — that the search for an untouched indie paradise would only lead to more of the same, that Chicago or Chapel Hill would eventually go the way of Seattle.

But the search for space could still be realised in time, since the past could never really be colonised by the present. In early folk and blues recordings by artists like Elizabeth Cotten and Lead Belly, Beck heard the distant echo of a world without global franchises, Fox News or MTV. 'Their voices speak so directly to us of all the things we've lost with the advent of mass media and global communication,' he said. 'It used to be you'd go to different parts of the world and things would be developing their own rich traditions. Now it's all melding together and kind of homogenizing, but at the same time completely splintered.'[7] With *Odelay*, Beck had made an album that drew on these traditions while reflecting the melding and splintering they'd since undergone. But by 1998, he'd begun to feel that his postmodern constructions were simply not built to last the way the old music was. 'It's the difference between a Styrofoam cup and an old porcelain crafted thing,' he said.[8] Beck's third album, *Mutations*, was made with one eye on posterity. Computers and samplers were banished from the sessions; the songs were mostly played live in the studio on guitars, upright bass and pedal steel and recorded vérité-style by Radiohead producer Nigel Godrich.

'A lot of blues, popular standards, folk music,' said Mercury Rev's Jonathan Donahue, listing his influences for Richard Kingsmill. 'Maybe even some jazz and classical. It's not necessarily all rock and roll and rap music or heavy metal. Certainly not alternative modern rock music. It tends to be more roots-based.'[9] Nineteen-ninety-eight's *Deserter's Songs* was, as its title implied, Mercury Rev's farewell to alternative rock and the decade that spawned it. Images of leaving ran through the album, from 'Hudson Line' ('gonna leave the city, gonna catch the Hudson Line'), to the closing 'Delta Sun Bottleneck Stomp', a marching-band rag with movie-score strings, which saw Donahue 'waving goodbye' to a world whose relentless appetite for novelty demands that the past be destroyed. 'Constructing new ideals, old ones laid to rust,' he sang, 'nothing seems so real.'[10] Musically, the album bolstered the band's earlier psychedelic sound with elements of folk, country and jazz — styles that predated not only alternative rock, but rock and roll itself. 'How does that old song go?' sang Donahue in 'Holes'.[11] A lonely be-bop trumpet answered him, softly soloing over the song's cinematic blues.

Artists like Beck and Mercury Rev abandoned the sound of the nineties because they suspected it was shallow and disposable. But Beck was also aware, as he admitted in an interview with Ben Thompson, that the same might once have been said about Lead Belly. 'Funny thing about time,' he said in 1998, 'your context always changes. The has-beens never had it so good, 'cause we'll always repackage you some other way.' Beck's admiration for hip-hop, his long career as a junk-store hound, and his recent work with the Dust Brothers had taught him that you couldn't really plan for posterity, that the best you could hope for was to be 'obsolete and part of the elements — the minerals of the now scene'.[12] This knowledge had helped him cope, in 1996, with the flood of second-wave grunge bands that threatened to keep his own music off the radio. When music writer Eric Weisbard asked him if he felt any resentment toward Bush and Better Than Ezra, Beck laughed. 'In twenty years we're going to be digging that — fifth-generation style, that'll be the style,' he said. 'I'm really into collecting vinyl. The wanna-be Dylans that probably never sold more than 2000 copies. The Stones rip-offs. At this point they're almost more interesting than the original. That might be the case in twenty years.' Beck slipped into an impersonation of a 2018 hipster, making chitchat in a record store. 'Hey, did you hear the group from 1997 who were ripping off Silverchair?'[13]

We Miss Rock Stars

Samantha Maloney, formerly of the post-hardcore band Shift, had been invited to replace Patty Schemel as Hole's drummer not long after recording was completed on *Celebrity Skin*. At twenty-two, she was the youngest member of the band — three years Melissa Auf der Maur's junior and born a full decade after Courtney Love and Eric Erlandson. This inter-Gen X generation gap revealed itself when the band did a short promotional tour of Australia and piled, en masse, into a radio studio for a co-host segment on triple j. The members of Hole were asked to select one song each and one as a group — Erlandson vacillated between Mudhoney and Sonic Youth, and eventually picked Spiritualized; Love raved about PJ Harvey but settled on New Order's 1981 single 'Temptation'; Auf der Maur chose Split Enz's 'I Got You' (for the 'new wave slickness'); while Maloney picked Mötley Crüe's 'Shout at the Devil'. Released in 1983, the song would have reached Love and Erlandson's ears when they were entering their twenties — Love was already singing with Faith No More; her future guitarist had discovered the Stooges and Johnny Thunders. Both would have heard 'Shout at the Devil' as an abomination, symbolic of all that punk rock would one day hopefully destroy. Maloney, on the other hand, heard the song for the first time when she was nine years old. Mötley Crüe was to her what Kiss was to Love and Erlandson's age group — an eternal promise of youthful freedom and fun, guilt-free rock and roll from an era when such things were still possible. 'The songs were so *rock*!' she said, raising a fist. 'And they put on this *amazing* stage show.'[1]

As the song's sub-'Wild Thing' riff blared out of the monitors for what was very likely the first time in the station's twenty-five-year history, Love told a story about a recent close encounter she'd had with the hair-metal monsters. As it turned out, Tommy Lee's sister had auditioned for Hole following Patty Schemel's departure. She was pretty good, but they couldn't take her on. 'She kept on saying, "Sorry, I didn't have time to listen to the song, we just got off tour with the Scorpions!"' The mere fact that the Scorpions still played, let alone the idea that Tommy Lee's sister now toured with them, was enough to crack the band up. 'That whole world exists!' said Love, incredulous. Despite reports of its having been killed by grunge, hair metal had never quite given up the ghost. 'It's a low-burning flame,' said Auf der Maur with a smile. Maloney told of how she still occasionally saw aspiring glam-metal singers stalking the streets of Hollywood with their heavily made-up girlfriends in tow. 'They're still holding on,' she said, 'you know, like "maybe one day …"'[2]

The idea that these washed-up rockers might live to see their scene back on top was, of course, plainly ridiculous. Glam metal was dead. It had to die because — as anyone who'd lived through the music wars of 1991 could tell you — it was sexist, stupid and materialistic. 'In the hair band world there was no room for girls,' Love explained. 'Girls were like the prize.' Love characterised the musical culture of glam metal as non-progressive in both a political and a musical sense — she recalled trying to talk to LA singers about punk in the eighties and getting mostly blank looks. 'The Stooges, maybe, *maybe* you could find a really evolved hair guy who knew who Iggy was.' But this was hardly surprising, since most of the musicians who gravitated to this world weren't really into music at all. 'They were in it for the cash,' she said. 'It was pretty see-through,' remarked Kingsmill. Hole had seen through it — as had Nirvana, Soundgarden, Pearl Jam and L7. By the time those bands broke through to the mainstream in 1992, it was as though the veil had been lifted — LA metal was revealed for what it had always been: a shallow, materialistic pseudo-rebellion. Warrant's Jani Lane saw the writing on the wall in February of that year, when he walked into his label's offices and saw his band's block-mounted poster being taken down off the wall and replaced by Nirvana's. Two years later, he was contemplating flannel, and the music industry was acting as though neither his band nor the style they typified had ever existed. 'That formula is dead,' said one Geffen song-plugger in 1995. 'We've all walked away from it. Nothing aged faster than that.'[3] The nineties had arrived, rock had been improved.

But rock and roll hates perfection, and Courtney Love was rock and roll to the core. 'I don't want utopia,' she said in 1992, 'I want cacophony.' Here Love predicted the alt-fatigue that would set in two years later, when the musically curious, bored by the ubiquity of grunge, returned to the underground in search of more surprising stuff. But Love's premonition about what was to come for alt rock a few years hence also anticipated something else, something none of the indie alternatives — post-rock, alt-country or emo — could offer in 1999. 'My God!' she'd exclaimed, 'if the charts were just and fair and the Pixies and Nirvana and Hole were the most popular bands, I'd probably start listening to Poison.'[4] Now, Love found herself agreeing with her drummer that 'Shout at the Devil' sounded pretty badass, and wondering if there might be a reason why LA's hair-metal scene stubbornly refused to die. 'There's something about it that apparently we're missing at the moment,' she said, 'and that's a kind of *rock stardom,* maybe.'[5] This statement went some way beyond the purely reactionary one she'd made in 1992, in which she'd suggested that she might start listening to glam metal again just because nobody else was. In 1999, however, Love was implying that there was something necessary about rock stars like Tommy Lee and Axl Rose, some essential role they played in the culture that might necessitate their return.

In Los Angeles, younger musicians with fond memories of the Crüe and Guns N' Roses in their heyday had already begun to pursue this idea — 1998 saw the arrival of a number of self-consciously hedonistic scarf-on-the-mic-stand bands, including Buckcherry and Satellite Beach. Dave Grohl, who was in the city in the middle of the year, auditioning players for a new line-up of the Foo Fighters, couldn't believe what he was seeing. 'People there are trying to recreate that whole eighties G N' R thing which I hate even more now than I did in 1991,' he said. 'I met all these people who were trying to save rock and roll because they were superhero rock stars. But the music they made sucked shit.'[6] People like Samantha Maloney or Buckcherry's Josh Todd might have been too young to know what it felt like to be in a band and know that your music would never get played on the radio because you weren't from LA and didn't wear leather pants, but Grohl did, and so, for that matter, did Courtney Love. 'I mean it was a terrible period,' she admitted. 'I moved to Los Angeles in the middle of Guns N' Roses and all I wanted to do was FUCK THEM UP. 'Cause they made me mad.' But, Love went on to admit, for some reason, she'd been thinking a lot about Axl Rose of late. 'We miss … rock stars!' she said. 'He was a rock star!' Her bandmates agreed. In the end, the final song on Hole's wish list, the one thing Love, Erlandson, Auf der Maur and Maloney could agree on was Guns N' Roses' 'Sweet Child o' Mine'. 'We're not being ironic!' Love insisted.[7]

In 1991, Soundgarden's Matt Cameron had been refused service at a 'Kill Rock Stars' T-shirt stand because its operator suspected him of *being* a rock star. Twelve months later, Eddie Vedder had been forced to confront the possibility that he too may have been transformed, against his will, into one of these hideous creatures. 'I hate rock stars,' he'd said. 'And here I am being turned into one.' By this point, John Frusciante had decided he was not about to let the same thing happen to him. Sometime between his spectacular act of career sabotage on *Saturday Night Live* and the Japanese leg of the Chili Peppers world tour, Frusciante concluded that he owed it to himself — to the nine-year-old John who had thrown his Kiss records out of the window in 1979 — to quit the band. He spend the next six years, by his own account, doing almost nothing, with 'no obligation to do anything for anybody or for myself', before realising, in mid 1998, that he *did* in fact have a responsibility, a responsibility he'd abandoned all those years ago when he walked out on the tour. 'Now,' he said in 1999, 'I think the rock star, his role in our society, is a very beautiful thing, and the best kind of thing for a child to experience.'[8] Alt rock had killed rock stars. Now, it wanted them back.

Bigger Than Satan

Gregg Alexander still believed in rock stars. The twenty-six-year-old frontman of the New Radicals told *Rolling Stone* in January 1999 that rock stardom still offered the best platform for those who felt they had an important message to share with the youth of the world. 'The problem is,' he explained, 'no-one's using it for anything other than their own selfish benefit.'[1] Alexander had already been through his selfish phase. His major-label debut, *Michigan Rain*, released in 1991 ('before the suicide chic thing' as he put it) had laid his broken heart bare, and became something of a cult favourite as a result — Rivers Cuomo's decision to delve deeper into his own emotional world after Weezer's debut had been inspired to a large degree by his exposure to Alexander's work. But by 1998, the singer had decided this kind of subjective wallowing was a cop-out. 'It's so much easier to scream "I want to kill myself" than to have a sense of hope and find a way out of the darkness,' he told cable TV network VH1.[2]

With the New Radicals' first single, 'You Get What You Give', Alexander aimed to do exactly that. The song was a bright pop-soul confection in the mould of Todd Rundgren's 'I Saw the Light' — the lyrics insisting that there was 'one chance left' for the kids to change the world. In the video, Alexander and his bandmates loitered in a suburban shopping mall while greedy yuppies and corporate clones went about their business and teenagers with no shopping agenda looked bored. At a signal from Alexander, the teens sprang into action, taking control of the mall. They helped themselves to CDs and sundaes, danced on the escalators and liberated the dogs in the pet store from their cages. A kid dropped a fishing net from the mezzanine, ensnaring several yuppies, store managers and rich baby boomers. The teens dragged them back to the pet store, locked them up in the dog cages, and celebrated their reclamation of public space by dancing to the New Radicals.

The video was plainly ridiculous — things like this didn't happen in America in 1999. But Alexander knew why. TV host Jerry Springer had explained how it worked on an episode of his show devoted to 'Shock Rock' in 1998. Rock music, he said, was art, and 'art, no matter how outrageous, is the safest of all outlets for whatever ails society at a given moment, and better that anger be expressed in a song than in the streets, better with a guitar than a gun'.[3] Alexander also believed that music was a safe outlet. 'Rock and roll is a controlled environment' he told *Mojo* magazine.[4] But unlike Springer, Alexander saw this as a problem. The last line of 'You Get What You Give's chorus, 'You've got the music in you' was no disco cliché, but a reminder that the freedom promised in rock songs was a real possibility, that we had merely been fooled into buying it instead of doing it. Real change, Alexander insisted, would remain impossible as long as our obsession with media spectacles and celebrity culture remained in place, as long as we allowed entertainment to realise our desires by proxy, in songs, and not in the streets.

As far as Alexander was concerned, the success of 'You Get What You Give' had already proved that this was the case. The song, he said, tackled a number of 'real issues' — the lack of accountability in the corporate world, the private takeover of public space, and the disenfranchisement of youth from politics. But the only part of the song the rock media wanted to talk to him about was the rap in the last verse: 'Fashion shoots with Beck and Hanson / Courtney Love and Marilyn Manson / you're all fakes / run to your mansions / come around / we'll kick your ass in!'[5] Alexander claimed that the song was a pop booby-trap, and the entertainment media had fallen for it. Marilyn Manson, however, wasn't buying this for a second. 'If I ever see him,' the singer told MTV, 'I'll crack his head open.'[6] Manson wasn't bothered by the accusation that he was a fake — his whole persona was fake to the core, and proud of it. What hurt, he said, was being included in the same sentence as Courtney Love.

Alexander could be forgiven for lumping Manson and Love in with one another, since the two were, at the time of the song's release, about to embark on a tour together. The name of the venture, 'Beautiful Monsters', summed up Love's new rock star ideal, while her co-headliner appeared to embody it. Manson's music was loud and defiantly lowbrow, his image and stage show reeked of sex and subversion, and his lifestyle, to hear him tell it, was not so much a return to the cock-rock bullshit of the eighties as a cross between the Marquis de Sade's *120 Days of Sodom* and a Mötley Crüe video. If Manson was PC, it was only in the sense that he refused to discriminate — all people were, to him, playthings. Was it true that he covered a fan in lunchmeat and urinated on her? 'Ah,' he replied, calling the scene to mind. 'A deaf girl.' When the interviewer looked surprised, Marilyn widened his blue-tinted eyes. 'I'm not going to *not* exploit a deaf person, just because she's deaf!' He paused, and adjusted his feathers. 'I think it was ham.'[7]

Manson appeared to enjoy being interviewed in a way that few other rock singers of the nineties had done — every time a camera was pointed at him, his brain started working overtime on new ways to amuse himself, delight his fans and offend those who needed offending. 'I think if there was a devil, he'd worship me,' he said. 'Because I'm better looking.' This was Manson's way of denying he was a Satanist. He was, however, somewhat like Jesus. Manson had set out to become a cartoon corruptor of the youth of America by self-consciously embracing everything their parents hated. When his wish came true, and the media started blaming him for teenage delinquency, Manson slipped effortlessly into the second act of the movie of his life, in which he became 'a poster-boy for fear', as he later put it, and shortly afterward, a media martyr — the spectacular video for his 1999 single 'I Don't Like the Drugs (But the Drugs Like Me)' showed him pinned to a crucifix made of TVs. Manson's God-baiting had by this point created an environment that suited the singer perfectly. When he travelled south for the annual Big Day Out festival in Australia and New Zealand, Christian activists, parents' groups and right-wing politicians sprang into action, calling for his concerts to be cancelled. But, when asked about this in interviews, Manson looked more surprised and hurt than angry. 'I thought Christianity was all about loving your enemies and turning the other cheek,' he said, with a sad shake of the head. 'That's something they don't seem to do very much.' Manson insisted that he was more Christian than the Christians — and that the moral majority was picking on the wrong rock star. 'I'm *bigger* than Satan,' he reminded Channel V. 'But Courtney *is* Satan.'[8]

Manson and Love had announced their co-headlining tour in November 1998. 'What better role models to lead the youth of America into the next millennium than us?' said Manson. 'It had to be done.' The singer insisted that he and Love had a great deal of respect for one another, and that the comment he made apropos 'You Get What You Give' was nothing more than friendly rivalry. Courtney Love, he explained, was very competitive, and he was determined to give as good as he got. He later told the *San Francisco Examiner* that he'd decided to do the tour because he thought, 'Well, here's a chance to show Courtney the difference between being a celebrity and being a real rock star. We're just going to blow her off the stage — my show will be the biggest and greatest rock show of the 1990s.'[9] But the size of Manson's show soon became a real problem, not so much because he was blowing Courtney Love off the stage, but because he was blowing her budget. The tour's expenses were shared, so Hole ended up having to pay for Manson's increasingly baroque production. 'Every time he wants another cannon or another Kabuki screen,' Love said, 'we get the bill.' Manson, in turn, resented having to pay for her private chef and yoga teacher.

After Manson tore up a Bible one night on stage, Love registered her disapproval on the following evening. 'I just want to say to fans of the Christian religion that there are some nice things about it,' she said, taking a drag of her cigarette. 'There really are! And Marilyn can tear up the Bible all he wants, but there's good things in the Bible. Good things. Like not killing people and not sleeping with other people's husbands.' After this, things turned ugly. Love fought with Manson's girlfriend, the actress Rose McGowan, and then pretended not to know who she was in a TV interview ('Is she the one with the upturned nose? There's so many girls hanging around him'). Manson began insulting Hole onstage, asking the audience if they'd had time to enjoy a nap during the band's set, and referring to them as 'the older people on this tour — the grandmothers.' Hole dropped out of the Beautiful Monsters roadshow in March. Manson renamed it the 'Rock is Dead' tour, and announced that he would complete the remaining dates alone.

Eighteen days later, on 20 April, a pair of senior students at Columbine High School named Eric Harris and Dylan Klebold marched into their school's cafeteria with sawn-off shotguns and pipe-bombs and killed twelve students and one teacher, before committing suicide. Neither was a Manson fan, but when early reports suggested the two were members of a 'goth subculture' and listened to 'dark' music, the news media quickly concluded that Manson was in some way to blame. The singer denied this, with a degree of eloquence that surprised many of his critics. In an op-ed piece published in the May issue of *Rolling Stone*, Manson argued that he had been made a convenient scapegoat for a society that refused to accept responsibility for having created monsters like Harris and Klebold. 'From Jesse James to Charles Manson, the media, since their inception, have turned criminals into folk heroes,' he wrote. 'They just created two new ones when they plastered those dipshits Dylan Klebold and Eric Harris's pictures on the front of every newspaper. Don't be surprised if every kid who gets pushed around has two new idols.'[10] Nevertheless, Manson decided to cancel the last five shows out of respect for the victims' families, and to defuse any accusation that he might be using the publicity to make money. After a final date in Iowa, the Rock is Dead tour was dead.

Manson's name for his tour — a name which was already being used by Korn and White Zombie at the time — gave some indication of the difficulties faced by those who hoped to revive the rock star in 1999. To be a rock star was to swim against the tide of history, since many felt that rock itself would not survive the millennium. 'We've heard all the rock music,' said Ian Brown, 'there is no new rock music.'[11] While the Woodchuck Nation headed for the hills, the music industry did its best to anticipate the future, which, as everybody knew, would be digital. Major labels began clearing alt rock bands from their rosters to make room for dance-pop acts and post-Prodigy stadium techno. Meanwhile, bands did their best to keep up by incorporating 'electronica' into their music (as the Red Hot Chili Peppers had considered doing in 1998), doing webcasts and online interviews, or — at the very least — embellishing their album titles and artwork with digital junk, as Garbage did for its second album, *Garbage 2.0.* Thom Yorke, burned out on guitars after six months of touring, denied that Radiohead was 'a fucking rock group', and made a guest appearance on DJ Shadow and James Lavelle's UNKLE project. The Jon Spencer Blues Explosion followed up on the promise of its 1996 remix album by recording with techno star Alec Empire and hip-hop producer Dan the Automator — who also collaborated with Damon Albarn on a sci-fi concept album called *Deltron 3030.* The experience got Albarn thinking about an electronic project of his own. Sitting on the couch one night, watching music TV, he and cartoonist Jamie Hewlett came up with the idea for a completely artificial band. 'Something manufactured,' he explained, 'that's actually good.'[12]

Musical Hell

In April 1999, Ben Folds Five released their third album, *The Unauthorized Biography of Reinhold Messner*. The record appeared in stores minus a tune called 'Carrying Cathy', which Folds had recorded, but decided to leave on the shelf, because it was too emotionally affecting. 'I thought that maybe I was guilty of being manipulative,' he said. 'It was moving everybody, but I thought that I was going to go to musical hell for some reason if I did that.' Folds had a long-standing policy of using sad chords responsibly. When he wrote a melancholy song like 'Brick', he was always careful not to push it into emotional overload, to make the music louder in the chorus, or start screaming — although if he had, he would probably have sold a lot more records. "Cause that's been the whole climate of the radio in the last five or ten years,' he explained. 'You have to build it to this boil and then scream your guts out in the middle, or there's got to be some big point where you just let it rip.'[1]

Here, Folds described Fred Durst's favourite thing about rock music in the late nineties, the thing he heard in Tool and Rage Against the Machine that made him want to start a band, the sound he shared with Korn and the Deftones that made him feel part of a movement — what he described as 'the big build-up'. 'You know it's coming … here it comes … Then it's like, Boom! People are just out of it, man!'[2] Durst had been paying close attention to the way fans reacted to these moments over the past two years, as well as to the other things they seemed to like in Limp Bizkit's music — the big guitar riffs, the aggressive, accusatory lyrics, the angry songs he wrote about ex-girlfriends. 'Whatever they reacted to the most,' he explained, 'that's what I took and put into the new songs.'[3]

Durst would have an opportunity to showcase this new material when Limp Bizkit played at Woodstock '99 in July, along with Korn, Metallica, the Red Hot Chili Peppers and Rage Against the Machine. One song in particular, he felt, was certain to go down a treat with the Woodstock crowd. 'Break Stuff' began with a brutally simple metal riff and an equally elemental lyric about waking up to 'one of those days' when 'everything is fucked and everybody sucks'.[4] A catchy, playground-chant chorus led into a big build-up to end all big build-ups, where Durst warned about what would happen if people kept pissing him off, while guitarist Wes Borland illustrated his state of mind with squiggles of atonal noise. After thirty seconds of this, the tension became unbearable and Durst sounded like he was about to snap — which of course he was. 'If my day keeps goin' this way I might' — and here the band stopped down — 'break your fuckin' face tonight!' Durst smiled, imagining a crowd of 200,000 people getting air as he said these words, and crashing back down on the dirt as the band slammed back into the main riff. 'It's gonna be insane!' he warned.[5]

Limp Bizkit played Woodstock '99 at around 9pm on the second night of the festival, right after Alanis Morissette. Toward the end of her performance, Limp Bizkit fans moved up to the front of the mosh pit and started throwing plastic bottles, yelling at her to get off. After she had, Verne 'Mini-Me' Troyer appeared on stage to introduce the next act. 'You wanted the worst, you got the worst — Limp Bizkit!' Troyer stood aside as Durst, wearing his trademark backwards baseball cap and baggy pants, sauntered up to the mic. The singer had been told by festival organisers that the crowd had been getting rough. Fans had torn the plywood cladding from the sound control tower, using the fragments as makeshift crowd-surfing surfboards. Medical staff had treated concert goers for bruises, lacerations and even broken bones sustained in the crush near the front of the stage. There had also been reports of women being groped and raped in the mosh pit during Morissette's show. With all this in mind, Woodstock staff had urged Durst to calm the crowd, or at least not provoke them.

Nothing about the first half of Limp Bizkit's set suggested that Durst had payed any attention to this advice — the band played hard and heavy, and its frontman worked the crowd into a frenzy. But Durst did eventually stop down to deliver a public service announcement of sorts: 'They're telling us to get you motherfuckers to mellow out,' said the singer, as he surveyed the crowd. 'I say Alanis Morissette already did that!' A huge cheer went up. 'Now I don't want anybody to get hurt, but I don't think you should mellow out either.' Borland cranked out the riff from 'Break Stuff', and Durst appealed to the crowd once more. 'How many people have ever woke up in the morning and just decided you're gonna break some shit?' he asked.[6] As the audience let out another roar, the band started playing their new song. Just as Durst had predicted, the reaction was insane. Fans laid into what was left of the control tower wall with renewed vigour, and the already violent mosh pit turned into a seething mass of arms and legs. More bones were broken, more scalps lacerated by flying bottles. Dozens of kids staggered out of the mosh with blood-soaked T-shirts, head wounds and dislocated shoulders, while others were carried out on stretchers. Another woman was raped, dozens more groped or molested. Durst couldn't see exactly what was going on from the stage; but he could feel the anger coming from the crowd, and he knew it felt good. 'It's time to take all that negative energy,' he said, 'and put it the fuck out!'

Durst thought of himself as an artist and an entertainer, but also as a medium. He sensed that his audience was angry, and that he had a talent for expressing their anger. When he sang about having a shit day and wanting to break stuff, and his fans recognised these feelings in themselves and shouted along, he figured he'd provided them with a form of release; a public service, as Trent Reznor — one of the unwitting godfathers of nu metal — had once put it. But when Reznor had found himself in this situation, he'd baulked at it, as had many other groups of the past decade. For Nirvana, Pearl Jam, Liz Phair, Faith No More, Beck, and even the Smashing Pumpkins, the audience's acceptance of the emotional material they presented on stage was a problem. In fact, the bigger the audience became, and the more enthusiastically they accepted the message, the more of a problem it became. There was something grotesque about having fifty thousand people sing along to a song about one's feelings, something that seemed to degrade both the quality of the song and — more importantly — the dignity of the audience.

Having realised this, most of these artists had attempted to bring the process to a halt, or at least slow it down. When Faith No More's audience demanded rap-metal, the band gave them seventies soul — or simply told them to shut up. When Nirvana's fans wanted to mosh, the band played Lead Belly. When Trent Reznor found himself faced with 10,000 kids at Lollapalooza screaming along with a set of words he'd written at one of the lowest points of his life, he responded by going back into the studio to record an album he hoped they'd find almost unlistenable. Liz Phair was so troubled by the mass acceptance of her innermost thoughts that she almost stopped writing songs. Eventually, she came up with a compromise whereby she would keep playing music, but keep her feelings to herself — a classicist approach that Rivers Cuomo, similarly troubled by the new cult status of *Pinkerton*, had by now also embraced. Beck, having seen 'Loser' become an anthem for a generation, had decided this was perhaps the worst possible thing that could happen to a song, and had since pursued a far more oblique approach to songwriting. Now, Radiohead, having come to the same conclusion, were in the process of dismantling their music beyond all recognition. Like Ben Folds, Thom Yorke had begun to feel that melodies were the cheapest kind of emotional manipulation. But where Folds simply resolved to lay off the screaming and the loud choruses, Yorke had by this point ditched the tune, the singing, the guitar, and the drums, and was about to do the same with the song. All, he felt, would do nothing more than guarantee him a place in musical hell.

The problem was that rock on a mass scale tended, by its very nature, to eradicate the possibility of free thought and free expression. This hadn't been a problem for Freddie Mercury, Paul Stanley or Jon Bon Jovi, all of whom viewed their work as popular entertainment, and saw no major conflict between their music and the political and social order of the day. But alternative rock bands defined themselves and their art against mass culture; their fans treasured it for this reason. This alternative culture could not, therefore, become mass, for the same reason that individuality could not become popular. Cobain envied Freddie, but he could not allow his music to become a rally in favour of failure in the way that Queen had staged rallies in favour of victory. It seemed unfair, both to himself and to his fans, who admired him, after all, because he seemed able to think for himself.

Fred Durst, too, took pride in the fact that he was different. He'd had a long time to get used to the idea. 'I was a fucking outcast, man!' he said of his high school days in Jacksonville, Florida. The source of Durst's trouble was music; his first love was Michael Jackson, followed by hip-hop, a preference that would have earned him few admirers anywhere in America outside of the Bronx in 1981 — when rap was still an underground phenomenon — and none at all in Jacksonville. 'My white friends called me "nigger-lover",' he explained. 'Being from such a hillbilly place, a lot of white kids had a serious problem with me.'[7] Over time, Durst honed his skills as a rapper, which didn't win him any new friends, though it did occasionally get him laid. He also learned, as Courtney Love had, to enjoy feeling as though he was part of a minority, and therefore special. But no sooner had he got used to this state of affairs than disaster struck — in the unlikely form of Rick Rubin. In 1986, Rubin's Def Jam Records released the Beastie Boys' '(You Gotta) Fight for Your Right (To Party)', which went to number seven on the Billboard charts, making it the first rap record to enter the US Top Ten. After that, it seemed like everybody in Jacksonville was into hip-hop, and Fred Durst didn't feel so special anymore. 'I was like, "great, now the rednecks and preps who wanted to beat me up for listening to hip-hop are making a joke out of it".'[8]

Over a decade later, Durst was still pissed about it. Limp Bizkit's first single, 'Counterfeit', expressed the rage and disappointment of a music fan betrayed by the mass acceptance of his subculture, and his disgust at the shallow trend-hoppers who had robbed it of its meaning. 'I wonder what it's like to be a clone,' he rapped, 'doin' nothin' on your own.'[9] This song, for some reason, seemed to appeal to exactly the kind of people Durst spat about in the lyrics, who turned up in droves to Limp Bizkit concerts and yelled along to all the words. 'Ironic?' he said, in 1999. 'Of course it's fucking ironic. I'm like, you're standing there singing my shit, but this song is about people like you who act like they get it, but they don't get it.' 'Counterfeit', it seemed, had gone the way of Nirvana's 'In Bloom' or Pulp's 'Mis-Shapes'. A song which raged against mass conformity and the herd mentality had been accepted by the masses, and thus robbed it of its meaning.

But here Durst parted ways with most other alternative rock bands. Where Nirvana, Pulp, Beck and Radiohead, faced with this same situation, had attempted to disrupt it by complicating their music and challenging their audiences, Durst simply channelled the anger he felt back into his performance while essentially giving his listeners what they had come to expect from him. He could do this because, unlike his predecessors — and some of the people in his own band — he saw no real conflict between art and business, and cared far less about whether the fans got the message than he did about whether or not they got the album. In June 1999, Zev Borow asked the members of Limp Bizkit where they hoped to be in June 2009. 'Making beats,' replied DJ Lethal. 'Probably not in this band,' said Borland. 'At between ten and twenty million units sold,' said Durst.[10]

Borow, like most writers who met Durst around this time, noted his extraordinary aptitude for business — the singer had a knack for schmoozing and deal-making that not only set him dramatically apart from his alt rock contemporaries, but from most major rock artists of the past three decades. His real peers, not coincidentally, were to be found among hip-hop CEOs like Puff Daddy, although he also shared much in common with Paul Stanley of Kiss. Like Stanley, Durst found that his ability to be realistic about the music business, to see his fans as units and his audiences as markets, equipped him to cope with stadium rock in a way that Eddie Vedder, Kurt Cobain and other indie-rock-reared singers could not. Stephen Malkmus had expressed his disdain for the Smashing Pumpkins' stadium tendencies by saying 'they give you what they want, if that's what you want'. For Durst, this was simply business, and business was real, and if the singer had learned nothing else from hip-hop, it was the importance of being real. 'Reality bites,' he sang in 'Counterfeit', 'but that's what life is.'[11] Durst had accepted that his job was to give people what they wanted — the big riffs, the big build-up, the song they all loved but didn't quite get. If this made him pop, so be it. 'Pop means popular,' he reminded Borow, 'which is fine by me.'[12]

Durst's ability to be realistic allowed him to seize and take hold of something that had always lain within alt rock's grasp — the power to lead a mob. Cobain had felt that he owed it to his audience *not* to do this — the revolution he'd mooted in his draft for 'Smells Like Teen Spirit' could only be brought about by a youth constituency whose individual members had learned to think for themselves. Durst, like all good businessmen, believed he was giving the audience what it wanted. Grunge had mobilised a teen army, but had dissipated its energy by re-routing it into totally unrealistic goals, or confusing it with surreal word games. Limp Bizkit's group therapy doubled as market research, and the research showed that the fans were angry with their girlfriends and wanted to break stuff. At Woodstock '99, Limp Bizkit fans were able to realise their goals in reality. Durst, meanwhile, could rest assured that whatever his fans did in his name was beyond his control, since he believed that his job was to provide them with a means to express their rage, not to tell them what to do. 'There are no motherfuckin' rules here,' he said from the stage.[13]

As she watched the fans scramble up the control tower and rip it to shreds, webzine writer Julie Wiskirchen found herself thinking — not for the first time that weekend — of the French Revolution, or at least the version of it she'd seen in *Les Misérables*. 'They were storming the Bastille like Jean Valjean,' she wrote in her Woodstock diary, 'except he did it to gain independence and their act showed their pure, unquestioning allegiance to Fred. The mob rules.'[14] Durst himself certainly seemed to have a sense that he and his fans were making history at Woodstock '99. 'The whole world is watching us,' he reminded them. There could be no doubt about this — like everything else in the nineties, rock festivals only became real if they were on TV. Accordingly, every aspect of Woodstock '99 was filmed: from the stage to the artists' tents to the garbage-strewn fields outside. Even when they weren't being stared down by a camera or interviewed for MTV, the Woodstockers would have been all too aware that the event was being filmed for posterity. Those being carried out of the mosh pit on stretchers would have seen, up in the sky, a plane trailing a banner that read: 'WOODSTOCK '99 CD AND VIDEO, AVAILABLE THIS FALL.'

Party Malfunction

On the afternoon of the second day of Woodstock '99, the festival's film tent offered a screening of Danny Boyle's *Trainspotting*. Julie Wiskirchen had already seen it, but since there were no good bands on at the time, she decided it was a better option than standing outside in the heat — not to mention the smell. 'I remember wanting to retch the first time I saw the Worst Toilet in Scotland scene,' she wrote in her diary. 'This time, that toilet looked pretty good compared to some of the overflowing porta-potties I'd seen that morning.'[1] The festival's promoters appeared to have seriously underestimated the number of toilets required for a three-day event with almost a quarter of a million people camping on-site. There weren't nearly enough, they weren't emptied often enough, and they were all in one place — which, for those who'd missed out on a prime camping spot, meant a long walk in the heat, and a twenty-minute wait when they got there. By the Saturday, many people had decided it wasn't worth the effort, and elected to go behind their tent, or behind someone else's tent — or wherever they happened to be standing. Showers were also a problem; there were only a hundred heads on the whole site, which meant more long queues. To make matters worse, they'd been installed in an area with no proper drainage, on a patch of slightly elevated ground near the main campsite. The water ran straight down the hill over the faeces-strewn ground, and by Saturday night, the tents were awash in rivers of mud and human waste.

These were just the worst of a series of indignities that had confronted festival-goers at Griffiss Air Force Base. The ticket information came with a warning that guests were not to bring their own food or drinks (because the organisers were worried about 'spoilage'). So having spent $150 on their tickets, patrons were obliged to pay another fifteen for a slice of microwaved pizza, five for a beer, and four for a bottle of water. It was almost forty degrees Celsius that weekend, so people bought a lot of drinks, and their money was spent in no time. There were fourteen ATMs on site, but these ran out of cash on Saturday. Many simply stopped drinking, and let dehydration run its course. Tired and exhausted, they found themselves even less inclined to attempt the kilometre-long walk to the toilets or showers which, considering the filthy state of the ground and the site in general, meant that the festival-goers soon resembled the dun-coloured subhumans in the Smashing Pumpkins' 'Bullet with Butterfly Wings' video clip. Tired, hungry, thirsty, dirty and somewhat degraded, the social conventions that usually guided their behaviour soon broke down. This state of affairs suited the rapists and sociopaths in the crowd, who felt they had no reason not to do what they liked with people who appeared to be somewhat less than human.

The next morning, Wiskirchen woke to an ugly sight. 'The field was covered in garbage,' she wrote, 'plastic bottles and pizza boxes everywhere. A river of muck ran down the middle of the field and people had assembled a trash bridge to cross it.' Many people, she noted, had decided to go home — tired, hungry, dirty, and sick of being ripped off, they elected to cut their losses and miss seeing that night's performance by the Red Hot Chili Peppers. But Wiskirchen decided to stick it out, because she'd heard a rumour, which had been since confirmed by the organisers, that there was a 'secret headliner' scheduled to appear after the Chili Peppers. The names being thrown around — Bob Dylan, Guns N' Roses, the Artist Formerly Known as Prince — were tantalising enough to convince her to put up with the heat, the smell, and a fairly lacklustre afternoon of performances by Creed, Jewel and Godsmack.

The Red Hot Chili Peppers appeared on stage at 9pm. John Frusciante — who had rejoined the soul circle following his rock star epiphany of 1998 — sported very long hair and a beard, Kiedis wore a silver wig and a school uniform, while Flea had dyed his hair turquoise for the occasion, but otherwise wore nothing but his bass.

As the band played 'Under the Bridge', festival staff passed candles out into the crowd. By the end of the song, these had been used to light some of the garbage piles, and soon the field was scattered with bonfires. Fragments of the 'Peace Wall' — the perimeter fence around the site — were torn down and used as kindling, and a corner of the stage also started burning. Kiedis looked out into the crowd and saw naked, mud-covered people dancing around bonfires while others beat on upturned bins. 'It looks like *Apocalypse Now* out there,' he said.[2] The band closed with a cover of Jimi Hendrix's 'Fire', which, by a strange coincidence, they'd been asked to perform by festival organisers — as way of leading into a 'video tribute' to Hendrix, which ended with a synchronised laser display.

After that, nothing happened. No Axl Rose, no Artist Formerly Known As, no Dylan or Doors or any of the other legends of rock whose names had been bandied about as potential secret headliners. Just a hundred thousand exhausted, dehydrated people standing in a smouldering, rubbish-strewn field, staring at a blank screen and an empty stage. In what seemed like no time at all, the final remnants of the Peace Wall were broken off and fed into the bonfires, as was much of the main stage. A mob capsized the sound tower, while others attacked the merch and food stands, looting T-shirts and CDs and freely distributing drinks and pizza among the crowd. More fires were lit, trailers exploded, and the on-site MTV crew fled the scene, fearing for their lives.

On Monday morning, TV news crews arrived at Griffiss Air Base and interviewed some of the vendors and stallholders about what had happened the night before. 'This is a war zone,' said a thirty-eight-year-old man named Michael Sozek. 'You didn't get this with the old Woodstock crowd. This new rock and roll is all about a bunch of butt-heads.' A younger man with a shaved head and a pierced eyebrow told of how he'd tried to fend off looters with a piece of broken pipe. 'It really bothered me,' he said, 'because this is supposed to be about peace, and it was destruction for no reason.'[3] Festival promoter John Scher told the *Washington Post* that he was 'bummed big time. I don't know if we'll ever know why these kids did this.'[4] But even those who blamed the kids felt that Scher was at least partly at fault. Sozek said he thought the promoter had been 'too greedy'. Another vendor, Bill Hemsley, said he thought the violence was a case of 'haves versus have nots. They were trapped in here. When they ran out of money, they took what they wanted.'[5] Tom Morgan, of the festival security consultancy Crowdsafe, had no doubt that Scher and the festival board were entirely to blame. 'It's the organiser's responsibility to protect people,' he insisted. 'You cannot blame the victims for an environment they can't control.'[6]

In an article published in the *New York Times*, Rage Against the Machine's Tom Morello took the media to task for what he described as 'the frenzied demonisation of youth' in the wake of Woodstock '99, insisting that the real problems with the festival had nothing to do with young people and their angry music — which after all had not resulted in a bloodbath at Ozzfest or the Family Values tour — but with a badly organised event.[7] But he went on to strike a more hopeful note, suggesting that the kids who rioted at Woodstock '99 had simply got fed up with being exploited, and had effectively taken the festival over. This, as he pointed out, was far closer to the real 'spirit of Woodstock' than the popular cliché — which for most people simply meant 'peace and love' and kids sitting in the dirt with flowers in their hair. Many of the festival-goers interviewed in the early hours of Monday morning had seen the riot in similar terms. One girl said the violence was 'a way of getting back at them. They took advantage of us.'[8]

It wasn't hard to see why this idea would appeal to Morello — festival capitalism breeding the forces of its own destruction. But it seemed to some a little too hopeful; the violence at Woodstock spoke more of desperation than revolution. If there was a collective spirit at work, it was not so much that of Paris '68 or Woodstock '69 as the 'Woodstock for the eighties' envisaged by J. D. in *Heathers* — a final, self-destructive act as an 'ultimate protest against a society that degrades us. Fuck you all!'[9] There was also, as Anthony Kiedis noted when he looked out into the crowd, something apocalyptic about it — as though the kids, having realised the end was coming, had simply decided that all bets were off and anything goes. In any case, it was hard to ascribe any lofty goals to the actions of people who had simply been pushed until they snapped. And yet this, as Morello knew, was how revolutions got started. Not with songwriters or intellectuals or ideologues, but with masses of angry, frustrated people burning trash and looting stores.

At Woodstock '99, Perry Farrell — who had curated the festival's Rave Hangar — witnessed the realisation of something he'd hoped to see at the very first Lollapalooza in 1991. At the end of that show, he'd stood on the edge of the stage and demanded a riot. Nothing had happened because, as he told David Fricke, the kids were 'too happy with life'. They were being entertained, and the entertainment was good. They had rock and roll and beer and drugs and a ride home. What incentive could they possibly have to take up arms against their oppressors when they didn't feel oppressed? The following year saw the beginnings of Lollapalooza's commercial success and the end of its revolutionary goals. It was the year that Farrell taught corporations that there was a serious market for youth culture. 'That's the bad news,' he said. Woodstock '94 had been an ironic, second-hand experience for exactly this reason; the 'us versus them' feeling which had made the 1969 festival meaningful was gone, because there seemed to be no adversary, nothing to complain about. People paid to see good bands, the good bands appeared. Everybody had a good time, but left feeling as though nothing had really happened. Woodstock '99 was different, because it was a bad festival. In 1991 and 1994, the kids had been too happy with life to cause trouble. In 1999, they were made just unhappy enough to want to tear the place apart.

'I don't think it was an anti-Woodstock statement,' said Michael Lang, one of the organisers of the original festival. 'I think it was an anti-establishment statement.'[10] Lang's words pointed to some of the challenges involved in interpreting and understanding Woodstock '99, and demonstrated how much had changed since he organised the first 'Aquarian Exposition' on Max Yasgur's farm thirty years earlier. In those days, it had all seemed a lot simpler. Taking off your clothes, smoking a joint, listening to Jefferson Airplane — these things could still be seen as 'anti-establishment' to a generation that had grown up in a conservative post-war climate. Rock and roll, drugs and festivals represented freedom; parents, the government and the draft represented the enemy. But Woodstock '69 represented the end of this idea, rather than its realisation. The festival itself was, as Simon Frith has pointed out, one of the most comprehensive and ambitious attempts to exploit the new youth culture for profit to date; its success paved the way for the institutionalisation of rock in the 1970s and 1980s. By the time the children of the Woodstock Generation came of age in the 1990s, the situation was quite different. When older rock journalists spoke of Nirvana and Pearl Jam taking on 'the establishment', one had the sense they were using an old word to describe a new problem, just as Lang was when he offered his thoughts on Woodstock '99. What was 'the establishment' at the end of the 1990s? It seemed far less likely that it was the police or Bill Clinton than that it was MTV, David Geffen, John Scher, Limp Bizkit or rock and roll itself. In 1999, an anti-Woodstock statement *was* an anti-establishment statement.

In the sixties, the counterculture had often used the term 'the machine' when it wanted to describe the enemy. This slightly paranoid piece of terminology, borrowed from the Beats, served as a shorthand for the forces of oppression in general, but also referred more specifically to the insidious tie-up between government and industry that kept America at war in Vietnam. Rage Against the Machine retained both the word and its significance, and also inherited many of the problems associated with it. The problem with the machine was its size and complexity, and the extent to which people had come to rely on it, to think of it as necessary to the point where it seemed natural. Now that the enemy was so diffuse, so widespread, and so inextricably tied up in everyday life, the challenge for youth was to find a purchase, something specific to attack, and something to attack it with that could not simply be used — as grunge had — to further exploit them. The members of Rage Against the Machine were never more aware of how difficult this could be than they were at events like Woodstock '99, where they performed immediately after Limp Bizkit. The energy the two bands stirred up was quite similar — which was no coincidence. Limp Bizkit, like Korn, took their musical template directly from Rage. But where Durst gave his fans easy targets to hit, Rage set themselves the more difficult task of connecting the crowd's energy to action that could not be resolved at the show; that could only be realised in the wider world.

'We try to build a bridge between people who get into our music and lyrics, and ways they can get their hands dirty and act,' said Tom Morello in November 1999.[11] Morello saw no problem with playing 'parking-lot rock' as long as the riot was not confined to the parking lot. The key was to make something happen. But he also made it clear that he didn't see the fans as 'empty glasses' waiting to be filled with ideas; he sought to provoke them to think, rather than telling them what to do.[12] Morello believed that, by doing exactly this, Rage had already created a culture of free thought within its fan community. 'Rage Against the Machine fans are intelligent, pissed off, and they've got their own ideas about things,' he said. 'We're constantly surprised by what our fans do on their own — whether it's combating the use of sweatshops or showing solidarity with the Zapatistas or supporting [Native American activist] Leonard Peltier here in the States.' There was nothing artificial about this process — Zack de la Rocha believed that the fury expressed by fans at a Korn or Limp Bizkit show was symptomatic of wider problems in the world, the very same ones he wrote about in his lyrics. 'All this alienation has roots,' he said. 'It's not just TV or boredom or bad parents.'[13] Rage's task was to connect the dots — to show that Jonathan Davis's otherwise inexplicable failure to be satisfied by his new silver Adidas trackpants, could be traced, via an invisible thread, to a sweatshop in Manila, and on from there, via a labyrinth of buyouts and mergers, to a boardroom in Manhattan. From this point of view, it became clear why Morello saw fans chasing MTV out of a festival as encouraging. If they weren't quite attacking the source of the problem, they were at least getting closer.

2000

War Music

Human civilisation defied the predictions of doomsday cults and techno-paranoia merchants by stubbornly continuing to exist after the millennium. Planes did not fall out of the sky; nuclear missiles did not spontaneously launch themselves. On 1 January 2000, people woke up to find the world much as they had left it on New Year's Eve 1999. The twentieth century, on the other hand, was gone for good. Sonic Youth sent it off with a double album released on their own SYR label, featuring the band playing modernist avant-garde scores by John Cage, Christian Wolff, Steve Reich, Pauline Oliveros and Yoko Ono. The 1990s also obediently rolled over and died, and this also did not pass without comment from Sonic Youth. 'Nevermind (What Was It Anyway)', was a sleepy-eyed elegy for the alternative nation and its crossover dreams from a band who'd seen it all. In 1985, underground music was underground. In 1990, small flowers began to crack concrete. By the end of 1991, alternative bands had broken through to the surface, and were on their way to the stars. Now, in 2000, Kim Gordon wondered what had been achieved by it all. 'Boys go to Jupiter to get more stupider,' she rapped. 'Girls go to Mars, become rock stars.'[1]

'When the youth culture feeding-frenzy began in the early nineties,' wrote Naomi Klein in January 2000, 'few of us asked — at least not right away — why it was that these scenes were proving so packageable, so unthreatening — and so profitable. Many of us had been certain that we were doing something subversive and rebellious, but ... what was it again?'[2] Lest they allow themselves to be fooled again, Klein offered her readers a reliable litmus test, which would determine 'whether a movement genuinely challenges the structure of economic and political power'. 'One need only measure how affected it is by goings-on in the fashion and advertising industries,' she said. 'If … it continues as if nothing had happened, it's a good bet it's a real movement.'[3] In their 1998 hit, 'Walking on the Sun', Smash Mouth warned that the youth revolt of the 1990s was disappearing fast because 'fashion is smashin' the true meaning of it'.[4] Klein raised the possibility that the ska punks ought to have placed their faith in something less easily smashed.

As such, the jury was still out, in 2000, on the worldwide anti-globalisation movement with which bands like Primal Scream, Radiohead and Rage Against the Machine had aligned themselves. The fashion and advertising industries had already picked up on youth culture's militant mood — a scan of the malls and mosh pits at the dawn of the millennium suggested a rag-tag anti-capitalist army in training for a coming guerrilla war, T-shirts with *detourned* corporate logos hung over low-slung camouflage cargo pants, aerodynamic goggles perched on shaved domes. To some extent, this was just camping-as-usual. After all, camouflage — as Warhol demonstrated in 1986 — was just another pattern, like soup cans or dollar bills or the face of Chairman Mao.

But the posing also gave notice of real intent and, at this stage, the movement itself showed no signs of being compromised by the recuperation of its imagery. There was, as Klein revealed in her book *No Logo*, a new spirit of revolt and unrest at large in youth culture. Online forums and communities had helped speed the flow of alternative information, and allowed it to easily bypass the official channels. As a result, young people in America had moved on from the identity politics and therapy culture of the early nineties, and begun to identify the real roots of their feelings of alienation and disenfranchisement. They had followed the thread from the sweater they bought at Gap, past the closed-down factory out of town, all the way to the death-trap warehouse in Singapore where it had been stitched together. The anti-sweatshop movement drew more recruits every day — its adherents organised large-scale boycotts of brands who exploited cheap third-world labour, while adbusters and culture-jammers defaced their billboards and hacked their ads. Street artists, T-shirt designers and online 'cyberterrorists' used the power of brand recognition, carefully fostered by the new global corporations, against the brands themselves. Klein put this new mood down to a populace pushed too far — as the corporate takeover of public life became ever more invasive and pervasive, increasingly extreme methods had become necessary to break its stranglehold. 'It's this coalition of disparate interest groups who are all pissed off because they've been disenfranchised by politicians, who are only listening to corporate lobby groups,' said Radiohead's Thom Yorke, who eagerly devoured Klein's book in the weeks following its release. 'It's not based on the old left/right politics … it's a new form of dissent.'[5]

In *No Logo*, Klein scuppered the grungestalgia already being peddled by those end-of-decade lists, insisting that the Seattle scene had, in the end, produced nothing but money, and a warning to those who go chasing it. 'Seattle, long-dead and forgotten as anything but a derivative fad, now serves as a cautionary tale about why so little opposition to the theft of cultural space took place in the early to mid nineties.'[6] A story published in *Spin* in March 2000 revealed a very different Seattle scene emerging from the rubble of the old one. Kurt Cobain had fantasised in his journal about a 'violent uprising of your children, littering the floors of Wall Street with revolutionary debris'.[7] Now, six years after his death, something like this seemed to be taking place. Journalist RJ Smith reported on an anarchist disruption of the World Trade Organisation meeting in Seattle six months earlier with the purpose of, as one participant put it, '[making] a break with the whole dying mess'. According to Smith, the organisers saw 'only the most total of upheavals as likely to make much difference', since 'all attempts at reform that everybody that's older than them has tried has only led to a world that's more harsh, more exploited'. On the day of the summit meeting, the black-hooded activists made their way through Seattle's retail hub, smashing store windows and destroying millions of dollars' worth of property. 'Whose streets?' they chanted. 'Our streets!' One by one, they trashed the brand kings — Nike, McDonald's and Planet Hollywood — each target carefully chosen for its crimes against the environment, its incursions into public space, or its ruthless exploitation of the third world. 'Stop it, goddammit,' begged a bystander. 'Why are you doing this?' 'We're doing this for everybody, OK?' replied one of the activists. The Seattleite might miss his frappuccino or his Air Jordans for a little while, but in the end he'd come to see that these — like all the other commodities in his life, had simply enslaved him, and that he could only realise his potential by destroying them.[8]

'You are not your grande latte,' said Brad Pitt, lending his vocals to the Dust Brothers' 1999 single 'This is Your Life', 'You are not the car you drive.'[9] The song had been recorded for the soundtrack to David Fincher's *Fight Club*, in which Pitt — as anarchist heartthrob Tyler Durden — leads a city full of service-industry drones, first in an existential revolt against consumerism, and then in a terrorist plot to destroy the ruling class. The film was another sign of Klein's 'Bad Mood Rising', and another indicator of how much had changed since 1991. In that year's *Generation X*, Douglas Coupland described his narrator, Andy, discovering some kind of foamy gunk in his dogs' mouths. He eventually realises it's human fat, sucked out of the thighs of ageing yuppies into plastic bags, and dumped in the bins behind the clinic down the road, where his dogs had simply torn the bags open and helped themselves. Andy allows himself a rueful smile as he cleans the stuff out of their snouts. 'This world,' he says to himself, 'I tell you.'[10] In *Fight Club*, Tyler takes a more proactive approach. He steals the yuppie lipo-fat himself, takes it back to his squat, and renders it down into luxury handmade soaps, which he then sells back to those same yuppies for a small fortune. He uses the cash to fund his anarchist plot, and uses the soap's chemical by-products to build bombs. The film ends with Edward Norton and Helena Bonham Carter holding hands and watching the results of Tyler's handiwork — one by one, the charges go off, one by one, the city's high-rise buildings explode and topple to the ground. As the Pixies' 'Where Is My Mind' plays on the soundtrack, Norton offers his girlfriend a faint apology. 'You met me at a very strange time in my life,' he says.[11]

Entertain Us

Rob Gordon, the disgruntled record store owner played by John Cusack in the 2000 film *High Fidelity*, is stickering new arrivals while listening to the new Belle and Sebastian album. Suddenly this quiet moment is interrupted by the arrival of Barry — and his Monday Morning Mixtape, which leads off with Katrina and the Waves' impossibly perky new wave hit 'Walking on Sunshine'. Barry — played with great gusto by comedian Jack Black (who'd been seen mugging his way through the video for Beck's 'Sexx Laws') — boogies up and down the record aisles, blissfully unaware of just how badly he's misjudged his boss's mood — until Rob hurls himself over the counter and snaps the Monday Morning Mixtape off in mid-flow. Barry makes no secret of his disgust. 'Go ahead,' he says with a dismissive wave, 'put on some more Old Sad Bastard Music, see if I care.' 'I don't wanna listen to Old Sad Bastard Music, Barry,' says Rob, as if to a small child. 'I just want something I can *ignore*.'[1]

Rob, like his younger employees, is a music lover. But where Dick and Barry's love for music is characterised by a certain irrational zeal, Rob's is tempered by his responsibilities. Dick can waste all his time obsessing over the latest import indie sensation, and Barry can alienate the store's customers with his high-minded principles, because they're both young, irresponsible and unattached. Rob, on the other hand, has a long-term relationship to maintain and a business to run. He still takes music very seriously. But when his girlfriend is giving him a hard time at home and the daily grind of running the store is getting him down, he doesn't want to be challenged by exciting new sounds — to be made to think or argue or discuss or dance. He just wants something he can put on in the background while he slaps stickers on CDs. In this respect at least, Rob bears a strong resemblance to his creator, Nick Hornby, the UK music journalist and author who wrote the novel from which *High Fidelity* was adapted. One could imagine that Rob would have about as much time for Radiohead's fourth album, *Kid A*, as Hornby did when he reviewed it, six months after the film's release. '*Kid A* demands the patience of the devoted,' wrote Hornby. 'Both patience and devotion become scarcer commodities once you start picking up a pay cheque.'[2]

No one would have described *Kid A* as an easy listen. The opening track, 'Everything in Its Right Place', might have seemed, at first, as though it could serve as music to sticker CDs to, with its warm electric keyboard motif and steady pulsing beat. But 'Everything' turned out to be an intro for a song that never arrived. Johnny Greenwood played not one note on his guitar, Phil Selway left his drumsticks on the stool and let a mechanised kickdrum keep the beat. Thom Yorke sang, but his singing went nowhere, while computers smashed and scrambled his words, spitting them back out in unintelligible vowel-clusters. By the second track, 'Kid A', these random word-generators appeared to have replaced Yorke entirely — the lead vocal was taken by a droning droid singing about 'heads on sticks' and 'shadows at the end of my bed'.[3] The band, meanwhile, was still missing in action. Some relief was at hand on 'The National Anthem', which opened with a fuzz-bass riff and hip-hop drum pattern that might not have been out of place on *OK Computer*. But if this slight return to business as usual had gotten the customers' heads nodding, the atonal jazz freak-out that followed would have cleared the store in a flash. This pattern was repeated throughout the rest of the record — the band seemed to be back together again on the Smiths-like 'How to Disappear Completely', only to disappear completely on 'Treefingers', which had no singing, no guitar , no drums, no bass and only the barest scrap of a melody. 'Optimistic' sounded like Radiohead, 'Idioteque' sounded like Thom Yorke crooning softly to himself next to the bass bin at a rave.

To say that Radiohead's fans (among whom Hornby counted himself) were not expecting this was not to suggest that they were hoping to hear more of the same. 'Whatever Radiohead do next,' wrote Nick Carr in his quickie biography of the group, 'expect the unexpected. Radiohead will continue to defy categorization.'[4] Admirers like Carr would not have wished to hear a retread of *OK Computer* when they popped *Kid A* into the CD player, nor would they have appreciated it if they had. Consistency was for AOR grunge bands like Matchbox 20, ('We're not pushing the boundaries,' said the band's singer Rob Thomas in July 2000, 'we're taking up some space there in the middle. I want to do that consistently)',[5] or for Limp Bizkit — a band the Deftones' Chino Moreno guessed would be all but forgotten in five years time because they seemed unwilling or unable to change their sound. Radiohead was a progressive band for progressive people, their fans admired them for their creativity and their willingness to reinvent themselves. For producer Steve Lillywhite, it was exactly this ability to innovate that made Radiohead a great band, and legitimised their inclusion in rock's hall of fame. In 1998, Lilywhite had been making an album with festival-circuit favourites, the Dave Matthews Band. 'We tried to be a bit like Radiohead, who we love to death,' he explained, 'the way they change things with every album. Or the Beatles. Great bands change things every time.'[6] This would not have been news to Thom Yorke, who read Ian MacDonald's *Revolution in the Head* — an eye-opening account of the Beatles' recording sessions — every night while working on *Kid A*.[7]

But with *Kid A*, some felt, Radiohead had gone a bit too far. 'The bad news,' wrote the *NME*'s Steven Wells, 'is that the new Radiohead album has been ruthlessly purged of anything that might even vaguely resemble a good pop song.'[8] Critics like Wells complained that the band had virtually innovated itself out of existence, by tampering with the three things that made great bands great: the songs, the guitar playing and the singing. In truth, Radiohead hadn't abandoned any of these completely — most of the tracks on *Kid A* had a melody and a vocal, and clocked in at between three and a half and four minutes, and at least half of them featured Jonny Greenwood playing guitar. As Yorke pointed out, if Radiohead had really wanted to alienate their audience with unlistenable noise, they would have done a much better job of it. Nevertheless, *Kid A* had fucked with the formula just enough to annoy people, and this gave Yorke no small amount of pleasure.

'We're extremely chuffed,' he told Simon Reynolds, 'because two days ago Jonny did an interview with a Brazilian newspaper, and the first question was "What do you think of Noel and Liam from Oasis saying *Kid A* was a monumental piece of cowardice?" I don't even know what that means, but who cares, we were like, "YES! We've finally pissed them off!"'[9]

The Gallaghers' one-line review was echoed by Nick Hornby's longer one in *The New Yorker*, which described *Kid A* as 'a failure of courage'.[10] This was a piece of Britpop rhetoric that required some unpacking. In the Oasis/Hornby universe, experimental music was a sheltered workshop for fragile aesthetes, who would never realise their potential because they were too frightened of the real world (i. e. the marketplace) to stick their necks out and write a hit. This argument was first heard at the start of the decade coming out of the mouths of crossover stars like the Stone Roses and Bobby Gillespie (which was where Noel Gallagher had picked it up). It had made some sense at the time, when the UK indie scene had become dangerously parochial and small-minded. And it had served as a useful way to puncture the pious bubble of grunge two years later. But in the sorry aftermath of Britpop, it was less convincing. Indeed, it was exactly this kind of thinking, the 'Make It Big At All Costs ethos', as Simon Reynolds put it, that had sunk British rock into its current quagmire. The conflation of artistic success with popular acclaim fostered by Suede, Pulp, Blur and Oasis had brought forth the idea that experimentation was a form of elitism. Long after Britpop itself had expired, English rock bands dutifully stayed away from sonic innovation — lest they be accused of snobbery — and stuck with the classics, the Beatles and the Stones, strings and horns, verse and chorus. In this context, for Radiohead to release an album of clicks, drones, cut-up vocals and avant-classical arrangements could be seen as quite brave. Little wonder then, that Thom Yorke was bemused by the Gallagher brothers' accusations of cowardice, or that he took some measure of pride in having provoked them.

But while Noel and Liam pilloried Radiohead for opting out of success, other critics accused the band of a much more serious dereliction of duty. 'You fucking snob,' wrote Steven Wells in his *NME* review. 'Why not just do your job properly? You know the score.

Hook, verse, chorus, verse …'[11] Wells, like Hornby, had no problem with Radiohead messing about in the studio and kicking against the pricks, as long as they gave him something to nod his head to at the end of a long hard day. What else could they do? Bands might imagine that they could use music to change everyday life, but as the *NME*'s Andrew Collins argued in 'Are Radiohead Dirty Great Hypocrites?' this was nothing more than a conceit. 'Rock and roll is the wrong place to look for acts of true subversion,' he wrote.[12] Meanwhile, in the real world, people had to get on with their lives and their jobs, and these real people were under no such illusions about what music really was for — not to destroy the system, but to ease our way through it. This, Wells insisted, was the least that could be expected of songwriters — to give people a catchy tune to play in the background while they cooked dinner or did their shopping or stuck price tags on CDs. And when the world turned chilly, the band would still be there, to 'sing a song / a song to keep us warm', as Thom Yorke did on *OK Computer*. But it was precisely this that Yorke had neglected to do this time around. 'Thom, listen up man!' wrote Wells, 'Pop songs are good! They make the world go round, they put a spring in your step and they give the grocer's boy something to whistle.'[13]

History does not record whether or not Thom Yorke was paying attention when Wells delivered his advice. But it's not hard to imagine what he might have made of it if he had. He would no doubt have agreed that pop songs made the world go around. He'd seen the way that the success of 'Creep' in 1994 had placed him and his band at 'the sharp end of the sexy sassy MTV eye-candy lifestyle thing they're trying to sell to the rest of the world, make them aspire to'.[14] As the song sold, it helped to sell the lifestyle, and the lifestyle helped to sell all kinds of things — sneakers, cars, hair dye, soft drinks and health insurance. He would have seen, too, the way that other alternative bands and their record companies had begun to streamline this process by licensing pop songs for 'secondary uses' — The Verve's 'Bitter Sweet Symphony' sold Nikes, Blur's 'Song 2' sold Fox Sports, Harvey Danger's 'Flagpole Sitta' sold the high school horror movie *Disturbing Behavior*, and Republica's 'Ready to Go' sold Mitsubishi hatchbacks. These things being fairly expensive, the people who bought them worked hard to be able to afford them. They delivered groceries, worked in call centres, sold used CDs, pulled lattes at Starbucks, and picked up their pay cheques — and when they trudged up the road to the Tube station at 7am on a Monday, they would need a little something to put a spring in their step. Here, music would come to their rescue, as it would later in the evening, when they realised that despite all their hard work and conscientious shopping, the sexy sassy lifestyle remained out of reach. In such moments, they might need to hear a song that told them it was OK to feel like a loser, like a creep, like a weirdo, like they didn't belong. When they felt down, songs like these could lift them up; when they felt cold, songs like these could keep them warm. When the weekly round of work, sleep and leisure became meaningless to the point of being absurd, a great song could make it all seem — as the Verve did in 1998 — like a bittersweet symphony. And as long as songwriters did their jobs, there would always be songs, songs that — at their best — served the amazing dual purpose of advertising dreams while providing consolation for their disappearance. In this way, pop songs made the world go around.

But while Yorke would no doubt have seen that this was true, he would not have agreed that it was good. Yorke, the road worrier, the paranoid android, could not greet the news that his songs helped MTV sell sneakers and grocer's boys deliver groceries without wondering where exactly the sneakers and the groceries had come from. Reading Naomi Klein's *No Logo* had given him some idea, his subsequent involvement in the anti-globalisation movement and the campaign to drop third world debt had filled in the blanks. And then of course, there was the question that had bothered Yorke since 1996 — having been stitched in sweatshops, pimped on MTV, sold, bought, delivered, consumed and thrown away, where does all this stuff *go*? In Don DeLillo's 1998 novel, *Underworld*, waste disposal specialist Brian Glassic stands gazing at the Fresh Kills Landfill on Staten Island, 'three thousand acres of mountained garbage, contoured and road-graded, with bulldozers pushing waves of refuse onto the active face'. In the distance, Glassic sees the twin towers of the World Trade Center, and he knows this is no coincidence. 'All the great works of transport, trade and linkage were directed in the end toward this culminating structure … where all the sodden second thoughts came runnelling out, the things you wanted ardently and then did not.'[15] To say that pop songs helped the world go around was another way of saying that pop songs helped this stinking pile grow bigger by the day. 'Never trust a melody, because melodies sell people things they don't need.' This, according to *Spin*'s Charles Aaron, was the lesson Kurt Cobain learned from punk.[16] Whether Thom Yorke inherited this philosophy — along with the stripy shirt and the blond mop top — from Cobain in 1992, or figured it out at some later point on his own, there could be no doubt that he had learned it by 1999. 'All melody,' he said, 'was pure embarrassment.'[17] On *OK Computer*, he and the band had worked hard to couch his musings on 'global hideousness' in uplifting melodies. But while touring the album the following year, he'd come to realise that the latter had a way of cancelling out the former. *OK Computer* was a manifesto for the disgusted, which was all too easily co-opted to sell the thing it raged against; 'Paranoid Android' was a song that said that everything was wrong with the world, but its catchy riff and timely solo made you feel, by the end, that everything was going to be alright. The un-whistle-ability of *Kid A* was the result of a concerted effort on the band's part to find something that would not let the listener off the hook quite so easily. 'The whole point of *Kid A*,' wrote David Fricke in *Rolling Stone*, 'is that there are no sure things, in pop or anything else.'[18] In this, the band's refusal to put guitar solos, choruses and catchy refrains in the places where people expected to find them was crucial. 'The refrain creates a territory which can be inhabited by the listener,' wrote Greg Hainge, 'the punctual structures of most pop songs … follow this rule to the letter, and can thus shelter the listener from the terrifying sense of alienation that the chaos of the modern world and global politics can instil in individuals *even when* this very chaos, alienation and dysfunction forms the thematic content of the songs.'[19] If Radiohead were going to make music about alienation, they had to make sure that alienation was built into the structure of the music rather than merely described in words. The repeated insistence, from the album's critics, that *Kid A* lacked warmth suggested they'd been successful. 'If you set out making music or sounds to alienate people then that can express as much as drawing them in,' explained Yorke.

'Extreme sounds go with extreme emotions, or do we not have those? Am I simply in the business of creating wallpaper to emptiness?'[20]

Extreme sounds for extreme emotions was not, in itself, a new idea in the nineties. This, after all, was what Kurt Cobain had set out to do with *In Utero*, Trent Reznor with *Broken*, Billy Corgan with *Mellon Collie*, Eddie Vedder with *Vitalogy*. All had responded to the commodification of their music, and of alternative music in general, by trying to create something non-recuperable, something that denied the pop marketplace the comforting assurances it had been expecting. All trusted that, in doing so, they could rely on one thing as a marker and a guarantee of their authenticity — their personality, as represented by their singing voice. Even after their personalities became commodities, they clung steadfastly to the idea that they could survive this process by being, in Fiona Apple's memorable phrase, 'as purely me as I can be[21]'. But in doing so, they vastly underestimated the mass media's appetite for self-hood. Every time the entertainment industry co-opted some aspect of their appearance or sound, they reaffirmed their self-hood by reaching for some deeper, truer, more honest revelation. When this was in turn transformed into spectacle ('The Real Eddie Vedder!'), they dug deeper, and so on, until there was no longer 'any more room to be real', as Corgan put it in 1995. These singers had laboured under the false assumption that there was something in their personalities that was, by nature, dangerous or threatening to the entertainment industry. In fact, the opposite was true. The human face, and the voice that comes out of it, was the most seductive 'refrain' of all. Whatever horrors the artist threw at his audience's feet, they could take solace in the fact that there was, at the centre of it all, a warm, honest human being with a soulful voice and piercing blue eyes. Selling this to a generation burned out on artifice and irony was like selling water in the desert.

Thom Yorke had spent a great deal of time singing songs about his feelings over the past decade, and, like his alt-rock counterparts in America, had experienced the alienating effects of having those songs reproduced for, and consumed by, millions of people. 'It was someone else's property,' he said. 'I was never sure who exactly, so I had no-one (or everyone) to blame.' As a result, Yorke soon found that the sound of his own voice, having been bought and sold many times over, was no longer available to him. 'It did my head in that whatever I did with my voice, it had that particular set of associations. And there were lots of similar bands coming out at the time, and that made it even worse.'[22] While Radiohead had been biding their time, other groups had emerged to fill the gap in the market. Listeners who wanted more of the histrionic vocals and wild lead playing heard on songs like 'Paranoid Android' and 'My Iron Lung' could content themselves with Devon-based prog rock kings, Muse, who recorded their 2000 album *Showbiz* with *The Bends* producer John Leckie. Meanwhile, those still waiting for Thom Yorke to write another 'Fake Plastic Trees' could make do with Travis, or with Coldplay's *Parachutes*, which contained at least four of the things. This was good news for record companies and radio programmers, but bad news for Thom Yorke, who now found that when he opened his mouth to sing, he sounded more like Muse's Matt Bellamy trying to sound like Thom Yorke than Thom Yorke. 'I couldn't stand the sound of me even more,' he said.

This was the same problem Eddie Vedder had been faced with in 1994, when he caught Scott Weiland stealing his act, and was still dealing with in 2000, when Creed's Scott Stapp was making a small fortune with a singing voice that sounded uncannily like Vedder's. MTV's claymation comedy segment, *Celebrity Deathmatch*, pitted the two grunge crooners against each other. 'It's my voice!' growled Vedder. 'But it's my voice too!' wailed Stapp. In the end, Vedder settled the matter by sticking his arm down Stapp's throat and yanking out his vocal cords.[23] Meanwhile, back in the real world, the Yorke vs Bellamy grudge match was settled far more amicably when Yorke simply walked away and let Bellamy keep it. By the end of 1999, Thom Yorke was no longer interested in singing like Thom Yorke, and not even sure if he wanted to sing at all. When it came time to record *Kid A*, he drastically rethought the role that his voice played in Radiohead's music. By doing this, he found a number of escape routes from the more standard forms of rock emoting he'd employed on *OK Computer*, which he felt had since become a cliché, but also managed to call time on the commodification of his personality, the audience's constant need to be reassured by the presence of a 'real' Thom Yorke, and the industry's eagerness to provide them with one. 'Most interviews you do,' Yorke explained, 'there's this constant subtext which is "Is this you?" By using other voices, I guess it was a way of saying obviously, it isn't me.' And what if it was? Yorke saw the expression of personality — in rock and elsewhere — as vastly overrated. 'I can't stand endless self-revelation,' he admitted. 'Honesty is kind of a bullshit quality, really.'[24]

'This is the real me, ladies,' sang Beck on 'Broken Train', 'you won't find a shelter here.'[25] *Midnite Vultures* was, in many ways, Beck's own *Kid A* — the music's synthetic textures and wild juxtapositions worked against easy identification, while Beck's pop art lyrics ('Bed and Breakfast and away weekends / *Sports Illustrated* Moms'[26]), heavy use of vocal effects (like the vocoder on 'Get Real Paid') and pastiche impersonations of other singers (Snoop Dogg on 'Hollywood Freaks'; Prince on 'Debra') made it almost impossible. But unlike Radiohead, Beck had made a party album, because while he liked the idea of making alienating music in principle, ('that John Cage thing', as he put it), in practice, he found pop impossible to resist.[27] 'You'd need to surrender all earthly pleasures and weaknesses,' he said. 'How can you not be seduced by an AC/DC guitar riff? Or a fat beat from a gap band song? These are musical hamburgers. These are pleasures we can't deny ourselves.'[28]

Self-denial was one of the things Radiohead were accused of following the release of *Kid A* (almost as often as they were said to be self-indulgent). Hornby described them as 'a band that has come to hate itself'.[29] Certainly, in rock's prevailing fin de siècle/fin de globe mood, the austerity and minimalism of *Kid A* could seem like a form of self-flagellation. Even as Thom Yorke was trying to disappear completely, Weezer's Rivers Cuomo was rediscovering the joys of making a spectacle of himself. After the Vans Warped tour of Summer 2000, Cuomo abandoned the 'alternative tradition, where you're not supposed to shred too much on the guitar', and embraced the trappings of party metal — pink Ibanez axes, stadium shows, 'woah-oh' choruses — with all the relish of a born-again carnivore tucking into his first hamburger in ten years.

Beck's fast-food metaphor was very much to the point. The hamburger was the ultimate symbol of mass-produced fun in the post-war world. As such, it became an ambassador for consumer ideology, and a key weapon in what Bill Hicks described as 'the Americanisation of the world'.[30] Hicks's onetime friend Denis Leary had his archetypal American asshole guzzling burgers while his convertible guzzled gas, throwing the Styrofoam containers out the window, secure in the knowledge that no one could stop him, 'because we got the bomb'.[31] But this routine was two years old by the time it became a hit, and somewhat out of date. By 1993, the asshole no longer needed the bomb, because the evil empire was gone — its citizens had come around to the asshole's way of thinking, not because they'd been threatened with bombs, but because they'd been promised burgers. 'Sweet dreams are coming true,' went the new McDonald's ads, 'and there's no difference between me and you.' In 1995, Blur cheekily celebrated this new state of affairs with a logo for their song 'Globe Alone', the words formed out of beef in a cartoon bun.[32] Who, in this new world united under golden arches, would be churlish enough to worry about where the Styrofoam containers went, or who really paid for all that cheap meat? Even if you knew — if you'd spent some time in the underground, been to those meetings, read the alternative information — could you really deny yourself the pleasure?

Cypher — the character played by Joe Pantoliano in the Wachowski brothers' 1999 film, *The Matrix* — has spent a decade underground. He knows without a doubt that the world of freedom and fun before his eyes is a lie, constructed to conceal suffering and exploitation on a monstrous scale. But with what appears to be a perfectly cooked steak in front of him, and a nice glass of red beside it, he is less inclined to care. 'I know this steak doesn't really exist,' he says, hoisting a succulent slice of rump aloft on his fork. 'But after nine years, you know what I've realised? Ignorance is bliss.'[33] As he chews, a harpist plays dinner music, a lovely glissando like the one heard in the final moments of *Kid A*. 'Red wine and sleeping pills,' sings Thom Yorke. 'Cheap sex and sad films / help me get where I belong.'[34] The Matrix, in the Wachowskis' film, is the very same 'wallpaper for emptiness' Yorke said he could not make, the 'something I can ignore' that Radiohead refused to provide. Yorke understood, as few of his peers did, that the role of pop music was directly analogous to that of fast food in the twenty-first century. Musical hamburgers, like actual hamburgers, sold a lifestyle, and that lifestyle had consequences. Yorke knew because he'd seen them — the misery of the developing world, the poverty and violence of the third world, the garbage piling up, the landscape disappearing. Pop songs helped this world go around, but it was a bad world, spinning too fast, and out of control. 'Ice age coming, ice age coming,' he chanted, like a crank with a painted sign outside a Tube station. 'Women and children first.'[35]

This, as his critics pointed out, was not his job. But there are jobs, and then there are responsibilities, and being a singer in an alternative rock band had always fallen in some curious zone between the two — a 'non-service industry', as Frank Black, one of Yorke's all-time heroes, had put it back in 1990. The commercialisation of the underground in the 1990s had turned a lot of would-be revolutionaries into employees, but if singing in a band resembled a McJob, it was still a strange one — like working at a fast-food restaurant where the customers ask for burgers and leave with a slice of homemade vegetarian lasagne and an armful of literature about the evils of factory farming and the corporate takeover of the mass media. Was it the slacker's job to give them all this stuff? No. Was it his responsibility? Without a doubt. So it was for Thom Yorke. The singer was painfully aware that it was his job to write hits, things to ignore, songs to keep us warm. Nevertheless he decided — for reasons that had to do with everything in the world besides money — that it was his responsibility to make trouble. At the end of the decade, the cranky voice of denial that issued from *Kid A* formed the only reasonable response to the demand bolted to the wall of the Hard Rock Hotel and Casino: Here we are now, entertain us.

Acknowledgments

This book was written all over the place — on trains and planes, in pubs and cafes, while sleeping on friends' couches and cluttering up their kitchen tables. Everywhere I went, I picked up some precious little scrap of information — people told me stories and gave me advice, lent me books, copied albums for me or sent me links to interviews on YouTube or sites where people post scans of old magazines. For all of this, I am extremely grateful, especially to the following people: Blake Thompson and Alexis Vogelzang, Vladimir Stoiljkovic, Colin Fraser, Claudia Monteiro, Alicia Brown, Dan Buhagiar, Monique Schafter, Rei Cheatham, Zan Rowe, Chris Scaddan, Elmo Keep, Marc Fennell, Kate Crawford, Lawrence Greenwood, Bastian Fox Phelan, Denise Hurley, Dom Alessio, Dan Bishton and Sasha Pavey, Bella Ann Townes, Sam Miller, Ben Fletcher, Jess Keeley, Sarah Blasko, Dave Hunt and Natalie Kemp, James Francis Drinkwater and Lottie Consalvo Drinkwater, Jutta Tischendorf, Tom Tilley, Peta Ridley, Vanessa Lynch and Adam Welch, Nathan Bloxsom, Michael 'Timmy' Rosenthal, Emma Burrows, Ann-Katherine Weldy, Arthur Lawrence, John, Judith and Alexander Wregg, Julia Gregg, Marissa and Shane Hurst, Robert and Frances Schuftan, Kirsten Morley, Nicole Cheek and Max Lavergne, Dave McDonald, Shona Devlin and Grzegorz Gozdz, Kate Jinx, Carl Johns and Emily Farrell, Mitchell Kerley, Brittany Smeed, Marcus Westbury, Jan Pier Brands, Natasha Taylor, Nicole Dijk, Yuri Landman, Bettina Rech, and Gesine 'Zeitgeisty' Kühne. I'm especially grateful to Olga Drenda for giving me her small but perfect collection of UK music mags, and for her thoughtful and intelligent correspondence, which ranged all over the place from *My*

379

So-Called Life to *Velvet Goldmine*, Suede to *Slacker*. I also owe an enormous debt to Richard Kingsmill, for entrusting his considerable archive of 90s music interviews to me, and to Ella Piltz, who helped to copy and transcribe them. And I'm very grateful to Jo Mackay, who saw the potential in this project at the start and had the patience and perseverance to see it through to the end, to Susan Morris-Yates, Kathy Hassett, Matt Stanton and Brad Cook, who worked very hard to make it the best book it could be, and to Cath Haridy, Mel Bampton, Kelly Fagan and Kirsten Doert, for telling everybody what's going down, in every city in every town.

My greatest thanks, however, go to Kirileigh Lynch, who put up with a lot of nonsense during the two years it took to write this book. For all the times you listened to stuff and told me what you thought, for all those small kitchen parties where we cranked Faith No More or Green Day or Oasis and plotted the ultimate demise of The Man, for that other time when you forced me to go outside because I hadn't left the house in four days. For all of this, and much more — thank you, babe.

Endnotes

Trust the Kids

1. Peter Kane, *Q*, July 1990
2. *Rolling Stone*, May 1990
3. John Wilde, *Melody Maker*, December 1989
4. ibid.
5. Interview with Ian Brown and John Squire, 1989 http://youtu.be/EK7FsV9Oj98
6. Peter Kane, *op. cit.*
7. John Wilde, *Melody Maker*, December 1989
8. ibid.
9. Nick Kent, *The Dark Stuff: Selected Writings on Rock Music*, Faber, 2007
10. Peter Kane, op. cit.
11. John Wilde, op. cit.
12. Peter Kane, op. cit.
13. ibid.
14. Roger Morton, *NME,* May 1990
15. ibid.
16. Tony Wilson, *24 Hour Party People: What the Sleeve Notes Never Tell You*, Channel Four Books, 2002
17. Peter Kane, op. cit.
18. Simon Williams, *NME*, October 1990
19. ibid.
20. Steve Lamacq, *NME,* January 1990
21. James Brown, *Spin*, May 1990
22. Peter Kane, op. cit.

New Sounds for a New World

1. Naomi Klein, *No Logo*, Picador, 2002
2. 'First on MTV' promo, August 1990, You Tube (video removed)
3. Dick Hebdige, 'Guilt Trips', *Art and Text*, May 1990
4. Steven Wells, *NME*, July 1990
5. Matt Snow, *Q*, November 1992
6. Matt Snow, *Q*, September 1991
7. Hanif Kureshi and Jon Savage, *The Faber Book of Pop*, Faber, 1995
8. Dave Thompson, *Red Hot Chili Peppers — By the Way: The Biography*, 2004
9. Interview with Faith No More on CNN *Showbiz Today* http://youtu.be/P9SIk5oaeN4
10. ibid.

11. Richard Kingsmill , Interview with Billy Gould, triple j, 1998
12. Kim Neeley, *Rolling Stone*, September 1990
13. CUSM review singles, *NME*, July 1990
14. Kim Neeley, *Rolling Stone*, September 1990
15. ibid.
16. Interview with Faith No More on CNN *Showbiz Today* http://youtu.be/P9SIk5oaeN4
17. ibid.
18. ibid.
19. Amy Raphael, *Never Mind the Bollocks: Women Rewrite Rock*, Virago, 1995
20. ibid.

We Wanna Be Free

1. David Cavanagh, *My Magpie Eyes are Hungry for the Prize: The Creation Records Story*, Virgin Books, 2011
2. James Brown, *NME*, September 1991
3. David Cavanagh, op. cit.
4. Jack Barron, *NME*, October 1990
5. ibid.
6. Primal Scream, 'Come Together', *Screamadelica*, Creation LP, 1991
7. Hanif Kureshi and Jon Savage, op. cit.
8. Peter Kane, *Q*, July 1990
9. *Rolling Stone*, May 1990
10. David Cavanagh, op. cit.
11. Primal Scream, 'Loaded', *Screamadelica*, Creation LP, 1991

We're the Load of Crap

1. Michael Azerrad, *Our Band Could Be Your Life: Scenes from the American Indie Underground 1981–1991*, Little Brown, 2002
2. ibid.
3. Richard Kingsmill, interview with Mark Arm, triple j, 1990
4. Steven Wells, *NME*, July 1990
5. Michael Azerrad, op. cit.
6. Richard Kingsmill, op. cit.
7. Azerrad, op. cit.
8. Interview with Ian Brown and John Squire, 1989 http://youtu.be/EK7FsV9Oj98
9. Azerrad, op. cit.

10. J. Mascis, *The Dinosaur Jr J Files*, triple j music special
11. Sonic Youth, 'Teenage Riot', Enigma / Blast First single, 1988
12. Superchunk, 'Slack Motherfucker', *Superchunk*, Matador LP, 1990
13. Richard Linklater, *Slacker*, Orion Pictures, 1990

Male, White, Corporate Oppression

1. Dave Kendall, interview with Sonic Youth, MTV *120 Minutes*, 1990 http://youtu.be/WPFMxTVTp-U
2. Ibid.
3. Richard Kingsmill, interview with Bob Mould, triple j, 1990
4. ibid.
5. Dave Kendall, op. cit.
6. Keith Cameron, *NME*, June 1990
7. ibid.
8. Kim Gordon, *Spin*, September 1989
9. ibid.
10. Sonic Youth, 'Kool Thing', DGC single, 1990
11. Dave Kendall, op. cit.
12. *NME*, June 1990

The Non-Service Industries

1. John Wilde, *Melody Maker*, October 1990
2. ibid.
3. Tim Ritchie, interview with the Pixies, triple j, 1989
4. Simon Reynolds, *Blissed Out: The Raptures of Rock*, Serpents Tail, 1990
5. Interview with the Pixies, Canadian TV, 1989 http://youtu.be/-N2b3k3DreA
6. John Wilde, *Melody Maker*, October 1990
7. David Quantick, *NME*, July 1991
8. Tim Ritchie, op. cit.
9. John Wilde, *Melody Maker*, October 1990
10. David Quantick, *NME*, July 1991
11. ibid.
12. Tim Ritchie, op. cit.
13. ibid.
14. Kim Deal interview, WPRB, 1989, http://youtu.be/Jw0rXecoKbw
15. David Quantick, *NME*, October 1990
16. ibid.

Double Seriousness

1. The Soup Dragons, 'I'm Free', Big Life single, 1990
2. Sean Dickson, *NME*, July 1990
3. Jack Barron, *NME*, April 1990
4. Chris Heath, *Q*, April 1990
5. ibid.
6. Jack Barron, *NME*, October 1990
7. Betty Page, *Vox*, October 1990
8. Jack Barron, *NME*, April 1990
9. Mick Middles, *Shaun Ryder: Happy Mondays, Black Grape and other Traumas*, Independent Music Press, 1997
10. Chris Heath, *Q*, April 1990
11. ibid.

12. Mick Middles, op. cit.
13. Nick Kent, 'The Mancunian Candidates', 1989
14. Happy Mondays, 'Loose Fit', *Pills 'n' Thrills and Bellyaches*, Factory LP, 1990
15. ibid.
16. Stud Brothers, *Melody Maker*, March 1990
17. Nick Kent, *The Dark Stuff: Selected Writings on Rock Music*, Faber, 2007
18. Mick Middles, op. cit.
19. Chris Heath, op. cit.
20. ibid.
21. Billy Bragg, *NME*, December 1990
22. ibid.

Freedom Isn't Free

1. *Flashback*, Paramount Pictures, 1990
2. Steven Wells, *NME*, July 1989
3. ibid.
4. Simon Williams, *Spin*, February 1990
5. Jesus Jones, 'Right Here, Right Now', Food Records / EMI single, 1990
6. Steven Wells, op. cit.
7. ibid.
8. Jesus Jones, op. cit.
9. RL Borsage, *Rolling Stone*, February 1991
10. George Bush address, 8 August 1990
11. ibid.
12. RL Borsage, op. cit.
13. Pixies, 'Stormy Weather', *Bossa Nova*, 4AD LP, 1990
14. Michael Azerrad, *Rolling Stone*, November 1990
15. Happy Mondays, 'Loose Fit', *Pills 'n' Thrills and Bellyaches*, Factory LP, 1990
16. John Katz, *Rolling Stone*, March 1991
17. Danny Shechter, *Spin*, April 1995
18. Gavin Martin, *NME*, May 1991
19. Happy Mondays, op. cit.
20. US Army Recruitment TV commercial, 1989, http://youtu.be/NPXi_wx2luo
21. Bob Mack, *Spin*, May 1991
22. Jesus Jones, op. cit.

A Popular Consensus

1. David Quantick, *NME*, 1991
2. Matt Snow, *Q*, November 1992
3. Matt Snow, *Q*, September 1991
4. ibid. David Quantick, *Spin*, September 1991
5. Charlie Rose, CBS News, 1991 http://www.youtube.com/watch?v=gagQlrAaLHM
6. Kurt Cobain, *Journals*, Paw Prints, 2008
7. *NME*, February 1990
8. The Smashing Pumpkins Fan Collaborative, band chronology http://www.spfc.org/band/chronology.html?year=1988
9. Anthony Decurtis, *Rolling Stone*, January 1990
10. Legs McNeil, *NME*, January 1990
11. Dave Markey, *1991: The Year Punk Broke*, Tara Films, 1992

12. Ronald Edsforth, *Popular Culture and Political Change in America*, State University of New York Press, 1991
13. Herbert Schiller, *Culture Inc.*,Oxford University Press, 1991
14. David Wild, *NME*, March 1991
15. ibid.
16. Hanif Kureshi and Jon Savage, op. cit.
17. Michael Azerrad, *Our Band Could Be Your Life: Scenes from the American Indie Underground 1981–1991*, Little Brown, 2002
18. *NME*, March 1990
19. Kurt Cobain, *Nevermind, it's an interview*, DGC, 1993
20. Grant Alden, *Spin*, September 1992
21. Daniel Fidler, *Spin*, September 1991
22. IPU Convention flyer, image from www. olyblog.net
23. ibid.
24. Ann Magnusson, *Spin*, February 1992

Last Chance

1. Dean Kuipers, *Spin*, 1990
2. Dele Fedele, *Melody Maker*, 1989
3. Jane's Addiction, *Ritual de lo Habitual*, Warner Bros LP, 1990, liner notes by Perry Farrell
4. Jane's Addiction, 'Been Caught Stealing', *Ritual de lo Habitual*, Warner Bros LP, 1990
5. Jane's Addiction, 'Stop', *Ritual de lo Habitual*, Warner Bros LP, 1990
6. Jane's Addiction, 'Ain't no Right', *Ritual de lo Habitual*, Warner Bros LP, 1990
7. Kurt Loder, Interview with Perry Farrell, MTV, 1990 http://youtu.be/zVCap56Dydk
8. ibid.
9. Celia Farber, *Spin*, September 1991
10. Kurt Loder, Interview with Perry Farrell, MTV, 1990
11. Jim Greer, *Spin*, July 1991
12. *Rock Legends on Film*, interview with Perry Farrell, 1991, http://youtu.be/0gHiVl8ac1g
13. Jim Greer, *Spin*, July 1991
14. David Fricke, *Rolling Stone*, September 1991
15. Allan Moyle, *Pump Up the Volume*, New Line Cinema, 1990
16. David Fricke, op. cit.

Spending Our Children's Inheritance

1. Tim Ritchie, interview with the Pixies, triple j, 1989
2. Rob Jovanovic, *Nirvana: The Recording Sessions*, Firefly, 2004
3. Keith Cameron, *Mojo*, March 2011
4. Steve Lamacq, *NME*, September 1991
5. Keith Cameron, *NME*, September 1991
6. ibid.
7. Chris Mundy, *Rolling Stone*, January 1992
8. Keith Cameron, *NME*, September 1991
9. ibid.
10. ibid.

11. Dave Markey, *1991: The Year Punk Broke*, Tara Films, 1992
12. Julian Dibbell, 'Classic Rock', in Douglas Rushkoff (ed), *The Gen X Reader*, Ballantine Books, 1994
13. Nirvana, *Nevermind*, DGC LP, 1991
14. Donna Gaines, *Teenage Wasteland: Suburbia's Dead End Kids*, University of Chicago Press, 1998
15. Geoffrey T Holtz, *Welcome to the Jungle: The Why Behind Generation X*, St Martin's Press, 1995
16. Kurt Cobain, *Journals*, Paw Prints, 2008
17. Kurt Cobain, *Nevermind, it's an interview*, DGC, 1993
18. Barney Hoskyns, *Waiting for the Sun*, Backbeat Books, 2009
19. Kurt Cobain, *Journals*, Paw Prints, 2008
20. ibid.
21. ibid.
22. ibid.
23. Kurt Cobain, *Nevermind, it's an interview*, DGC, 1993
24. ibid.
25. Keith Cameron, *Mojo*, March 2011
26. Kim Neeley, *Rolling Stone*, 1992
27. Nirvana, 'Smells Like Teen Spirit', DGC single, 1991
28. Kurt Cobain, *Journals*, Paw Prints, 2008
29. Mary-Ann Hobbs, *NME*, November 1991
30. Nirvana, op. cit.
31. Mary-Ann Hobbs, op. cit.
32. John Harris, *The Last Party: Britpop, Blair and the Demise of English rock*, Fourth Estate, 2003
33. ibid.
34. Simon Williams, *Melody Maker*, April 1991
35. Danny Kelly, *NME*, July 1991
36. ibid.

Dealing with Things

1. Penelope Spheeris, *Wayne's World*, Paramount Pictures, 1992
2. Michael Azerrad, *Rolling Stone*, April 1992
3. Steven Wells, *NME*, March 1992
4. Kim Neeley, *Rolling Stone*, October 1991
5. Interview with Pearl Jam, New York 1991, http://youtu.be/9D8KZ5sfUcE
6. Kim Neeley, *Rolling Stone*, October 1991
7. ibid.
8. Pearl Jam, 'Once', *Ten*, Epic LP, 1991
9. Pearl Jam, 'Footsteps', *Ten*, Epic LP, 1991
10. Douglas Coupland, *Generation X: Tales for an Accelerated Culture*, St Martin's Press, 1991
11. Matt Snow, *Q*, November 1993
12. ibid.
13. Interview with Pearl Jam, New York 1991, http://youtu.be/9D8KZ5sfUcE
14. Richard Kingsmill, interview with Stone Gossard, triple j, 1998
15. Travis Hoy, *Seattle Post-Intelligencer*, December 2008

16. Interview with Pearl Jam, New York 1991, http://youtu.be/9D8KZ5sfUcE
17. Simon Reynolds, *Bring the Noise*, Faber, 2007
18. *Spin*, letters, September 1992

Learning and Hugging

1. Interview with Pearl Jam, New York 1991, http://youtu.be/9D8KZ5sfUcE
2. ibid.
3. Red Hot Chili Peppers, TV interview with Erica Ehm, 1991, http://youtu.be/ZACdJdeHQkI
4. ibid.
5. Jerry Seinfeld, *Rolling Stone*, May 1991
6. 'Amazing Interview', 1991, http://youtu.be/zElZdKBQNKg
7. Dave Thompson, *Red Hot Chili Peppers — By the Way: The Biography*, 2004
8. Anthony Keidis with Larry Sloman, *Scar Tissue*, Hyperion, 2004
9. Red Hot Chilli Peppers, 'Give it Away', Warner Bros single, 1991
10. Bob Mack, *Spin*, December 1991
11. Anthony Keidis with Larry Sloman, op. cit.
12. *NME*, February 1990
13. ibid.
14. Red Hot Chili Peppers, TV interview with Erica Ehm, 1991 http://youtu.be/ZACdJdeHQkI
15. Jerry Seinfeld, op. cit.
16. Mötley Crüe, *Decade of Decadence*, Elektra, 1991
17. Bob Mack, *Spin*, December 1991
18. ibid.
19. Robert Hughes, *Culture of Complaint: The Fraying of America*, Oxford University Press, 1993

Platform Double Suede

1. Kurt Cobain, *Nevermind, it's an interview*, DGC, 1993
2. Johan Kugelberg, *Spin*, July 1992
3. ibid.
4. Stuart Maconie, *NME*, July 1991
5. John Wozniak interview, Songfacts, http://www.songfacts.com/detail.php?id=20085
6. Jefferson Morley, *Washington Post*, 1988
7. Celia Farber, *Spin*, May 1991
8. ibid.
9. ibid.
10. Walter Russell Mead, *Rolling Stone*, 1991
11. ibid.
12. Jefferson Morley, *Washington Post*, 1988
13. Steven Daly and Nathaniel Wice, *Alt. Culture: An A-to-Z guide to the '90s*, Harper Perennial, 1995
14. Elizabeth Moran, 'Bradymania', in Douglas Rushkoff (ed), *The Gen X Reader*, Ballantine Books, 1994
15. Celia Farber, op. cit.
16. ibid.

17. ibid.
18. Johan Kugelberg, op. cit.
19. Stuart Bailie, *NME*, July 1991
20. David Thomas, *Spin*, May 1993

Useless Generation

1. Ad for 'Our Price Music', *Vox*, July 1992
2. Steve Lamacq, *NME*, October 1990
3. Simon Frith, *Sound Effects*, Constable, 1983
4. Simon Dudfield, *NME*, October 1990
5. Steven Wells, *NME*, January 1991
6. ibid.
7. ibid.
8. ibid.
9. ibid.
10. David Quantick, *NME*, 1992
11. Steve Lamacq, *NME*, May 1991
12. Greil Marcus, *Double Trouble: Bill Clinton and Elvis Presley in a land of no alternatives*, Picador, 2001
13. Steve Lamacq, *NME*, May 1991
14. David Quantick, op. cit.
15. ibid.
16. ibid.
17. Steve Lamacq, op. cit.
18. ibid.
19. James Brown, *NME*, June 1991

Mass Rioting in America

1. Alan Light, *Rolling Stone*, August 1992
2. ibid.
3. ibid.
4. Kurt Loder, Interview with Ice T, MTV, 1992
5. Ice T and Body Count interviewed at Club C5, 1992 http://youtu.be/XseyD-ipJ9U
6. Alan Light, *Rolling Stone*, August 1992
7. Charlton Heston on 'Cop Killer', You Tube http://www.youtube.com/watch?v=u6lwNyCo7O8
8. Alan Light, op. cit.
9. ibid.
10. Mike Heck, the ROC, August 1992
11. Alan Light, op. cit.
12. MTV News report, April 1992
13. Peter Watson, *A Terrible Beauty*, Phoenix, 2002
14. ibid.
15. JK Gailbraith, *The Culture of Contentment*, Houghton Mifflin Harcourt, 1993
16. Greil Marcus, op. cit.
17. Faith No More interview, *NME*, January 1993
18. Alan Light, *Rolling Stone*, August 1992

Mega Distribution

1. Keith Cameron, *NME*, September 1991
2. John Norris, interview with L7, MTV 'L7 Interview part two', http://youtu.be/1wtj05Q5YNs
3. Simon Frith, *Sound Effects*, Constable, 1983

4. Michael Tunn, interview with L7, 1992, You Tube http://youtu.be/tVCLUZrIYe0
5. John Norris, interview with L7, MTV 'L7 Interview part two'
6. Ricki Rachtman, interview with L7, MTV *Headbangers' Ball*, 1992 http://youtu.be/LvSZgrM7wSk
7. Steven Wells, *NME*, March 1992
8. John Norris, op. cit.
9. Steven Wells, *NME*, March 1992
10. L7, 'Shitlist', *Bricks are Heavy*, Slash LP, 1992
11. Michael Tunn, interview with L7, 1992, http://youtu.be/tVCLUZrIYe0
12. L7, 'Pretend We're Dead', *Bricks are Heavy*, Slash LP, 1992
13. ibid.
14. Michael Azerrad, *Our Band Could Be Your Life: Scenes from the American Indie Underground 1981–1991*, Little Brown, 2002
15. Keith Cameron, *NME*, September 1991
16. Sindi Valsamis, *NME*, January 1991
17. Ricki Rachtman, op. cit.
18. Terry Jones, *Smile I-D: Fashion and Style*, Taschen, 2001
19. Steven Daly and Nathaniel Wice, op. cit.
20. Ricki Rachtman, op. cit.

A Small Victory

1. Red Hot Chili Peppers, 'Under the Bridge', *Saturday Night Live*, http://youtu.be/AMxQzGA2hA8
2. RJ Smith, *Spin*, August 1999
3. ibid.
4. Interview with Mike Bordin and Mike Patton, Italy, 1992, http://youtu.be/XSVb_aiVH0s
5. Billy Gould, TV interview, January 1992, http://youtu.be/AMxQzGA2hA8
6. Vanessa Warwick, interview with Mike Patton and Roddy Bottum, Prague, MTV *Headbangers' Ball*, 1992 http://youtu.be/xRPJv3yIMgQ
7. Richard Kingsmill, interview with Billy Gould, triple j, 1998
8. Interview with Mike Bordin and Mike Patton, Italy, 1992, http://youtu.be/XSVb_aiVH0s
9. Richard Kingsmill, op. cit.
10. ibid.
11. Frank Owen, *Spin*, December 1990
12. Faith No More, *NME*, January 1993
13. Frank Owen, op. cit.
14. Faith No More, *NME*, January 1993

Be True to Yourself

1. Jon Katz, *Rolling Stone*, September 1992
2. ibid.
3. ibid.
4. Kim Neeley, *Rolling Stone*, July 1992
5. Mark Blackwell, *Spin*, June 1992
6. Grant Adler, *Spin*, September 1992
7. Keith Cameron, *NME*, September 1991
8. Mark Cooper, *Q*, April 1993

9. Anthony Keidis with Larry Sloman, *Scar Tissue*, Hyperion, 2004
10. Keith Cameron, *NME*, February 1992
11. Regina Joseph, *Spin*, August 1992
12. Maxwell Hudson, *Spin*, October 1992
13. Jon Bon Jovi, *Q*, November 1994

A White Man's Mentality

1. Jonathan Gold, *Spin*, September 1993
2. Stone Temple Pilots, 'Sex Type Thing', Atlantic single, 1993
3. Katherine Turman, *Spin*, September 1993
4. Thurston Moore, *Ray Gun*, June 1993
5. Katherine Turman, op. cit.
6. Jonathan Gold, *Spin*, op. cit.
7. Jon Katz, *Rolling Stone*, August 1992
8. Steven Daly and Nathaniel Wice, *Alt. Culture*, Harper Perennial, 1995
9. Kurt Cobain, *Journals*, Paw Prints, 2008
10. Jon Katz, op. cit.
11. Denis Leary, 'Asshole', A&M single, 1993
12. Jon Katz, op. cit.
13. Bikini Kill, 'This is not a Test', *The CD version of the First Two Records*, Kill Rock Stars, 1994
14. ibid.

Your Whole Fucking Culture

1. Camille Paglia, *Spin*, September 1991
2. Barbara O'Dair (ed), *The Rolling Stone Book of Women in Rock*, Random House, 1997
3. Maria Raha, *Cinderella's Big Score: Women of the Punk and Indie Underground*, Seal Press, 2005
4. Bikini Kill, op. cit.
5. Emily White, *The Chicago Reader*, September 1992
6. ibid.
7. ibid.
8. ibid.
9. Bikini Kill, Zine no. 2
10. Emily White, op. cit.
11. Fugazi, *In on the Kill Taker*, Dischord Records, 1993
12. Dana Nasrallah, *Spin*, November 1992
13. ibid.
14. Ada Calhoun, bikinikillarchive. wordpress.com/stories
15. ibid.
16. Ann Japenga, *New York Times*, November 1992

Dirty

1. Michael Azerrad, *Rolling Stone*, July 1992
2. Sonic Youth, '100%' *Dirty*, DGC LP, 1992
3. Sonic Youth, 'Swimsuit Issue', *Dirty*, DGC LP, 1992
4. Sonic Youth, 'Youth Against Fascism', *Dirty*, DGC LP, 1992
5. Glenn O'Brien, 'Mike Kelley', www.interviewmagazine.com
6. Roseanne Arnold, *People*, October 1991
7. Richard Zoglin, *Time*, 1989
8. Steven Daly and Nathaniel Wice, op. cit.

9. Emily White, op. cit.
10. Kaya Oakes, *Slanted and Enchanted: The Evolution of Indie Culture*, Henry Holt and Co, 2009
11. Courtney Love, letter to Kim Gordon, posted by www.lettersofnote.com
12. Babes in Toyland, 'Lashes', *Spanking Machine*, Twin Tone LP, 1989
13. Everett True, *Melody Maker*, March 1990
14. ibid.
15. Daniel Fidlerm, *Spin*, September 1992
16. Naomi Wolf, *The Beauty Myth*, Random House, 1991
17. Kurt Cobain, liner notes, *Incesticide*, DGC LP, 1992
18. Courtney Love, *Newsweek*, November 1992

None of Our Business

1. Kim Neeley, *Rolling Stone*, July 1992
2. Chris Roberts, *Melody Maker*, January 1989
3. Keith Cameron, *Mojo*, March 2011
4. Kurt Cobain, *Nevermind, it's an interview*, DGC, 1993
5. Kurt Cobain, liner notes, *Incesticide*, DGC LP, 1992
6. Kurt Cobain, *Nevermind, it's an interview*, DGC, 1993
7. Richard Kingsmill, interview with Steve Albini, triple j,1993
8. Steve Lamacq, *NME*, April 1992
9. Simon Reynolds, *Bring the Noise*, Faber, 2007
10. PJ Harvey, *Rid of Me*, Island LP, 1993
11. Richard Kingsmill, op. cit.
12. ibid.

Fragments

1. Douglas Coupland, *Generation X: Tales for an Accelerated Culture*, 1991
2. Naomi Klein, op. cit.
3. Dick Hebdige, op. cit.
4. Peter Watson, op. cit.
5. McDonald's TV Commercial, 1990, You Tube (clip removed)
6. Hugh Gallagher, '7 Days and Nights Alone with MTV', in Douglas Rushkoff (ed), *The Gen X Reader*, Ballantine Books, 1994
7. Stuart Maconie, *Select*, April 1993
8. Stephen Dalton, *NME*, November 1992
9. Blur, 'Sunday Sunday', *Modern Life is Rubbish*, Food Records/EMI LP, 1993
10. David Nolan and Martin Roach, *Damon Albarn: Blur, Gorillaz and other fables*, Independent Music Press, 2007
11. Beastie Boys review singles, *NME*, March 1992
12. *NME*, March 1992
13. *No Distance Left to Run*, Pulse Films, 2010
14. *NME*, March 1992
15. *NME*, March 1992
16. Chris Global, *NME*, January 1992
17. Keith Cameron, *NME*, 1992
18. Liz Evans, *NME*, January 1992

19. Mark Blackwell, *Spin*, April 1993
20. Nolan and Roach, op. cit.
21. Chris Global, *NME*, January 1992/Keith Cameron, *NME*, 1992
22. Stud Brothers, op. cit.
23. Jonathan Bernstein, *Spin*, March 1993
24. ibid.
25. Stud Brothers, op. cit.
26. Anthony Haden-Guest, 'Damien Hirst', www.interviewmagazine.com
27. Simon Williams, *Melody Maker*, April 1991
28. Danny Kelly, *NME*, July 1991
29. John Harris, op. cit.
30. ibid.
31. Andrew Collins, *NME*, November 1991
32. Kurt Cobain, *Journals*, Paw Prints, 2008
33. Craig Marks, *Spin*, July 1993
34. Will Lovelace, *No Distance Left to Run*, Pulse Films, 2010
35. Blur Interview, London, 1992 http://youtu.be/Y3cycQBi0ls
36. John Harris, op. cit.
37. *Rolling Stone*, February 1997
38. Blur interview, op. cit.

What Pop Stars are For

1. Richard Kingsmill, interview with Frank Black, triple j, 1993
2. Richard Kingsmill, interview with Kim Deal, triple j, 1993
3. Beck, 'Pay No Mind (Snoozer)', *Mellow Gold*, DGC LP, 1993
4. Charles Aaron, *Spin*, April 1994
5. William Leith, *The Independent*, March 1993
6. ibid.
7. ibid.
8. Phil Sutcliffe, *Q*, November 1992
9. William Leith, op. cit.
10. ibid.
11. ibid.
12. John Mulvey, *NME*, August 1991
13. Steve Lamacq, *NME*, February 1992
14. ibid.
15. ibid.
16. Richard Kingsmill, interview with Brett Anderson, triple j, 1996
17. Jim Greer, *Spin*, April 1993
18. Jonathan Poneman, *Spin*, September 1992
19. Jon Savage, *Time Travel*, Chatto and Windus, 1996
20. Craig Marks, *Spin*, September 1993
21. Radiohead, 'Creep', EMI single, 1992
22. Chris Mundy, *Rolling Stone*, January 1992
23. Amy Raphael, op. cit.
24. Nick Johnstone, *Radiohead*, Omnibus Press, 1997
25. Radiohead, 'Creep', EMI single, 1992

Check Out America

1. Urge Overkill, 'Positive Bleeding', DGC 1993
2. Liz Phair, 'Fuck and Run', *Exile in Guyville*, Matador LP, 1993

3. Liz Phair, 'Soap Star Joe', *Exile in Guyville*, Matador LP, 1993
4. Richard Kingsmill, interview with Liz Phair, triple j, 1999
5. Amy Raphael, op. cit.
6. Rob Trucks, *Village Voice*, June 2008
7. ibid.
8. ibid.
9. Amy Raphael, op. cit.
10. *Harper's Bazaar*, September 1994
11. Rob Trucks, op. cit.
12. Adrian Deevoy, *Q*, March 1994
13. Nils Bernstein, *Ray Gun*, March 1993
14. Richard Kingsmill, interview with Liz Phair, 1999
15. Michael Azerrad, *Spin*, December 1994

Alternative to Alternative

1. Smashing Pumpkins interview part 1, You Tube (account deleted)
2. Dave Kendall, interview with Smashing Pumpkins, MTV http://youtu.be/a6KIrbtY0I4
3. Smashing Pumpkins interview part 1, You Tube
4. Dave Thompson, *Creem*, January 1994
5. Billy Corgan interview on WNUR, 1988, You Tube (clip removed)
6. 'Interview, 1991', You Tube
7. Dave Thompson, *Creem*, January 1994
8. ibid.
9. ibid.
10. Billy Corgan, Smashing Pumpkins interview, 1992 http://youtu.be/BHV-H0w2TjM
11. Michael Snyder, *San Francisco Chronicle*, October 1993
12. Michael Azerrad, *Spin*, December 1994
13. Todd Snider, 'Talkin' Seattle Grunge Rock Blues', Aimless Records single, 1994
14. Bill Wyman, 'Not From the Underground', *Chicago Reader*, January 1994
15. Steve Albini, 'Three Pandering Sluts and one Music Press Stooge', *Chicago Reader*, February 1994
16. ibid.
17. Dave Thompson, op. cit.
18. ibid.
19. Smashing Pumpkins, 'Cherub Rock', *Siamese Dream*, Virgin LP, 1993
20. Dave Thompson, op. cit.
21. Michael Azerrad, *Spin*, December 1994
22. ibid.

In the Shade

1. Charles Aaron, *Spin*, April 1994
2. Interview with Kim Deal, 1994, http://youtu.be/09S0wgzvxio
3. Richard Kingsmill, interview with Kim Deal, triple j, 1993
4. ibid.
5. Claude Rajotte, interview with the Breeders, *Musique Plus*, November 1993

6. Mark Kates, *Spin*, October 1993
7. Andy Darlington, *Hot Press*, October 1993
8. Jude Rodgers, *The Guardian*, May 2009
9. Richard Kingsmill, interview with Kim Deal, triple j, 1993
10. ibid.

Family Values

1. Niall Crumlish, *Hot Press*, October 1993
2. Stud Brothers, *Melody Maker*, August 1993
3. ibid.
4. Nirvana, 'Radio Friendly Unit Shifter', *In Utero*, DGC LP, 1993
5. Nirvana, 'Heart Shaped Box', DGC single, 1993
6. Stud Brothers, *Melody Maker*, August 1993
7. Interview with Kurt Cobain, Much Music, 1993 (You Tube, clip removed)
8. ibid.
9. Stud Brothers, op. cit.
10. Amy Raphael, op. cit.
11. Four Non-Blondes, 'What's Up', Interscope single, 1993
12. Stud Brothers, op. cit.
13. Everett True, *Melody Maker*, December 1993
14. ibid.

The Job We Never Wanted

1. Matt Snow, *Q*, November 1993
2. ibid.
3. ibid.
4. Jim Greer, *Spin*, 1993
5. Matt Snow, op. cit.
6. Stuart Maconie, Select, April 1993
7. ibid.
8. Ben Stiller, *Reality Bites*, Universal Studios, 1994
9. Bruce Pavitt, *Spin*, April 1995
10. Pavement, 'Cut Your Hair', *Crooked Rain, Crooked Rain*, Matador LP, 1994
11. ibid.
12. Mark Prindle and Jame Lathram, interview with Scott Kannberg and Mark Ibold, WUNC, North Carolina, 1994
13. Jim Greer, op. cit.
14. Evan Dando and Juliana Hatfield, *Spin*, December 1993
15. Keith Cameron, *NME*, March 1992
16. Pavement, 'Cut Your Hair', 1994
17. Richard Kingsmill, interview with Steven Malkmus, triple j, 1994
18. ibid.
19. Tim Nye, *Bomb*, Fall 1994
20. ibid.
21. Mark Prindle and Jame Lathram, opcit
22. Krist Novoselic, MTV News, October 1993
23. Kaya Oakes, op. cit.
24. Pavement, 'Filmore Jive', *Crooked Rain, Crooked Rain*, Matador LP, 1994
25. Richard Linklater, *Dazed and Confused*, 1994
26. Richard Kingsmill, op. cit.

27. Mark Prindle and Jame Lathram, opcit
28. Michael Roberts, *Westward*, October 1994
29. Weezer, 'Buddy Holly', DGC single, 1994
30. Weezer interview, Public Access TV, 1994 http://youtu.be/z3kVM0HJY04

I'm in the Band

1. Pamela Des Barres, *Interview*, March 1994
2. ibid.
3. 'The Making of *Live Through This*', MTV special, 1994 http://youtu.be/Cb9B1K3j-kY
4. Pamela Des Barres, op. cit.
5. ibid.
6. Richard Kingsmill, interview with Hole, triple j, 1999
7. Pamela Des Barres, op. cit.
8. interview with Courtney Love, backstage at MTV VMAs, 1994, (You Tube, account deleted)
9. Caitlin Moran, *Melody Maker*, February 1994
10. Hole, 'Doll Parts', DGC single, 1994
11. Interview with Courtney Love, Backstage at the MTV VMAs, 1994, You Tube
12. Lisa Carver, *Rollerderby*, November 1993
13. Pamela Des Barres, op. cit.

Usual Torments

1. Everett True, *Melody Maker*, December 1993
2. Allan Jones, *Melody Maker*, April 1994
3. Craig Marks, *Spin*, December 1994
4. ibid.
5. KSTW News, April 1994, You Tube (clip removed)
6. ibid.
7. ibid.
8. Courtney Love reads Kurt Cobain's suicide note, triple j archive, 1994
9. MTV news
10. KSTW News, op. cit.
11. *NME*, April 1994
12. David Stubbs, *Melody Maker*, April 1994
13. ibid.
14. Courtney Love reads Kurt Cobain's suicide note, triple j archive, 1994
15. David Stubbs, op. cit.
16. MTV News report, April 1994
17. Bruce Handy, *Time*, April 1994
18. Krist Novoselic, on the death of Kurt Cobain, triple j archive, 1994
19. Everett True, *Melody Maker*, April 1993
20. ibid.
21. Kurt Cobain suicide note
22. David Stubbs, op. cit.
23. Jeff Giles, *Newsweek*, April 1994
24. Kurt Cobain suicide note
25. Steve Kulick, *Melody Maker*, April 1994
26. Craig Marks, *Spin*, December 1994

The Kingdom of the Pleasing

1. James Brown, *Live Forever*, BBC, 2003 http://youtu.be/_DhdIurkiKs

2. *MCM Backstage: Blur*, You Tube http://youtu.be/rDfF7ATDfwI
3. ibid.
4. David Nolan and Martin Roach, op. cit.
5. Blur interview, You Tube
6. *MCM Backstage: Blur*, You Tube http://youtu.be/rDfF7ATDfwI
7. MTV News report, April 1994
8. *The O-Zone*, interview with Damon Albarn, 1994 http://youtu.be/khOsZlA9QI0
9. ITV, interview with Damon Albarn, 1994, You Tube (clip removed)
10. Granada TV documentary on Oasis, You Tube http://youtu.be/p2YrhgiaZJg

A New Smell

1. Kaya Oakes, op. cit.
2. Dave Markey, *1991: The Year Punk Broke*, Tara Films, 1992
3. Billie Joe Armstrong, *MTV News*, 1994 http://youtu.be/Y3cycQBi0ls
4. Helen Razer, interview with Green Day, triple j, 1994
5. ibid.
6. Interview with Green Day, MTV, *120 Minutes*, 1994 http://youtu.be/tmXzkG5ZfeM
7. Kaya Oakes, op. cit.
8. Billie Joe Armstrong, MTV News, 1994
9. Green Day radio interview, 1994 http://youtu.be/NF4oilEmY54
10. Billie Joe Armstrong, *MTV News*, 1994 http://youtu.be/Y3cycQBi0ls
11. John Ginoli, *Deflowered: My Life in Pansy Division*, Cleis Press, 2009
12. Billie Joe Armstrong, *MTV News*, 1994 http://youtu.be/Y3cycQBi0ls
13. John Ginoli, op. cit.
14. *Spin*, letters, February 1995
15. Simon Frith, *Sound Effects*, Constable, 1983
16. Raymond Williams, *Culture and Society 1780-1950*, Pelican, 1952

Problems, Traumas, Whatever

1. Richard Kingsmill, interview with Steven Malkmus, triple j, 1994
2. ibid.
3. Joshua Berger, *Plazm*, July 1994
4. ibid.
5. Jon Wiederhorn, *Melody Maker*, August 1990
6. Amy Raphael, op. cit.
7. *NME*, February 1990
8. Joshua Berger, op. cit.
9. Eric Weisbard, *Spin*, 1995
10. Robin Reinhardt, *Spin*, February 1990
11. Interview with Trent Reznor, 1994, You Tube http://youtu.be/m-8nXCgFLGo
12. Nine Inch Nails, The Downward Spiral, Interscope LP, 1994
13. Nine Inch Nails, 'Mister Self-Destruct', *The Downward Spiral*, Interscope LP, 1994

14. Nine Inch Nails, 'Heresy', *The Downward Spiral*, Interscope LP, 1994
15. Jane's Addiction, 'Ain't No Right', *Ritual de lo Habitual*, Warner Bros LP, 1990
16. Nine Inch Nails, 'Hurt', *The Downward Spiral*, Interscope LP, 1994
17. Joshua Berger, op. cit.
18. Nine Inch Nails, 'Burn', *Natural Born Killers soundtrack*, Interscope LP, 1994
19. Andrew Collins, *Q*, December 1994
20. Keith Cameron, *NME*, March 1992
21. Chris Mundy, *NME*, November 1992
22. Jon Savage, op. cit.
23. Greil Marcus, *Double Trouble: Bill Clinton and Elvis Presley in a land of no alternatives*, Picador, 2001
24. Joshua Berger, op. cit.
25. Lawrence Grossberg, 'The Media Economy of Rock Culture', in Simon Frith (ed), *Sound and Vision: The Music Video Reader*, Routledge, 1993
26. Joshua Berger, op. cit.

This Year Sucked

1. Beavis and Butt-head, *Spin*, December 1994
2. Michael Jarrett, 'Concerning the Progress of Rock and Roll', in Anthony de Curtis (ed) *Present Tense: Rock and Roll and Culture*, Duke University Press, 1992
3. Beavis and Butt-head, op. cit.
4. Lynn Chiam, *BIGO*, April 1994
5. Kurt Cobain, unsent letter to MTV, published by www.lettersofnote.com 2011
6. William Burroughs, *Nova Express*, Grove Press, 1964
7. Steven Daly and Nathaniel Wice, op. cit.
8. ibid.
9. Joshua Berger, *Plazm*, 1994
10. Robert Hilburn, *LA Times*, November 1994
11. Kim Neeley, *Rolling Stone*, July 1992
12. Jeff Giles, *Newsweek*, April 1994
13. Steven Daly and Nathaniel Wice, op. cit.
14. Jon Bon Jovi, *Q*, November 1994
15. Pearl Jam, 'Blood', *Vs*, Epic LP, 1993
16. Steven Daly and Nathaniel Wice, op. cit.
17. Steve Kulick, *Melody Maker*, April 1994
18. Steven Daly and Nathaniel Wice, op. cit.
19. Jonathan Gold, *Spin*, September 1993
20. Lawrence Grossberg, op. cit.
21. Pearl Jam, 'Not For You', *Vitalogy*, 1994
22. Robert Hilburn, *LA Times*, November 1994
23. Steve Kulick, *Melody Maker*, April 1994
24. Robert Hilburn, *LA Times*, November 1994

My So-called Life

1. Guy Debord, *Panegyric*, Verso, 2004
2. Simon Ford, *The Situationist International*, Black Dog Press, 2005
3. ibid.
4. ibid.

5. Guy Debord, *The Society of the Spectacle*, Zone Books, 1991
6. ibid.
7. Simon Ford, op. cit.
8. Guy Debord, op. cit.
9. Rob Jovanovic, *Beck: On a Backwards River*, Virgin Books, 2000
10. Douglas Rushkoff, op. cit.
11. Mark Blackwell, *Spin*, August 1992
12. John Norris, interview with L7, MTV 'L7 Interview part two' http://youtu.be/1wtj05Q5YNs
13. Amy Raphael, op. cit.
14. Kennedy, interview with Elastica, MTV *Alternative Nation*, 1995 http://youtu.be/RLj5DbH4pw0
15. *Reality Bites*, op. cit.
16. Craig Marks, *Spin*, September 1993
17. Helen Razer, interview with Beck, triple j, 1995
18. Radiohead, 'My Iron Lung', EMI single, 1995
19. Alan Moyle, op. cit.
20. Nine Inch Nails, 'Hurt', 1994, *The Downward Spiral*, Interscope LP, 1994
21. *My So-Called Life*, ABC productions, 1994
22. Stud Brothers, *Melody Maker*, October 1994
23. Radiohead, *The Bends*, EMI LP, 1995

The Best Year

1. Mark Kates, interview with Oasis, 2FM, June 1994 http://youtu.be/rU72fgDIxIo
2. Beavis and Butt-head, MTV, August 1994
3. 'Wibbling Rivalry', Interview with Oasis, August 1994 http://youtu.be/wWU2ZQjQI-s
4. ibid.
5. Granada TV, interview with Oasis, 1994 http://youtu.be/p2YrhgiaZJg
6. Mark Kates, interview with Oasis, 2FM, June 1994
7. James Brown, *Live Forever*, BBC, 2003 http://youtu.be/_Dhd1urkiKs
8. Stuart Maconie, *Q*, November 1994
9. 'Wibbling Rivalry', Interview with Oasis, August 1994 http://youtu.be/wWU2ZQjQI-s
10. Mark Kates, op. cit.
11. Stuart Maconie, *Q*, November 1994
12. Interview with Oasis, *Much Much Music*, 1994 http://youtu.be/ExUFPzZzavo
13. Oasis, 'Whatever', Creation, 1994
14. Zoe Ball, interview with Oasis, *The O-Zone*, October 1994 http://youtu.be/E7MNpvShZk8
15. ibid.
16. 'Wibbling Rivalry', op. cit.
17. Interview with the Stone Roses, *Q*, March 1995
18. *Mojo*, January 1995
19. Interview with the Stone Roses, *Q*, March 1995

20. Zoe Ball, interview with Oasis, *The O-Zone*, October 1994
21. Donna Matthews, interview with Noel Gallagher, MTV, November 1994 http://youtu.be/HQC60sGsnXU

Classic Rock Now

1. Stud Brothers, *Melody Maker*, October 1994
2. Radiohead, 'My Iron Lung' EMI, 1995
3. Sean Hughes, *NME*, November 1992
4. David Bennun, *Melody Maker*, February 1995
5. ibid.
6. Stud Brothers, *Melody Maker*, November 1994
7. Hanif Kureshi and Jon Savage, op. cit.
8. Andrew Mueller, *NME*, April 1995
9. ibid.
10. David Bennun, op. cit.
11. Jennifer Nine, *NME*, March 1995

Bored-Furious, Stop-Start

1. *Melody Maker*, Classifieds, 1993
2. Kennedy, interview with Elastica, MTV *Alternative Nation*, 1995 http://youtu.be/RLj5DbH4pw0
3. Jon Savage, *Time Travel*, Chatto and Windus, 1996
4. ibid.
5. 'Justine Talks about Suede', 1995, You Tube http://youtu.be/H9d-qXaxAos
6. Jon Savage, op. cit.
7. Julian Dibbell, op. cit.
8. Simon Reynolds, *Bring the Noise*, Faber, 2007
9. Tom Barman, *Mojo*, March 1995
10. Supergrass, 'Alright', Parlophone single, 1995
11. The Boo Radleys, 'Wake Up Boo!' Creation single, 1995
12. Martin Carr, *Ray Gun*, October 1995
13. Peter Shapiro, *Spin*, 1995
14. Jennifer Nine, *NME*, February 1995
15. ibid.
16. ibid.

The Future of Rock

1. Interview with Butch Vig, *Volume*, May 1995
2. Simon Williams, *NME*, May 1995
3. *Ray Gun*, October 1995
4. Interview with Butch Vig, *Volume*, May 1995
5. ibid.
6. *Rolling Stone*, December 1996
7. Interview with Butch Vig, AOL, May 1995
8. Eric Schumacher, *Rolling Stone*, November 1995
9. *Ray Gun*, October 1995
10. Dan Dinello, *Pop and all that Junk*, Alternative Press, 1995
11. Rob Sheffield, *Spin*, 1994

12. Liesegang, *Spin*, November 1995
13. Eric Weisbard, *Spin*, February 1996

The Future's Been Sold

1. *Britpop Now*, BBC TV, August 1995
2. Steve Sutherland, *NME*, September 1995
3. John Harris, op. cit.
4. Steve Sutherland, *NME*, September 1995
5. Amy Raphael, op. cit.
6. ibid.
7. Steve Sutherland, op. cit.
8. ibid.
9. ibid.
10. Interview with Blur, MTV UK, 1995
11. Steve Sutherland, op. cit.
12. David Sprague, *Rolling Stone*, December 1995
13. Keith Cameron, *NME*, October 1994
14. ibid.
15. Damien Hirst, quoted in exhibition catalogue, Tate Britain
16. Blur, 'Sing', *Leisure*, EMI / Food LP 1991
17. Steve Sutherland, *op. cit.*

What You Want, if That's What You Want

1. Alison Stewart, MTV News, July 1995
2. ibid.
3. Richard Kingsmill, interview with Steven Malkmus, 1995
4. ibid.
5. Michael Azzarad, *Spin*, December 1994
6. Smashing Pumpkins interview, Planet Rock profiles, 1995
7. ibid.
8. Amy Raphael, op. cit.
9. Richard Kingsmill, interview with Dave Grohl, 1995
10. ibid.
11. Amy Raphael, op. cit.
12. Smashing Pumpkins interview, Planet Rock profiles, 1995
13. Lee Baxandall, *Radical Perspectives in the Arts*, Pelican, 1972
14. 'The Making of Bullet with Butterfly Wings', You Tube
15. Smashing Pumpkins, 'Fuck You (an ode to no-one)', Virgin, 1995
16. Smashing Pumpkins, 'Bullet with Butterfly Wings', Virgin, 1995
17. 'The Making of Bullet with Butterfly Wings', You Tube http://youtu.be/EtcFs4iWlXo
18. Lance Bangs, *Slow Century*, Matador Records DVD, 2000
19. ibid.
20. Rob Jovanovic, *Beck: On a Backwards River*, Fromm Intl, 2001
21. ibid.
22. Bangs, op. cit.

Intergalactic Pop Megastar

1. Jarvis Cocker, Glastonbury Diary, 1995
2. ibid.

3. Pulp, 'Common People', Island, 1995
4. Andrew Smith, *The Face*, June 1995
5. Steve Sutherland, *NME*, September 1995
6. *Select*, September 1995
7. Andrew Smith, op. cit.
8. ibid.
9. Single reviews, *NME*, September 1991
10. Pulp, 'Mis-shapes', Island, 1995
11. Roger Morton, *Vox*, February 1996
12. Oasis, 'Bring it On Down', *Definitely Maybe*, Creation LP 1994
13. James Brown, *Live Forever*, BBC, 2003 http://youtu.be/_DhdlurkiKs
14. John Harris, op. cit.
15. ibid.
16. *Vox*, May 1995
17. Andrew Smith, op. cit.
18. Roger Morton, op. cit.
19. ibid.
20. David Stubbs, *Melody Maker* Christmas issue, December 1995

These People are Losers

1. *Spin*, letters, November 1996
2. Richard Kingsmill, *The J-Files Compendium*, ABC Books, 2002
3. ibid.
4. *Rolling Stone*, April 1996

A Mutually Exploitative Situation

1. Lynne Snowden, *Spin*, 1996
2. Rich Drees, interview with Doug Pray, *Times Leader*, March 1997
3. ibid.
4. Doug Pray, *Hype*, Lion's gate, 1996
5. Naomi Klein, op. cit.
6. Keith Cameron, *NME*, 1991
7. Naomi Klein, op. cit.
8. Douglas Rushkoff, op. cit.
9. Interview with Zack de la Rocha, MTV Buzz Bin, 1996
10. Interview with Tom Morello, MTV Buzz Bin, 1996
11. Richard Kingsmill, *The J-Files Compendium*, 2002
12. Amy Raphael, *Vox*, 1996
13. Interview with Tom Morello, *LA Times*, 1996
14. Amy Raphael, Vox, April 1996
15. Sandy Masuo, *Ray Gun*, 1996
16. R.J. Smith, *Spin*, October 1996

I Am My Own Scene

1. Interview with Gwen Stefani, 1996, You Tube http://youtu.be/zgf4uMBrl60
2. Jonathan Bernstein, *Spin*, November 1996
3. Daly and Wice, op. cit.
4. Interview with Gwen Stefani, 1996, accesshollywood.com
5. Ben Folds Five, 'Underground', Passenger/Caroline, 1995
6. Frank Black, 'Freedom Rock', 4AD, 1995
7. Rob Jovanovic, op. cit.

8. Interview with Frank Black, 1995, You Tube http://youtu.be/CBHWpQPgX_8
9. Michael Tunn, interview with Beck, triple j, 1996
10. Douglas Rushkoff, op. cit.
11. *Spin*, letters, 1996
12. Ad for 'Simple Shoes', *Spin*, October 1996
13. Daly and Wice, op. cit.
14. Mark Saltveit, 'Whatever', 1994
15. No Doubt, 'Different People', Interscope, 1996
16. Daly and Wice, op. cit.

Learning from Las Vegas

1. *Spin*, 1996
2. Peter Conrad, *Modern Times, Modern Places*, Thames & Hudson, 1998
3. Douglas Rushkoff, op. cit.
4. Steven Wells, *NME*, March 1992
5. Jim De Rogatis, *Milk It*, Da Capo Press, 2003
6. Woodstock '94 Multimedia Center, www.well.com/woodstock/
7. Naomi Klein, op. cit.
8. Kevin Smith, *Mallrats*, View Askew Productions, 1994
9. No Doubt, 'Tragic Kingdom', 1996
10. Doug Pray, op. cit.
11. Michael Azerrad, *Our Band Could Be Your Life: Scenes from the American Indie Underground 1981–1991*, Little Brown, 2002
12. Doug Pray, op. cit.
13. Andrew Hultkrans, *Mondo 2000*, 1994
14. Matt Sturges, 'It is ironic, isn't it?' www.fgk.hanua.net/articles/ironic
15. R.J. Smith, *Spin*, 1996
16. Elizabeth Gilbert, *Spin*, August 1996

Flux and Chaos

1. Rob Jovanovic, op. cit.
2. Beck, 'Devil's Haircut', DGC single 1996
3. John Norris, Interview with the Dust Brothers, MTV, 1996
4. Michael Tunn, interview with Beck, triple j, 1996, http://youtu.be/e4XZJBUwjxc
5. Beck, 'High Five', DGC single 1996
6. Rob Jovanovic, op. cit.
7. Eric Weisband, *Spin*, August 1996
8. Michael Tunn, op. cit.
9. Douglas Coupland, op. cit.
10. Beck, 'Hot wax', *Odelay*, DGC LP, 1996
11. Jovanovic, op. cit.
12. Eric Weisband, op. cit.

This is How I Feel, This is Who I Am

1. Peter Weir, *Spin*, November 1996
2. Kurt Loder, interview with Fiona Apple, MTV, 1996
3. Fiona Apple, 'Criminal', Sony, 1996
4. *Nan Goldin: In My Life*, Whitney Museum of American Art, 1997
5. Scott Frampton, *CMJ New Music Monthly*, September 1996

Junkie's Promise

1. Interview with Nan Goldin, Whitney Museum of Modern Art, 1996
2. Naomi Wolf, *The Beauty Myth*, 1990
3. *Ray Gun*, October 1995
4. Quentin Tarentino, *Pulp Fiction*, 1994
5. Mark Ehrman, in Daly and Wice, *Alt. Culture*, Harper Perennial, 1995
6. Mark Cooper, *Q*, 1993
7. Amy Raphael, op. cit.
8. David Fricke, *Rolling Stone*, February 1997
9. Kurt Loder, interview with Perry Farrell, 1991, You Tube http://youtu.be/hIrlb3e8EZE
10. Mark Ehrman, op. cit.
11. Irvine Welsh, *Trainspotting*, Secker & Warburg, 1993
12. Danny Boyle, *Trainspotting*, 1996
13. ibid.

Dan Abnormal

1. 'Movie Connections: *Trainspotting*', You Tube http://youtu.be/x2gSmOwftB0
2. John Harris, op. cit.
3. Interview with Damon Albarn, *The O-Zone*, 1997
4. Richard Kingsmill, interview with Blur, triple j, 1997
5. Matt Pinfield, interview with Blur, MTV *120 Minutes*, 1997
6. ibid.
7. Will Lovelace, op. cit.
8. Richard Kingsmill, interview with Blur, triple j, 1997
9. ibid.
10. Ben Thompson, *Seven Years of Plenty*, Griffn Skye 1998
11. ibid.
12. *Spin*, 1997
13. Richard Kingsmill, op. cit.

The Year of the Women

1. Scott Frampton, *CMJ New Music Monthly*, September 1997
2. Interview with Kim Deal, 1993, You Tube http://youtu.be/Qx44MeV94BQ
3. Scott Frampton, op. cit.
4. Maria Raha, *Cinderella's Big Score*, Seal Press, 2005
5. Meredith Brooks, 'Bitch', Capitol, 1997
6. Ann Powers, *Spin*, November 1997
7. ibid.
8. Meredith Brooks, op. cit.
9. Ann Powers, op. cit.
10. Maria Raha, op. cit.
11. Frampton, op. cit.
12. *Roseanne*, 1997, http://youtu.be/CeTjUhAxabM
13. Joy Press, *The Wire*, January 2002
14. ibid.
15. Eric Weisband, *Spin*, August 1996
16. Sleater-Kinney, 'It's Enough', Kill Rock Stars, 1996

Happy Thoughts for Your Next Album

1. Interview with Radiohead, *Q*, August 1997
2. Nick Johnston, *Radiohead*, Omnibus Press, 1998
3. Claire Kleinedler, 'Addicted to Noise', February 1997
4. Radiohead, 'No Surprises', Capitol, 1997
5. Radiohead, 'Electioneering', 1997
6. Claire Kleinedler, 1997
7. Interview with Radiohead, *Q*, 1997
8. Radiohead, 'Karma Police', Capitol, 1997
9. Radiohead, 'Fitter, Happier', Capitol, 1997
10. Radiohead, 'No Surprises', Capitol, 1997
11. Radiohead, 'Subterranean Homesick Alien', Capitol, 1997
12. Oasis, 'Roll With It', Creation, 1995
13. Kleinedler, op. cit.

Veganistic Views

1. Phil Sutcliffe, *Q*, March 1998
2. ibid.
3. *Rolling Stone*, Music Box, interview with Blink 182, 1998, http://youtu.be/zCbGMoDUfCk
4. ibid.
5. Interview with Blink 182, *Much Music*, 1998
6. Steve Tauschke, interview with Blink 182, 1995
7. *Rolling Stone*, Music Box, interview with Blink 182, 1998
8. Jeffrey Rotter, *Spin*, 1998
9. Blink 182, 'Dammit', MCA/ Cargo 1998
10. Steve Tauschke, *True Punk*, July 1997
11. *Spin*, 1998
12. *Spin*, 1998
13. Steve Tauschke, op. cit.
14. Greil Marcus, *Lipstick Traces*, 1990
15. Kurt Cobain, *Journals*, Paw Prints, 1998
16. *Rolling Stone*, Music Box, op. cit.
17. Coen Brothers, *The Big Lebowski*, 1998
18. Sex Pistols Australian Press Conference 1997, http://youtu.be/TArn_MFfswE

Watching this World

1. Wim Wenders, *Wings of Desire*, Orion, 1987
2. The Goo Goo Dolls, 'Iris', Warner Bros, 1998
3. Steve Sutherland, *NME*, 1995
4. The Eels, 'Susan's House', Dreamworks, 1996
5. *Rolling Stone*, *The Decades of Rock*, Chronicle Books, 2001
6. Robert Hughes, op. cit.
7. Dave Eggers, *A Heartbreaking Work of Staggering Genius*, Simon & Schuster 1999
8. Pavement, 'Shady Lane', Matador 1997
9. Fiona Apple, MTV Video Music Awards, http://youtu.be/GSLwYrPbuts

The Eye of the Storm

1. *Melody Maker* Christmas Issue, 1995
2. *Q*, January 1995
3. Ben Thompson, op. cit.
4. James Brown, op. cit.
5. Richard Kingsmill, interview with Jarvis Cocker, triple j, 1998
6. ibid.
7. Adam Higginbottom, *Select*, October 1995
8. *Vox*, February 1996
9. Charles Aaron, *Spin*, May 1998
10. Pulp, 'This is Hardcore', Island, 1998
11. ibid.
12. ibid.
13. Richard Kingsmill, interview with Jarvis Cocker, 1998
14. Pulp, 'Dishes', Island, 1998
15. David Denby, *New York Magazine*, April 1998
16. Supervert, *John Currin: Oeuvres*, ICA London, 1995
17. Stephen Dalton, *NME*, March 1998
18. Pulp, 'The Day After the Revolution', Island, 1998
19. Jim De Rogatis, *The Flaming Lips: Staring at Sound*, Broadway, 2004

Rap Metal, Rap Metal

1. *Kerrang!*, July 1997
2. Fans interviewed by MTV at Korn Konference, 1998
3. John Doran, *NME*, May 1998
4. Frank Owen, *Spin*, December 1990
5. Chris Roberts, *Melody Maker*, January 1989
6. Richard Kingsmill, interview with Steven Malkmus, triple j, 1994
7. Faith No More present the Billboard Top Ten, 1990
8. Alan Moyle, *Empire Records*, 1995
9. Fans interviewed by MTV at Korn Konference, 1998
10. Richard Kingsmill, *The J-Files Compendium*, 2002
11. *Kerrang!* June 1998
12. ibid.
13. Korn, 'Blind', Immortal/Epic, 1994
14. Richard Kingsmill, *The J-Files Compendium*, 2002
15. Korn, 'Daddy', Epic, 1995
16. Richard Kingsmill, *The J-Files Compendium*, 2002

The Bums Will Always Lose

1. Richard Kingsmill, interview with Courtney Love, triple j, 1999
2. Mark Schone, *Spin*, July 1998
3. Richard Kingsmill, op. cit.
4. Ibid.
5. *Rolling Stone*, February 1999
6. Mark Schone, op. cit.
7. ibid.

8. Interview with Smashing Pumpkins, Planet Rock Profiles, 1995
9. Smashing Pumpkins *Adore* interview part 1, http://youtu.be/JyMug_FOVP0

Fields Outside

1. Gomez, 'Get Miles', Hurt/Virgin, 1998
2. Barney Hoskins, *Mojo*, December 1998
3. John Mulvey, *NME*, May 1998
4. Ben Thompson, op. cit.
5. Barney Hoskyns, *Mojo*, December 1998
6. ibid.
7. Ben Thompson, op. cit.
8. ibid.
9. Richard Kingsmill, interview with Mercury Rev, 1998
10. Mercury Rev, 'Delta Sun Bottleneck Stomp', v2, 1998
11. Mercury Rev, 'Holes', v2, 1998
12. Ben Thompson, op. cit.
13. Eric Weisbard, *Spin*, August 1998

We Miss Rock Stars

1. Richard Kingsmill, interview with Hole, triple j, 1999
2. ibid.
3. Lynne Snowden, *Spin*, February 1996
4. Daly and Wice, op. cit.
5. Richard Kingsmill, op. cit.
6. Zev Borow, *Spin*, December 1999
7. Richard Kingsmill, op. cit.
8. RJ Smith, *Spin*, August 1999

Bigger Than Satan

1. *Rolling Stone*, January 1999
2. Interview with Gregg Alexander, VH1, 1999
3. *Jerry Springer's Wildest Shows Ever*, 1998
4. *Mojo*, May 1999
5. The New Radicals, 'You Get What You Give', MCA, 1999
6. Interview with Marilyn Manson, MTV, 1999
7. Interview with Marilyn Manson, Channel V, 1999
8. ibid.
9. Interview with Marilyn Manson, *San Fransisco Examiner*, 1999
10. Marilyn Manson, *Rolling Stone*, May 1999
11. Ian Brown, Plastic, 1998
12. Nolan and Roach, op. cit.

Musical Hell

1. Richard Kingsmill, interview with Ben Folds, triple j, 1999
2. *Kerrang!* July 1997
3. G Beato, *Spin*, April 1999
4. Limp Bizkit, 'Break Stuff', Interscope, 1999
5. *Spin*, 1999
6. Julie Wiskirchen, Woodstock tour diary, 1999, apeculture.com
7. Kerrang!
8. Charles Aaron, *Spin*, 1999

9. Limp Bizkit, 'Counterfeit', Interscope, 1997
10. *Spin*, 1999
11. Limp Bizkit, 'Counterfeit', Interscope, 1997
12. Zev Borow, *Spin*, August 1999
13. Julie Wiskirchen, op. cit.
14. ibid.

Party Malfunction

1. Julie Wiskirchen, op. cit.
2. David Moodie, *Spin*, October 1999
3. 5 Live News report, July 1999
4. *Washington Post*, July 1999
5. Alona Wartofsky, *Washington Post*, July 1999
6. Crowdsafe report, 1999
7. Tom Morello, *New York Times*, 1999
8. *Spin*, 1999
9. *Heathers*, New World Pictures, 1989
10. Washington Post, July 1999
11. Interview with Rage Against the Machine, MTV, November 1999
12. ibid.
13. *Spin*, 1999

War Music

1. Sonic Youth, 'Nevermind (What Was It Anyway?)', DGC, 2000
2. Naomi Klein, op. cit.
3. ibid.
4. Smash Mouth, 'Walkin' On The Sun', Interscope, 1998
5. Simon Reynolds, *Bring the Noise*, Faber, 2007
6. Naomi Klein, op. cit.
7. Kurt Cobain, op. cit.
8. R.J. Smith, *Spin*, March 2000
9. The Dust Brothers featuring Brad Pitt, 'This is Your Life', Restless, 1999
10. Douglas Coupland, op. cit.
11. David Fincher, *Fight Club*, 20ᵗʰ Century Fox, 1999

Entertain Us!

1. Stephen Frears, *High Fidelity*, Worling Title Films, 2000
2. Nick Hornby, *The New Yorker*, July 2000
3. Radiohead, 'Kid A', EMI, 2000
4. Nick Carr, op. cit.
5. Gavin Edwards, *Spin*, July 1999
6. Chris Norris, *Spin*, July 1998
7. Simon Reynolds, op. cit.
8. Steven Wells, *NME*, October 2000
9. Simon Reynolds, op. cit.
10. Nick Hornby, op. cit.
11. Steven Wells, op. cit.
12. Andrew Collins, *NME*, October 2000
13. Steven Wells, op. cit.
14. Simon Reynolds, op. cit.
15. Don De Lillo, *Underworld*, Picador, 1998
16. Charles Aaron, *Spin*, 1994
17. Simon Reynolds, *The Wire*, July 2001
18. David Fricke, *Rolling Stone*, July 2000
19. Greg Hainge, 'To(rt)uring the Minotaur', in Joseph Tate, *The Music and Art of Radiohead*, Ashgate Publishing, 2005
20. Zev Borrow, *Spin*, November 2000
21. Sia Michel, *Spin*, July 1997
22. Simon Reynolds, op. cit.
23. *Celebrity Death Match*, MTV, 2000
24. *Spin*, 2000
25. Beck, 'Broken Train', DGC, 1999
26. ibid.
27. Neil Strauss, *Spin*, January 1997
28. John Norris, *Spin*, December 1999
29. Nick Hornby, op. cit.
30. Stephen Dalton, *NME*, November 1992
31. Denis Leary, 'Asshole', A&M, 1993
32. Blur, 'The Great Escape', EMI, 1995
33. Wachowski Brothers, *The Matrix*, Village Roadshow, 1999
34. Radiohead, 'Motion Picture Soundtrack', EMI, 2000
35. Radiohead, 'Idiotheque', EMI, 2000

Printed by RR Donnelley at Glasgow, UK